# The Economics of Money and Financial Markets

# The Economics of Money and Financial Markets

Edited by Leo Morris

STATES ACADEMIC PRESS
www.statesacademicpress.com

States Academic Press,
109 South 5th Street,
Brooklyn, NY 11249, USA



ISBN: 978-1-63989-515-1

**Cataloging-in-Publication Data**

The economics of money and financial markets / edited by Leo Morris.
p. cm.
Includes bibliographical references and index.
ISBN 978-1-63989-515-1
1. Money. 2. Capital market. 3. Money market. 4. Finance. 5. Financial institutions. I. Morris, Leo.
HG221 .E26 2022
332.4--dc23

For information on all States Academic Press publications
visit our website at www.statesacademicpress.com

STATES
ACADEMIC PRESS

# Contents

# Preface

The purpose of the book is to provide a glimpse into the dynamics and to present opinions and studies of some of the scientists engaged in the development of new ideas in the field from very different standpoints. This book will prove useful to students and researchers owing to its high content quality.

Money is a standard unit that functions as a recognized medium of exchange for transactional purposes. The main functions of money are unit of account, store of value and standard of deferred payment. Hence, any item or verifiable record that fulfills these functions can be considered money. Money market is a system of finance where short-term financial assets with a maturity up to one year are traded. A financial market is a place where people trade financial securities, derivatives, and instruments such as shares, debentures, bonds, commodities, and currencies. The topics included in this book on money and financial markets are of utmost significance and bound to provide incredible insights to readers. It is a valuable compilation of topics, ranging from the basic to the most complex advancements in this field. This book will provide comprehensive knowledge to the readers.

At the end, I would like to appreciate all the efforts made by the authors in completing their chapters professionally. I express my deepest gratitude to all of them for contributing to this book by sharing their valuable works. A special thanks to my family and friends for their constant support in this journey.

**Editor**

# 1

# Do Firm's Organisational Slacks Influence the Relationship between Corporate Lobbying and Corporate Financial Performance? More Is Not Always Better

**Woon Leong Lin**

Faculty of Economics and Management, Universiti Putra Malaysia; Selangor 43400, Malaysia; linwoonleong@gmail.com

**Abstract:** A political involvement in any organisation has often proved to be profitable for such firms that are seeking support and favourable regulatory conditions. Though many studies have investigated the effect of the corporate lobbying activities on the organisations, no clear results have been achieved. In this study, we have investigated the lobbying expenditure of some of the most famous United States (US)-based companies, which support the U.S. government during 2007–2016. Primarily, we tested the relationship between the corporate lobbying and the Corporate Financial Performance (CFP), with the help of a dynamic panel data analysis, which is based on the System Generalised Methods of the Moment (SYS-GMM). The results of this study indicated that the corporate lobbying did not increase the probability of gaining more support from the government in comparison to the firms that did not use any lobbying techniques. Furthermore, the findings showed that corporate lobbying is a component of the zero-sum political agenda that cannot be accurately evaluated and does not contribute towards the improvement of the CFP. This study introduced the important component of organisational slack and noted that the corporate lobbying could significantly destroy the CFP if the organisational slack was high.

**Keywords:** corporate lobbying; corporate financial performance; organisational slack; system GMM

**JEL Classification:** C51; F14

---

## 1. Introduction

Lobbying, of any type, is always used for acquiring some political advantage in the United States (US). Even the Congressional historical records have stated that the American Revolutionary veteran groups lobbied the Congress during the 1790s, which was much before any primary lobbying-related regulations were implemented in 1876 (Byrd 1991). Currently, the growth and the scale of the lobbying practices are very substantial. In the USA, the political campaign costs have increased significantly. The report submitted by The Centre for Responsive Politics (https://www.opensecrets.org/lobby/) stated that the lobbying costs that were spent by the various organisations in 2016 were >$3.2 billion, where the Top-5 firms were responsible for 40% of the overall costs. Amongst the Top-5 companies, Gump et al. spent ≥$36 million, followed by the Podesta Group ($24 million), Van Scoyoc Associates ($21 million), Holland and Knight ($19 million), and the Squire Patton Boggs ($18 million). Many organisations partake in lobbying. In comparison to the alternative techniques of seeking a political influence, like the contributions made by the corporate Political Action Committees (PACs), many organisations used the lobbying activities to acquire a political advantage (Chen et al. 2015). The corporate lobbying involves the various political activities that are employed by the corporations to influence the legislators at different governmental levels. At the federal level, the corporate lobbying includes any form of communication which is made on the behalf of the client to the various members of the Congress, like the staffers, White House staff, The President, or other high-level employees regarding the modification, formulation, or the adoption of any legislative decision (The Centre for Public Integrity).[1] This was controlled by the Lobbying Disclosure Act of 1995.

Many economists have stated that the firms that lobbied for political connections could acquire many economic benefits (Roberts 1990; Stratmann 2005; Fisman 2001; Jayachandran 2006; Faccio and Parsley 2009; Hochberg et al. 2009; Igan et al. 2009; Richter et al. 2009; Cooper et al. 2010; Yu and Yu 2011; Hill et al. 2013). Also, Richter et al. (2009) suggested that an important factor that led to corporate lobbying included the desire to acquire subsidies for the R and D sector, which was considered to be a very risky investment when compared to the capital investment. Earlier studies indicated that engaging in any political process could act as insurance against the economic crisis. Faccio et al. (2006) noted that the firms that had a political connection in 35 countries were very likely to derive government bailouts during economic distress as compared to the non-connected organisations. The rationale behind this observation was that, since the government actions and regulations directly affected the company's business condition, political lobbying could help the companies to derive important information regarding the regulatory agenda, acquire political information for altering their business decisions in time, and encourage (or discourage) the regulatory decisions that could be beneficial (or detrimental) to the company, if possible. Due to regular communication, this information helps the government make better decisions. However, corporate lobbying acts as an instrument by the organisations for interfering in the policy formation process, which directly affects the lobbying interests. For instance, the various companies involved in the controversies, scandals, or lawsuits (like Phillip Morris, WorldCom, Enron, and Halliburton) had spent a lot of money on lobbying (Chen et al. 2015).

It is very surprising that the various empirical studies ignored the effect of corporate lobbying on the financial performance of the organisation. Lobbying was seen to be the biggest type of political involvement in corporate America. With regards to its financial effect, corporate lobbying was 20-times higher than the PAC or the soft-money contribution made every election cycle. Furthermore, many corporations, business-related groups, or trade associations are responsible for the huge amount of money spent on lobbying. Many individual organisations also spend a lot of money every year. Additionally, many researchers, investigating the corporate political activities, have investigated the different types of expenditures by the corporate-affiliated PACs. This also involved the problem of limited variation and a narrow political activity, i.e., sponsorship of the PACs (Andres 1985; Masters and Keim 1985; Grier and Munger 1991; Grier et al. 1994; Humphries 1991; McKeown 1994; Mitchell et al. 1997). In their study, Milyo et al. (2000) described the "inordinate attention to the PACs", by stating that the data regarding the contribution was available and the PACs could be linked easily to their industrial or corporate sponsors. Furthermore, Sabato (Morris and Sabato 1984) noted that the PACs are formed by the groups that are not capable of establishing a governmental affair or a legislative lobbying department. On the other hand, many companies have a good lobbying division and no PAC. Brasher and Lowery (2006) warned that this type of investigation was narrow and suggested that the empirical studies regarding the PAC behaviour could not be generalised, but they should have focused more on corporate lobbying. Ansolabehere et al. (2003) observed that the major distinction was that since the PAC finances are because of individual contributions and not by corporations, the PAC expenditure cannot be considered as 'corporate'. However, corporate lobbying is considered to be a corporate expense, which helps in improving the firm's performance. Hence, many corporations indulge in corporate lobbying. Similar to the alternative techniques of acquiring political influence, like the PAC contribution, lobbying is another popular method that is used by the corporations for exercising the political strategies (Chen et al. 2015). Based on these parameters, in

---

[1] Reported by the Centre for Public Integrity.

this study, we have focused on the effect of the corporate lobbying on the financial performance of the corporations.

Here, we have also determined the dominating effect amongst the above-mentioned countervailing forces, and the circumstances surrounding it. Firstly, we have analysed the corporate lobbying expenses and compared them to the PAC contributions. We attempted to determine the causal effects of the corporate lobbying on the Corporate Financial Performance (CFP). We analysed all of the firms from which they could obtain the financial data, including many firms that were not very politically active. This helped us to derive the benefits from the data's panel structure, which helped us further control the various time-invariant and firm-specific variables after we had compared the firms that lobbied and those that did not. A few researchers (Nichols 2007; Angrist and Pischke 2010) stated that this technique was used for addressing the bias that occurred because of unobserved confounders, which were commonly seen in the studies that rely solely on the observational data. This study also used another identification strategy, wherein another moderating variable was introduced for examining the effect of the organisation's slack on the association between the CFP and corporate lobbying. Here, we evaluated the impact of the lobbying activities on the CFP, while controlling the inherent endogeneity by using many alternative methods.

We have also postulated that the total costs (or benefits) of the corporate lobbying varied with regards to the organisational slack. The slack resources included the spare assets and the capabilities of the company, which could be reclaimable for the re-deployment. It also includes the hidden and underutilised spare resources that can be reused and recaptured for many tasks. Though several governmental policies and regulations affect the firms, the marginal advantage derived due to the lobbying activities can be determined by the different factors that affect the demand and supply of the firm's products or services. Hence, every lobbying activity shows a different effect on the CFP. Very few studies used this approach. In this study, we examined the association between the corporate lobbying activities and the CFP based on organisational slack.

We used the data from various Fortune magazines' American Most Admired Corporation (AMAC) firms for a 10-year period (2007–2016) and evaluated whether the corporate lobbying was advantageous to the shareholders. We also determined if the organisational slack controlled the association between the CFP and the corporate lobbying. This study showed no significant relationship between the CFP and the corporate lobbying activities. Furthermore, this neutral association could also be partially due to the fact that the lobbying expenditure by the company was unable to provide a few tangible benefits or helped the firm acquire additional governmental contracts and improved the probability of getting the bill passed in the Congress. This indicated that agency expenditure (i.e., an inefficient use of the corporate funds) for the lobbying activities dominated the strategic benefits of the lobbying. Secondly, we also noted the positive relationship between the lobbying activities and the organisational financial slack on the CFP that firms' organisational slack acts as a moderator of the impacts of corporate lobbying on performance; firms that are efficient in utilizing their available resources will be able to register better links between corporate lobbying and firm performance.

These findings showed significant implications. Firstly, the results indicated that the lobbying costs were higher than the benefits, thereby supporting the agency's perspective in comparison to the stewardship viewpoint. Secondly, the results highlighted the endogenous and dynamic nature of the association between the CFP and the lobbying activities. These results suggested that the control of the endogeneity was important for investigating the effect of the various lobbying activities. Thirdly, we noted that the impact of the lobbying activities was heterogeneous for the firms and that the moderating variable of organisational slack could enhance the relationship between the CFP and the lobbying activities.

The remaining paper is organised in the following manner: Section 2 includes the literature review and the hypothesis development, whereas Section 3 discusses all the acquired data and the methodology used. Sections 4 and 5 describes and analyses all of the empirical results, while the discussions and conclusions are presented in Sections 6 and 7.

## 2. Literature Review and the Hypotheses Development

### *2.1. Literature Review*

Many lobbying activities help in seeking protection against the foreign competition. In his study, Schuler (1996) has stated that the lobbying activities in the U.S. steel industry helped to shape the trade policy. Also, Gawande and Bandyopadhyay (2000) mentioned that the U.S. protection pattern was influenced by the lobbying expenditure and the lobbying competition, thus, the protection was 'sold'. Lee and Baik (2010) made a similar argument where they stated that the companies that were engaged in the lobbying activities could buy trade protection against the foreign competition. Many academic institutions also engaged in lobbying activities. De Figueiredo and Silverman (2006) noted that, during particular circumstances, the academic institutions acquired an average return of $11–36 for every dollar that was spent for lobbying. Lastly, many firms (and/or the associated individuals) that contributed to the various political campaigns and acquired significant subsidies from the successful administration had to face several allegations (i.e., Solyndra incident). On the other hand, no conclusive empirical evidence is present, which shows the relationship between the lobbying activities and the CFP. Many studies have shown a negative/positive or neutral relationship between the lobbying activities and the CFP.

#### 2.1.1. Positive Association

According to Chen et al. (2015) and Brown (2016), lobbying could positively affect the CFP, wherein the organisations engaging in the lobbying activities could derive better returns in comparison to the firms that did not. Hill et al. (2013)noted that the shareholders incorporated the lobbying activities pursued by the managers in the share prices of the company. Alexander et al. (2009) showed that the firms that lobbied for the American Jobs Creation Act (2004) acquired $11–$36 for every dollar that was spent for lobbying. De Figueiredo and Silverman (2006) provided an empirical evidence for this scenario, wherein a majority of the educational institutions did not receive any return for their corporate lobbying activities. Fisman (2001) used a novel event study-based approach for investigating the 1997 Indonesian financial crisis and estimating the effect of the political connections on the Indonesian firms. The researcher noted that the politically-connected companies could derive benefits due to their connections. Many studies have indicated that the political connections helped the companies to acquire additional benefits, like regulatory reforms (Stigler 1971), a better tax regime (De Soto 1989), and a preferential treatment by the various government-owned organisations (Backman 1999).

#### 2.1.2. Negative Association

Many studies provided empirical evidence that supported this negative association. Furthermore, the political connections and lobbying activities also have many detrimental effects on the companies, especially during political turmoil. For instance, Gul (2006) noted that, after the occurrence of the Asian financial crisis, the politically connected companies in Malaysia had to pay a higher audit fee in comparison to their non-connected associates. The researcher stated that the Malaysian government could not financially support the politically-connected firms after this financial crisis. Aggarwal et al. (2012) observed that the companies which donated funds to the political candidates had to face many cash-flow issues, which showed long-term negative effects. The researchers also noted that these donating companies engage in a higher acquisition, which was characterised by a lower return in comparison to other acquisitions that were made by the non-donating companies. Hadani and Schuler (2013) also observed that the company's political investments were negatively associated with the market value of the company and the returns on the sales. The researchers claimed that the personal managerial bias and imperatives, in addition to the firm-level profit-maximising objectives, drove the company's political behaviour. Aggarwal et al. (2012) measured the political activities of the companies, but excluded the lobbying activities, whereas Hadani and Schuler (2013) combined all political activities, like the lobbying and the different PACs. The lobbying expenditure and the political donations are different forms of political investment with regards to their influence and scale of expenditure (Yu and Yu 2011; Aggarwal et al. 2012). Coates (2012) also observed a negative effect of the lobbying activities on the corporate value.

#### 2.1.3. No Impact or a Mixed Outcome

Two studies did not observe any relationship between the CFP and the corporate lobbying. In one study, Ansolabehere et al. (2004) did not observe any benefit from the various campaign donations, whereas Hersch et al. (2008) stated that the lobbying activities did not generate any financial capital. Two studies determined multiple outcomes and noted a mixed outcome. Faccio et al. (2006) mentioned that the politically connected firms could pursue the bailout policies in their favour, but they showed a poor operational performance. Tu et al. (2013) observed that, although the connected firms had to a pay a lower premium than the other firms during the privatisation, they showed a lower stock and operating performance during the post-privatisation period.

### 2.2. *Organisational Slack*

The basic organisational slack definition presented by Bourgeois (1981) and which has been used by many other studies (Meyer 1982; Sharfman et al. 1988), stated that:

> *'Slack includes the potential or actual resources which help any organisation successfully adapt to changes. It also provides a means for the organisations to adopt certain strategies to the external environments'. (p. 30)*

These resources comprise a surplus of inputs, such as labour and equipment, which are not functioning at maximum level due to unwise investments in technology know-hows that could have generated better profits and incomes (Meyer 1982; Tan 2003). The definition by Bourgeois (1981) indicates that companies may amass slack resources for future use in case of any environmental changes. Furthermore, these slack resources help organisations to waive short-term returns in support of longer-term profits by generating avenues for chasing current and future competitive prospects (Sharfman et al. 1988). This is because slack resources can be used in an elective fashion for determining competitive and market prospects, although some researchers consider these slack resources unnecessary (Dimick and Murray 1978). However, some organisational slack could be beneficial to the company, wherein a company can develop a financial cushion that can shield the company against any cash flow deficiency or unexpected losses (Rajagopalan and Spreitzer 1997).

Slack resources can help firms to implement strategies for improving efficiency and profitability and to prosper in the long run (Nystrom et al. 2002; Tan and Peng 2003; Adams and Lamont 2003; Bogetoft and Hougaard 2004), because such resources, although not optimally deployed, can provide the mechanisms for effective learning, thereby providing the potential for further enhancements of alignment skills (Levinthal and March 1993). Sharfman et al. (1988) point out that slack resources are especially important during turbulent times since slack resources can buffer the technical cores of corporations during such turbulence (Moreno et al. 2009). This is because slack resources offer organisations a surplus of time as well as the possibility of experimenting with these resources (Geppert 1996). Together, these studies support the notion of Bourgeois (1981), who states that slack represents resource cushions that can be used to counteract threats as well as develop opportunities.

The emerging concept of slack in financial resources was introduced in Barnard's (Barnard 1938) 'inducement-contribution ratio' scheme. Nevertheless, the model failed to secure recognition, until Cyert and March (1963) applied the financial resource slack concept to management models and practices. Organisational slack was utilised to describe the strategic and political behaviours of top management teams (Bourgeois and Singh 1983), their risk-taking behaviours (Bromiley 1991; Palmer and Wiseman 1999; Singh 1986; Wiseman and Bromiley 1996), environmental initiatives (Bowen 2002), and the performances of firms (Greenley and Oktemgil 1998). Discretionary organisational resources enable firms to develop slack (Seifert et al. 2004) and organise uncommitted resources into outputs

(Nohria and Gulati 1996). For an organisation with various slack resources (i.e., excess labour and raw material, excessive work-in-process inventories, surplus productive or plant capacity), the most discretionary of slack resource types would be the excess or slack in financial resources (Austin et al. 1996). Slack in financial resources is defined in this research as utilisable financial capital that could be diverted or else allocated by an organisation in pursuit of its goals (George 2005). Such capital is typically denoted by measures of the capital at hand (namely, net profits after optional expenses and taxes), which is normally treated as a key corporate monetary resource (Austin et al. 1996). The available literature on societal engagement contends that measures of profitability remain the strongest indicators of the "availability of resources for the potential funding of social and environmental investments" (Julian and Ofori-dankwa 2013, p. 1321). Nonetheless, there is a continuing argument on the ideal level of organisational slack, since some academics believe that a 'surplus of slack' is linked to a lack of competence (Wu and Tu 2007).

The idea of the organisational slack was based on the concept of the inducement-contribution ratio, which was initially proposed by Barnard (1938). Cyert and Cyert and March (1963) were the first to apply this concept to the management-related theories and practices. Organisational slack can be defined as the resources that are acquired by an organisation and are not included in the necessary expenditure. On the other hand, some resources have to be used in an unrestricted manner. This also includes many techniques in which the energy and the resources are used for pursuing some organisational objectives that can be channelled into many other things. If the resources have to be considered as slack, then they must be easily visible to the company manager and should be deployable during need. However, other resources are more recoverable and visible, while some are not. Also, different slacks require a different level of flexibility and discretion. As the discretionary level of the resources increases, they are used in many scenarios and contingencies, and they also provide a broader range of tools that can be used by the managers (Sharfman et al. 1988). Conversely, the less discretionary resources are used as a protection in some scenarios, i.e., during rising demands or an excess capacity. Finally, organisational slack is a capital-based firm resource (i.e., human resource, physical, financial, and organisational), which is used by the firms for implementing strategies and improving the organisational efficiency and/or the effectiveness. It is also used as a mechanism for effective learning, which provides a potential for enhancing the alignment skills.

Many studies showed that the firms having higher organisational slacks could engage in some political activities (Schuler and Rehbein 1997) and derive the associated benefits (Hillman et al. 2004). Also, the slack resources were seen to significantly affect the corporate political activities, like lobbying. Furthermore, studies observed that the organisations were more probable to follow the legitimate practices if they had higher financial resources (Seifert et al. 2004). If the organisations aim to influence the different legislatures and lobby for acquiring legitimacy from the administration, then, the firms with a better performance and/or higher slack resources were very likely to mobilise the resources and use them for lobbying.

The organisational slack resources can be measured using a ratio of free cash flow (FCF) to revenue, for approximating the organisation's liquidity (Griffin and Mahon 1997). Cash flow was considered to be more suitable to measure organisational slack as compared to accounting return in this study, since cash flow denotes the uncommitted money that is accessible for corporate lobbying and other discretionary activities. Numerous companies have profit but lack cash flow (George 2005). Here, this study converted the FCF value to its log value. This variable was generally skewed and it could violate the assumption of normality. This study used the DataStream database for determining the FCF value and the formula is as follows:

$$\text{FCF} = (\text{net profit} + \text{interest expenses} + \text{non-cash expenses}) - \text{increase in the working capital} - \text{capital expenditure}$$

$$\text{Organisational slack} = \text{FCF}/\text{total of net sales}$$

### 2.3. *Hypotheses Development*

#### 2.3.1. Corporate Lobbying and the Firm Performance

According to the stewardship theory, corporate lobbying is an integral component of the organisational strategy. This theory also states that the corporate political activities must positively affect the company's profits. Based on this theory, the lobbying expenditure has a higher Return on Investment (ROI). In their study, Alexander et al. (2009) mentioned that, under specific circumstances, lobbying generated a 22% ROI. Empirical evidence showed that firms, which conduct lobbying-related activities for achieving a specific goal, are generally successful. Many individuals or groups who are affected by the current or the pending governmental activities or legislations provide vital information to the government about the various lobbying activities. This information helps the government to make better and informed decisions. Some studies noted this relationship in other scenarios. Richter et al. (2009) observed that the lobbying was related with a low corporate tax rate in a majority of the publicly-traded companies. Lee and Baik (2010) noted that the disbursements provided by the U.S. government to the domestic firms in the anti-dumping petition were related to the lobbying activities. Bonardi et al. (2006) investigated some U.S. electric utilities and noted that the firm's lobbying activities were related to the permitted rate of returns by the Public Utilities Commission (PUCs). According to Brown (2016), the lobbying activities were associated with a high Return on Assets (ROA), Return on Invested Capital (ROIC), and a Return on Equity (ROE) in some of the Fortune-500 firms. Hence, we proposed that:

**Hypothesis 1.** *Corporate lobbying has a positive effect on the CFP.*

#### 2.3.2. Corporate Lobbying, Organisational Slack, and CFP

In this study, we also investigated the effect of the organisational slack on the association between the CFP and the lobbying activities. As mentioned above, the slack resources are described as excessive resources that generate some organisational output (Nohria and Gulati 1996). The buffer argument stated that the presence of organisational slack is related to the increase in the corporate lobbying. The proponents of the slack theory argued that this encouraged the strategic behaviour, helped the companies adapt to the new environment, fostered a long-term thinking, and helped in the exploration of many uncertain investment opportunities, which would otherwise not be used (Bourgeois and Singh 1983; Rajagopalan and Spreitzer 1997). A higher organisational slack is related to high data acquisition costs and difficulty in monitoring, while economists agreed that lobbying protected the company's benefits. Hence, many companies conduct lobbying for acquiring the governmental support and surviving in the market (Melitz 2005). Some researchers (Richter 2010; Houston et al. 2014) stated that the political influence increases the firm's access to the debt and the equity finance. Hence, many firms lobby for improving their access to the capital. The availability of the organisational slack is an important criterion for developing a corporate political strategy. The bigger firms have the necessary slack resources for conducting corporate lobbying and influencing the legislators at different governmental levels. Also, firms with a higher organisational slack can exploit the scale economy-related benefits and generate a significant effect on the CFP. Hence, we proposed that:

**Hypothesis 2.** *Corporate lobbying is more positively related to the CFP when the firms have a high organisation slack and less positively when organisation slack levels are low.*

## 3. Data and Empirical Design

### 3.1. *Data and Sample Selection*

In this study, we have focused solely on America's Most Admired Companies (AMAC), since the data for such companies is very easily available. A new list for the Fortune companies is established every year in March (in 2017, 341 companies listed) and the data was collected for a period between 2007 and 2016. We collected lobbying expenditure data for the period between 2007 and 2016 for the firms from the Centre for Responsive Politics (CRP). The CRP is a non-profit group that operates in Washington D.C. and studies the effect of lobbying activities on the legislative procedure. This group maintains a public access database for the lobbying expenditure and campaign contribution at www.opensecrets.org. The CRP also provides the lobbying expenditure of the publicly-traded firms. This study manually compared the data for all the firms for determining which of the firms were included in the Fortune list for 2007–2016. In order to avoid from the error of sample selection bias, this study does not need a balanced panel. Therefore, the number of firms in our sample dataset varies from year to year and the estimation approach uses as many observations as available. Besides, to exploit the dynamic dimension of our database (i.e., to include the lagged dependent variable) we have to observe firms over at least five consecutive years. We combined the data with the DataStream for extracting the public firm-related data. As the CRP did not use any company identifiers, we manually verified the names of all public firms for ensuring that the CRP lobbying and DataStream data matched and excluded those firms that were without provide complete information. Finally, due to a lack of relevant data for the CFP and lobbying expenditure, eventually, this decreased the sample population to 134 firms. Our final unbalanced panel sample comprises 2494 observations over the 2007–2016 periods.

### 3.2. *Empirical Design*

Here, we developed a dynamic panel model of the lagged levels for the dependent variables and have used the two-step Generalised Methods of the Moment (GMM) technique (Blundell and Bond 1998; Blundell et al. 2001) along with the error correction system (Windmeijer 2005). The use of this methodology could be justified based on the fact that the conventional fixed effects estimator was biased when the lagged dependent variable was used as a regressor. Furthermore, this technique also takes into consideration the probable endogeneity of a few dependent variables. The researchers stated that the alternative consistent estimators having a lagged dependent variable are valid only if the explanatory variables are exogenous.

They also used a novel methodology, i.e., system-GMM, for two main reasons. First, it is possible that the CFP is endogenous and it affects the corporate lobbying activities that are conducted and it is also simultaneously affected by the corporate lobbying. Second, many relevant factors motivate the corporate lobbying; however, they are not included or observed in the model. All these factors include various intangibles like the management quality and the company attitude. In this model, we considered that the ROA, ROE, and ROA were endogenous, since these factors responded to the changes in the corporate lobbying variable, which was pre-determined. Furthermore, the system-GMM method shows the minimal bias and the highest precision when the N factor in the data (in our study refers to the number of the firms) is high and the series is moderately or very persistent, in comparison to other commonly used estimators, i.e., a fixed or differing effects (Soto 2009).

Corporate lobbying requires a lot of expenditure within a short period of time, while the results with respect to governmental support are realised later (Chen et al. 2015). This delay in the gain of the lobbying activities indicates that the lobbying initiatives require significant internal or external changes with regards to their restructuring and reorganising, to help the firms become more familiar with the novel corporate political strategies. The dynamic effects can be incorporated in the panel data model by including the lagged dependent variable. This was seen to be a common strategy that was used by several researchers who investigated the firm performance in the industrial organisations (Chen et al. 2015; Keele and Kelly 2006). The introduction of a lagged dependent variable indicates that the standard estimators are highly inconsistent. The consistent estimators are determined with the help of the GMM approach, which was described earlier (Arellano and Bond 1991). It converts the equation into the differences and then applying a lagged value of the endogenous variables as tools, wherein the instrument number differs for every time period. This procedure was used for deriving the estimates of the dynamic model, with the help of the Stata ver. 15.0. These GMM estimates are seen to be inconsistent if no serial correlation exists. This problem is also noted in the model that was based on the second-order serial correlation seen in the first difference model. Furthermore, we have also reported a diagnostic test for the first and the second order serial correlation, along with the Hansen test for instrumental validity.

### 3.3. *Corporate Lobbying and CFP*

This study used the empirical model, described below, for investigating the relationship between the CFP and corporate lobbying.

$$\begin{aligned} CFP = {} & \alpha Prio\_CFP_{it} + \beta_1 Corporate\_Lobbying_{it} + \beta_2 Firm\_Size_{it} \\ & + \beta_3 Leverage_{it} + \beta_4 Advertisment\_Intensity_{it} + \beta_5 Revenue_{it} + Year\_Effects_{it} + \varepsilon_{it} \end{aligned}$$

Corporate lobbying is the variable of interest, which is present on the right-hand side of the model. The *ln* Lobbying refers to the natural logarithm of the total expenditure (in dollars) of the firm's lobbying activities in the given year. Firm performance is the dependent variable. For understanding the behaviour between a dependent (i.e., CFP) and an independent variable (i.e., corporate lobbying), it is important to apply appropriate techniques for measuring the dependent variable and determining its actual effect. If it is not measured properly, then the effect will not be clear. CFP can be measured using two techniques, i.e., accounting (market-based) or economic performance measures. Here, this study has used accounting-based measures, like the Return on Assets (ROA) and the Return on Equity (ROE), to measure CFP.

The first measure included the ROA, which was commonly used in other studies (Coles et al. 2008; Adams and Ferreira 2009; Masulis and Mobbs 2011). ROA was defined as the company's operating income divided by the total assets. The main dependent variable includes the natural logarithm of the ROA. It also describes the organisation's profitability and assesses the management's ability to create revenue by using the firm's assets. ROA represents the competent manner in which the company resources are used for generating income. It also presents the efficiency of the company's management in generating an income from its resources (Khrawish 2011). Wen (2010) stated that a high ROA indicates the efficiency of a company in utilising its funds.

ROE is a different financial value that indicates the amount of the income that was generated by the company in comparison to a total of the shareholder equity that was capitalised or recorded on the company's financial statement. It indicates the rate of the return made on the various resources invested by the stakeholders in the bank. Furthermore, ROE is a way to determine the efficient manner in which the company management utilises the shareholders' resources. Hence, a better ROE value indicates the efficient utilisation of the shareholders' investment. For measuring the robustness, this study used a second measure of the CFP, i.e., ROIC, which was defined as the company's operating income divided by the total equity.

This study used a comprehensive set of various control variables noted in the literature that were associated with the CFP. The firm size could be defined as a natural logarithm of the total assets. We also calculated the leverage as a ratio of the book value of the long-term debt to the total assets. The earlier firm profitability was measured based on the lagged CFP (i.e., lagged ROA, lagged ROE, or a lagged ROIC). The adverting intensity refers to the expense scaled by the total assets. We also used the reputation index as a control variable, as the sample was derived from the AMAC, which could significantly affect the CFP (Sánchez and Sotorrío 2007).

### 3.4. *Effect of Organisational Slack on the Relationship between the Corporate Lobbying and CFP*

The researchers used another model for testing the effect of the different company characteristics on the association between the CFP and the corporate lobbying.

$$CFP = \alpha Prio\_CFP_{it} + \beta_1 Corporate\_Lobbying_{it} + \beta_3 Slack_{it} + \beta_2 (Corporate\_Lobbying*Slack)_{it} + \beta_3 Firm\_Size_{it} + \beta_4 Leverage_{it} + \beta_5 Advertisment\_Intensity_{it} + \beta_6 Revenue_{it} + Year\_Effects_{it} + \varepsilon_{it}$$

We used the factor analysis for characterising the major firm attributes, i.e., organisational slack. Thereafter, we included the interaction between the variables for corporate lobbying and organisational slack in the empirical analysis for determining the differential effect of the lobbying on the CFP. We also calculated the organisational slack using the free cash flow and the sale amount. Many other studies used the CFP as a precursor of the slack resources, instead of the measure of the slack alone (Singh 1986; Sharfman et al. 1988). Buchholtz et al. (1999) disapproved of the use of the accounting returns for measuring the slack resources based on the fact that the income and the profit margin cannot reveal the number of the firm's resources, which were committed, and how much was available for discretionary purposes. We agreed that the profits are not indicative of the firm's slack resources, and hence, we have proposed that the cash flow must capture the concept of the resources that are available for the discretionary purpose. The cash flow can be defined as the firm's operative income, which is determined before the depreciation and minus the nondiscretionary expenditure, like the interest on the debt, taxes, or dividends (Lehn and Poulsen 1989). Thereafter, we derived the measure of the operational complexity based on the advertisement intensity, firm size, and leverage (Coles et al. 2008). Subsequently, we used the reputation index as a control variable, as the sample was collected from the AMAC, and this could significantly affect the CFP.

## 4. Empirical Results

Tables 1 and 2 present the descriptive statistics for the variables used in this study. The researchers noted that the relationship between these variables had a statistical significance (based on the *t*-value) and fulfilled the expectations of this study. This could be seen from the control variables that were associated with the other variables. Moreover, the correlation matrix showed that all of the study variables did not show the problem of multicollinearity as they showed a value ≥0.80. Also, the analysis of the Variance Inflation Factors (VIF) (1.48) showed no multicollinearity issue in this data, as the VIF values were further away from the maximal threshold value, i.e., 10.

**Table 1.** Descriptive statistics.

| Variable | Unit of Measurement | Obs | Mean | Std. Dev | Min | Max |
|---|---|---|---|---|---|---|
| *ln*roa | Log Net income before extraordinary items to total asset of firm | 1294 | 3.762 | 0.170 | 0.000 | 4.404 |
| *ln*roe | Log Net income before extraordinary items to total equity of firm | 1294 | 5.488 | 0.189 | 0.000 | 6.620 |
| *ln*roic | Log Net income before extraordinary items to total equity and debt of firm | 1294 | 4.147 | 0.203 | 0.000 | 4.814 |
| *ln*cpa | Log of total amount of lobbying to total net sales of firm | 1294 | 7.419 | 1.834 | −2.303 | 10.635 |
| *ln*freecash | Log Free cash flow to total of net sales | 1294 | 5.383 | 0.167 | 0.000 | 6.216 |
| *ln*lev | Long term debt of firms to total equity | 1294 | 1.135 | 0.660 | 0.113 | 6.899 |
| *ln*totalasset | Log of total asset of firm | 1294 | 10.460 | 1.267 | 7.282 | 13.632 |
| *ln*adv | Log advertising expenses to total net sales of firm | 1245 | 2.816 | 0.788 | −0.713 | 4.775 |

Notes: All statistics are based on original data values.

**Table 2.** Correlation.

| | *ln*roa | *ln*roe | *ln*roic | *ln*cpa | *ln*freecash | *ln*lev | *ln*totalasset | *ln*adv |
|---|---|---|---|---|---|---|---|---|
| *ln*roa | 1 | | | | | | | |
| *ln*roe | 0.332 *** | 1 | | | | | | |
| *ln*roic | 0.726 | 0.400 *** | 1 | | | | | |
| *ln*cpa | 0.153 *** | 0.088 *** | 0.162 *** | 1 | | | | |
| *ln*freecash | 0.099 *** | 0.038 | 0.080 *** | 0.005 | 1 | | | |
| *ln*lev | −0.265 *** | −0.112 | −0.117 *** | 0.101 *** | −0.088 *** | 1 | | |
| *ln*totalasset | −0.072 *** | −0.027 | −0.093 *** | 0.315 *** | 0.009 | 0.205 *** | 1 | |
| *ln*adv | 0.039 | 0.002 | 0.021 | −0.076 *** | 0.074 | 0.096 *** | −0.005 | 1 |

Notes: All statistics are based on original data values. The *p*-values ***, ** and * indicate significance at 1%, 5%, and 10% levels, respectively.

### *4.1. Testing the Effect of the Corporate Lobbying on the CFP*

Here, this study has presented the empirical results of the association between the CFP and corporate lobbying in 2 steps. In Step 1, we have provided a direct evidence regarding the dynamic relationship of the corporate lobbying and CFP (i.e., ROA, ROE, and ROIC); and, in Step 2, they directly tested the interactive effect of the organisational slack and corporate lobbying on the CFP. Tables 3–5 present the static and dynamic results, along with the fixed effect model and the system-GMM results for the ROA, ROE, and the ROIC, which were estimated using the corporate lobbying for evaluating the effect after overlooking the dynamic corporate lobbying–CFP relation and heterogeneity. The results were validated for the misspecification tests (i.e., Hansen test for other restrictions along with a second-order serial correlation test, i.e., AR 2 test), which helped in confirming the appropriateness of using the system-GMM model specification. Furthermore, the positive and significant coefficient for the lagged dependent variable validated the persistence of the CFP, which was seen to significantly rely on its past value. As shown in Tables 3–5, the positive and significant coefficient for the lagged dependent variable for the system-GMM was present between the fixed effects and the pooled OLS. Similar results were noted earlier (Bond et al. 2001), where the researchers applied an effective and unbiased system GMM. Hence, in this study, we used the system-GMM two-step[2] estimator for all calculations and the Hansen test for the other restrictions. Thus, we concluded that the system-GMM was an effective model specification. Irrespective of the estimation technique used, the control variables showed the following effect on the CFP (i.e., ROA, ROE, and ROIC). The total revenue of firms showed a positive effect on the CFP. We observed a negative effect of the total asset and the leverage on the CFP. We also noted a mixed relationship between the advertising intensity and the CFP.

**Table 3.** Corporate lobbying and Corporate Financial Performance (CFP) (Return on Assets (ROA)) (N = 134 firms; T = 10; period = 2007–2016).

| | Static | | Dynamic | | |
|---|---|---|---|---|---|
| | OLS | Fixed Effect | OLS | Fixed Effect | Syetem GMM |
| Variables | Model 1 | Model 2 | Model 3 | Model 4 | Model 5 |
| $ln\text{roa}_{t-1}$ | | | 0.326 ** | 0.257 ** | 0.131 *** |
| | | | (0.146) | (0.129) | (0.0329) |
| *ln*cpa | 0.0202 *** | 0.0262 | 0.00911 *** | 0.00952 *** | −0.00583 |
| | (0.00617) | (0.0164) | (0.00301) | (0.00339) | (0.00383) |
| *ln*lev | −0.0710 *** | −0.0605 *** | −0.0468 *** | −0.0513 *** | −0.0290 *** |
| | (0.00819) | (0.0131) | (0.0138) | (0.0140) | (0.0109) |
| *ln*totalasset | −0.0117 *** | −0.0176 ** | −0.00964 *** | −0.0101 * | −0.0164 |
| | (0.00330) | (0.00826) | (0.00345) | (0.00551) | (0.0202) |
| *ln*adv | 0.0182 *** | 0.00534 | 0.0166 *** | 0.0158 ** | −0.0287 |
| | (0.00561) | (0.00902) | (0.00549) | (0.00687) | (0.0225) |
| Year | Yes | Yes | Yes | Yes | Yes |
| Constant | 3.806 *** | 3.838 *** | 2.558 *** | 2.853 *** | 3.599 *** |
| | (0.0455) | (0.0983) | (0.561) | (0.493) | (0.261) |
| Observations | 1245 | 1245 | 1114 | 1114 | 1114 |
| R-squared | 0.132 | | 0.334 | | |
| Number of code | | 134 | | 134 | 134 |
| AR1 | | | | | −3.420 (0.001) |
| AR2 | | | | | 0.300 (0.761) |
| Hansen Test | | | | | 15.680 (0.547) |
| Difference Hansen Test | | | | | 1.600 (0.809) |

Notes: The standard errors are reported in parentheses, except for Hansen test, AR (1), AR (2), and Difference-in-Hansen which are *p*-values. ***, ** and * indicate significance at 1%, 5%, and 10% levels, respectively. Time dummies are included in the model specification, but the results are not reported to save space. System GMM model is estimated by using the Blundell and Bond (1998) dynamic panel system GMM estimations and Roodman (2009)—Stata xtabond2 command.

2 Estimations were carried out using the Stata module Xtabond2 developed by Roodman (2009). System GMM was implemented as a one-step estimator with Windmeijer-corrected cluster-robust errors.

**Table 4.** Corporate lobbying and CFP (ROE) (N = 134 firms; T = 10; period = 2007–2016).

| | Static | | | Dynamic | |
|---|---|---|---|---|---|
| | OLS | Fixed Effect | OLS | Fixed Effect | Syetem GMM |
| Variables | Model 1 | Model 2 | Model 3 | Model 4 | Model 5 |
| *ln*roe$_{t-1}$ | | | 0.316 | 0.316 *** | 0.339 *** |
| | | | (0.303) | (0.0878) | (0.0215) |
| *ln*cpa | 0.0112 *** | 0.0107 | 0.00725 ** | 0.00725 *** | 0.00135 |
| | (0.00176) | (0.00327) | (0.00366) | (0.00242) | (0.00361) |
| *ln*lev | 0.0113 | −0.00178 | 0.0103 | 0.0103 | −0.0540 |
| | (0.0450) | (0.0656) | (0.0456) | (0.0411) | (0.0380) |
| *ln*totalasset | −0.0117 *** | −0.0114 | −0.00920 | −0.00920 ** | 0.00238 |
| | (0.00435) | (0.00749) | (0.00615) | (0.00452) | (0.0152) |
| *ln*adv | 0.00193 | −0.000505 | 0.00131 | 0.00131 | −0.0837 ** |
| | (0.00381) | (0.00755) | (0.00420) | (0.00572) | (0.0388) |
| Year | Yes | Yes | Yes | Yes | Yes |
| Constant | 5.524 *** | 5.541 *** | 3.762 ** | 3.796 *** | 3.881 *** |
| | (0.0284) | (0.0512) | (1.653) | (0.510) | (0.210) |
| Observations | 1245 | 1245 | 1114 | 1114 | 1114 |
| R-squared | 0.026 | | 0.117 | | |
| Number of code | | 134 | | 134 | 134 |
| AR1 | | | | | −1.11 (0.268) |
| AR2 | | | | | 0.970 (0.330) |
| Hansen Test | | | | | 17.85 (0.598) |
| Difference Hansen Test | | | | | 2.39 (0.664) |

Notes: The standard errors are reported in parentheses, except for Hansen test, AR (1), AR (2), and Difference-in-Hansen which are *p*-values. ***, ** and * indicate significance at 1%, 5%, and 10% levels, respectively. Time dummies are included in the model specification, but the results are not reported to save space. System GMM model is estimated by using the Blundell and Bond (1998) dynamic panel system GMM estimations and Roodman (2009)—Stata xtabond2 command.

**Table 5.** Corporate lobbying and CFP (Return on Invested Capital (ROIC)) (N = 134 firms; T = 10; period = 2007–2016).

| | Static | | | Dynamic | |
|---|---|---|---|---|---|
| | OLS | Fixed Effect | OLS | Fixed Effect | Syetem GMM |
| Variables | Model 1 | Model 2 | Model 3 | Model 4 | Model 5 |
| *ln*roic$_{t-1}$ | | | 0.395 *** | 0.352 ** | 0.119 *** |
| | | | (0.144) | (0.143) | (0.0351) |
| *ln*cpa | 0.0249 *** | 0.0312 | 0.0104 *** | 0.0109 ** | −0.00384 |
| | (0.00702) | (0.0209) | (0.00390) | (0.00480) | (0.00407) |
| *ln*lev | −0.0342 *** | −0.0401 * | −0.0201 | −0.0233 | −0.0373 *** |
| | (0.0129) | (0.0239) | (0.0140) | (0.0174) | (0.0140) |
| *ln*totalasset | −0.0228 *** | −0.0281 *** | −0.0169 *** | −0.0176 *** | −0.0758 ** |
| | (0.00401) | (0.0105) | (0.00505) | (0.00659) | (0.0298) |
| *ln*adv | 0.0127 * | −0.00302 | 0.0125 ** | 0.0122 | −0.0507 ** |
| | (0.00693) | (0.0123) | (0.00621) | (0.00864) | (0.0234) |
| Year | Yes | Yes | Yes | Yes | Yes |
| Constant | 4.253 *** | 4.299 *** | 2.569 *** | 2.789 *** | 4.672 *** |
| | (0.0538) | (0.122) | (0.619) | (0.605) | (0.374) |
| Observations | 1245 | 1245 | 1114 | 1114 | 1114 |
| R-squared | 0.076 | | 0.302 | | |
| Number of code | | 134 | | 134 | 134 |
| AR1 | | | | | −1.11 (0.268) |
| AR2 | | | | | 0.970 (0.330) |
| Hansen Test | | | | | 17.85 (0.598) |
| Difference Hansen Test | | | | | 2.39 (0.664) |

Notes: The standard errors are reported in parentheses, except for Hansen test, AR (1), AR (2), and Difference-in-Hansen which are *p*-values. ***, ** and * indicate significance at 1%, 5%, and 10% levels, respectively. Time dummies are included in the model specification, but the results are not reported to save space. System GMM model is estimated by using the Blundell and Bond (1998) dynamic panel system GMM estimations and Roodman (2009)—Stata xtabond2 command.

The model that was used in the study defines the measures for corporate lobbying. As seen in the study, a few biases can arise if the researchers overlooked the dynamic corporate lobbying-CFP relationship (i.e., fixed-effects model) and the unobservable heterogeneity (i.e., pooled OLS model). As shown in Table 3, a positive relationship (based on the OLS estimate—model 1 and 3, based on fixed-effects estimate—model 2) was noted between the corporate lobbying and ROA, while a neutral relationship was seen between the system-GMM (model 5) and the dynamic fixed-effects model (model 4). On the other hand, Tables 4 and 5 also showed same results, with a significant relationship between corporate lobbying and ROE and ROIC for all models. Hence, the dynamics must be considered before determining the CFP and the corporate lobbying relationship. As biased results could be generated with the help of the OLS estimate and the fixed-effects model, the researchers have highlighted these system-GMM results. With regards to the relationship between the CFP and the corporate lobbying, the ROA, ROE, and ROIC were unaffected by corporate lobbying. The resultant data did not show any effect on the H1, indicating that there was no effect of the corporate lobbying on the CFP. Thus, the researchers verified the presence of a neutral relationship between the CFP and the corporate lobbying activities. Similar results were noted in the earlier empirical studies (Ansolabehere et al. 2004; Cao et al. 2018; Faccio et al. 2006; Hersch et al. 2008).

### *4.2. Testing the Interactive Effect of Corporate Lobbying and the Organisational Slack on CFP*

This study has also investigated the interactive effects of the corporate lobbying and the organisational slack on the CFP. Tables 6–8 show the regression analysis for the system-GMM estimator. The Arellano and Bond test for autocorrelation supported the overall model validity, as it provided evidence for the presence of the 1st-order autocorrelation (ar1) and the absence of the second-order autocorrelation (AR2), whereas the Hansen test supported the consistency of all GMM instruments. It could be seen that this estimation controlled the potential correlation between the regressors and the unobserved factors. Tables 6–8 present the results for the conventional determinants of the financial performance (i.e., ROA, ROE, and ROIC). Furthermore, the CFP was seen to be unaffected by the corporate lobbying.

**Table 6.** Effects of corporate lobbying and organisational slack on the variable financial performance (ROA) (N = 134 firms; T = 10; period = 2007–2016).

| | System GMM | | |
|---|---|---|---|
| **Variables** | **Model 1** | **Model 2** | **Model 3** |
| *ln*roa$_{t-1}$ | 0.337 *** | 0.333 *** | 0.230 *** |
| | (0.0519) | (0.0505) | (0.0642) |
| *ln*cpa | | −0.00227 | 3.043 * |
| | | (0.00308) | (1.613) |
| *ln*freecash | −0.00568 | −0.00528 | 4.512 * |
| | (0.00613) | (0.00620) | (2.400) |
| (*ln*cpa**ln*freecash) | | | −0.567 * |
| | | | (0.300) |
| *ln*lev | −0.0281 *** | −0.0277 *** | −0.0396 ** |
| | (0.0103) | (0.0103) | (0.0164) |
| *ln*totalasset | 0.00432 | 0.00412 | 0.00473 |
| | (0.0222) | (0.0221) | (0.0233) |
| *ln*adv | −0.0476 ** | −0.0455 ** | −0.0693 *** |
| | (0.0204) | (0.0208) | (0.0252) |
| Year | −0.00609 | −0.00660 | −0.0113 |
| | (0.0162) | (0.0162) | (0.0201) |
| Constant | 2.642 *** | 2.664 *** | −21.15 |
| | (0.343) | (0.342) | (12.89) |
| Observations | 1114 | 1114 | 1114 |
| Number of code | 134 | 134 | 134 |
| AR1 | −4.13 (0.000) | −4.10 (0.000) | −4.16 (0.000) |
| AR2 | 0.72 (0.472) | 0.71 (0.480) | 0.23 (0.818) |
| Hansen Test | 31.59 (0.064) | 30.90 (0.480) | 21.35 (0.318) |
| Difference Hansen Test | 6.76 (0.239) | 8.30 (0.140) | 4.12 (0.532) |
| Number of instrument | 35 | 35 | 35 |

Notes: All models are estimated by using the Blundell and Bond (1998) dynamic panel data system GMM estimations and Roodman (2009)—Stata xtabond2 command. The standard errors are reported in parentheses, except for Hansen test, AR (1), AR (2), and Difference-in-Hansen which are *p*-values. ***, ** and * indicate significance at 1%, 5%, and 10% levels, respectively. Time dummies are included in the model specification, but the results are not reported to save space. The instruments employed in the first-differenced equation are two or more lags of the levels of the endogenous variables, while one lag of the first-difference of the endogenous variables is used as instrument in the difference equation.

**Table 7.** Effects of corporate lobbying and organisational slack on the variable financial performance (ROE) (N = 134 firms; T = 10; period = 2007–2016).

| | System GMM | | |
|---|---|---|---|
| Variables | Model 1 | Model 2 | Model 3 |
| *ln*roe$_{t-1}$ | 0.117 *** | 0.104 *** | 0.0671 ** |
| | (0.0123) | (0.0124) | (0.0270) |
| *ln*cpa | | −0.000254 | 37.16 * |
| | | (0.00826) | (21.35) |
| *ln*freecash | −0.00106 | −0.00140 | 55.16 * |
| | (0.00982) | (0.00945) | (31.70) |
| *(lncpa*lnfreecash)* | | | −6.905 * |
| | | | (3.973) |
| *ln*lev | −0.180 *** | −0.203 *** | −0.296 *** |
| | (0.0194) | (0.0230) | (0.0646) |
| *ln*totalasset | −0.155 * | −0.125 | −0.0240 |
| | (0.0837) | (0.0885) | (0.141) |
| *ln*adv | −0.190 *** | −0.143 * | −0.145 |
| | (0.0661) | (0.0772) | (0.133) |
| Year | Yes | Yes | Yes |
| Constant | 7.169 *** | 6.829 *** | −290.1 * |
| | (0.983) | (1.023) | (170.2) |
| Observations | 1114 | 1114 | 1114 |
| Number of code | 134 | 134 | 134 |
| AR1 | −1.10 (0.270) | −1.10 (0.2.73) | −1.74 (0.081) |
| AR2 | 0.48 (0.630) | 0.33 (0.740) | −1.29 (0.196) |
| Hansen Test | 21.02 (0.458) | 18.66 (0.544) | 7.51 (0.991) |
| Difference Hansen Test | 8.30 (0.414) | 6.47 (0.264) | 1.74 (0.884) |
| Number of instrument | 35 | 35 | 35 |

Notes: All models are estimated by using the Blundell and Bond (1998) dynamic panel data system GMM estimations and Roodman (2009)—Stata xtabond2 command. The standard errors are reported in parentheses, except for Hansen test, AR (1), AR (2), and Difference-in-Hansen which are *p*-values. ***, ** and * indicate significance at 1%, 5%, and 10% levels, respectively. Time dummies are included in the model specification, but the results are not reported to save space. The instruments employed in the first-differenced equation are two or more lags of the levels of the endogenous variables, while one lag of the first-difference of the endogenous variables is used as instrument in the difference equation.

**Table 8.** Effects of corporate lobbying and organisational slack on the variable financial performance (ROIC) (N = 134 firms; T = 10; period = 2007–2016).

| | System GMM | | |
|---|---|---|---|
| Variables | Model 1 | Model 2 | Model 3 |
| *ln*roic$_{t-1}$ | 0.307 *** | 0.305 *** | 0.106 ** |
| | (0.058) | (0.061) | (0.064) |
| *ln*cpa | | −0.0002 | 7.289 ** |
| | | (0.003) | (2.987) |
| *ln*freecash | −0.003 | −0.003 | 10.810 ** |
| | (0.007) | (0.007) | (4.439) |
| (*ln*cpa***ln*freecash) | | | −1.356 ** |
| | | | (0.556) |
| *ln*lev | −0.031 * | −0.032 ** | −0.076 *** |
| | (0.016) | (0.0159) | (0.0195) |
| *ln*totalasset | −0.0495 | −0.042 | −0.022 |
| | (0.031) | (0.031) | (0.038) |
| *ln*adv | −0.061 *** | −0.059 *** | −0.075 ** |
| | (0.020) | (0.023) | (0.032) |
| Constant | No | 3.550 *** | −53.840 ** |
| | | (0.493) | (23.900) |
| Year | Yes | Yes | Yes |
| Observations | 1114 | 1114 | 1114 |
| Number of code | 134 | 134 | 134 |
| AR1 | −3.89 (0.000) | −3.92 (0.000) | −4.34 (0.000) |
| AR2 | −0.48 (0.634) | −0.48 (0.635) | −1.60 (0.110) |
| Hansen Test | 26.87 (0.108) | 27.04 (0.0.078) | 19.46 (0.303) |
| Difference Hansen Test | 6.17 (0.290) | 8.06 (0.153) | 2.18 (0.824) |
| Number of instrument | 35 | 35 | 35 |

Notes: All models are estimated by using the Blundell and Bond (1998) dynamic panel data system GMM estimations and Roodman (2009)—Stata xtabond2 command. The standard errors are reported in parentheses, except for Hansen test, AR (1), AR (2), and Difference-in-Hansen which are *p*-values. ***, ** and * indicate significance at 1%, 5%, and 10% levels, respectively. Time dummies are included in the model specification, but the results are not reported to save space. The instruments employed in the first-differenced equation are two or more lags of the levels of the endogenous variables, while one lag of the first-difference of the endogenous variables is used as instrument in the difference equation.

Tables 6–8 present the results of the regression model that was used for investigating the proposed hypotheses. In both the tables, the interactions occurring between the organisational slack and the corporate lobbying along with their effect on the CFP were determined using Model 3 in Tables 6–8. We relied on the Model 3 for testing Hypothesis 2, since it was a completely specified model that accurately depicted the effects of every variable. The model includes the interaction term between corporate lobbying and organisational slack. According to Brambor et al. (2006), it is not necessary to interpret the individual term of the corporate lobbying and organisational slack, since these coefficients are not our main concern. Hypothesis 2 was proposed for predicting whether the organisational slack could positively moderate the association between the corporate lobbying and the CFP. When the organisational slack increased, the positive relationship between the CFP and the corporate lobbying also became stronger. However, the findings of this study showed an opposite result that the organisational slack negatively moderated this relationship and do not support the Hypothesis 2. As seen in the Model 3 in Tables 6–8 for the ROA, ROE, and ROIC, a significant and negatively coefficient was noted for the interaction between the organisational slack and the corporate lobbying ($\beta_{ROA} = -0.567$, $p$ value $< 0.10$; $\beta_{ROE} = -6.905$, $p$ value $< 0.10$; $\beta_{ROIC} = -1.356$, $p$ value $< 0.05$). These results showed that the detrimental effect of the corporate lobbying on the CFP when interacting with organisational slack. This finding is inconsistent with Hypothesis 2.

Furthermore, a significant interaction was noted between the financial slack and corporate lobbying. A further exploration of this effect has been described in Figures 1 and 2. Based on the Model 3 results shown in Tables 6–8, we applied the Aiken et al. (1991) strategy for plotting all significant interactive effects ($p$-value lower than 0.05) for depicting the moderating effects properly. Figures 1–3 illustrate the effect of the corporate lobbying on the corporate lobbying for the 2 levels (i.e., low and high) of organisational financial slack. A standard deviation value that was greater or lesser than the mean could indicate the higher or lower level of all moderating variables, respectively.

As shown in Figure 1, when the corporate lobbying increased by a value of 1 standard deviation lower than the mean to 1 value above the mean, the ROA decreased from 3.31 to 2.93 in the case of the firms with a high level of organisational slack, whereas the ROA increased from 2.86 to 3.18 for the firms with a low level of organisational slack. In other words, when the corporate lobbying expenditure increased from 1 standard deviation value below the mean to 1 value above the mean, the ROA for the firms with a higher slack showed an 16.06% decrease, whereas, in the case of the firms with a lower slack, the ROA increased by 15.32%. Hence, Figure 1 showed that the effect of the corporate lobbying varied from low to high, while the corporate lobbying and ROA relationship shifted from negative to positive. The organisational slack moderated the effect of the corporate lobbying on the CFP, and a strong negative relationship could be seen between the parameters in the case of the companies with a higher level of organisational slack.

With regards to the moderation effect, Figure 1 showed the negative effect of the corporate lobbying on the ROA when the organisational slack was high. On the other hand, this relationship was positive when the level of organisational slack was low. These results verified the moderating effect of the organisational slack; while the interaction pattern between the parameters was seen to be inconsistent when compared to the prediction. Thus, the Hypothesis 2 could not be proved. Similar results are explained in Figures 2 and 3 for ROE and ROIC, respectively, thus support this view on corporate lobbying by demonstrating that the effect of corporate lobbying is negative when organisational slack is high, but positive when organisational slack is low. In conclusion, based on the meaning of ROA, ROE, and ROIC, our findings indicate that firms with high corporate lobbying are expected to achieve high profit when organisational slack is low.

**Figure 1.** Effects of CPA on ROA: Contingent on Organisational Slack.

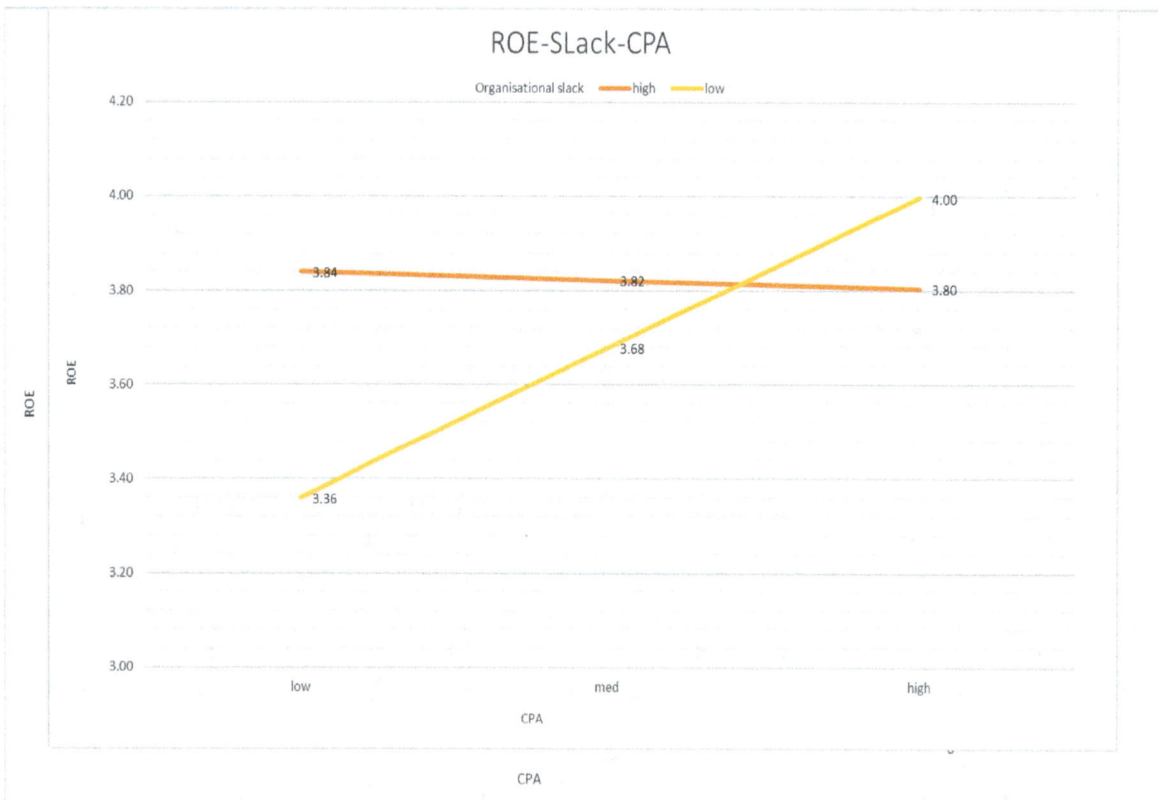


**Figure 2.** Effects of CPA on ROE: Contingent on Organisational Slack.

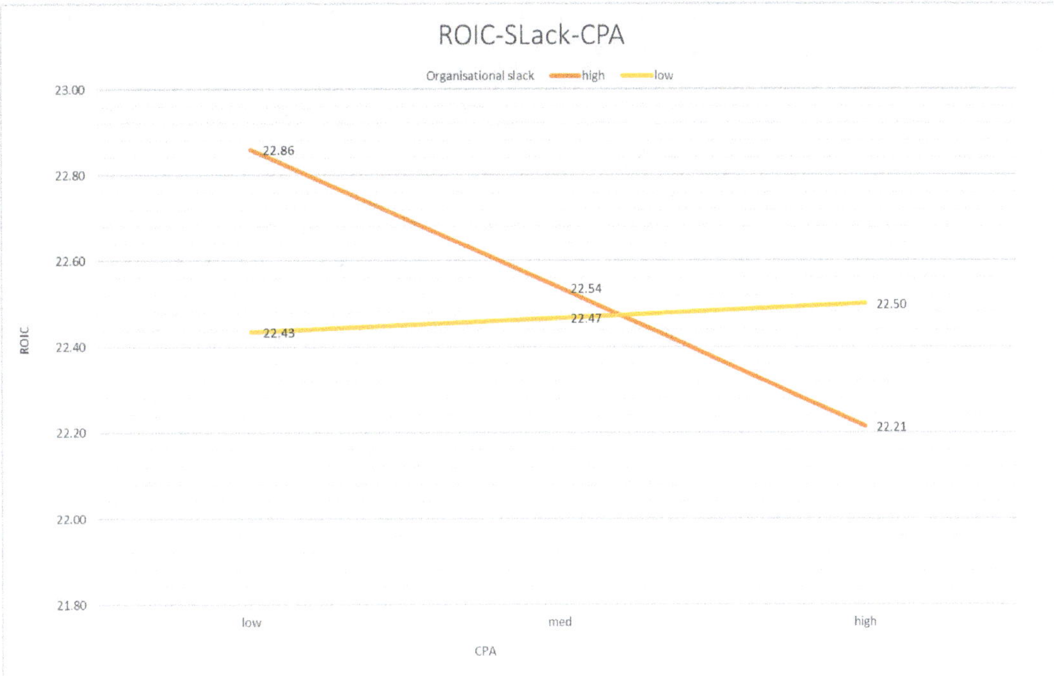


**Figure 3.** Effects of CPA on ROIC: Contingent on Organisational Slack.

## 5. Selection Bias

In order to correct for potential selection bias, a Heckman Two-Step procedure was estimated (Heckman 1979). The Heckman model is warranted when samples are non-random and there is a chance that omitted variables from a broader sample of firms will bias results. In the two-step procedure, the first equation is a selection equation where the control variables are regressed on the selection variable, in this case, corporate lobbying, the result is a correction factor, known as the Inverse Mills Ratio (Bascle 2008). The Mills coefficient is then added to the original equation as an additional right-hand variable to adjust for the selection bias. However, if the Inverse Mills Ratio coefficient is insignificant ($p > 0.05$), then there is no selection bias, and the original results are unbiased due to selection. In both Heckman equations, the Inverse Mills Ratio was insignificant (Lamda = −4.707, $p = 0.071$ for corporate lobbying), and therefore, selection bias is not present in the included sample.

## 6. Discussion

There has been an increasing interest in the lobbying and other political activities of the various organisations. Till date, the academics and the financial press have focused primarily on the weaker measure of the political activities, i.e., PAC contributions. However, the PAC contributions are a very small percentage of the total corporate political activities. Furthermore, as they are made by the individuals, they cannot be included as corporate expenses. This study has noted that the lobbying expenses are the biggest type of corporate political activity in America. This is determined by the number of the companies that are engaged and the amount of money spent. These factors showed that the lobbying activities were significantly higher than the corporate PACs and the soft money donations (banned). Therefore, this study used the publicly-accessible data about the corporate lobbying activities for investigating the financial effect of the corporate political activities.

This study examined the relationship between the CFP and the corporate lobbying activities with an aim to determine the moderating role of organisational slack. Many recent studies have indicated that the relationship between the corporate lobbying and the CFP was slightly positive, however, some researchers stated that further investigation was necessary for clarifying the role played by the omitted variables that could interfere in the relationship. This debate is still open and new models are required, which can address these issues. This study has tried to explain the lobbying activity interface after analysing the role played by organisational slack.

This study has presented several results describing the relationship between the corporate lobbying and the CFP. Firstly, while taking into consideration the dynamic data for the system-GMM estimation and regression, the researchers noted that the lobbying expenses were not significantly correlated with the CFP. Secondly, this study investigated the two-way interaction between the lobbying and the organisational slack, after using the CFP as a dependent variable. The results showed that organisational slack negatively interacts with the corporate lobbying, which indicates the synergy. Also, the interaction between the corporate lobbying and logistic slack generated a detrimental effect on the CFP, thereby rejecting H2. These results were robust to the different measures of the CFP, i.e., ROA or ROIC.

All of the results in this study have contributed to the theory in many ways. We noted that the corporate lobbying does not necessarily improve the CFP, which was explained using the political market theory, as it emphasised on the political competition, suggesting that the corporate lobbying activities could be an important component of the zero-sum political game, which cannot be accurately evaluated. This political marketplace theory regards corporate lobbying as an exchange in the policy arena that occurs between the policy demanders, like various interest groups or firms, on one hand, and the legislators, policy suppliers, regulators, etc. on the other hand (Bonardi et al. 2006). Many firms compete with one another for limited access to public officials (Hillman and Hitt 1999). Due to the increasing number of political rivals, the specific firms find it difficult to forward a particular public policy agenda successfully (Hall and Wayman 1990; Baumgartner et al. 2009). Similar results were noted by Baumgartner et al. (2009), who stated that the lobbying expenditure was not related to the public policy success. They also concluded that they could not observe any relationship between the resources and the policy results.

To explain further, though some managers believe that they can alter the political scenario, in actual reality, the firms cannot successfully predict the decisions of the policymakers, since policymaking involves personal, party, state, national, or media influences (Keim 2001). This factor, along with the rational decisions of the corporate decision-makers, increases the strategic uncertainty related to the corporate lobbying or its ability to produce the desired outcome, like an improved CFP (Hart 2010). Due to this uncertain influence, the corporate lobbying was seen to be less successful than what is presumed.

In this paper, we have extended the contingency theory to include corporate lobbying and the CFP. The contingency theory claims that external and internal factors have an impact on organisational structure and management. In this perspective, we applied this theory to demonstrate that corporate lobbying is highly situational determined firm performance and organisational slack as influential factor. The contingency theory has highlighted the significance of obtaining a fit or a congruency between the corporate lobbying and the level of organisational slack of the firm. The idea of organisational slack as an important driver of corporate lobbying originates from behavioural theory. As shown by this study, the amount of organisational benefits that can be obtained from corporate lobbying is contingent on the organisational slack when the resources level is low. Firms with low slack might see political activities as the only solution to rectify their financial woes (Hillman et al. 2004). We argued that firms with limited organisational slack have the potential of increasing their profits through lobbying on public policy protection, for instance through high tariffs for imported goods using the "infant industry protection" argument, but do not have the purchasing power. The level of organisational slack of a firm may influence its decision to seek political favours. The lesser a firm is in slack, the more sensitive it is to government's policies. Firms may seek political favor or intervention when trying to secure a government project and may ask for a subsidy.

*Limitations and Future Research*

Similar to other studies, this paper also has some limitations. Firstly, as the data used here was historical, the causalities could not be easily surmised. Though we have tested all of the equations within the model that showed a delayed effect on the political activity (reverse of the proposed hypothesis), they noted no evidence regarding this relationship. This raises a few questions regarding the causal relationships described in the empirical studies without experimentation. Secondly, since this field is very concentrated, the number of companies included was very small (N = 134). Though the estimations can be improved in this panel data set (N = 1294), increasing the sample size would be better. The future studies will have many techniques at their disposal for improving the published literature and determining the perfect category in which this study can be fit. This could be done by qualitatively studying the relationship that exists between the firm-level lobbying and the CFP. For instance, a massive case study can be carried out in many industries for expanding the scope of the corporate lobbying literature. This project would be empirical and also based on a theory. This phenomenon has not been researched in this area.

## 7. Conclusions

In this study, we investigated organisational slack as a main contingency that controls the effects of corporate lobbying on CFP. We argued that firms with low organisational slack will seek a political solution to their limited resources. We find that the relationship between corporate lobbying and CFP is negatively moderated by organisational slack. With these results, this study emphasizes the importance of examining organisational slack in understanding the firm's performance implications of corporate lobbying and covers the way for a comprehensive understanding of contingencies when corporate lobbying is financially beneficial.

**Funding:** This research was funded by Universiti Putra Malaysia grant number GP-IPS 9536600.

**Conflicts of Interest:** The author declares no conflict of interest.

## References

Adams, Renee B., and Daniel Ferreira. 2009. Women in the boardroom and their impact on governance and performance. *Journal of Financial Economics* 94: 291–309. [CrossRef]

Adams, Garry L., and Bruce T. Lamont. 2003. Knowledge management systems and developing sustainable competitive advantage. *Journal of Knowledge Management* 7: 142–54. [CrossRef]

Aggarwal, Rajesh K., Felix Meschke, and Tracy Yue Wang. 2012. Corporate political donations: Investment or agency? *Business and Politics* 14: 1–38. [CrossRef]

Aiken, Leona S., Stephen G. West, and Raymond R. Reno. 1991. *Multiple Regression: Testing and Interpreting Interactions*. Thousand Oaks: Sage.

Alexander, Raquel, Stephen W. Mazza, and Susan Scholz. 2009. Measuring rates of return for lobbying expenditures: An empirical analysis under the American Jobs Creation Act. *Journal of Law and Politics* 25: 401–57.

Andres, Gary J. 1985. Business involvement in campaign finance: Factors influencing the decision to form a corporate PAC. *PS: Political Science & Politics* 18: 213–20.

Angrist, Joshua D., and Jörn-Steffen Pischke. 2010. The credibility revolution in empirical economics: How better research design is taking the con out of econometrics. *Journal of Economic Perspectives* 24: 3–30. [CrossRef]

Ansolabehere, Stephen, John M. De Figueiredo, and James M. Snyder Jr. 2003. Why is there so little money in US politics? *Journal of Economic Perspectives* 17: 105–30. [CrossRef]

Ansolabehere, Stephen, James M. Snyder Jr., and Michiko Ueda. 2004. Did firms profit from soft money? *Election Law Journal* 3: 193–98. [CrossRef]

Arellano, Manuel, and Stephen Bond. 1991. Some tests of specification for panel data: Monte Carlo evidence and an application to employment equations. *The Review of Economic Studies* 58: 277–97. [CrossRef]

Austin, James, Walter Cohn, and John Quelch. 1996. Pathways to business success in sub-Saharan Africa. *Journal of African Development* 2: 57–76.

Backman, Michael. 1999. *Asian Eclipse: Exposing the Dark Side of Business in Asia*. Hoboken: Wiley.

Barnard, Chester I. 1938. *The Functions of the Executive*. Cambridge: Harvard University Press.

Bascle, Guilhem. 2008. Controlling for endogeneity with instrumental variables in strategic management research. *Strategic Organization* 6: 285–327. [CrossRef]

Baumgartner, Frank R., Jeffrey M. Berry, Marie Hojnacki, David C. Kimball, and Beth L. Leech. 2009. *Lobbying and Policy Change: Who Wins, Who Loses, and Why*. Chicago: University of Chicago Press.

Blundell, Richard, and Stephen Bond. 1998. Initial conditions and moment restrictions in dynamic panel data models. *Journal of Econometrics* 87: 115–43. [CrossRef]

Blundell, Richard, Stephen Bond, and Frank Windmeijer. 2001. Estimation in dynamic panel data models: Improving on the performance of the standard GMM estimator. In *Nonstationary Panels, Panel Cointegration, and Dynamic Panels*. Bingley: Emerald Group Publishing Limited, pp. 53–91.

Bogetoft, Peter, and Jens Leth Hougaard. 2004. Super efficiency evaluations based on potential slack. *European Journal of Operational Research* 152: 14–21. [CrossRef]

Bonardi, Jean-Philippe, Guy L. F. Holburn, and Richard G. Vanden Bergh. 2006. Nonmarket strategy performance: Evidence from US electric utilities. *Academy of Management Journal* 49: 1209–28. [CrossRef]

Bond, Stephen, Anke Hoeffler, and Jonathan Temple. 2001. *GMM Estimation of Empirical Growth Models*. Oxford: Economics Group, Nuffield College, University of Oxford.

Bourgeois, L. Jay, III. 1981. On the measurement of organizational slack. *Academy of Management Review* 6: 29–39. [CrossRef]

Bourgeois, L. Jay, III, and Jitendra V. Singh. 1983. Organizational Slack and Political Behavior Among Top Management Teams. In *Academy of Management Proceedings*. No. 1. Briarcliff Manor: Academy of Management, August, vol. 1983, pp. 43–47.

Bowen, William. 2002. An analytical review of environmental justice research: what do we really know? *Environmental Management* 29: 3–15. [CrossRef] [PubMed]

Brambor, Thomas, William Roberts Clark, and Matt Golder. 2006. Understanding interaction models: Improving empirical analyses. *Political Analysis* 14: 63–82. [CrossRef]

Brasher, Holly, and David Lowery. 2006. The corporate context of lobbying activity. *Business and Politics* 8: 1–23. [CrossRef]

Bromiley, Philip. 1991. Testing a causal model of corporate risk taking and performance. *Academy of Management Journal* 34: 37–59.

Brown, Richard S. 2016. Lobbying, political connectedness and financial performance in the air transportation industry. *Journal of Air Transport Management* 54: 61–69. [CrossRef]

Buchholtz, Ann K., Allen C. Amason, and Matthew A. Rutherford. 1999. Beyond resources: The mediating effect of top management discretion and values on corporate philanthropy. *Business & Society* 38: 167–87.

Bourgeois, L. Jay, III, and Jitendra V. Singh. 1983. Organizational slack and political behavior within top management groups. Paper presented at Academy of Management Annual Meeting, Dallas, TX, USA, August 14–17; pp. 43–49.

Byrd, Peter. 1991. *British Defence Policy: Thatcher and Beyond*. London: Philip Allan.

Cao, Zhiyan, Guy D. Fernando, Arindam Tripathy, and Arun Upadhyay. 2018. The economics of corporate lobbying. *Journal of Corporate Finance* 49: 54–80. [CrossRef]

Chen, Hui, David Parsley, and Ya-Wen Yang. 2015. Corporate lobbying and firm performance. *Journal of Business Finance & Accounting* 42: 444–81.

Coates, John C., IV. 2012. Corporate politics, governance, and value before and after citizens united. *Journal of Empirical Legal Studies* 9: 657–96. [CrossRef]

Coles, Jeffrey L., Naveen D. Daniel, and Lalitha Naveen. 2008. Boards: Does one size fit all? *Journal of Financial Economics* 87: 329–56. [CrossRef]

Cooper, Michael J., Huseyin Gulen, and Alexei V. Ovtchinnikov. 2010. Corporate political contributions and stock returns. *The Journal of Finance* 65: 687–724. [CrossRef]

Cyert, Richard M., and James G. March. 1963. *A Behavioral Theory of the Firm*. Englewood Cliffs: Prentice-Hall, Inc., vol. 2, pp. 169–87.

De Figueiredo, John M., and Brian S. Silverman. 2006. Academic earmarks and the returns to lobbying. *The Journal of Law and Economics* 49: 597–625. [CrossRef]

De Soto, H. 1989. *The Other Path*. New York: Harper & Row, p. 17133.

Dimick, David E., and Victor V. Murray. 1978. Correlates of substantive policy decisions in organizations: The case of human resource management. *Academy of Management Journal* 21: 611–23.

Faccio, Mara, and David C. Parsley. 2009. Sudden deaths: Taking stock of geographic ties. *Journal of Financial and Quantitative Analysis* 44: 683–718. [CrossRef]

Faccio, Mara, Ronald W. Masulis, and John J. McConnell. 2006. Political connections and corporate bailouts. *The Journal of Finance* 61: 2597–635. [CrossRef]

Fisman, Raymond. 2001. Estimating the value of political connections. *American Economic Review* 91: 1095–102. [CrossRef]

Gawande, Kishore, and Usree Bandyopadhyay. 2000. Is protection for sale? Evidence on the Grossman-Helpman theory of endogenous protection. *Review of Economics and Statistics* 82: 139–52. [CrossRef]

George, Gerard. 2005. Slack resources and the performance of privately held firms. *Academy of Management Journal* 48: 661–76. [CrossRef]

Geppert, Mike. 1996. Paths of managerial learning in the East German context. *Organization Studies* 17: 249–68. [CrossRef]

Greenley, Gordon E., and Mehmet Oktemgil. 1998. A comparison of slack resources in high and low performing British companies. *Journal of Management Studies* 35: 377–98. [CrossRef]

Grier, Kevin B., and Michael C. Munger. 1991. Committee assignments, constituent preferences, and campaign contributions. *Economic Inquiry* 29: 24–43. [CrossRef]

Grier, Kevin B., Michael C. Munger, and Brian E. Roberts. 1994. The determinants of industry political activity, 1978–1986. *American Political Science Review* 88: 911–26. [CrossRef]

Griffin, Jennifer J., and John F. Mahon. 1997. The corporate social performance and corporate financial performance debate: Twenty-five years of incomparable research. *Business & Society* 36: 5–31.

Gul, Ferdinand A. 2006. Auditors' response to political connections and cronyism in Malaysia. *Journal of Accounting Research* 44: 931–63. [CrossRef]

Hadani, Michael, and Douglas A. Schuler. 2013. In search of El Dorado: The elusive financial returns on corporate political investments. *Strategic Management Journal* 34: 165–81. [CrossRef]

Hall, Richard L., and Frank W. Wayman. 1990. Buying time: Moneyed interests and the mobilization of bias in congressional committees. *American Political Science Review* 84: 797–820. [CrossRef]

Hart, David M. 2010. Political theory of the firm. In *Oxford Handbook of Business and Government*. Edited by David Coen, Wyn Grant and Graham Wilson. Oxford: Oxford University Press, pp. 173–90.

Heckman, James J. 1979. Sample selection bias as a specification error. *Econometrica* 47: 153–61. [CrossRef]

Hersch, Philip, Jeffry M. Netter, and Christopher Pope. 2008. Do campaign contributions and lobbying expenditures by firms create "political" capital? *Atlantic Economic Journal* 36: 395–405. [CrossRef]

Hill, Matthew D., G. Wayne Kelly, G. Brandon Lockhart, and Robert A. Van Ness. 2013. Determinants and effects of corporate lobbying. *Financial Management* 42: 931–57. [CrossRef]

Hillman, Amy J., and Michael A. Hitt. 1999. Corporate political strategy formulation: A model of approach, participation, and strategy decisions. *Academy of Management Review* 24: 825–42. [CrossRef]

Hillman, Amy J., Gerald D. Keim, and Douglas Schuler. 2004. Corporate political activity: A review and research agenda. *Journal of Management* 30: 837–57. [CrossRef]

Hochberg, Yael V., Paola Sapienza, and Annette Vissing-Jørgensen. 2009. A lobbying approach to evaluating the Sarbanes-Oxley Act of 2002. *Journal of Accounting Research* 47: 519–83. [CrossRef]

Houston, Joel F., Liangliang Jiang, Chen Lin, and Yue Ma. 2014. Political connections and the cost of bank loans. *Journal of Accounting Research* 52: 193–243. [CrossRef]

Humphries, Craig. 1991. Corporations, PACs and the strategic link between contributions and lobbying activities. *Western Political Quarterly* 44: 353–72. [CrossRef]

Igan, Deniz, Prachi Mishra, and Thierry Tressel. 2009. *A Fistful of Dollars: Lobbying and the Financial Crisis*. Washington, DC: International Monetary Fund, Research Department.

Jayachandran, Seema. 2006. The jeffords effect. *The Journal of Law and Economics* 49: 397–425. [CrossRef]

Julian, Scott D., and Joseph C. Ofori-dankwa. 2013. Financial resource availability and corporate social responsibility expenditures in a sub-Saharan economy: The institutional difference hypothesis. *Strategic Management Journal* 34: 1314–30. [CrossRef]

Keele, Luke, and Nathan J. Kelly. 2006. Dynamic models for dynamic theories: The ins and outs of lagged dependent variables. *Political Analysis* 14: 186–205. [CrossRef]

Keim, Gerald. 2001. Managing business political activities in the USA: Bridging between theory and practice. *Journal of Public Affairs: An International Journal* 1: 362–75. [CrossRef]

Khrawish, Husni Ali. 2011. Determinants of commercial banks performance: Evidence from Jordan. *International Research Journal of Finance and Economics* 81: 148–59.

Lee, Seung-Hyun, and Yoon-Suk Baik. 2010. Corporate lobbying in antidumping cases: Looking into the continued dumping and subsidy offset act. *Journal of Business Ethics* 96: 467–78. [CrossRef]

Lehn, Kenneth, and Annette Poulsen. 1989. Free cash flow and stockholder gains in going private transactions. *The Journal of Finance* 44: 771–87. [CrossRef]

Levinthal, Daniel A., and James G. March. 1993. The myopia of learning. *Strategic Management Journal* 14: 95–112. [CrossRef]

Masters, Marick F., and Gerald D. Keim. 1985. Determinants of PAC participation among large corporations. *The Journal of Politics* 47: 1158–73. [CrossRef]

Masulis, Ronald W., and Shawn Mobbs. 2011. Are all inside directors the same? Evidence from the external directorship market. *The Journal of Finance* 66: 823–72. [CrossRef]

McKeown, Timothy J. 1994. The epidemiology of corporate PAC formation, 1975–1984. *Journal of Economic Behavior & Organization* 24: 153–68.

Melitz, Marc J. 2005. When and how should infant industries be protected? *Journal of International Economics* 66: 177–96. [CrossRef]

Meyer, Alan D. 1982. Adapting to environmental jolts. *Administrative Science Quarterly* 27: 515–37. [CrossRef] [PubMed]

Milyo, Jeffrey, David Primo, and Timothy Groseclose. 2000. Corporate PAC campaign contributions in perspective. *Business and Politics* 2: 75–88. [CrossRef]

Mitchell, Neil J., Wendy L. Hansen, and Eric M. Jepsen. 1997. The determinants of domestic and foreign corporate political activity. *The Journal of Politics* 59: 1096–113. [CrossRef]

Moreno, Antonia Ruiz, Luis Miguel Molina Fernandez, and Francisco Javier Lloréns Montes. 2009. The moderating effect of slack resources on the relation between quality management and organisational learning. *International Journal of Production Research* 47: 5501–23. [CrossRef]

Morris, Thomas R., and Larry Sabato. 1984. *Virginia Government and Politics: Readings and Comments*. Richmond: Virginia Chamber of Commerce.

Nichols, Austin. 2007. Causal inference with observational data. *Stata Journal* 7: 507.

Nohria, Nitin, and Ranjay Gulati. 1996. Is slack good or bad for innovation? *Academy of Management Journal* 39: 1245–64. [CrossRef]

Nystrom, Paul C., Keshavamurthy Ramamurthy, and Alla L. Wilson. 2002. Organizational context, climate and innovativeness: adoption of imaging technology. *Journal of Engineering and Technology Management* 19: 221–47. [CrossRef]

Palmer, Timothy B., and Robert M. Wiseman. 1999. Decoupling risk taking from income stream uncertainty: A holistic model of risk. *Strategic Management Journal* 20: 1037–62. [CrossRef]

Rajagopalan, Nandini, and Gretchen M. Spreitzer. 1997. Toward a theory of strategic change: A multi-lens perspective and integrative framework. *Academy of Management Review* 22: 48–79. [CrossRef]

Richter, Ulf Henning. 2010. Liberal thought in reasoning on CSR. *Journal of Business Ethics* 97: 625–49. [CrossRef]

Richter, Brian Kelleher, Krislert Samphantharak, and Jeffrey F. Timmons. 2009. Lobbying and taxes. *American Journal of Political Science* 53: 893–909. [CrossRef]

Roberts, John. 1990. *Postmodernism, Politics and Art*. Manchester: Manchester University Press.

Roodman, David. 2009. How to do xtabond2: An introduction to difference and system GMM in Stata. *The Stata Journal* 9: 86–136. [CrossRef]

Sánchez, José Luis Fernández, and Ladislao Luna Sotorrío. 2007. The creation of value through corporate reputation. *Journal of Business Ethics* 76: 335–46. [CrossRef]

Schuler, Douglas A. 1996. Corporate political strategy and foreign competition: The case of the steel industry. *Academy of Management Journal* 39: 720–37.

Schuler, Douglas A., and Kathleen Rehbein. 1997. The filtering role of the firm in corporate political involvement. *Business & Society* 36: 116–39.

Seifert, Bruce, Sara A. Morris, and Barbara R. Bartkus. 2004. Having, giving, and getting: Slack resources, corporate philanthropy, and firm financial performance. *Business & Society* 43: 135–61.

Sharfman, Mark P., Gerrit Wolf, Richard B. Chase, and David A. Tansik. 1988. Antecedents of organizational slack. *Academy of Management Review* 13: 601–14. [CrossRef]

Singh, Jitendra V. 1986. Performance, slack, and risk taking in organizational decision making. *Academy of Management Journal* 29: 562–85.

Soto, Marcelo. 2009. *System GMM Estimation with a Small Sample*. UFAE and IAE Working Papers 780.09. Bellaterra: Unitat de Fonaments de l'Anàlisi Econòmica (UAB) and Institut d'Anàlisi Econòmica (CSIC).

Stigler, George J. 1971. The theory of economic regulation. *The Bell Journal of Economics and Management Science* 2: 3–21. [CrossRef]

Stratmann, Thomas. 2005. Some talk: Money in politics. A (partial) review of the literature. In *Policy Challenges and Political Responses*. Boston: Springer, pp. 135–56.

Tan, Justin. 2003. Curvilinear relationship between organizational slack and firm performance: Evidence from Chinese state enterprises. *European Management Journal* 21: 740–49. [CrossRef]

Tan, Justin, and Mike W. Peng. 2003. Organizational slack and firm performance during economic transitions: Two studies from an emerging economy. *Strategic Management Journal* 24: 1249–63. [CrossRef]

Tu, Guoqian, Bingxuan Lin, and Feng Liu. 2013. Political connections and privatization: Evidence from China. *Journal of Accounting and Public Policy* 32: 114–35. [CrossRef]

Wen, W. 2010. Ownership Structure and Bank Performance in China: Does Ownership Concentration Matter? (October 30, 2010). Available online: https://ssrn.com/abstract=1747655 (accessed on 27 December 2018).

Windmeijer, Frank. 2005. A finite sample correction for the variance of linear efficient two-step GMM estimators. *Journal of Econometrics* 126: 25–51. [CrossRef]

Wiseman, Robert M., and Philip Bromiley. 1996. Toward a model of risk in declining organizations: An empirical examination of risk, performance and decline. *Organization Science* 7: 524–43. [CrossRef]

Wu, Jianfeng, and Rungting Tu. 2007. CEO stock option pay and R&D spending: A behavioral agency explanation. *Journal of Business Research* 60: 482–92.

Yu, Frank, and Xiaoyun Yu. 2011. Corporate lobbying and fraud detection. *Journal of Financial and Quantitative Analysis* 46: 1865–91. [CrossRef]

# 2

# Political Connections and Stock Price Crash Risk: Empirical Evidence from the Fall of Suharto

**Iman Harymawan [1,*], Brian Lam [2], Mohammad Nasih [1] and Rumayya Rumayya [3]**

[1] Department of Accountancy, Universitas Airlangga, Surabaya 60286, Indonesia; mohnasih@feb.unair.ac.id
[2] Division of Business and Management, BNU-HKBU United International College, Zhuhai 519087, China; brianmolam@uic.edu.hk
[3] Department of Economics, Universitas Airlangga, Surabaya 60286, Indonesia; rumayya@feb.unair.ac.id
* Correspondence: harymawan.iman@feb.unair.ac.id

**Abstract:** This study examines the relationship between firm-level political connections and stock price crash risk in Indonesia. It employs the difference-in-difference design to deal with the self-selection bias issue regarding the choice of the firms to become a politically connected firm. We use the sudden resignation of the former President of Indonesia, Suharto, to show that politically connected firms are associated with lower stock price crash risk and that the risk for these politically connected firms increased after Suharto resigned. Furthermore, we found evidence that these negative associations are more pronounced in firms with more complex firm structures.

**Keywords:** politically connected firms; stock price crash risk; complex firm structure

**JEL Classification:** D72; G10; L10

---

## 1. Introduction

Previous studies have found that firms with political connections receive preferential treatment to finance, enjoy lower debt and equity costs, and have more procurement contracts (Claessens et al. 2008; Boubakri et al. 2012; Houston et al. 2014; Goldman et al. 2013; Harymawan 2018). Other studies have shown, however, that connected firms pay higher audit fees to auditors and charge higher prices for debt to debtholders as a cost of political connections (Bliss and Gul 2012; Gul 2006). Grier et al. (1994) have also examined the benefit–cost model across industries and the contributions of political action committees in each industry, finding that industries with higher potential benefits from government connections contribute more to their connections.

This study extends these prior findings in the political connections literature by investigating the effect of political connections on firms' stock price crash risk. Recent studies have provided evidence that establishing political connections (i.e., hiring a politician as a director) can decrease the firm's stock price crash risk (Luo et al. 2016; Hu and Wang 2018). In contrast, Lee and Wang (2017) and Tee (2018) have shown that connected firms tend to have a higher stock price crash risk. Meanwhile, Roberts (1990) found a relationship between committee seniority in the US Congress and the distribution of federal benefits. He also found that the stock market reacted significantly to the death of Senator Henry Jackson, especially across his various constituent interests. Using the unexpected resignation of former Indonesian President, Suharto, this study was able to investigate the stock price crash risk of connected firms in the period before and after his resignation. This unique event provides a better setting than a simple relationship model for answering the question of whether connected firms have a higher or lower stock price crash risk than unconnected firms.

Investigating the relationship between political connections and stock price crash risk in the pre- and post-Suharto era provides us with a better research setting for several reasons. First, as Fisman (2001) shows, during the Suharto era, political connections in Indonesia were centralized, which provides a better proxy than a decentralized country for evaluating political connections; measuring the value of political connections in a country with decentralized political decision-making is more complex due to the variety of connection types. Second, the unexpected resignation of Suharto is an exogenous event which allows us to make clearer estimates when evaluating the relationship between political connections and stock price crash risk.

In this study, we first employed some univariate tests to describe our data and test the hypotheses. The correlation matrix shows that firms connected to Suharto have a significantly higher stock price crash risk. Then we compared the mean between a group of connected versus non-connected firms. The results also show that firms with Suharto connections had a significantly higher mean of stock price crash risk than firms with no connections.

In the multivariate analyses, we used the ordinary least square regression to test the hypotheses. We found that firms with political connections had a negative and significant association with stock price crash risk. To deal with the endogeneity issue, this study employed the difference-in-difference model, using the unexpected resignation of Suharto as a natural experiment. We found that in the period prior to the Suharto resignation, connected firms were more likely to have a lower stock price crash risk. Interestingly, we found that after Suharto resigned, there was a positive and significant association between political connections and stock price crash risk.

This study contributes to the existing literature of political connections in several ways. Prior studies have examined the relationship between political connections to stock price crash risk (citation). This study adds to this literature by being the first in providing evidence on how political connections affect stock price crash risk by comparing when the political connections are in and out of power. In addition, this study also extends the literature by examining the role of firm complexity on the relationship between political connections and stock price crash risk. For practitioners, this study provides useful information about the changes of stock price crash risk of politically connected firms between pre and post political power. For a regulator, these findings provide an insight that political activities disclosure might help the investor to reduce the information asymmetry between firms and stakeholders to reduce the likelihood of stock price crash risk for politically connected firms in the period post to political power resignation. The remainder of this article discusses the institutional setting of political connections in Indonesia and presents the hypotheses, data, methods, results, discussion, and conclusion.

## 2. Literature Review

### *2.1. Corporate Governance in Indonesia*

Since the late 1970s, Indonesia has experienced economic transformation from state-owned enterprise and a small and traditional business-dominated economy to modern private enterprise. Unfortunately, rather than signaling the development of entrepreneurship and healthy business sectors, the transformation marked the beginning of an era where political connections in business became increasingly widespread, with Suharto's cronies at the center. The success of these politically connected firms heavily depended on their ability to acquire and maintain relationships with Suharto's regime in order to secure special privileges from the state.

As noted by McLeod (2000), these privileges included import protection, import licenses, no-bid contracts from government and state-owned enterprises, cheap loans from the state and central banks, rights to extract natural resources, tax relief, and even the right to collect taxes.

At first, the majority of these politically well-connected firms were dominated by the Sino-Indonesian (of Chinese descent) business elites who had been close to Suharto since the 1950s. Suharto's administration granted them special rights to monopolize the import and distribution of sugar, rice, forestry products, and automobiles. Over time, two other elite groups emerged: the well-connected pribumi enterprises and businesses owned by Suharto's children. These three groups formed a core group of cronies in Suharto's regime (Schwarz 1994).

Hill (2000) has shown that the 20 largest conglomerates in 1993, with a total turnover valued at around 21% of GDP, were all connected to Suharto. Three of those twenty conglomerates were owned by Suharto's children. Claessens et al. (1999) has also shown that in 1996 Suharto's cronies controlled 417 listed and non-listed companies on the Indonesian stock market. Together, these companies contributed 16.6% of total stock market capitalization.

### 2.2. *After the Fall of Suharto*

In 1998, Indonesia was severely hit by a financial crisis. The crisis started in Thailand and South Korea and then spread throughout Asia. During the crisis, the rupiah depreciated by 30%, exports declined, the inflation rate escalated to almost 100%, the poverty rate doubled to over 27%, and economic growth contracted to almost 14% (Hofman et al. 2004). The financial crisis then evolved into a political crisis which led to the resignation of Suharto after 32 years in power. Pangestu and Habir (2002) have argued that the favorable treatment to politically connected firms created moral hazard and caused the crisis as these firms became reckless in their business practices, violating legal lending limits and generating non-performing loans.

Sato (2004) has found that the performance of Suharto-connected firms varied after the crisis. The firms that survived were those established in the 1970s and ranked among the top 20 or top 30 richest in the 1980s and 1996. In contrast, the firms that suffered severely were younger firms established in the 1980s and either ranked in the top 20 in 1996 or else outside the top 20 in the 1980s but inside the top 10 in 1996. Carney and Hamilton-Hart (2015) also found that a significant number of large firms shrank tremendously in 1996 and fell outside the top 200, including the firms of Suharto's children. Ultimately, Suharto's old, well-established cronies seemed to successfully reconsolidate their businesses and actively reconnect with current political actors and government officials in the post-Suharto administration, who were possibly motivated to secure the benefits they had gained under the Suharto government (Winter 2013).

### 2.3. *Stock Price Crash Risk*

Conceptually, stock price crash risk is premised on the tendency of managers to withhold bad news, which leads to bad news being stockpiled in firms. At a certain point, it becomes too costly or impossible for managers to withhold the bad news any longer. When such a point arrives, all the hidden bad news is revealed to the market at once, resulting in a significant stock price drop, that is, a stock price crash (Kim et al. 2011). Extant studies have investigated various determinants of stock price crash. For instance, Kim et al. (2011) found that corporate tax avoidance enables managers to hoard bad news, which leads to the risk of a stock price crash. He and Ren (2019) have provided evidence that financial constraints are positively associated with future stock price crash risk, via both bad news hoarding and default risk channels. Chen et al. (2016) have found that firms with a higher degree of earnings smoothing are more prone to stock price crashes. For their part, Chauhan et al. (2017) have shown that stock liquidity, which is identified through the threat of intervention and price informativeness, decreases stock price crash risk as it works as a governance mechanism to discipline managers for withholding bad news. In addition, prior research has shown that firms' corporate social responsibility significantly mitigates stock price crash risk (Lee 2016). Our research extends this stream of literature by examining the relationship between stock price crash risk and political connections, using the sudden resignation of Suharto to address the self-selection bias issue.

### 2.4. *Hypothesis Development*

There are two possible relationships between politically connected firms and stock price crash risk. The first possibility is that firms with political connections are more likely to have higher stock price crash risk. Prior literature has suggested that politically connected firms can derive significant benefits in terms of financing, whereas non-politically connected firms are more likely to suffer from financing constraints (Luo and Zhen 2008). To meet financing requirements, managers are encouraged to whitewash financial statements and hide negative information. These actions may result in an increase in information asymmetry, and the accumulation of bad news may eventually lead to a stock price crash. He and Ren (2019) have also argued that if the institutional setting of the country is not well developed (i.e., inefficient stock market, weak corporate governance, etc.), it will increase the ability of firms to hoard bad news. This situation (hoarding bad news) thus increases the stock price crash risk of connected firms. Based on this, we could say there is a positive association between political connections and stock price crash risk, which is the first possible relationship.

On the other hand, Hu and Wang (2018) have also found that with the preferential access of financing, politically connected firms can reduce bad news hoarding activities to avoid government regulation and maintain access to government subsidies. In this way, the degree of information asymmetry can be reduced, thus decreasing the likelihood of a stock price crash. Furthermore, He and Ren (2019) have argued that if a country has a good institutional setting (i.e., efficient stock market, good governance, pro-business policies, etc.) there is a lower probability of firms hoarding bad news, therefore decreasing stock price crash risk. From this, we could argue that politically connected firms actually have a lower stock price crash risk. Based on above discussion on the possible relationships between politically connected firms and stock price crash risk, the formal hypothesis is as follows:

**Hypothesis 1 (H1).** *There is a relationship between firms with political connections and the level of stock price crash risk.*

Fisman (2001) has found that politically connected firms in Indonesia strongly relied on the benefits from their connections under the Suharto regime and often had privileged access to financing. Suharto's resignation in 1998 represented a fundamental transition in Indonesia's political economy at the national level. The shift is evidenced by the decline in the number of people with military and state backgrounds and the rise of those with private sector backgrounds in Indonesia's political elite (Poczter and Pepinsky 2016). Leuz and Oberholzer-Gee (2006) have also found that political connections can lose their value through election losses. Connected firms thus need to be more responsive to market pressures since they can no longer rely on the same benefits from their connections (Harymawan and Nowland 2016). Suharto's resignation and the subsequent regime change triggered financial and operational shocks for politically connected firms. They then needed to face all kinds of market pressures by themselves, resulting in a higher stock price crash risk. Therefore, we predict that the resignation of Suharto increased the need for politically connected firms to respond to market pressures, resulting in a higher stock price crash risk.

**Hypothesis 2 (H2).** *After Suharto resigned, the risk of a stock price crash for firms with political connections increased.*

The complexity of firm structure may affect stock price crash risk. We measured the complexity of firm structure according to the number of subsidiaries owned by the company. As the number of subsidiaries increases, so too do the benefits derived from political connections.

**Hypothesis 3 (H3).** *The negative relationship between stock price crash risk and political connections is more pronounced for firms with a more complex firm structure.*

## 3. Methodology

### 3.1. Data

Our sample covers the period from 1995 to 2001. We obtained political connection data from the Indonesia Capital Market Directory (ICMD) and information on the total number of subsidiaries from Osiris. Accounting and financial data were retrieved from Compustat Global. We deleted observations with missing Compustat data, stock prices, returns, and trading volume data when estimating our crash risk measures and control variables. We excluded the year of Suharto's resignation (1998) to achieve an unambiguous pre-event and post-event period for the main tests, especially for the difference-in-difference test. The main sample includes 730 firm-year observations.

### 3.2. Measuring Stock Price Crash Risk

We followed Hutton et al. (2009) and Kim et al. (2016) to construct the three measures of stock price crash risk. Our first measure was the firm-specific return crashes. The indicator variable CRASH equals one for a firm-year that experiences one or more crash weeks during the fiscal year and zero otherwise.

To calculate the first measure of crash likelihood for each firm-year, we first estimated the weekly returns by firm and by year with the following regression model:

$$\begin{aligned} rj,k = \alpha j + \beta 1jrm,k - 2 + \beta 2jrm,k - 1 + \beta 3jrm,k + \beta 4jrm,k{+}1 + \beta 5jrm,k + 2 \\ + \beta 6jri,k - 2 + \beta 7jri,k - 1 + \beta 8jri,k + \beta 9jri,k + 1 + \beta 10jri,k + 2 + \varepsilon jk, \end{aligned} \quad (1)$$

where $rj,k$ is the return on stock $j$ in week $k$, $rm,k$ is the return on the value-weighted market index in week $k$ provided by the Center for Research in Security Prices, and $ri,k$ is the return on the Fama–French value-weighted industry index in week $k$. As in Dimson 1979, the lead and lag terms for the market and industry indexes were used to control for nonsynchronous trading. The firm-week return was measured by the natural logarithm of one plus the residual return in Equation (1), with at least 26 weekly return observations available per firm-year. Crash weeks are firm-week returns which are below 3.2 standard deviations of the mean firm-week return of the fiscal year.

For the second measure, we used the volatility of below-mean versus above-mean returns (DUVOL) for each firm-year. The variable DUVOL was calculated by the natural logarithm of the ratio of the standard deviation of weekly returns below the annual mean divided by the standard deviation of weekly returns above the annual mean.

For the third measure, we used the negative skewness of firm-specific weekly returns (NCSKEW). For each firm-year, we multiplied minus one to the third power of weekly returns and then divided it by the third power of the standard deviation of weekly returns. Appendix A presents a summary of all variables used in this research.

### 3.3. Main Model

To test our hypotheses, we performed multiple regression tests with a series of control variables to ensure the results were not subject to some crucial factors which have systematic effects on the cross-sectional variation in stock price crash risk.

To examine our first hypothesis (H1), we estimated the following linear regression, which regresses stock crash risk (*CRASH, DUVOL,* or *NCSKEW*) on political connection (*PCON*) and the control variables.

$$DepVart = \beta 0 + \beta 1\ PCONt + \sum \beta i\ Xt + \sum \beta j\ YRDt + \sum \beta k\ INDDt + et, \quad (2)$$

where *DepVar* is *CRASH, DUVOL,* or *NCSKEW*; *X* is a set of the control variables, *YRD* is the year dummy, and *INDD* is the industry dummy.

To examine our secondhypothesis (H2), we estimated the following linear regression, which regresses stock crash risk (*CRASH, DUVOL,* or *NCSKEW*) on the difference-in-differences dummy (*DID*), political connection (*PCON*), and control variables.

$$DepVart = \beta 0 + \beta 1\ DIDt + \beta 22\ PCONt + \sum \beta i\ Xt + \sum \beta j\ YRDt + \sum \beta k\ INDDt + et, \quad (3)$$

where *DepVar* is *CRASH, DUVOL,* or *NCSKEW*. *X* is a set of the control variables, *YRD* is the year dummy, and *INDD* is the industry dummy.

To examine our third hypothesis (H3), we estimated the linear regression using Equation (1), which regresses stock crash risk (*CRASH, DUVOL,* or *NCSKEW*) on the political connection (*PCON*). However, this time we divided the full sample into complex and less-complex subsamples. In the complex subsample, the total number of subsidiaries was greater than the median. In the less-complex subsample, the total number of subsidiaries was not greater than the median.

### *3.4. Sample Selection*

Our sample consisted of listed companies from Indonesia, covering the period from 1995 to 2001. We adopted the two-digit Standard Industrial Classification (SIC) system to classify the different industrial sectors and removed observations that did not have firm-specific control variables. The final sample for the main model contained 730 firm-year observations. Continuous variables were winsorized at 1% or 99% to control for the effects of outliers.

## 4. Empirical Analysis

Table 1 presents the sample distribution for the period 1995–1997 and 1999–2001. We excluded the year of Suharto's resignation (1998) to achieve an unambiguous pre-event and post-event period for the main tests, especially for the difference-in-difference test. Among the 730 firm-year observations, the number of firms with political connections was 149 and those without political connections 581.

**Table 1.** Sample distribution.

| Year | Number of Firms with Political Connections | Number of Firms without Political Connections | Total |
|---|---|---|---|
| 1995 | 13 | 29 | 42 |
| 1996 | 23 | 62 | 85 |
| 1997 | 29 | 106 | 135 |
| 1999 | 27 | 126 | 153 |
| 2000 | 28 | 125 | 153 |
| 2001 | 29 | 133 | 162 |
| Total | 149 | 581 | 730 |

Note: We excluded the year of Suharto's resignation (1998) to achieve an unambiguous pre- and post-event period for the difference-in-difference model.

Table 2 presents descriptive statistics for the period 1995–1997 and 1999–2001, totaling 730 firm-year observations. All variables are defined in the appendix. The sample mean of *PCON* is 0.204, indicating that about 20% of the sample was connected politically to Suharto and the remaining 80% was not. The dependent variables (*CRASH, DUVOL,* and *NCSKEW*) and variable of interest (*PCON*) are presented in current-year values. The control variables are presented in lag-one-year values because lag-one-year values of these variables are used in the regression model.

**Table 2.** Summary statistics (n = 730).

| Variables | Mean | Std | Min | Q1 | Median | Q4 | Max |
|---|---|---|---|---|---|---|---|
| *CRASH* | 0.563 | 0.496 | 0.000 | 0.000 | 1.000 | 1.000 | 1.000 |
| *DUVOL* | −0.066 | 0.298 | −1.026 | −0.251 | −0.079 | 0.100 | 2.092 |
| *NCSKEW* | −0.114 | 1.068 | −3.861 | −0.608 | −0.139 | 0.268 | 17.407 |
| *PCON* | 0.204 | 0.403 | 0.000 | 0.000 | 0.000 | 0.000 | 1.000 |
| $SIZE_{(t-1)}$ | 4.800 | 1.446 | 1.328 | 3.763 | 4.666 | 5.743 | 8.865 |
| $ROA_{(t-1)}$ | −0.013 | 0.193 | −1.175 | −0.065 | 0.028 | 0.083 | 0.473 |
| $LEVERAGE_{(t-1)}$ | 0.477 | 0.317 | 0.000 | 0.242 | 0.468 | 0.646 | 1.613 |
| $MTB_{(t-1)}$ | 1.323 | 2.252 | −8.558 | 0.385 | 0.908 | 1.711 | 23.928 |
| $NCSKEW_{(t-1)}$ | −0.089 | 1.257 | −8.230 | −0.545 | −0.107 | 0.326 | 10.310 |
| $DTURN_{(t-1)}$ | 0.001 | 0.004 | −0.022 | −0.001 | 0.000 | 0.001 | 0.026 |
| $SIGMA_{(t-1)}$ | 0.063 | 0.038 | 0.015 | 0.036 | 0.055 | 0.078 | 0.421 |
| $RET_{(t-1)}$ | 0.554 | 2.551 | −0.979 | −0.465 | −0.146 | 0.555 | 21.187 |
| Observations | | | | | | | |

This table presents summary statistics for our sample for the period 1995–1997 and 1999–2001.

Table 3 presents the Pearson correlations. It displays the correlations between dependent variables, the independent variable, and the control variables. The significance level is denoted at 10%, 5%, and 1%.

Table 4 presents the characteristics of politically connected and non-politically connected firms. We observed that firms with political connections are in general larger in terms of total assets than those without political connections. These politically connected firms also have higher leverage.

Table 5 presents the regression results for the relationship between political connection and stock price crash risk. The coefficient of political connection (*PCON*) was negative and significant for all three risk models (*CRASH* and *DUVOL* at the 1% level and *NCSKEW* at the 5% level) after controlling the firm-specific control variables. This result was consistent with our prediction, which is that the stock price crash risk is lower for politically connected firms. Therefore, hypothesis 1 is supported.

To use the difference-in-difference model, we needed to test whether the parallel trend assumption holds. The visual inspection method was not appropriate for this study because the main dependent variable (stock crash) is an indicator variable. Therefore, we conducted a formal test on the parallel trend. Our sample contained three pre-treatment periods and three post-treatment periods. Following Autor (2003), we specify the following model:

$$Yit = B_{-2}D_{it} + B_{-1}D_{it} + B_1D_{it} + B_2D_{it} + B_3D_{it} + \text{Firm Fix Effects} + \text{Year Fixed Effects} + e_{it}, \quad (4)$$

where $Y$ is the outcome for firm $i$ at time $t$. We included the interactions of the time dummies and the political connection indicator for the first two pre-Suharto-resignation periods and dropped the one for the year of Suharto's resignation. Therefore, all the other interactions are shown with reference to this omitted period. If the coefficients $B_{-2}$ and $B_{-1}$ were not significant, then the difference in differences was not significantly different between the politically connected firms and non-politically connected firms in the pre-Suharto-resignation periods, indicating that the parallel trend assumption holds.

As we included all the Suharto-connected firms as a treatment group and all the non-Suharto-connected firms as a control group during the sample period, the random sampling assumption for the treatment group and control group was not a concern in our study.

Table 6, panel A presents regression results testing the parallel trend. The coefficients for *PCON1996* and *PCON1997* were insignificant, indicating that the parallel trend assumption holds. Besides, it can be observed from the coefficients for *PCON1999*, *PCON2000*, and *PCON2001* that the increased stock crash risk for Suharto-connected firms fades across the years in the post-Suharto period.

**Table 3.** Pearson correlations (n = 730).

| Variables | [1] | [2] | [3] | [4] | [5] | [6] | [7] | [8] | [9] | [10] | [11] | [12] |
|---|---|---|---|---|---|---|---|---|---|---|---|---|
| [1] *CRASH* | 1.000 | | | | | | | | | | | |
| [2] *DUVOL* | 0.303 *** | 1.000 | | | | | | | | | | |
| [3] *NCSKEW* | 0.296 *** | 0.851 *** | 1.000 | | | | | | | | | |
| [4] *PCON* | 0.042 | −0.096 *** | −0.069 * | 1.000 | | | | | | | | |
| [5] $SIZE_{(t-1)}$ | 0.168 *** | −0.064 * | 0.008 | 0.391 *** | 1.000 | | | | | | | |
| [6] $ROA_{(t-1)}$ | 0.053 | −0.029 | −0.022 | −0.002 | 0.044 | 1.000 | | | | | | |
| [7] $LEVERAGE_{(t-1)}$ | −0.068 * | 0.044 | 0.043 | 0.093 ** | 0.132 *** | −0.589 *** | 1.000 | | | | | |
| [8] $MTB_{(t-1)}$ | 0.070 * | −0.013 | 0.006 | 0.063 * | 0.141 *** | 0.191 *** | −0.115 *** | 1.000 | | | | |
| [9] $NCSKEW_{(t-1)}$ | −0.059 | 0.060 | 0.064 * | −0.082 ** | −0.008 | −0.061 | 0.029 | −0.000 | 1.000 | | | |
| [10] $DTURN_{(t-1)}$ | 0.077 ** | −0.020 | 0.005 | 0.018 | 0.051 | 0.027 | −0.054 | 0.058 | −0.041 | 1.000 | | |
| [11] $SIGMA_{(t-1)}$ | −0.151 *** | 0.113 *** | 0.045 | −0.065 * | −0.328 *** | −0.136 *** | 0.170 *** | −0.081 ** | −0.029 | −0.054 | 1.000 | |
| [12] $RET_{(t-1)}$ | 0.007 | −0.012 | −0.049 | 0.051 | −0.030 | 0.165 *** | −0.035 | 0.209 *** | −0.117 *** | −0.007 | 0.239 *** | 1.000 |

* $p < 0.10$, ** $p < 0.05$, *** $p < 0.01$.

**Table 4.** Characteristics of politically connected and non-politically connected firms.

| Variables | Firms with Political Connections | Firms without Political Connections | Coef | t-Value |
|---|---|---|---|---|
| | N = 149 | N = 581 | | |
| *CRASH* | 0.604 | 0.552 | 0.052 | −1.131 |
| *DUVOL* | −0.123 | −0.052 | −0.071 *** | 2.601 |
| *NCSKEW* | −0.258 | −0.077 | −0.182 * | 1.854 |
| $SIZE_{(t-1)}$ | 5.916 | 4.514 | 1.402 *** | −11.458 |
| $ROA_{(t-1)}$ | −0.014 | −0.013 | −0.001 | 0.065 |
| $LEVERAGE_{(t-1)}$ | 0.535 | 0.462 | 0.074 ** | −2.533 |
| $MTB_{(t-1)}$ | 1.601 | 1.252 | 0.350 * | −1.692 |
| $NCSKEW_{(t-1)}$ | −0.293 | −0.037 | −0.256 ** | 2.220 |
| $DTURN_{(t-1)}$ | 0.001 | 0.001 | 0.000 | −0.492 |
| $SIGMA_{(t-1)}$ | 0.058 | 0.064 | −0.006 * | 1.761 |
| $RET_{(t-1)}$ | 0.811 | 0.488 | 0.323 | −1.381 |

The asterisks *, *** denote significance at the 10%, 5%, and 1% levels (two-tailed), respectively.

**Table 5.** Main results: results of regression of political connections on stock price crash risk.

| Variables | (1) | | (2) | | (3) | |
|---|---|---|---|---|---|---|
| | *CRASH* | | *DUVOL* | | *NCSKEW* | |
| *PCON* | −0.366 *** | −2.92 | −0.087 *** | −2.95 | −0.276 ** | −2.54 |
| $SIZE_{(t-1)}$ | 0.275 *** | 4.47 | 0.010 | 0.68 | 0.053 | 1.18 |
| $ROA_{(t-1)}$ | −0.119 | −0.12 | 0.058 | 0.91 | 0.256 | 1.16 |
| $LEVERAGE_{(t-1)}$ | −0.741 *** | −2.65 | 0.010 | 0.19 | 0.090 | 0.49 |
| $MTB_{(t-1)}$ | 0.035 | 0.64 | 0.001 | 0.31 | 0.013 | 0.77 |
| $NCSKEW_{(t-1)}$ | −0.069 | −1.16 | 0.007 | 0.80 | 0.031 | 1.07 |
| $DTURN_{(t-1)}$ | 6.830 | 0.39 | −4.586 *** | −2.97 | −12.449 *** | −2.98 |
| $SIGMA_{(t-1)}$ | −5.672 * | −1.93 | 0.666 | 1.48 | 1.465 | 1.23 |
| $RET_{(t-1)}$ | 0.041 | 1.57 | −0.000 | −0.02 | −0.004 | −0.39 |
| Constant | 2.261 * | 1.70 | 0.109 | 0.30 | 1.832 | 0.89 |
| Year FE | Yes | | Yes | | Yes | |
| Industry FE | Yes | | Yes | | Yes | |
| Observations | 704 | | 730 | | 730 | |
| $R^2$ | | | 0.151 | | 0.118 | |
| Adjusted $R^2$ | | | 0.078 | | 0.042 | |
| Pseudo R2 | 0.120 | | | | | |

Notes: This table presents regression results testing the effect of political connections on stock price crash risk. The second column displays t statistics. Standard errors were clustered by firm and year. The asterisks *, **, *** denote significance at the 10%, 5%, and 1% levels (two-tailed), respectively.

**Table 6. Panel A.** Test on parallel trend; **Panel B.** Difference-in-difference results.

| Panel A | | | | | | |
|---|---|---|---|---|---|---|
| | (1) | | (2) | | (3) | |
| | *Crash* | | *DUVol* | | *NCSkew* | |
| *PCON1996* | 0.258 | 0.40 | −0.073 | −1.02 | −0.271 | −0.99 |
| *PCON1997* | 0.063 | 0.10 | −0.050 | −0.73 | −0.118 | −0.45 |
| *PCON1999* | 1.662 *** | 2.81 | 0.222 *** | 3.32 | 0.551 ** | 2.15 |
| *PCON2000* | 0.976 * | 1.72 | 0.196 *** | 2.88 | 0.488 * | 1.87 |
| *PCON2001* | 0.591 | 1.04 | 0.107 | 1.57 | 0.480 * | 1.84 |
| Constant | −11.897 | −0.02 | −0.804 *** | −2.86 | −3.286 *** | −3.06 |
| Year FE | Yes | | Yes | | Yes | |
| Firm FE | Yes | | Yes | | Yes | |
| Observations | 765 | | 886 | | 886 | |
| $R^2$ | | | 0.317 | | 0.248 | |
| Adjusted $R^2$ | | | 0.129 | | 0.041 | |
| Pseudo $R^2$ | 0.138 | | | | | |

Notes: this table presents regression results testing the parallel trend. The second column displays t statistics. Standard errors are clustered by firm and year. The asterisks *, **, *** denote significance at the 10%, 5%, and 1% levels (two-tailed), respectively.

**Table 6.** *Cont.*

| Panel B | | | | | | |
|---|---|---|---|---|---|---|
| Variables | (1) | | (2) | | (3) | |
| | *CRASH* | | *DUVOL* | | *NCSKEW* | |
| *DID* | 2.142 *** | 2.74 | 0.284 *** | 3.84 | 0.933 *** | 2.64 |
| *PCON* | −1.576 * | −1.79 | −0.251 *** | −2.61 | −0.816 *** | −2.92 |
| $SIZE_{(t-1)}$ | 0.281 *** | 4.61 | 0.010 | 0.74 | 0.054 | 1.27 |
| $ROA_{(t-1)}$ | −0.203 | −0.22 | 0.045 | 0.87 | 0.213 | 1.13 |
| $LEVERAGE_{(t-1)}$ | −0.835 *** | −3.25 | −0.004 | −0.08 | 0.045 | 0.26 |
| $MTB_{(t-1)}$ | 0.041 | 0.70 | 0.002 | 0.42 | 0.015 | 0.82 |
| $NCSKEW_{(t-1)}$ | −0.051 | −0.94 | 0.008 | 1.10 | 0.036 | 1.41 |
| $DTURN_{(t-1)}$ | −0.147 | −0.01 | −5.234 *** | −3.97 | −14.581 *** | −2.71 |
| $SIGMA_{(t-1)}$ | −5.082 | −1.61 | 0.713 * | 1.65 | 1.620 | 1.40 |
| $RET_{(t-1)}$ | 0.043 * | 1.73 | 0.000 | 0.18 | −0.003 | −0.30 |
| Constant | 2.637 ** | 2.21 | 0.163 | 0.50 | 2.010 | 1.03 |
| Year FE | Yes | | Yes | | Yes | |
| Industry FE | Yes | | Yes | | Yes | |
| Observations | 704 | | 730 | | 730 | |
| $R^2$ | | | 0.188 | | 0.148 | |
| Adjusted $R^2$ | | | 0.116 | | 0.073 | |
| Pseudo R2 | 0.142 | | | | | |

Notes: This table presents regression results testing the effect of Suharto's resignation on stock price crash risk. The second column displays t statistics. Standard errors are clustered by firm and year. The asterisks *, **, *** denote significance at the 10%, 5%, and 1% levels (two-tailed), respectively.

Table 6, panel B presents the regression results for the effect of the fall of Suharto on the relationship between political connection and stock price crash risk. The coefficient for differences in differences (*DID*) is positive and significant at the 1% level for all three risk models after controlling the firm-specific control variables and country-level control variables. This result is consistent with our prediction, which is that the stock price crash risk of politically connected firms increased after the fall of Suharto. Therefore, hypothesis 2 is supported.

Table 7 reports the results of the sensitivity test for Table 5 on the regression of stock price crash risk on political connection because this test includes the year in which Suharto resigned, 1998. The coefficient of political connection (*PCON*) for all three models was negative (*CRASH* at the 1% level, and *NCSKEW* at the 10% level), indicating that political connection lowers stock price crash risk. The significance level for *NCSKEW* and *DUVOL* in Table 7 was lower than in Table 5. This is because the inclusion of observations for 1998, the year in which Suharto resigned, may have introduced some noise into the regression model.

Table 8 reports the results of the sensitivity test for Table 5 on the regression of stock price crash risk on *DID* because this test includes the year in which Suharto resigned, 1998. The coefficient of *DID* for all three models was significantly positive, indicating that the stock price crash risk of politically connected firms increased after the fall of Suharto.

To investigate whether a political connection exerts distinct impacts on stock price crash risk when interacting with the differential complexity of firm structure (H3), the full sample was divided into two subsamples according to the complexity of firm structure. Table 9 presents the regression results for the effect of complexity of firm structure on the relationship between political connection and stock price crash risk. The coefficient for political connection (*PCON*) was negative and significant at the 1% level for all three risk models for complex firms after controlling the firm-specific control variables. This result was consistent with our prediction, which is that the negative relationship between political connection and stock price crash risk is more pronounced for firms with complex firm structures. Therefore, hypothesis 3 is supported. In addition, we also tested (non-tabulated results) whether the negative associations between political connection and stock price crash risk in complex firms are due to the size effect (Dang et al. 2018). Hence, we run similar regression model except we exclude the *SIZE* variable. We find that the coefficients of *PCON* are still negative.

**Table 7.** Results of regression of political connections on stock price crash risk (including year of Suharto's resignation, 1998).

| Variables | (1) | | (2) | | (3) | |
|---|---|---|---|---|---|---|
| | *CRASH* | | *DUVOL* | | *NCSKEW* | |
| *PCON* | −0.373 *** | −3.32 | −0.059 | −1.54 | −0.200 * | −1.65 |
| $SIZE_{(t-1)}$ | 0.255 *** | 4.85 | 0.002 | 0.11 | 0.016 | 0.33 |
| $ROA_{(t-1)}$ | −0.283 | −0.32 | 0.049 | 0.85 | 0.230 | 1.28 |
| $LEVERAGE_{(t-1)}$ | −0.591 ** | −2.22 | 0.011 | 0.28 | 0.045 | 0.34 |
| $MTB_{(t-1)}$ | 0.050 | 1.10 | 0.001 | 0.24 | 0.010 | 0.98 |
| $NCSKEW_{(t-1)}$ | −0.087 | −1.50 | 0.009 | 0.95 | 0.038 | 1.15 |
| $DTURN_{(t-1)}$ | 5.944 | 0.42 | −1.445 | −0.52 | −2.049 | −0.22 |
| $SIGMA_{(t-1)}$ | −4.252 * | −1.80 | 0.616 * | 1.73 | 1.681 * | 1.91 |
| $RET_{(t-1)}$ | 0.040 | 1.63 | −0.001 | −0.37 | −0.003 | −0.31 |
| Constant | 1.737 | 1.25 | 0.113 | 0.38 | 1.616 | 1.00 |
| Year FE | Yes | | Yes | | Yes | |
| Industry FE | Yes | | Yes | | Yes | |
| Observations | 879 | | 886 | | 886 | |
| $R^2$ | | | 0.125 | | 0.088 | |
| Adjusted $R^2$ | | | 0.062 | | 0.022 | |
| Pseudo R2 | 0.111 | | | | | |

Notes: This table presents regression results testing the effect of political connections on stock price crash risk. The second column displays t statistics. Standard errors are clustered by firm and y ear. The asterisks *, **, *** denote significance at the 10%, 5%, and 1% levels (two-tailed), respectively.

**Table 8.** Difference-in-difference results (including year of Suharto's resignation, 1998).

| Variables | (1) | | (2) | | (3) | |
|---|---|---|---|---|---|---|
| | *CRASH* | | *DUVOL* | | *NCSKEW* | |
| *DID* | 2.441 *** | 3.46 | 0.274 *** | 4.18 | 0.961 *** | 2.80 |
| *PCON* | −1.496 *** | −2.66 | −0.190 ** | −2.38 | −0.662 *** | −2.78 |
| $SIZE_{(t-1)}$ | 0.262 *** | 5.23 | 0.002 | 0.15 | 0.018 | 0.38 |
| $ROA_{(t-1)}$ | −0.361 | −0.44 | 0.040 | 0.85 | 0.197 | 1.35 |
| $LEVERAGE_{(t-1)}$ | −0.657 ** | −2.50 | 0.002 | 0.07 | 0.017 | 0.14 |
| $MTB_{(t-1)}$ | 0.064 | 1.22 | 0.002 | 0.67 | 0.016 | 1.26 |
| $NCSKEW_{(t-1)}$ | −0.073 | −1.25 | 0.010 | 1.14 | 0.041 | 1.40 |
| $DTURN_{(t-1)}$ | 1.527 | 0.10 | −1.871 | −0.62 | −3.540 | −0.33 |
| $SIGMA_{(t-1)}$ | −3.713 | −1.54 | 0.644 * | 1.89 | 1.777 ** | 2.07 |
| $RET_{(t-1)}$ | 0.034 | 1.38 | −0.001 | −0.48 | −0.005 | −0.48 |
| Constant | 2.007 | 1.49 | 0.148 | 0.54 | 1.739 | 1.14 |
| Year FE | Yes | | Yes | | Yes | |
| Industry FE | Yes | | Yes | | Yes | |
| Observations | 879 | | 886 | | 886 | |
| $R^2$ | | | 0.161 | | 0.121 | |
| Adjusted $R^2$ | | | 0.100 | | 0.057 | |
| Pseudo R2 | 0.142 | | | | | |

Notes: This table presents regression results testing the effect of Suharto's resignation on stock price crash risk. The second column displays t statistics. Standard errors are clustered by firm and y ear. The asterisks *, **, *** denote significance at the 10%, 5%, and 1% levels (two-tailed), respectively.

**Table 9.** Results of regression for complex and less-complex firms.

| Variables | *CRASH* | | | | *DUVOL* | | | | *NCSKEW* | | | |
|---|---|---|---|---|---|---|---|---|---|---|---|---|
| | (1) | | (2) | | (3) | | (4) | | (5) | | (6) | |
| | Complex Firms | | Less-Complex Firms | | Complex Firms | | Less-Complex Firms | | Complex Firms | | Less-Complex Firms | |
| ***PCON*** | −0.610 *** | −9.48 | −0.028 | −0.07 | −0.154 *** | −3.09 | −0.103 * | −1.73 | −0.601 *** | −3.14 | −0.237 | −1.19 |
| $SIZE_{(t-1)}$ | 0.296 * | 1.68 | 0.166 | 1.52 | −0.005 | −0.18 | 0.030 | 1.46 | 0.055 | 0.68 | 0.075 | 1.25 |
| $ROA_{(t-1)}$ | 0.312 | 0.24 | −0.067 | −0.05 | 0.046 | 0.40 | 0.066 | 0.78 | 0.251 | 0.60 | 0.222 | 0.99 |
| $LEVERAGE_{(t-1)}$ | −2.047 ** | −2.43 | −0.110 | −0.18 | −0.042 | −0.36 | 0.006 | 0.11 | 0.015 | 0.04 | 0.071 | 0.53 |
| $MTB_{(t-1)}$ | 0.077 | 1.21 | 0.062 | 0.76 | 0.006 | 1.31 | 0.004 | 0.54 | 0.029 | 1.03 | 0.021 | 1.20 |
| $NCSKEW_{(t-1)}$ | −0.071 | −0.50 | −0.053 | −0.44 | −0.002 | −0.14 | 0.011 | 0.53 | 0.017 | 0.28 | 0.046 | 1.02 |
| $DTURN_{(t-1)}$ | −21.782 | −0.53 | 30.546 | 0.92 | −5.211 ** | −2.50 | −1.083 | −0.24 | −19.726 *** | −2.72 | 2.715 | 0.17 |
| $SIGMA_{(t-1)}$ | −5.253 | −1.07 | −6.479 *** | −2.87 | 0.569 | 0.67 | 0.553 | 1.33 | 1.053 | 0.35 | 1.182 | 1.26 |
| $RET_{(t-1)}$ | 0.037 | 0.83 | 0.067 ** | 2.33 | −0.007 | −1.27 | 0.008 | 1.50 | −0.019 | −0.70 | 0.017 | 1.24 |
| Constant | 3.415 ** | 2.24 | 2.929 * | 1.69 | 0.343 | 0.92 | −0.197 | −0.88 | 2.270 | 1.07 | −0.308 | −0.62 |
| Year FE | Yes | | Yes | | Yes | | Yes | | Yes | | Yes | |
| Industry FE | Yes | | Yes | | Yes | | Yes | | Yes | | Yes | |
| Observations | 299 | | 372 | | 315 | | 397 | | 315 | | 397 | |
| $R^2$ | | | | | 0.278 | | 0.165 | | 0.167 | | 0.151 | |
| Adjusted $R^2$ | | | | | 0.148 | | 0.058 | | 0.016 | | 0.042 | |
| Pseudo R2 | 0.197 | | 0.131 | | | | | | | | | |

Notes: this table presents regression results testing the effect of political connections on stock price crash risk in complex and less-complex subsamples. Complex is a subsample where the total number of subsidiaries is greater than the median. Less-complex is a subsample where the total number of subsidiaries is not greater than the median. The second columns displays t statistics. Standard errors are clustered by firm and year. The asterisks *, **, *** denote significance at the 10%, 5%, and 1% levels (two-tailed), respectively.

To ensure that the assignment of observations into the treatment group and control group was random, we adopted the coarsened exact matching (CEM) method. We set each covariate into five equal bins, or strata. Eight covariates were input into the CEM model. Table 10, panel A presents the matching CEM summary. Out of a total of 171 strata generated by the CEM model, 36 strata contained both connected and unconnected observations. A total of 109 out of 149 connected observations were matched with 403 out of 581 unconnected observations.

**Table 10. Panel A.** Coarsened exact matching method—matching summary. Number of strata: 171; Number of matched strata: 36. **Panel B.** Coarsened exact matching method—diagnosis of matching quality. **Panel C.** Coarsened exact matching method—difference-in-difference results.

| **Panel A** | | |
|---|---|---|
| | *PCON* = 0 | *PCON* = 1 |
| All | 581 | 149 |
| Matched | 403 | 109 |
| Unmatched | 178 | 40 |

| **Panel B** | | |
|---|---|---|
| | Pre-match L1 statistics | Post-match L1 statistics |
| *SIZE* | 0.391 | 0.230 |
| *ROA* | 0.156 | 0.144 |
| *LEVERAGE* | 0.195 | 0.163 |
| *MTB* | 0.107 | 0.138 |
| *NCSKEW* | 0.153 | 0.149 |
| *DTURN* | 0.151 | 0.098 |
| *SIGMA* | 0.203 | 0.123 |
| *RET* | 0.069 | 0.083 |

| **Panel C** | | | | | | |
|---|---|---|---|---|---|---|
| Variables | (1) | | (2) | | (3) | |
| | *Crash* | | *DUVol* | | *NCSkew* | |
| *DID* | 1.077 ** | 2.10 | 0.312 *** | 3.13 | 1.158 *** | 2.67 |
| $PCON_{(t-1)}$ | 0.591 *** | 3.11 | −0.257 ** | −2.05 | −0.871 ** | −2.37 |
| $SIZE_{(t-1)}$ | 0.294 *** | 5.91 | 0.009 | 0.82 | 0.061 * | 1.69 |
| $ROA_{(t-1)}$ | −1.337 ** | −2.18 | 0.047 | 0.60 | 0.146 | 0.68 |
| $LEVERAGE_{(t-1)}$ | −0.823 *** | −3.60 | 0.008 | 0.09 | −0.047 | −0.24 |
| $MTB_{(t-1)}$ | 0.083 | 0.85 | 0.007 | 1.08 | 0.050 ** | 2.23 |
| $NCSKEW_{(t-1)}$ | −0.099 | −0.56 | 0.032 * | 1.84 | 0.080 | 1.49 |
| $DTURN_{(t-1)}$ | −2.268 | −0.06 | −4.079 | −1.06 | −17.753 | −1.16 |
| $SIGMA_{(t-1)}$ | −6.599 | −1.35 | 0.549 | 0.76 | 2.651 | 1.20 |
| $RET_{(t-1)}$ | 0.211 | 1.55 | 0.035 *** | 2.77 | 0.087 *** | 3.43 |
| Constant | 3.019 * | 1.81 | 0.292 | 0.95 | 2.591 | 1.31 |
| Year FE | Yes | | Yes | | Yes | |
| Industry FE | Yes | | Yes | | Yes | |
| Observations | 475 | | 512 | | 512 | |
| $R^2$ | | | 0.242 | | 0.197 | |
| Adjusted $R^2$ | | | 0.143 | | 0.093 | |
| Pseudo $R^2$ | 0.124 | | | | | |

Notes: this table presents regression results testing the effect of Suharto's resignation on stock price crash risk. Standard errors are clustered by firm and year. The asterisks *, **, *** denote significance at the 10%, 5%, and 1% levels (two-tailed), respectively.

We used L1 statistics to measure the matching quality (Iacus et al. 2012; He et al. 2019). L1 statistics are the absolute difference in the value of covariates between the connected and unconnected firms. Table 10, panel B presents the diagnosis of the matching quality of the CEM method. The results show that the post-match L1 statistics were generally lower than the pre-match L1 statistics, indicating there is a significant improvement in the matching quality with CEM.

Table 10, panel C presents the result of the replication of the baseline model with the difference-in-difference model by the CEM method. The table reveals a consistent result with that in Table 6 Panel B, further supporting our hypothesis.

## 5. Conclusions

Establishing political connections can generate benefits and costs for firms. On the one hand, if politicians are involved in a firm, they can use their network and power to support that firm. However, this can also increase the firm's risk due to potential conflicts of interest. This study has focused on providing some evidence on the relationship between political connections and stock price crash risk in a country with centralized political decision-making. In general, we have shown that firms with political connections have a lower stock price crash risk. This finding indicates that political connections can reduce the probability of a firm experiencing a stock price crash. Using the difference-in-difference method, we found that firms with political connections have a higher stock price crash risk after their connections fall from power. This result implies that the cost of having political connections emerges only after these connections lose power. In addition, we also found that negative associations between political connections and stock price crash risk are more pronounced in firms with more complex firm structures. Despite the issue of the sample period, this study provides a better research setting which produces better information on how political connections affect the stock price crash risk of firms.

**Author Contributions:** Conceptualization, I.H., M.N., R.R., and B.L.; data curation, B.L.; formal analysis, I.H., M.N., R.R., and B.L.; methodology, I.H. and B.L.; software, I.H.; supervision, I.H., M.N., and R.R.; validation, I.H., M.N., and R.R.; visualization, I.H. and B.L.; writing—original draft, R.R.; writing—review and editing, I.H. and B.L.

**Funding:** This research was partially supported by the Ministry of Research Technology and Higher Education of Indonesia under the 2018 SIMLITABMAS Research Grant (PDUPT Scheme).

**Conflicts of Interest:** The authors declare no conflict of interest.

## Appendix A

**Table A1.** Variable definitions.

| Variable | Definition | Data Source |
|---|---|---|
| *CRASH* | 1 for a firm–year that experiences one or more firm-specific weekly returns falling 3.2 standard deviations below the mean firm-specific weekly returns over the fiscal year, with 3.2 chosen to generate frequencies of 0.1% in the normal distribution during the fiscal year period, otherwise 0 | Compustat |
| *DUVOL* | Down-to-up volatility of firm-specific weekly returns | Compustat |
| *NCSKEW* | Negative skewness of firm-specific weekly returns over the fiscal year period. | Compustat |
| *PCON* | 1 for a firm that is politically connected with Suharto, otherwise 0 | ICMD |
| *DTURN* | Average monthly share turnover over the current fiscal year period minus the average monthly share turnover over the previous fiscal year period, where monthly share turnover is calculated as the monthly trading volume divided by the total number of shares outstanding during the month | Compustat |
| *SIGMA* | Standard deviation of firm-specific weekly returns over the fiscal year period. | Compustat |
| *RET* | Mean of firm-specific weekly returns over the fiscal year period | Compustat |
| *SIZE* | Natural logarithm of the market value of equity | Compustat |
| *MTB* | Market value of equity divided by the book value of equity | Compustat |
| *LEVERAGE* | Total long-term debts divided by total assets | Compustat |
| *ROA* | Income before extraordinary items divided by lagged total assets | Compustat |

## References


Autor, David H. 2003. Outsourcing at will: The contribution of unjust dismissal doctrine to the growth of employment outsourcing. *Journal of Labor Economics* 21: 1–42. [CrossRef]

Bliss, Mark A., and Ferdinand A. Gul. 2012. Political connection and cost of debt: Some Malaysian evidence. *Journal of Banking & Finance* 36: 1520–27. [CrossRef]

Boubakri, Narjess, Omrane Guedhami, Dev Mishra, and Walid Saffar. 2012. Political connections and the cost of equity capital. *Journal of Corporate Finance* 18: 541–59. [CrossRef]

Carney, Richard W., and Natasha Hamilton-Hart. 2015. What Do Changes in Corporate Ownership in Indonesia Tell Us? *Bulletin of Indonesian Economic Studies* 51: 123–45. [CrossRef]

Chauhan, Yogesh, Satish Kumar, and Rajesh Pathak. 2017. Stock liquidity and stock prices crash-risk: Evidence from India. *The North American Journal of Economics and Finance* 41: 70–81. [CrossRef]

Chen, Changling, Jeong-Bon Kim, and Li Yao. 2016. Earnings Smoothing: Does It Exacerbate or Constrain Stock Price Crash Risk? *Journal of Corporate Finance*. [CrossRef]

Claessens, Stijn, Simeon Djankov, and Larry HP Lang. 1999. Who Controls East Asian Corporations, and the Implications for Legal Reform. *World Bank Policy Research*, 2054. [CrossRef]

Claessens, Stijn, Erik Feijen, and Luc Laeven. 2008. Political connections and preferential access to finance: The role of campaign contributions. *Journal of Financial Economics* 88: 554–80. [CrossRef]

Dang, Chongyu, Zhichuan Frank Li, and Chen Yang. 2018. Measuring firm size in empirical corporate finance. *Journal of Banking & Finance* 86: 159–76.

Fisman, Raymond. 2001. Estimating the Value of Political Connections. *The Amerian Economic Review* 91: 1095–102. [CrossRef]

Goldman, Eitan, Jörg Rocholl, and Jongil So. 2013. Politically connected boards of directors and the allocation of procurement contracts. *Review of Finance* 17: 1617–48. [CrossRef]

Grier, Kevin B., Michael C. Munger, and Brian E. Roberts. 1994. The determinants of industry political activity, 1978–86. *American Political Science Review* 88: 911–26. [CrossRef]

Gul, Ferdinand A. 2006. Auditors' response to political connections and cronyism in Malaysia. *Journal of Accounting Research* 44: 931–63. [CrossRef]

Harymawan, Iman. 2018. Why do firms appoint former military personnel as directors? Evidence of loan interest rate in militarily connected firms in Indonesia. *Asian Review of Accounting* 26: 2–18. [CrossRef]

Harymawan, Iman, and John Nowland. 2016. Political connections and earnings quality: How do connected firms respond to changes in political stability and government effectiveness? *International Journal of Accounting & Information Management* 24: 339–56. [CrossRef]

He, Guanming, and Helen Ren. 2019. Are Financially Constrained Firms Susceptible to a Stock Price Crash? Working Paper. Durham University, Durham/Stockton-on-Tees, UK. Available online: https://ssrn.com/abstract=3021307 (accessed on 21 June 2019).

He, Guanming, David Marginson, and Xixi Dai. 2019. Do voluntary disclosures of product and business expansion plans impact analyst coverage and forecasts? *Accounting and Business Research*, 1–33. [CrossRef]

Hill, Hal. 2000. *The Indonesian Economy*. Cambridge: Cambridge University Press.

Hofman, Bert, Ella Rodrick-Jones, and Kian Wie Thee. 2004. Indonesia: Rapid growth, weak institutions. Paper presented at World Bank Shanghai Conference, Shanghai, China, May 25–27. Available online: http://www.worldbank.org/wbi/reducingpoverty/case-Indonesia-PovertyReduction.html (accessed on 15 April 2019).

Houston, Joel F., Liangliang Jiang, Chen Lin, and Yue Ma. 2014. Political connections and the cost of bank loans. *Journal of Accounting Research* 52: 193–243. [CrossRef]

Hu, Guoliu, and Yu Wang. 2018. Political connections and stock price crash risk: The role of intermediary information disclosure. *China Finance Review International* 8: 140–57. [CrossRef]

Hutton, Amy P., Alan J. Marcus, and Hassan Tehranian. 2009. Opaque financial reports, R2, and crash risk. *Journal of Financial Economics* 94: 67–86. [CrossRef]

Iacus, Stefano M., Gary King, and Giuseppe Porro. 2012. Causal inference without balance checking: Coarsened exact matching. *Political analysis* 20: 1–24. [CrossRef]

Kim, Jeong-Bon, Yinghua Li, and Liandong Zhang. 2011. Corporate tax avoidance and stock price crash risk: Firm-level analysis. *Journal of Financial Economics* 100: 639–62. [CrossRef]

Kim, Jeong-Bon, Zheng Wang, and Liandong Zhang. 2016. CEO overconfidence and stock price crash risk. *Contemporary Accounting Research* 33: 1720–49. [CrossRef]

Lee, Ming-Te. 2016. Corporate Social Responsibility and Stock Price Crash Risk: Evidence from an Asian Emerging Market. *Managerial Finance* 42. [CrossRef]

Lee, Wei, and Lihong Wang. 2017. Do political connections affect stock price crash risk? Firm-level evidence from China. *Review of Quantitative Finance and Accounting* 48: 643–76. [CrossRef]

Leuz, Christian, and Felix Oberholzer-Gee. 2006. Political relationships, global financing, and corporate transparency: Evidence from Indonesia. *Journal of Financial Economics* 81: 411–39. [CrossRef]

Luo, Donglun, and Liming Zhen. 2008. Private control, political relationship and financing constrain of private listed enterprises. *Journal of Financial Research* 12: 164–78.

Luo, Jin-hui, Manning Gong, Yilong Lin, and Qifeng Fang. 2016. Political connections and stock price crash risk: Evidence from China. *Economics Letters* 147: 90–92. [CrossRef]

McLeod, Ross H. 2000. Soeharto's Indonesia: A Better Class of Corruption. *Agenda: A Journal of Policy Analysis and Reform*, 99–112. [CrossRef]

Pangestu, Mari, and Manggi Habir. 2002. *The Boom, Bust and Restructuring of Indonesian Banks.* IMF Working Paper WP/02/66. Washington: International Monetary Fund.

Poczter, Sharon, and Thomas B. Pepinsky. 2016. Authoritarian Legacies in Post–New Order Indonesia: Evidence from a New Dataset. *Journal Bulletin of Indonesian Economic Studies* 52: 77–100. [CrossRef]

Roberts, Brian E. 1990. A dead senator tells no lies: Seniority and the distribution of federal benefits. *American Journal of Political Science*, 31–58. [CrossRef]

Sato, Yuri. 2004. *Corporate Ownership and Management in Business in Indonesia: New Challenges, Old Problems.* Singapore: Institute of South East Asian Studies.

Schwarz, A. 1994. *A Nation in Waiting: Indonesia in the 1990s.* St. Leonards: Allen & Unwin.

Tee, Chwee Ming. 2018. Political connections and stock price crash risk: Evidence of institutional investors' heterogeneous monitoring. *Spanish Journal of Finance and Accounting/Revista Española de Financiación y Contabilidad*, 1–18. [CrossRef]

Winter, Jeffrey A. 2013. Oligarchy and Demoracy in Indonesia. *Indonesia* 96: 11–33. [CrossRef]

# 3

# The Impact of Financial Leverage on the Variance of Stock Returns

**David Yechiam Aharon** [1,*] **and Yossi Yagil** [2,3]

1 Department of Business Administration, Ono Academic College, Haifa 55000, Israel
2 Department of Business Administration, University of Haifa, Haifa 3498838, Israel; yyagil@univ.haifa.ac.il
3 Department of Business Administration, Western Galilee College, Akko 2412101, Israel
* Correspondence: dudi.ah@ono.ac.il

**Abstract:** This paper investigates the direct theoretical relationship between the variance of stock returns ($\sigma^2{}_E$) and financial leverage (L) considering both corporate and personal taxes. Using a dataset of U.S. industrial firms, we examine the variance of stock returns as a function of the firm's financial leverage. We demonstrate that (1) the variance of stock returns is positively related to the firm's financial leverage, (2) the relationship between the variance of stock returns and financial leverage is positive when corporate and personal taxes are also considered, and (3) with regard to the relationship between the variance of stock returns and financial leverage, using market measures of the latter tends to generate a higher coefficient of determination and a more accurate approximation of the theoretical relationship between financial leverage and the variance of stock returns.

**Keywords:** volatility; financial leverage; market imperfections; corporate taxes; personal taxes

**JEL Classification:** G30; G32

---

## 1. Introduction

Volatility, which is commonly measured by the standard deviation of stock returns, has received a great deal of attention in the literature, as it is the key factor in portfolio theory, option valuation, and asset pricing models. Volatility is important to academics, policy makers, and financial market participants. For policy makers, a volatile stock market can be a source for concern, because the instability of the stock market creates uncertainty, which may have an adverse effect on growth prospects. In fact, volatility can be helpful for the formulation of the economic policies, rules, and regulations related to the stock market. Investors use the variance of stock returns as a measure of risk to assess the performance of their past and future investments. Also, volatility has a central role in the pricing theories of derivatives. The Black-Scholes option pricing model treats volatility as the only parameter, among the strike price, time to expiration, interest rate, and stock price that must be forecasted. Finally, academics try to identify the factors that affect the volatility of stock returns and its role in determining capital structure valuation.

While the literature is replete with studies devoted to the characteristics of the variance of stock returns (henceforth: $\sigma^2{}_E$ or $\sigma_E$), there are very few studies to the best of our knowledge on the *direct* relationship between financial leverage (henceforth: L) and $\sigma_E$, a fortiori when both corporate and personal taxes exist. The closest type of studies that does refer to the impact of L on $\sigma_E$ is what is commonly named in the literature as "leverage effect" studies in which the impact of L on $\sigma_E$ is evident only *indirectly*. In such studies, financial leverage is provided as a potential explanation for the asymmetric $\sigma_E$ found under various market conditions. This possible explanation can be easily demonstrated based on the pioneering "leverage effect" works of Black (1976) and Christie (1982) described by Equation (1) below:

$$\sigma_E = \Delta E/E = \Delta V/E = (\Delta V/V) \times (V/E) = (\Delta V/V) \times [(E+D)/E)] = (\Delta V/V) \times L = \sigma_V \times (1 + L) \quad (1)$$

where V is the value of the firm, E is the value of outstanding equity, and D is the value of debt, so that V = E + D. According to this formulation, if debt is risk-free, a change in the value of the firm's assets ($\Delta V$) is passed entirely through to the equity: $\Delta E = \Delta V$. Thus, Equation (1) expresses the change in the value of a firm's stock caused by a given $\Delta V$. Meaning, $\sigma_E = \sigma_V(1 + L)$, where $\sigma_V$ is the standard deviation of asset returns, and $\sigma_E$ is the standard deviation of equity returns. An important and well documented empirical feature in many financial markets is the financial leverage effect (Black 1976; Christie 1982). According to the latter, a higher return reduces L (because a positive return increases the value of the equity, while the risk free debt is unchanged) and is therefore expected to lower the volatility of equity returns. In contrast, a lower return should have the opposite effect on $\sigma_E$. That is, an increase in L also increases $\sigma_E$.

To summarize, to the best of our knowledge, the existing studies in the literature have not tested the *direct* theoretical relationship between $\sigma_E$ and L when both corporate and personal taxes exist. The purpose of this study is to test directly whether and to what extent the theoretical relationship between $\sigma_E$ and L established in the literature holds in the real corporate world, particularly when corporate taxes and personal taxes are considered. To overcome the potential problem of measurement errors and for the sake of a sensitivity analysis, we use both book and market measures of leverage with two methods of calculating corporate and personal taxes. Finally, we test which of the risk free debt theoretical models (the perfect capital market model, the corporate taxes only model, or the theoretical model that includes both corporate and personal taxes) best describes the real relationship between $\sigma_E$ and L. We make this differentiation by comparing the observed parameters from the regression analysis with the theoretical values implied by each model. We contribute to the literature by employing a direct and thorough empirical test of the theoretical relationship between $\sigma_E$ and L. The direct test should fill a gap in the literature on capital structure theory and can assist portfolio managers, investors, and policy makers.

To emphasize, our study extends the literature in several aspects. First, we test three (rather than one) theoretical models in the context of the $\sigma_E$-L relationship. Second, we actually compare the OLS (Ordinary Least Squares) regression coefficients in all three models with their theoretical counterparts and examine whether the differences between these values are statistically significant—an important investigation that has not been conducted so far in the literature. Third, while prior studies simply employed a standard regression analysis of the relationship between $\sigma_E$ and L and some other variables, conducting what we call an indirect-test, we in contrast apply a direct test approach by testing the theoretical relationship between $\sigma_E$ and L directly. In addition, we employ direct estimates of the additional variables that are present in the theoretical models, such as corporate and personal taxes, and we also use both book and market leverage measures.

This paper is organized as follows. Section 2 provides a detailed scientific background of both theoretical and empirical studies of the relationship between $\sigma_E$ and L. Section 3 presents the main hypotheses and the methodology. In Section 4, we describe the sample, the selection process, and data sources used for the construction of the sample. Section 5 discusses the empirical results, while Section 6 concludes.

## 2. Scientific Background

Many of the recent studies about financial leverage (L) and volatility ($\sigma_E$) introduce the leverage effect hypothesis, which posits that stock returns and volatility are negatively correlated. One explanation for the negative relationship is that an increase in volatility leads to an increase in the expected return on the equity, which results in a decline in stock prices. An alternative explanation is referred to financial leverage, where a drop in stock prices leads to an increase in financial leverage, resulting in an increase in the volatility of stock returns.

Using a sample of 30 stocks, mostly Dow Jones Industrials, from 1964 to 1975, Black (1976) was the first to demonstrate the so-called leverage effect in the context of asymmetric equity volatility. He showed that stock volatility was negatively correlated with stock returns, meaning that volatility tends to grow as stock prices drop. He argues that a possible explanation for the negative relationship is due to a financial leverage effect, meaning when stock prices fall, financial leverage increases, leading to an increase in the volatility of stock returns. He also states that a similar effect may occur even if the firm has almost no debt because of the presence of so-called "operating leverage" (fixed costs that cannot be eliminated, at least in the short run). Therefore, a stylized fact is that financial leverage may be the factor accounting for this negative relationship. However, the empirical evidence for this effect is not conclusive. Moreover, crises, such as the 2008 subprime crisis (which is a debt crisis), may call for another reconsideration of the leverage effect discussed in the literature. On the one hand, in this subprime crisis, stock prices actually fell, leading to a higher financial leverage, but on the other hand, the crisis itself was a debt crisis, which caused a crash in bond prices, causing the opposite effect on the financial leverage. From this viewpoint, this study is motivated to test the direct $\sigma$E-L relationship to investigate the true effect of financial leverage.

Early studies, such as those of Christie (1982), Cheung and Ng (1992), and Duffee (1995), found that volatility seems to rise when stock prices go down and decline when stock prices go up. Schwert (1990) showed that stock market volatility increases during recessions and after a large drop in stock prices. He found that the higher the financial leverage of the market, the greater the volatility. Figlewski and Wang (2000) noted a strong leverage effect for falling stock prices, but for positive returns they found a very weak or even non-existent leverage effect. They called these findings the "down market effect", because it is much stronger when the market is falling. Titman and Wessels (1988) reported a negative association between earnings volatility and leverage. Lemmon et al. (2008) found a negative effect of cash flow volatility (measured by the standard deviation of historical operating income) on the leverage decisions of firms. Bollerslev et al. (2012) established a negative correlation between volatility and current and lagged returns, which lasts for several days, weak correlations between the returns and the lagged volatility, and strong correlations between high frequency returns and their absolute values. Their findings support the dual presence of a prolonged leverage effect at the intra-daily level and an almost instantaneous volatility feedback effect. Ait-Sahalia et al. (2013) used a natural estimate of the empirical correlation between daily returns and changes in daily volatility estimated from high frequency data. Using the well-known Heston model, they found that at high frequencies and over short horizons, the estimated "leverage parameter" is close to zero instead of being an expected strong negative value. At longer horizons, the effect is present, especially when using option-implied volatility. The authors also provided theoretical results to disentangle the biases involved in estimating the leverage parameter and isolated the sources one by one: Discretization bias, smoothing bias, estimation error, and noise correction error. In addition, they also considered the influence of price jumps on estimating the correlation between Brownian shocks to price and volatility. Using a simulation study, they successfully recovered the leverage parameter using a simple OLS regression.

To summarize, while there are numerous indirect studies that connect financial leverage with the volatility of stock returns, this study is motivated to test the direct effect of L on $\sigma_E$. To the best of our knowledge, this is the first study that implements in this manner such a test.

### 3. Theory, Hypotheses, and Methodology

Based on Modigliani and Miller (1958, 1963) capital structure theory, the standard deviation of equity returns ($\sigma_E$) is a function of the financial leverage of the firm (L) and the specific market imperfections considered. To derive the $\sigma_E$ expressions, we first present the formulations for the required return on equity ($K_E$). Yagil (1982) devised a general theoretical expression to describe $K_E$ as a function of the required return for an unlevered firm, the firm's financial leverage, the corporate and personal tax rates, and when debt is also risky and associated with bankruptcy costs:

$$K_E = K_U + [K_U [(1 - \Psi) - r(1 - T_C)(1 - T_E)]L, \quad (2)$$

where $K_E$ is the required return on equity for the levered firm, $K_U$ is t required return on equity for the unlevered firm, $\Psi$ equals $(1 - q - T)$, where q is the bankruptcy factor as a percentage of the firm's debt, T is the tax ratio given by the term $(1 - T_C)(1 - T_E)/(1 - T_D)$, $T_C$ is the corporate tax rate, $T_E$ is the personal tax rate applicable to equity holders, $T_D$ is the personal tax rate for debt holders, r is the required return on debt, and L is the financial leverage ratio of the firm given by D/E where D and E are the values of the debt and equity, respectively[1].

If capital markets are perfect, and debt is risk free, and neither corporate nor personal taxes exist, then $\Psi = 0$ and Equation (2) reduces down to:

$$K_E = K_U + [(K_U - r)L], \quad (3)$$

which is similar to Modigliani and Miller's proposition 2 for the cost of equity in the absence of taxes.

If debt is risk free and corporate taxes are the only market imperfection, then $\Psi$ from Equation (2) is reduced down to: $[1 - (1 - T_C)]$ or simply $T_C$ and the resulting relationship becomes:

$$K_E = K_U + [K_U(1 - T_C) - r(1 - T_C)]L, \quad (4)$$

which can also be organized as:

$$K_E = K_U + (1 - T_C)(K_U - r)L, \quad (5)$$

where Equation (5) is equivalent to the corporate tax expression in Modigliani and Miller (1963, p. 439). If in addition to corporate taxes, personal taxes also exist, while debt is still risk free, then $q = 0$ and $\Psi$ simply reduces to (1-T), and, consequently, Equation (2) reduces to the following:

$$K_E = K_U + T\,[K_U - r(1 - T_D)]L. \quad (6)$$

In theory, as the tax rate on interest income increases relative to the tax rate on equity income, bondholders demand relatively higher pretax returns to leave them equally well off on an after-tax basis. The resulting higher interest cost reduces the tax benefit from debt accruing to equity holders. As a result, the equity risk premium from leverage should increase with the personal tax penalty on interest income according to Miller (1977).

Next, we turn to the derivation of the variance (or standard deviation) for each of the K expressions above. The σE-L expressions corresponding to Equations (3), (5), and (6) are as follows:

$$\sigma_E = \sigma_U + \sigma_U L, \quad (7)$$

$$\sigma_E = \sigma_U + \sigma_U(1 - T_C)L, \quad (8)$$

$$\sigma_E = \sigma_U + \sigma_U(TL). \quad (9)$$

1 The general variance expression corresponding to the general K expression given by Equation (2), which incorporates both corporate and personal taxes as well as risky debt and bankruptcy costs is Equation (2a):

$$\sigma^2_E = \sigma^2_U [1 + (1 - \Psi)L]^2 + \sigma^2_D(1 - T_C)^2(1 - T_E)^2L^2 - 2\text{cov}(K_U, r) \quad (2a)$$

Next, we explain the methodology of testing the $\sigma$E-L theoretical models. We divide our tests into two main stages. In the first stage, we test the direct relationship between $\sigma_E$ and L using an ordinary least squares (OLS) regression analysis for the following three cases: No taxes, corporate taxes only, and both corporate and personal taxes. The second stage of our test will present comparative tests whose purpose is to determine which of the above three cases better corresponds to the real world relationship. We use two methods of testing: Method 1 and method 2. Method 1 involves the comparison of the observed $\gamma_0$, $\gamma_1$ (from each direct regression) with their theoretical counterparts, $\gamma_0{}^*$, $\gamma_1{}^*$.

The alternative test method (method 2) involves two stages. The first stage is the following regression estimation of Equation (7):

$$\sigma_E = \gamma_0 + \gamma_1[L]. \tag{10}$$

Using this estimation procedure, $\gamma_1$ should account for the effect of all market imperfections. Thus, in the second stage, we compare $\gamma_0$ with $\sigma_{U,}$ where $\sigma_U$ is derived from the corresponding model, and we compare $\gamma_1$ with the theoretical slope in the corresponding theoretical model. For example, for model (3a), where corporate and personal taxes are the only market imperfections, $\gamma_0$ should be equal to $\sigma_U$, where $\sigma_U = \sigma_E/(1 + TL)$, and $\gamma_1$ should be equal to $\sigma_U T$. Note that in all three cases (a perfect capital market, corporate taxes, and corporate and personal taxes), we should expect a positive slope, representing the positive relationship between $\sigma_E$ and L.

## 4. Data and Variable Measurement

### *4.1. Data*

We gathered the financial and market data from two main sources: The COMPUSTAT database and the Yahoo stock screener. Testing the various theoretical models outlined above requires a reference to the risk class issue. Theory states that the $\sigma_U$ should be identical across all firms in the same risk class. Consequently, an empirical problem that can arise is that $\sigma_U$ is supposed to be constant in the defined risk class, but, practically, it may vary across the companies in the same risk class. Taken to the extreme, $\sigma_U$ may practically even vary from one company to another. The empirical tradeoff involved then is between selecting a very small sample in order to maintain a homogenous risk class on the one hand, and the low statistical reliability that may be associated with a relatively small sample. Given this tradeoff, we selected our sample to consist of the industrial sector according to the GICS (Global Industry Classification Standards) definition of COMPUSTAT and, at the same time, is sufficiently large to obtain statistically reliable results. Furthermore, to reduce the "survival bias" discussed in the literature, our sample in the various years contains precisely the same set of companies (which naturally reduced the size of our initial sample). In addition, to minimize the potential measurement errors caused, among other things, by our relatively broad risk class assumption, we employed various sensitivity analyses and robustness tests discussed later in this study. Our sample time period ended at 2007 since the Haifa university subscription to COMPUSTAT expired at the end of 2007. Also, to focus on the most recent normal years available, the starting point year was defined here as 2003, since prior years to 2003 were associated with the rise and burst of the so called high tech bubble. The initial sample consisted of all 306 firms and companies covered by COMPUSTAT in the sample time period. We then required complete data in each sample year on the company's total debt, current liabilities, total equity, total taxes paid, pretax income, total dividend paid, and preferred stocks in each year and also the historical 60 monthly returns. This screening procedure reduced our sample to 182 firms. Since no data was available for estimating the "cov($K_U$,r)" term, our empirical analysis will be based on the debt risk free models described in the previous section. This is also consistent with the empirical approach adopted by many prior empirical studies, which only employed models in which debt is assumed to be risk free.

### 4.2. *Variable Measurement*

The variables in our study include the financial leverage (L), the standard deviation of stock returns ($\sigma_E$), and the tax rates—corporate and personal ($T_C$, $T_D$, and $T_E$). We gathered all of the required data from the balance sheets and income statements of each firm in each sample year and market data, such as stock prices and returns.

To test for the robustness of our results and overcome the potential problem of measurement errors, we used several estimates of the financial leverage and tax variables combined with different methods of estimating them.

#### 4.2.1. Financial Leverage

The literature is replete with financial leverage measures that include both market and book measures for equity and debt. Barclay et al. (2006) show how book leverage is theoretically preferred in regressions involving financial leverage. Using book values may be justified by a survey of Graham and Harvey (2001), who reports that managers focus on book values when considering the financial structure of the firm. Welch (2004) argues against book values, and Fama and French (2002) find different results for book and market leverage. On the other hand, Bowman (1980) has used various estimates of the financial leverage in terms of both book and market values, and concluded that the estimates are not statistically different from each other in terms of the relationship between risk and leverage. Thus, the literature is not unanimous about the optimal way of assessing the appropriate financial leverage measure. Appendix A provide a review of various proxies for financial leverage in the empirical literature.

Since financial leverage is a central variable in this study, we used two L measures based on the long-term debt of the firm: $Lev_1 = LTD/Equity_{BV}$ and $Lev_2 = LTD/Equity_{MV}$. We also used two other L measures to include current liabilities: $Lev_3 = (LTD + CL)/Equity_{BV}$ and $Lev_4 = (LTD + CL)/Equity_{MV}$. Lev denotes the financial leverage, LTD is long-term debt, Equity is the value of common equity, CL is the current liabilities, and the subscripts, BV and MV, stand for the book and market values, respectively. $Equity_{MV}$ includes the market value of common equity given by the product of the number of common shares outstanding and the mean of the 12 monthly closing stock prices. The estimate of the financial leverage (Lev) for each year is based on the mean value of the preceding five years. We constructed two such estimates—*Relative* and *Absolute*. The *Relative* Lev estimate for a given year is the mean value of the Lev variable across the preceding five years, while the *Absolute* Lev is given by the 5-year mean value of the "debt" numerator divided by the 5-year mean value of the "equity" denominator. Following previous relevant empirical works, we used the book value of debt. Additional estimates include using preferred equity in the "debt" component. The preferred stock estimates are not presented here, because the results with and without preferred stock remained similar. To summarize, eight different versions of the financial leverage variable are considered here—four using the *Absolute* method and four using the *Relative* method of leverage calculation. Each one of the eight leverages (both book and market measures) will be used to test the theoretical models. Accordingly, each one of them will be employed in the unlevering formulas.

#### 4.2.2. Corporate and Personal Taxes

Testing Equations (7)–(9) requires estimates of the corporate tax rate ($T_C$) and the personal tax rates applicable to the equity holders ($T_E$) and the debt holders ($T_D$). Most proxies for the corporate tax rate are based on the total income tax expense divided by the pre-tax income (Fan et al. (2012); Arena and Roper (2010); Dyreng et al. (2010); Butler et al. (1991)), or by assuming a constant corporate tax rate (DeAngelo et al. (2011); Kemsley and Nissim (2002); Marston and Perry (1996)). Following the first set of studies, we used the total tax expense divided by the pretax income as a proxy for the corporate tax variable. The estimate of the corporate tax rate ($T_C$) for each year is based on the mean value of the preceding five years. Again, we constructed two such estimates—*Relative* and *Absolute*.

The *Relative* $T_C$ estimate for a given year is the mean value of the $T_C$ variable across the preceding five years, while the *Absolute* $T_C$ is given by the 5-year mean value of the firm's total tax expense divided by the 5-year mean value of the firm's taxable income. Butler et al. (1991) set the outliers of corporate tax rates to 40%, because such rates are likely to be associated with non-recurring or unusual items. They state that this procedure is necessary for approximately 15% of the sample firms. We follow that procedure here for approximately 12% of the sample. We set the corporate tax rates that exceed 60% to the mean value plus two standard deviations, and the corporate tax rates that are less than 20% to the mean value minus two standard deviations.

The personal tax rate is a function of the tax rates faced by debt holders ($T_D$), and the tax rate faced by equity holders ($T_E$). Two factors determine the latter: The tax rates on dividend ($T_d$) and capital gains ($T_{cg}$) income. Following Dhaliwal et al. (2006) (henceforth: DHL), we set $T_D$ to the highest statutory tax rate on interest income. We also estimated $T_E$ according to DHL's modification of the tax rate on equity income to represent a weighted-average tax rate on dividend and capital gains income by the following term: $[d \cdot T_d + (1 - \mathrm{d}) \cdot \alpha \cdot T_{cg}]$, where $d$ is the amount per after-corporate tax dollar of earnings that is distributed to shareholders in the form of a dividend. $d$ represents the dividends paid for the most recent year divided by the average earnings over the prior three years, and accordingly, (1 − d) is the retention rate.

Following the procedure used by Dhaliwal et al. (2006), we winsorize $d$ at zero and one. $T_d$ is the personal tax rate on dividend income, set to equal $T_D$ for the years prior to 2003, and 15% thereafter. $T_{cg}$ is set to equal the top statutory tax rate on long-term capital gains income, which equals 20% for 1998 through to 2002 and 15% thereafter. $\alpha$ is the benefit of capital gains deferral. This benefit stems from the lower present value of future tax payments, especially if the capital gains are realized in future time periods when the investor's personal tax rate is lower than the corresponding tax rate in the present. A very informal rule is to multiply the statutory capital gains tax rate by 0.25 to capture the fact that the present value of the expected capital gains taxes is small[2].

Following Van Binsbergen et al. (2010); Graham (1999); Dhaliwal et al. (2006), we assumed that $\alpha = 0.25$. To summarize, the personal tax rate is a function of $T_D$, $T_d$, $T_{cg}$, and $d$, and equal to $(1 - T_E)/(1 - T_D)$.

## 5. Empirical Findings

### 5.1. Descriptive Statistics

Table 1 reports the descriptive statistics for our sample. The values reported are measured in $millions and include the mean, median (Med), standard deviation (SD), coefficient of variation (CV), minimum (Min), and maximum (Max). For example, the mean value of the total liabilities of the firms is $6720.1 million, and the mean value of their common equity is $2269.7 million. The standard deviations of these corresponding variables are $533.9 and $312.7 million, which reflect a coefficient of variation (CV) of 0.08 and 0.14, respectively.

Table 1 also reports our measurements for the financial leverage according to eight measures of L according to the *Relative* and *Absolute* computation methods.

The $\mathrm{Lev}_1$ rows in Table 1 present the descriptive statistics of the ratio of long-term debt to (book) equity, and the $\mathrm{Lev}_2$ rows report the descriptive statistics when the market value of equity is used. Similarly, the $\mathrm{Lev}_3$ rows present the descriptive results of the ratio of total debt to total (book) equity, and the $\mathrm{Lev}_4$ rows report these results when the market value of equity is used. For example, the mean value of long-term debt to total book equity by the relative computation method (*Relative* $\mathrm{Lev}_1$) is 0.84 and 0.51 by $\mathrm{Lev}_2$. Similarly, the mean value of $\mathrm{Lev}_3$ is 1.65 and 1.02 for $\mathrm{Lev}_4$. It is clear that market,

2 We would like to thank John Graham for clarifying this point to us.

rather than book measures, tend to generate lower L values, because the market value of equity is generally higher than the book value of equity.

Table 1 also reports the descriptive statistics for the measurement of the dependent variable ($\sigma_E$). $\sigma_E$ is the historical standard deviation (HSD) for each firm based on the monthly stock returns in five years prior to each sample year. The mean (median) value of $\sigma_E$ across the years is 0.114 (0.096) and the min–max range is 0.048–0.421. Additional descriptive statistics for other key variables, such as corporate ($T_C$) and personal taxes ($T_E$ and $T_R$), are also included in Table 1. For example, the mean value of the corporate tax rate by the *Absolute*-computation method (*Absolute* $T_C$) is 0.348, while by the *Relative*-computation method (*Relative* $T_C$) measure the corresponding mean value is 0.358 by the absolute corporate tax measure. Overall, the estimation of the corporate tax rate by either the *Absolute* or the *relative* computation methods yields similar $T_C$ measures for each of the sample years, and therefore we report here only the mean value across the years.

**Table 1.** Descriptive statistics of the corporate variables ($M).

| | Mean | Med | SD | CV | Min | Max |
|---|---|---|---|---|---|---|
| Total Liabilities | 6720.10 | 6705.60 | 533.9 | 0.08 | 6098.40 | 7556.30 |
| Common Equity | 2269.70 | 2280.80 | 312.7 | 0.14 | 1833.50 | 2693.20 |
| Total Assets | 8989.70 | 8872.40 | 834.6 | 0.09 | 7931.90 | 10,249.50 |
| Current Liabilities | 2931.60 | 2929.50 | 219.1 | 0.07 | 2657.20 | 3206.80 |
| Long-Term Debt | 2429.90 | 2272.40 | 365.8 | 0.15 | 2053.50 | 2998.80 |
| Deferred Taxes | 308.2 | 311.3 | 35.6 | 0.12 | 251.9 | 345.8 |
| Pref. Equity | 1.8 | 1.5 | 0.9 | 0.5 | 0.7 | 3 |
| Common Shares | 173.5 | 174.1 | 2.2 | 0.01 | 170.5 | 175.6 |
| Pretax Income | 517.2 | 501.6 | 148.3 | 0.29 | 341 | 709.4 |
| Tax Expense | 140.6 | 134.4 | 42.2 | 0.3 | 95.4 | 198 |
| *Relative* Lev1 | 0.84 | 0.81 | 0.06 | 0.07 | 0.77 | 0.92 |
| *Relative* Lev2 | 0.51 | 0.51 | 0.08 | 0.16 | 0.4 | 0.59 |
| *Relative* Lev3 | 1.65 | 1.61 | 0.09 | 0.05 | 1.56 | 1.78 |
| *Relative* Lev4 | 1.02 | 1.03 | 0.15 | 0.15 | 0.82 | 1.19 |
| *Absolute* Lev1 | 0.8 | 0.81 | 0.04 | 0.05 | 0.76 | 0.84 |
| *Absolute* Lev2 | 0.38 | 0.34 | 0.15 | 0.4 | 0.23 | 0.61 |
| *Absolute* Lev3 | 1.55 | 1.55 | 0.07 | 0.05 | 1.45 | 1.64 |
| *Absolute* Lev4 | 0.74 | 0.69 | 0.26 | 0.35 | 0.49 | 1.14 |
| $\sigma_E$ | 0.114 | 0.096 | 0.057 | 0.499 | 0.048 | 0.421 |
| Absolute $T_C$ | 0.348 | 0.347 | 0.067 | 0.193 | 0.209 | 0.519 |
| Relative $T_C$ | 0.358 | 0.354 | 0.078 | 0.219 | 0.205 | 0.572 |
| D | 0.205 | 0.17 | 0.222 | 1.078 | 0 | 1 |
| $T_E$ | 0.061 | 0.057 | 0.025 | 0.411 | 0.038 | 0.15 |
| $T_R$ | 1.445 | 1.451 | 0.038 | 0.027 | 1.308 | 1.481 |

Notes: Table 1 reports the descriptive sample statistics. All financial statement data are gathered from the COMPUSTAT database. The values reported are measured in $millions except for common shares outstanding. The reported statistics are the mean, median (med), standard deviation (SD), coefficient of variation (CV), minimum (min), and maximum (max). Lev1 is the ratio of LTD/$Equity_{BV}$, Lev2 is the ratio of LTD/$Equity_{MV}$, Lev3 is the ratio of (LTD + CL/$Equity_{BV}$), and Lev4 is the ratio of (LTD + CL/$Equity_{MV}$), where Lev denotes the financial leverage, LTD is long-term debt in book value, equity is the total value of common equity, CL is the current liabilities, and the subscripts, BV and MV, stand for book and market values, respectively. The estimate of the financial leverage for each year is based on the mean value over the preceding five years. Two such estimates have been constructed—Relative and Absolute. The relative Lev estimate for a given year is the mean value of the Lev variable across the preceding five years, while the Absolute Lev is given as the 5-year mean value of the "debt" numerator divided by the 5-year mean value of the "equity" denominator. $\sigma_E$ is the historical standard deviation (HSD) of stock returns based on 60 monthly observations. The *Relative* $T_C$ estimate for a given year is the mean value of the $T_C$ variable across the preceding five years, while the *Absolute* $T_C$ is given by the 5-year mean value of the firm's total tax expense divided by the 5-year mean value of the firm's taxable income. The table also reports the payout ratio (d), the personal tax rate ($T_E$), and the taxes ratio [($T_R$); $T_R = (1 - T_E)/(1 - T_D)$]. $T_E$ is the tax rate applicable to equity holders, and $T_D$ is the tax rate applicable to debt holders. $T_D$ is the highest statutory tax rate on interest income, which is 39.6% for 1998 through to 2000, 38.6% for 2001 through to 2002, and 35% thereafter. We estimate $T_E$ as a weighted-average tax rate on dividend and capital gains income using the following term: $T_E = [d \cdot T_d + (1 - d) \cdot \alpha \cdot T_{cg}]$, where d is the proportion of the net income distribution paid out in dividends, and (1 − d) is the retention ratio. Following the procedure devised by Dhaliwal et al. (2006), we winsorized at zero and one. $T_d$ is the personal tax rate on dividend income, set to equal the values of $T_D$ for the years prior to 2003, and 15% thereafter. $T_{cg}$ is set to equal the top statutory tax rate on long-term capital gains income, which equals 20% for 1998 through to 2002 and 15% thereafter. $\alpha$ is the benefit of capital gains deferral. Following Graham (1999) and Dhaliwal et al. (2006), we assume that $\alpha = 0.25$. The sample size (N) relevant to this table as well as to the subsequent tables is 182 companies.

*5.2. Regression Results*

Table 2 presents the findings for the tested models with respect to the following cases: Perfect capital markets, corporate taxes, and both corporate and personal taxes. The results are reported for two different L measures [$Lev_4$(Mv) and $Lev_3$(Bv)], which are based on the total debt of the firm. Using other L measures yields similar results. The statistics reported for each regression are the intercept, slope, R-squared, and the significance of the slope OLS coefficient by the null hypothesis HO: $\gamma_1 = 0$ vs. H1: $\gamma_1 \neq 0$. Since the intercept was significant at the 1% level in all cases, only the significance of the slope is reported in the tables. Additional tests comparing whether each regression parameter is equal to its theoretical counterpart in each sample year are provided in Tables 3 and 4.

**Table 2.** Regression results.

| Perfect Capital Market | | Mean | Median | SD | CV | Min | Max |
|---|---|---|---|---|---|---|---|
| | Intercept | 0.092 | 0.093 | 0.013 | 0.140 | 0.077 | 0.108 |
| $Lev_4$(Mv) Rel | Slope | 0.021 | 0.022 | 0.001 | 0.062 | 0.019 | 0.022 |
| | $R^2$ | 0.189 | 0.175 | 0.030 | 0.159 | 0.166 | 0.241 |
| HO: $\gamma_1 = 0$ | Slope Sig | 0.000 | 0.000 | 0.000 | 0.000 | 0.000 | 0.000 |
| | Intercept | 0.095 | 0.094 | 0.015 | 0.157 | 0.080 | 0.116 |
| $Lev_3$(Bv) Rel | Slope | 0.011 | 0.012 | 0.002 | 0.182 | 0.008 | 0.013 |
| | $R^2$ | 0.110 | 0.110 | 0.030 | 0.277 | 0.077 | 0.159 |
| HO: $\gamma_1 = 0$ | Slope Sig | 0.000 | 0.000 | 0.000 | 0.000 | 0.000 | 0.000 |
| **Corporate Taxes** | | **Mean** | **Median** | **SD** | **CV** | **Min** | **Max** |
| | Intercept | 0.093 | 0.092 | 0.013 | 0.143 | 0.078 | 0.110 |
| $Lev_4$(Mv) Rel | Slope | 0.032 | 0.032 | 0.003 | 0.093 | 0.027 | 0.035 |
| | $R^2$ | 0.184 | 0.175 | 0.037 | 0.200 | 0.149 | 0.246 |
| $\gamma_1 = 0$ | Slope Sig | 0.000 | 0.000 | 0.000 | 0.000 | 0.000 | 0.000 |
| | Intercept | 0.097 | 0.094 | 0.016 | 0.170 | 0.080 | 0.119 |
| $Lev_3$(Bv) Rel | Slope | 0.016 | 0.017 | 0.003 | 0.207 | 0.012 | 0.020 |
| | $R^2$ | 0.103 | 0.099 | 0.040 | 0.384 | 0.055 | 0.165 |
| HO: $\gamma_1 = 0$ | Slope Sig | 0.000 | 0.000 | 0.000 | 0.000 | 0.000 | 0.001 |
| **Corporate + Personal Taxes** | | **Mean** | **Median** | **SD** | **CV** | **Min** | **Max** |
| | Intercept | 0.093 | 0.092 | 0.013 | 0.143 | 0.078 | 0.110 |
| $Lev_4$(Mv) Rel | Slope | 0.022 | 0.022 | 0.002 | 0.105 | 0.018 | 0.024 |
| | $R^2$ | 0.190 | 0.181 | 0.037 | 0.194 | 0.154 | 0.252 |
| HO: $\gamma_1 = 0$ | Slope Sig | 0.000 | 0.000 | 0.000 | 0.000 | 0.000 | 0.000 |
| | Intercept | 0.096 | 0.093 | 0.017 | 0.175 | 0.079 | 0.119 |
| $Lev_3$(Bv) Rel | Slope | 0.011 | 0.012 | 0.002 | 0.223 | 0.008 | 0.014 |
| | $R^2$ | 0.111 | 0.107 | 0.041 | 0.367 | 0.061 | 0.174 |
| HO: $\gamma_1 = 0$ | Slope Sig | 0.000 | 0.000 | 0.000 | 0.000 | 0.000 | 0.001 |

Notes: Table 2 presents the regression results of: Model (1a): $\sigma_E = \sigma_U + \sigma_U$ [L] using the estimated regression equation given by: $\sigma_E = \gamma_0 + \gamma_1[L]$, Model (2a): $\sigma_E = \sigma_U + \sigma_U [(1 - T_C)L]$ using the estimated regression equation given by: $\sigma_E = \gamma_0 + \gamma_1[(1 - T_C)L]$, Model (3a): $\sigma_E = \sigma_U + \sigma_U$ [TL] using the estimated regression equation given by: $\sigma_E = \gamma_0 + \gamma_1[TL]$. $\sigma_E$ is the risk coefficient of the equity in terms of standard deviation; L is the financial leverage ($Lev_3$, $Lev_4$) of the firm using the *Relative* estimate (Rel) for a given year, which is the mean value of the Lev variable across the preceding five years, while the *Absolute* (Abs) is given by the 5-year mean value of the "debt" numerator divided by the 5-year mean value of the "equity" denominator. $Lev_3 = (CL + LTD)/Equity_{BV}$, $Lev_4 = (CL + LTD)/Equity_{MV}$ where Lev denotes the financial leverage, LTD is long-term debt, CL is the current liabilities, Equity is the value of common equity, and the subscripts, BV and MV, stand for book and market values, respectively. Slope sig refers to the usual null hypothesis: H0: $\gamma_1 = 0$ vs. H1: $\gamma_1 \neq 0$. The sample size (N) is 182 companies.

**Table 3.** Comparison results by method 1.

| Panel A | | 2007 | | | 2006 | | | 2005 | | | 2004 | | | 2003 | | |
|---|---|---|---|---|---|---|---|---|---|---|---|---|---|---|---|---|
| | | *Risk Free Debt Models* | | | | | | | | | | | | | | |
| **Lev$_4$(Mv) Rel** | | $\sigma_U{}^*$ | $\gamma_0$ | $\gamma_1$ | $\sigma_U{}^*$ | $\gamma_0$ | $\gamma_1$ | $\sigma_U{}^*$ | $\gamma_0$ | $\gamma_1$ | $\sigma_U{}^*$ | $\gamma_0$ | $\gamma_1$ | $\sigma_U{}^*$ | $\gamma_0$ | $\gamma_1$ |
| | **1a** | 0.051 | 0.077 | 0.019 | 0.053 | 0.082 | 0.021 | 0.057 | 0.093 | 0.022 | 0.059 | 0.101 | 0.022 | 0.061 | 0.108 | 0.022 |
| ***Rel* T$_C$** | **2a** | 0.060 | 0.077 | 0.028 | 0.063 | 0.082 | 0.033 | 0.069 | 0.093 | 0.033 | 0.073 | 0.100 | 0.036 | 0.077 | 0.108 | 0.035 |
| ***Abs* T$_C$** | **2a** | 0.060 | 0.078 | 0.027 | 0.063 | 0.082 | 0.032 | 0.069 | 0.092 | 0.035 | 0.072 | 0.101 | 0.033 | 0.076 | 0.110 | 0.032 |
| ***Rel* T$_C$** | **3a** | 0.052 | 0.077 | 0.019 | 0.054 | 0.081 | 0.023 | 0.059 | 0.093 | 0.023 | 0.062 | 0.099 | 0.025 | 0.065 | 0.108 | 0.024 |
| ***Abs* T$_C$** | **3a** | 0.052 | 0.078 | 0.018 | 0.054 | 0.082 | 0.022 | 0.058 | 0.092 | 0.024 | 0.061 | 0.101 | 0.023 | 0.064 | 0.110 | 0.022 |
| **Mean** | | 0.055 | 0.077 | 0.022 | 0.057 | 0.082 | 0.026 | 0.062 | 0.093 | 0.027 | 0.065 | 0.100 | 0.028 | 0.069 | 0.109 | 0.027 |
| **Median** | | 0.052 | 0.077 | 0.019 | 0.054 | 0.082 | 0.023 | 0.059 | 0.093 | 0.024 | 0.062 | 0.101 | 0.025 | 0.065 | 0.108 | 0.024 |
| **SD** | | 0.005 | 0.001 | 0.005 | 0.005 | 0.000 | 0.006 | 0.006 | 0.001 | 0.006 | 0.007 | 0.001 | 0.006 | 0.007 | 0.001 | 0.006 |
| **Min** | | 0.051 | 0.077 | 0.018 | 0.053 | 0.081 | 0.021 | 0.057 | 0.092 | 0.022 | 0.059 | 0.099 | 0.022 | 0.061 | 0.108 | 0.022 |
| **Max** | | 0.06 | 0.078 | 0.028 | 0.063 | 0.082 | 0.033 | 0.069 | 0.093 | 0.035 | 0.073 | 0.101 | 0.036 | 0.077 | 0.11 | 0.035 |
| **Lev$_3$(Bv) Rel** | | $\sigma_U{}^*$ | $\gamma_0$ | $\gamma_1$ | $\sigma_U{}^*$ | $\gamma_0$ | $\gamma_1$ | $\sigma_U{}^*$ | $\gamma_0$ | $\gamma_1$ | $\sigma_U{}^*$ | $\gamma_0$ | $\gamma_1$ | $\sigma_U{}^*$ | $\gamma_0$ | $\gamma_1$ |
| | **1a** | 0.036 | 0.081 | 0.008 | 0.039 | 0.083 | 0.012 | 0.044 | 0.094 | 0.013 | 0.046 | 0.104 | 0.012 | 0.048 | 0.116 | 0.010 |
| ***Rel* T$_C$** | **2a** | 0.046 | 0.081 | 0.011 | 0.050 | 0.085 | 0.015 | 0.057 | 0.096 | 0.019 | 0.060 | 0.106 | 0.017 | 0.063 | 0.118 | 0.014 |
| ***Abs* T$_C$** | **2a** | 0.046 | 0.080 | 0.012 | 0.049 | 0.083 | 0.017 | 0.056 | 0.094 | 0.020 | 0.059 | 0.107 | 0.017 | 0.063 | 0.119 | 0.013 |
| ***Rel* T$_C$** | **3a** | 0.037 | 0.080 | 0.008 | 0.040 | 0.085 | 0.010 | 0.046 | 0.095 | 0.014 | 0.049 | 0.106 | 0.012 | 0.051 | 0.118 | 0.010 |
| ***Abs* T$_C$** | **3a** | 0.053 | 0.079 | 0.008 | 0.057 | 0.082 | 0.012 | 0.065 | 0.093 | 0.014 | 0.069 | 0.106 | 0.012 | 0.073 | 0.119 | 0.009 |
| **Mean** | | 0.044 | 0.080 | 0.009 | 0.047 | 0.084 | 0.013 | 0.054 | 0.094 | 0.016 | 0.057 | 0.106 | 0.014 | 0.060 | 0.118 | 0.011 |
| **Median** | | 0.046 | 0.08 | 0.008 | 0.049 | 0.083 | 0.012 | 0.056 | 0.094 | 0.014 | 0.059 | 0.106 | 0.012 | 0.063 | 0.118 | 0.01 |
| **SD** | | 0.007 | 0.001 | 0.002 | 0.008 | 0.001 | 0.003 | 0.009 | 0.001 | 0.003 | 0.009 | 0.001 | 0.003 | 0.010 | 0.001 | 0.002 |
| **Min** | | 0.036 | 0.079 | 0.008 | 0.039 | 0.082 | 0.01 | 0.044 | 0.093 | 0.013 | 0.046 | 0.104 | 0.012 | 0.048 | 0.116 | 0.009 |
| **Max** | | 0.053 | 0.081 | 0.012 | 0.057 | 0.085 | 0.017 | 0.065 | 0.096 | 0.02 | 0.069 | 0.107 | 0.017 | 0.073 | 0.119 | 0.014 |

| Panel B | | 2007 | | 2006 | | 2005 | | 2004 | | 2003 | |
|---|---|---|---|---|---|---|---|---|---|---|---|
| **Lev$_4$(Mv) Rel** | | $\gamma_0 - \sigma_U{}^*$ | $\gamma_1 - \sigma_U{}^*$ | $\gamma_0 - \sigma_U{}^*$ | $\gamma_1 - \sigma_U{}^*$ | $\gamma_0 - \sigma_U{}^*$ | $\gamma_1 - \sigma_U{}^*$ | $\gamma_0 - \sigma_U{}^*$ | $\gamma_1 - \sigma_U{}^*$ | $\gamma_0 - \sigma_U{}^*$ | $\gamma_1 - \sigma_U{}^*$ |
| | **1a** | 0.026 * | −0.032 * | 0.029 * | −0.032 * | 0.036 * | −0.035 * | 0.042 * | −0.037 * | 0.047 * | −0.039 * |
| ***Rel* T$_C$** | **2a** | 0.017 * | −0.032 * | 0.019 * | −0.030 * | 0.024 * | −0.036 * | 0.027 * | −0.037 * | 0.031 * | −0.042 * |
| ***Abs* T$_C$** | **2a** | 0.018 * | −0.033 * | 0.019 * | −0.031 * | 0.023 * | −0.034 * | 0.029 | −0.039 * | 0.034 * | −0.044 * |
| ***Rel* T$_C$** | **3a** | 0.025 * | −0.033 * | 0.027 * | −0.031 * | 0.034 * | −0.036 * | 0.037 * | −0.037 * | 0.043 * | −0.041 * |
| ***Abs* T$_C$** | **3a** | 0.026 * | −0.034 * | 0.028 * | −0.032 * | 0.034 * | −0.034 * | 0.040 * | −0.038 * | 0.046 * | −0.042 * |
| **Mean** | | 0.022 | −0.033 | 0.024 | −0.031 | 0.030 | −0.035 | 0.035 | −0.038 | 0.040 | −0.042 |
| **Median** | | 0.025 | −0.033 | 0.027 | −0.031 | 0.034 | −0.035 | 0.037 | −0.037 | 0.043 | −0.042 |
| **SD** | | 0.005 | 0.001 | 0.005 | 0.001 | 0.006 | 0.001 | 0.007 | 0.001 | 0.007 | 0.002 |
| **Min** | | 0.017 | −0.034 | 0.019 | −0.032 | 0.023 | −0.036 | 0.027 | −0.039 | 0.031 | −0.044 |
| **Max** | | 0.026 | −0.032 | 0.029 | −0.03 | 0.036 | −0.034 | 0.042 | −0.037 | 0.047 | −0.039 |

**Table 3.** *Cont.*

| Panel B | | 2007 | | 2006 | | 2005 | | 2004 | | 2003 | |
|---|---|---|---|---|---|---|---|---|---|---|---|
| **$Lev_3$(Bv) Rel** | | $\gamma_0 - \sigma_U^*$ | $\gamma_1 - \sigma_U^*$ | $\gamma_0 - \sigma_U^*$ | $\gamma_1 - \sigma_U^*$ | $\gamma_0 - \sigma_U^*$ | $\gamma_1 - \sigma_U^*$ | $\gamma_0 - \sigma_U^*$ | $\gamma_1 - \sigma_U^*$ | $\gamma_0 - \sigma_U^*$ | $\gamma_1 - \sigma_U^*$ |
| | **1a** | 0.045 * | −0.028 * | 0.044 * | −0.027 * | 0.050 * | −0.031 * | 0.058 * | −0.034 * | 0.068 * | −0.038 * |
| ***Rel* $T_C$** | **2a** | 0.035 * | −0.035 * | 0.035 * | −0.035 * | 0.039 * | −0.038 * | 0.046 * | −0.043 * | 0.055 * | −0.049 * |
| ***Abs* $T_C$** | **2a** | 0.034 * | −0.034 * | 0.034 * | −0.032 * | 0.038 * | −0.036 * | 0.048 * | −0.042 * | 0.056 * | −0.050 * |
| ***Rel* $T_C$** | **3a** | 0.043 * | −0.029 * | 0.045 * | −0.030 * | 0.049 * | −0.032 * | 0.057 * | −0.037 * | 0.067 * | −0.041 * |
| ***Abs* $T_C$** | **3a** | 0.026 * | −0.045 * | 0.025 * | −0.045 * | 0.028 * | −0.051 * | 0.037 * | −0.057 * | 0.046 * | −0.064 * |
| **Mean** | | 0.037 | −0.034 | 0.037 | −0.034 | 0.041 | −0.038 | 0.049 | −0.043 | 0.058 | −0.048 |
| **Median** | | 0.035 | −0.034 | 0.035 | −0.032 | 0.039 | −0.036 | 0.048 | −0.042 | 0.056 | −0.049 |
| **SD** | | 0.008 | 0.007 | 0.008 | 0.007 | 0.009 | 0.008 | 0.009 | 0.009 | 0.009 | 0.010 |
| **Min** | | 0.026 | −0.045 | 0.025 | −0.045 | 0.028 | −0.051 | 0.037 | −0.057 | 0.046 | −0.064 |
| **Max** | | 0.045 | −0.028 | 0.045 | −0.027 | 0.05 | −0.031 | 0.058 | −0.034 | 0.068 | −0.038 |

Notes: Table 3 presents the *theoretical and observed* regression parameters according to the *direct* estimation by method 1 for each model using the *Relative* $Lev_3$ and $Lev_4$ financial leverage estimates. The first and second columns in Panel A describe the model and its variables' variants. Each year is divided into three columns. The first one reports the $\sigma_U$* derived by each model and the second and third columns report the *observed* values of $\gamma_0$ and $\gamma_1$ in each *direct* testing. Panel B presents the findings for the null hypothesis H0: $\gamma_0 = \sigma_U^*$; $\gamma_0 = \sigma_U^*$. The asterisk * indicates significance $\leq$ 5%. The sample size (N) is 182 companies.

**Table 4.** Comparison results by method 2.

| Panel A | | 2007 | | 2006 | | 2005 | | 2004 | | 2003 | |
|---|---|---|---|---|---|---|---|---|---|---|---|
| | | | | | | *Risk Free Debt Models* | | | | | |
| $Lev_4$(Mv) Rel | | Intercept $\gamma_0$* | Slope $\gamma_1$* | Intercept $\gamma_0$* | Slope $\gamma_1$* | Intercept $\gamma_0$* | Slope $\gamma_1$* | Intercept $\gamma_0$* | Slope $\gamma_1$* | Intercept $\gamma_0$* | Slope $\gamma_1$* |
| | **1a** | 0.051 | 0.051 | 0.053 | 0.053 | 0.057 | 0.057 | 0.059 | 0.059 | 0.061 | 0.061 |
| *Rel* $T_C$ | **2a** | 0.060 | 0.039 | 0.063 | 0.041 | 0.069 | 0.045 | 0.073 | 0.046 | 0.077 | 0.048 |
| *Abs* $T_C$ | **2a** | 0.060 | 0.039 | 0.063 | 0.041 | 0.069 | 0.045 | 0.072 | 0.047 | 0.076 | 0.048 |
| *Rel* $T_C$ | **3a** | 0.052 | 0.040 | 0.054 | 0.047 | 0.059 | 0.056 | 0.062 | 0.064 | 0.065 | 0.069 |
| *Abs* $T_C$ | **3a** | 0.052 | 0.041 | 0.054 | 0.048 | 0.058 | 0.057 | 0.061 | 0.065 | 0.064 | 0.070 |
| **Observed by** $Lev_4$(Mv) Rel **$\gamma_0$ $\gamma_1$** | | **0.077** | **0.019** | **0.082** | **0.021** | **0.093** | **0.022** | **0.101** | **0.022** | **0.108** | **0.022** |
| $Lev_3$(Bv) Rel | | Intercept $\gamma_0$* | Slope $\gamma_1$* | Intercept $\gamma_0$* | Slope $\gamma_1$* | Intercept $\gamma_0$* | Slope $\gamma_1$* | Intercept $\gamma_0$* | Slope $\gamma_1$* | Intercept $\gamma_0$* | Slope $\gamma_1$* |
| | **1a** | 0.036 | 0.036 | 0.039 | 0.039 | 0.044 | 0.044 | 0.046 | 0.046 | 0.048 | 0.048 |
| *Rel* $T_C$ | **2a** | 0.046 | 0.030 | 0.050 | 0.032 | 0.057 | 0.037 | 0.060 | 0.038 | 0.063 | 0.040 |
| *Abs* $T_C$ | **2a** | 0.046 | 0.030 | 0.049 | 0.032 | 0.056 | 0.037 | 0.059 | 0.039 | 0.063 | 0.040 |
| *Rel* $T_C$ | **3a** | 0.037 | 0.055 | 0.040 | 0.061 | 0.046 | 0.069 | 0.049 | 0.077 | 0.051 | 0.082 |
| *Abs* $T_C$ | **3a** | 0.053 | 0.039 | 0.057 | 0.044 | 0.065 | 0.050 | 0.069 | 0.057 | 0.073 | 0.061 |

**Table 4.** *Cont.*

| Panel A | | 2007 | | 2006 | | 2005 | | 2004 | | 2003 | |
|---|---|---|---|---|---|---|---|---|---|---|---|
| | | | | | | *Risk Free Debt Models* | | | | | |
| $Lev_4$(Mv) Rel | | Intercept $\gamma_0$* | Slope $\gamma_1$* | Intercept $\gamma_0$* | Slope $\gamma_1$* | Intercept $\gamma_0$* | Slope $\gamma_1$* | Intercept $\gamma_0$* | Slope $\gamma_1$* | Intercept $\gamma_0$* | Slope $\gamma_1$* |
| **Observed by** $Lev_3$(Bv) Rel $\gamma_0$ $\gamma_1$ | | **0.080** | **0.008** | **0.083** | **0.012** | **0.094** | **0.013** | **0.104** | **0.012** | **0.116** | **0.010** |
| **Panel B** | | **2007** | | **2006** | | **2005** | | **2004** | | **2003** | |
| | | | | | | *Debt risk free models* | | | | | |
| **$Lev_4$(Mv) Rel** | | $\gamma_0 - \gamma_0$* | $\gamma_1 - \gamma_1$* | $\gamma_0 - \gamma_0$* | $\gamma_1 - \gamma_1$* | $\gamma_0 - \gamma_0$* | $\gamma_1 - \gamma_1$* | $\gamma_0 - \gamma_0$* | $\gamma_1 - \gamma_1$* | $\gamma_0 - \gamma_0$* | $\gamma_1 - \gamma_1$* |
| | 1a | 0.026 * | −0.032 * | 0.029 * | −0.032 * | 0.036 * | −0.035 * | 0.042 * | −0.037 * | 0.047 * | −0.039 * |
| *Rel* $T_C$ | 2a | 0.017 * | −0.020 * | 0.019 * | −0.020 * | 0.024 * | −0.023 * | 0.028 * | −0.024 * | 0.031 * | −0.026 * |
| *Abs* $T_C$ | 2a | 0.017 * | −0.020 * | 0.019 * | −0.020 * | 0.024 * | −0.023 * | 0.029 * | −0.025 * | 0.032 * | −0.026 * |
| *Rel* $T_C$ | 3a | 0.025 * | −0.021 * | 0.028 * | −0.026 * | 0.034 * | −0.034 * | 0.039 * | −0.042 * | 0.043 * | −0.047 * |
| *Abs* $T_C$ | 3a | 0.025 * | −0.022 * | 0.028 * | −0.027 * | 0.035 * | −0.035 * | 0.040 * | −0.043 * | 0.044 * | −0.048 * |
| **Mean** | | 0.022 | −0.023 | 0.025 | −0.025 | 0.031 | −0.030 | 0.036 | −0.034 | 0.039 | −0.037 |
| **Median** | | 0.025 | −0.021 | 0.028 | −0.026 | 0.034 | −0.034 | 0.039 | −0.037 | 0.043 | −0.039 |
| **SD** | | 0.005 | 0.005 | 0.005 | 0.005 | 0.006 | 0.006 | 0.007 | 0.009 | 0.007 | 0.011 |
| **Min** | | 0.017 | −0.032 | 0.019 | −0.032 | 0.024 | −0.035 | 0.028 | −0.043 | 0.031 | −0.048 |
| **Max** | | 0.026 | −0.020 | 0.029 | −0.020 | 0.036 | −0.023 | 0.042 | −0.024 | 0.047 | −0.026 |
| **$Lev_3$(Bv) Rel** | | $\gamma_0 - \gamma_0$* | $\gamma_1 - \gamma_1$* | $\gamma_0 - \gamma_0$* | $\gamma_1 - \gamma_1$* | $\gamma_0 - \gamma_0$* | $\gamma_1 - \gamma_1$* | $\gamma_0 - \gamma_0$* | $\gamma_1 - \gamma_1$* | $\gamma_0 - \gamma_0$* | $\gamma_1 - \gamma_1$* |
| | 1a | 0.044 * | −0.028 * | 0.044 * | −0.027 * | 0.050 * | −0.031 * | 0.058 * | −0.034 * | 0.068 * | −0.038 * |
| *Rel* $T_C$ | 2a | 0.034 * | −0.022 * | 0.033 * | −0.020 * | 0.037 * | −0.024 * | 0.044 * | −0.026 * | 0.053 * | −0.030 * |
| *Abs* $T_C$ | 2a | 0.034 * | −0.022 * | 0.034 * | −0.020 * | 0.038 * | −0.024 * | 0.045 * | −0.027 * | 0.053 * | −0.030 * |
| *Rel* $T_C$ | 3a | 0.043 * | −0.047 * | 0.043 * | −0.049 * | 0.048 * | −0.056 * | 0.055 * | −0.065 * | 0.065 * | −0.072 * |
| *Abs* $T_C$ | 3a | 0.027 * | −0.031 * | 0.026 * | −0.032 * | 0.029 * | −0.037 * | 0.035 * | −0.045 * | 0.043 * | −0.051 * |
| **Mean** | | 0.036 | −0.030 | 0.036 | −0.030 | 0.040 | −0.034 | 0.047 | −0.039 | 0.056 | −0.044 |
| **Median** | | 0.034 | −0.028 | 0.034 | −0.027 | 0.038 | −0.031 | 0.045 | −0.034 | 0.053 | −0.038 |
| **SD** | | 0.007 | 0.010 | 0.008 | 0.012 | 0.009 | 0.013 | 0.009 | 0.016 | 0.010 | 0.018 |
| **Min** | | 0.027 | −0.047 | 0.026 | −0.049 | 0.029 | −0.056 | 0.035 | −0.065 | 0.043 | −0.072 |
| **Max** | | 0.044 | −0.022 | 0.044 | −0.020 | 0.050 | −0.024 | 0.058 | −0.026 | 0.068 | −0.030 |

Notes: Table 4 presents the *theoretical and observed* parameters of $\gamma_0$ and $\gamma_1$ by method 2 using the *Relative* $Lev_3$ and $Lev_4$ financial leverage estimates. Panel A presents the theoretical values while Panel B reports the comparison results for the differences between the *theoretical and observed* parameters. Panel A reports the theoretical $\gamma_0$* and $\gamma_1$* derived by each model and the last row in each group presents the *observed* parameters of $\gamma_0$ and $\gamma_1$ based on the estimation of Equation (10), which are the reference parameters for each model. Panel B presents the findings for the null hypothesis H0: $\gamma_0 = \sigma_U$*; $\gamma_0 = \sigma_U$*. The asterisk * indicates significance $\leq$5%. The sample size (N) is 182 companies.

The main results that emerge from Table 2 here imply a positive and significant relationship between $\sigma_E$ and L. This result holds in each case tested: The perfect capital market case (Equation (7)—Model (1a)), corporate taxes only (Equation (8)—Model (2a)), and both corporate and personal taxes (Equation (9)—Model (3a)). Though not reported here, the positive relationship also holds for each of the sample years and for all eight leverage estimates whether the *Absolute* or *Relative* method is employed. Note that the overall results tend to support the positive relationship between $\sigma_E$ and L, but the R-squared is higher when using market measures of L rather than book measures. For the case of a perfect capital market in Table 3, the mean value of R-squared is 0.189 for the *Relative* $Lev_4$ and 0.110 for its corresponding book measure (*Relative* $Lev_3$). For the corporate tax case, the mean value of R-squared is 0.184 for the *Relative* $Lev_4$ and 0.103 for its corresponding book measure (*Relative* $Lev_3$). Finally, for the corporate and personal taxes case, the mean value of R-squared is 0.190 for the *Relative* $Lev_4$ and 0.111 for its corresponding book measure (*Relative* $Lev_3$). We obtained similar results when the financial leverage is based on long-term debt ($Lev_1$, $Lev_2$) rather than total debt ($Lev_3$, $Lev_4$). A comparison between the book and market slope regression parameters in each case implies that the extra penalty for volatility with the use of book measures may be more moderate than using market measures. For example, the mean value of the slope measures for the $Lev_4$ across the years is 0.021 (the perfect capital market case), 0.032 (corporate taxes), and 0.022 (both corporate and personal taxes). Similarly, the mean value of the slope measures for $Lev_3$ is 0.011 (the perfect capital market case), 0.016 (corporate taxes), and 0.011 (both corporate and personal taxes).

### 5.3. *Comparative Analysis and Robustness Tests*

We test the degree to which the observed regression coefficients, $\gamma_0$ (intercept) and $\gamma_1$ (slope), in each model correspond to their theoretical model counterparts, designated here as $\gamma_0{}^*$ and $\gamma_1{}^*$. We use two methods to conduct this comparison—method 1 and method 2. In the first method, the corresponding explanatory variables are [L], [(1 − $T_C$)L], and [TL] for the perfect capital market case, the corporate taxes case, and both the corporate and personal taxes, respectively. Thus, in all three cases, the null hypothesis is H0: $\gamma_0 = \sigma_U{}^*$ and $\gamma_1 = \sigma_U{}^*$, where $\sigma_U{}^*$ is the theoretical value derived from each model.

In the second method, we first run the following cross-sectional regression model, which is the estimated regression of the perfect capital market case described earlier in Equation (7):

$$\sigma_E = \gamma_0 + \gamma_1[L]. \tag{11}$$

In the first step, we run Equation (11) to estimate the observed $\gamma_0$ and $\gamma_1$. In the second step, we compare the regression's $\gamma_0$ with $\gamma_0{}^*$, where $\gamma_0{}^*$ is the theoretical value derived from each model and $\gamma_1$ to $\gamma_1{}^*$ implied in each theoretical model. For the perfect capital market [model (1a)], $\gamma_0{}^* = \sigma_U = \sigma_E/(1 + L)$ and $\gamma_1{}^*$ is also $\sigma_U$. For the corporate taxes case [model (2a)] in Equation (8), $\gamma_0{}^* = \sigma_U = \sigma_E/[1 + (1\text{-}\ T_C)L]$ and $\gamma_1{}^*$ is $\sigma_U(1 - T_C)$. Finally, for the corporate and personal taxes case [model (3a)] in Equation (9), $\gamma_0{}^* = \sigma_U = \sigma_E/[1 + TL]$ and $\gamma_1{}^*$ is $\sigma_U T$. Similarly, we compare the regression $\gamma_0$ and $\gamma_1$ with the intercept and slope as detailed above.

Table 3 presents the theoretical values derived from each model according to two different measures of L, and the T tests for [$\gamma_0 - \gamma_0{}^*$] and [$\gamma_1 - \gamma_1{}^*$] in each year using each L measure. We mark the *p*-value, which is significant at least at the 5% level, with an asterisk, *. The last row of each group of models in Table 3 presents the observed parameters ($\gamma_0$ and $\gamma_1$) in the first stage of method 2. Every other row presents the implied theoretical values of the intercept and slope ($\gamma_0{}^*$ and $\gamma_1{}^*$) if the specific model holds true.

For example, looking at 2006, if model (2a) (the corporate taxes case) holds true, by the null hypothesis (under *Relative* $Lev_4$ and *Relative* $T_C$) $\gamma_0$* is 0.063 and $\gamma_1$* is 0.041. In other words, if model (2a) holds true, the observed parameters in the last row (0.082 and 0.021 for the intercept ($\gamma_0$) and slope ($\gamma_1$)) should not be statistically different from their theoretical values above ($\gamma_0$* is 0.063 and $\gamma_1$* is 0.021). Since the final results remain the same in all of our financial leverage estimates, we report here the findings using $Lev_3$ and $Lev_4$ only.

We begin by testing the approximation of the observed values relative to their theoretical counterparts using method 1. This method of comparison relies on the *direct* testing of each model outlined earlier (that is, (1a), (2a), and (3a)). Note that we test each model *directly* and then compare the observed parameters ($\gamma_0$ and $\gamma_1$) to the theoretical values ($\gamma_0$* and $\gamma_1$*) derived from each model. Given that we run the explanatory variables of L, $(1 - T_C)L$ and TL directly versus the standard deviation of equity returns, in all cases, both $\gamma_0$ and $\gamma_1$ should be equal to $\sigma_U$, where $\sigma_U$ is derived directly from the relevant model. A more detailed explanation is as follows. Equation (12) below is the theoretical model in which debt is risk free, and corporate tax is the only market imperfection (model (2a)):

$$\sigma_E = \sigma_U + \sigma_U[(1 - T_C)L]. \quad (12)$$

Testing this equation *directly* means that $\sigma_E$ is the dependent variable, and the term in the squared parentheses, $[(1 - T_C)L]$, is the explanatory variable. Accordingly, the specification model here is Equation (13) below:

$$\sigma_E = \gamma_0 + \gamma_1[(1 - T_C)L]. \quad (13)$$

Thus, if Model (2a) holds true, then both $\gamma_0$ and $\gamma_1$ should be equal to $\sigma_U$* (where $\sigma_U$ is derived from the theoretical model in Equation (7)). Hence, we compare the value of $\sigma_U$* with the observed intercept and slope (expressed by $\gamma_0$ and $\gamma_1$) obtained by the *direct* test we conducted.

Table 3 presents the results of the observed parameters of $\gamma_0$ and $\gamma_1$ (panel A) using method 1, and the significance for the [$\gamma_0 - \sigma_U$*] and [$\gamma_1 - \sigma_U$*] differences (panel B). All of the tests indicate significant gaps for [$\gamma_1 - \sigma_U$*] and mostly significant for [$\gamma_0 - \sigma_U$*]. The gaps are significant for the five years in the sample and for all eight leverage estimates whether the market or book measures are used and whether the *Absolute* or *Relative* method is employed for corporate taxes and financial leverage. While the majority of the differences are significant, using market measures generally minimizes the differences between the theoretical and actual values. For example, in 2007, the mean value of [$\gamma_0 - \sigma_U$*] is 0.022 using the *Relative* $Lev_4$ and 0.037 using its corresponding book measure—*Relative* $Lev_3$. Similarly, though not reported here, the mean value of [$\gamma_1 - \sigma_U$*] is −0.039 using the *Relative* $Lev_2$ and −0.043 using its corresponding book measure—*Relative* $Lev_1$. Long term debt measures illustrate similar results. Combining these results with the higher coefficient of determination may suggest that using market measures accords better with the theoretical models.

The results for method 2 presented in Table 4 are similar for the results of method 1 in Table 3. Most the results of the t tests conducted for the differences in the [$\gamma_0 - \gamma_0$*] gaps clearly show that the gaps are significant for the five years in the sample and for all leverage estimates whether the *Absolute* or *Relative* method is employed. As with the [$\gamma_0 - \gamma_0$*] gaps, we find that most of the [$\gamma_1 - \gamma_1$*] gaps are significant. Also, the gaps are relatively lower using market rather than book measures of L. For example, in 2006, the mean [$\gamma_0 - \gamma_0$*] gap is 0.025 for the market measure compared with 0.036 using the book measure of L. Similarly, the mean [$\gamma_1 - \gamma_1$*] gap is 0.025 and 0.030 (in absolute terms) for the market and book measures of L, respectively.

## 6. Summary and Conclusions

This paper contributes to a large body of research on capital structure theory by testing the direct theoretical relationship between the variance of stock returns ($\sigma^2_E$) and financial leverage (L). The purpose of this study and its motivation was to test the association between $\sigma_E$ and L when corporate and personal taxes exist. Using a sample of U.S. industrial firms traded on the New York

Stock Exchange, we provide empirical evidence that the association between $\sigma_E$ and L is affected by the level of corporate and personal level taxes.

The main findings of this research are as follows. First, $\sigma_E$ was positively related to financial leverage in all sample years tested, and this positive relationship was robust regardless of whether financial leverage was measured in book or market terms, and whether the tax estimates were based on *Relative* or *Absolute* methods of measurement. Second, the relationship between $\sigma_E$ and L was positive in all of the three theoretical models tested here: The perfect capital market, corporate tax model, and both corporate and personal tax model. Finally, using market measures generated better results in terms of R squared, and reduced the differences between the theoretical and actual parameters. These results might support and motivate the use of market measures of financial leverage rather than book measures.

Our study contributes to the existing literature in the following aspects: First, our research tested three theoretical models in the context of the σE-L relationship, and in this respect it extends prior studies. Second, for all of these three models, we compared the OLS regression coefficients with their theoretical counterparts and examined whether the differences between these values were statistically significant—an important investigation that has not been conducted so far in the literature. In addition, to test whether the σE-L relationship is positive, an attempt was also made to capture the degree to which the theoretical models were practically confirmed. Third, as emphasized earlier in this study, most prior studies only employed a standard regression analysis of the relationship between $\sigma_E$ and L and some other variables, conducting what we call here the indirect-test approach. Furthermore, taxes were excluded from these tested regressions. Our study, in contrast, was entirely devoted to testing the theoretical relationship between $\sigma_E$ and L—adopting what we call in this study the direct-test approach. In addition, we employed direct estimates of the additional variables that are present in the theoretical models, such as corporate and personal taxes, as well as both book and market leverage measures.

The comprehensive approach employed in this study may enhance the understanding of the nature of the theoretical relationship between $\sigma_E$ and L when both corporate and personal taxes exist, and may help comprehend the degree to which this theoretical relationship is confirmed in the real corporate world.

One limitation of this study, which may also be an opportunity for future research, is the incorporation of risk in addition to risk free debt. Future study should involve an estimation of the "cov($K_U$,r)" term, which will likely need an intensive data search, and the employment of methodological assumptions.

**Author Contributions:** The authors contributed equally to the paper in the context of research design, gathering data, empirical design and testing procedures as well as in writing the paper.

**Funding:** This research received no external funding.

**Acknowledgments:** We would like to thank the seminar participants at the University of Haifa for their comments and suggestions on an earlier draft of the paper. Remaining errors are our responsibility.

**Conflicts of Interest:** The authors declare no conflict of interests.

## Appendix A Summary of Financial Leverage Proxies

The table indicates the type of financial leverage from which the proxy was derived and the specific paper that obtained these proxies. Further information about the construction of the specific variable appears in the comments column.

**Table A1.** Summary of Literature Financial Leverage Proxies.

| Authors | Proxy for Financial Leverage | Comments |
|---|---|---|
| Faff et al. (2002, NAJE) | Total Liabilities/Total Equity | Equity and preferred stock are measured as market values, whereas liabilities are measured as book values |
| | (Total Liabilities + Preferred Stock)/Total Equity | Equity and preferred stock are measured as market values, whereas liabilities are measured as book values |
| Ghosh and Jain (2000, JCF) | (LTD + Current Liabilities)/(book value of debt + market value of equity) | Ghosh and Jain (2000, JCF) |
| Lang et al. (1996, JFE) | (Short term debt + Long term debt)/total assets | They used only book values rather than market values |
| Bradley et al.(1984, JF) | LTD/(LTD + Total EQUITY) | LTD-book value, equity-market value |
| Bowman (1980, JAR) | Four variations of book and market values | Equity is common stockholders' equity. Debt is equal to total assets minus common stockholders' equity |
| | | Market value of common stockholders' equity is calculated by the market value per share of common stock times the number of common shares outstanding |
| Breen and Lerner (1973, JF) | LTD/Common Equity | Ratio of only long term debt to common equity, the second measure of total debt to equity showed similar results and is not reported |
| | Total Debt/Common Equity | Book values |
| Rosenberg and McKibben (1973, JF) | Senior Securities/total assets | Based on Book valuesCalculated as a 5-year average |
| Errunza (1979, FM) | Total Debt/Total Assets | |
| Beaver et al. (1970, AR) | Total Senior Securities including current liabilities/Total Assets | |
| | LTD/Total Assets | |

## References


Ait-Sahalia, Yacine, Jianqing Fan, and Yingying Li. 2013. The leverage effect puzzle: Disentangling sources of bias at high frequency. *Journal of Financial Economics* 109: 224–49. [CrossRef]

Arena, Matteo P., and Andrew H. Roper. 2010. The effect of taxes on multinational debt location. *Journal of Corporate Finance* 16: 637–54. [CrossRef]

Barclay, Michael J., Clifford W. Smith Jr., and Erwan Morellec. 2006. On the debt capacity of growth options. *Journal of Business* 79: 37–58. [CrossRef]

Beaver, William, Paul Kettler, and Myron Scholes. 1970. The association between market determined and accounting determined risk measures. *The Accounting Review* 45: 654–82.

Black, F. 1976. Studies of Stock Market Volatility Changes. Paper Presented at the American Statistical Association, Business and Economic Statistics Section, American Statistical Association, Washington DC, WA, USA. pp. 177–81. Available online: http://www.citeulike.org/group/2384/article/7656400 (accessed on 6 March 2019).

Bollerslev, Tim, Natalia Sizova, and George Tauchen. 2012. Volatility in equilibrium: A symmetries and dynamic dependencies. *Review of Finance* 16: 31–80. [CrossRef]

Bowman, Robert G. 1980. The importance of a market-value measurement of debt in assessing leverage. *Journal of Accounting Research* 18: 242–54. [CrossRef]

Butler, Kirt C., Rosanne M. Mohr, and Richard R. Simonds. 1991. The Hamada and Conine Leverage Adjustments and the Estimation of Systematic Risk for Multisegment Firms. *Journal of Business Finance and Accounting* 18: 885–901. [CrossRef]

Bradley, Michael, Gregg A. Jarrell, and E. Han Kim. 1984. On the existence of an optimal capital structure: Theory and evidence. *The Journal of Finance* 39: 857–78. [CrossRef]

Breen, William J., and Eugene M. Lerner. 1973. Corporate financial strategies and market measures of risk and return. *The Journal of Finance* 28: 339–51. [CrossRef]

Cheung, Yin-Wong, and Lilian K. Ng. 1992. Stock price dynamics and firm size: An empirical investigation. *Journal of Finance* 47: 1985–97. [CrossRef]

Christie, Andrew A. 1982. The stochastic behavior of common stock variances: Value, leverage and interest rate effects. *Journal of financial Economics* 10: 407–32. [CrossRef]

DeAngelo, Harry, Linda DeAngelo, and Toni M. Whited. 2011. Capital structure dynamics and transitory debt. *Journal of Financial Economics* 99: 235–61. [CrossRef]

Dhaliwal, Dan, Shane Heitzman, and Oliver Zhen Li. 2006. Taxes, leverage, and the cost of equity capital. *Journal of Accounting Research* 44: 691–723. [CrossRef]

Duffee, Gregory R. 1995. Stock returns and volatility: A firm-level analysis. *Journal of Financial Economics* 37: 399–420. [CrossRef]

Dyreng, Scott D., Michelle Hanlon, and Edward L. Maydew. 2010. The effects of executives on corporate tax avoidance. *The Accounting Review* 85: 1163–89. [CrossRef]

Errunza, Vihang R. 1979. Determinants of financial structure in the central American common market. *Financial Management* 8: 72–77. [CrossRef]

Fama, Eugene F., and Kenneth R. French. 2002. Testing Tradeoff and Pecking Order Predictions about Dividends and Debt. *Review of Financial Studies* 15: 1–33. [CrossRef]

Faff, Robert W., Robert D. Brooks, and Ho Yew Kee. 2002. New evidence on the impact of financial leverage on beta risk: A time-series approach. *The North American Journal of Economics and Finance* 13: 1–20. [CrossRef]

Fan, Joseph P. H., Sheridan Titman, and Garry Twite. 2012. An International Comparison of Capital Structure and Debt Maturity Choices. *Journal of Financial and Quantitative Analysis* 47: 23–56. [CrossRef]

Figlewski, Stephen, and Xiaozu Wang. 2000. *Is the Leverage Effect a Leverage Effect?* Working Paper. New York: Stern School of Business, New York University.

Ghosh, Aloke, and Prem C. Jain. 2000. Financial leverage changes associated with corporate mergers. *Journal of Corporate Finance* 6: 377–402. [CrossRef]

Graham, John. 1999. Do personal taxes affect corporate financing decisions. *Journal of Public Economics* 73: 147–85. [CrossRef]

Graham, John R, and Campbell R Harvey. 2001. The theory and practice of corporate finance: Evidence from the field. *Journal of Financial Economics* 60: 187–243. [CrossRef]

Kemsley, Deen, and Doron Nissim. 2002. Valuation of the debt-tax shield. *Journal of Finance* 57: 2045–73. [CrossRef]

Lang, Larry, Eli Ofek, and RenéM Stulz. 1996. Leverage, investment, and firm growth. *Journal of financial Economics* 40: 3–29. [CrossRef]

Lemmon, Michael L., Michael R. Roberts, and Jaime F. Zender. 2008. Back to the beginning: Persistence and the cross-section of corporate capital structure. *Journal of Finance* 63: 1575–608. [CrossRef]

Marston, Felicia, and Susan Perry. 1996. Implied Penalties for Financial Leverage: Theory versus Empirical Evidence. *Quarterly Journal of Business and Economics* 35: 77–97.

Miller, Merton H. 1977. Debt and taxes. *Journal of Finance* 32: 261–75.

Modigliani, Franco, and Merton H. Miller. 1958. The Cost of Capital, Corporation Finance and the Theory of Investment. *The American Economic Review* 48: 261–97.

Modigliani, Franco, and Merton H. Miller. 1963. Corporate income taxes and the cost of capital: A correction. *The American Economic Review* 53: 433–43.

Rosenberg, Barr, and Walt McKibben. 1973. The prediction of systematic and specific risk in common stocks. *Journal of Financial and Quantitative Analysis* 8: 317–33. [CrossRef]

Schwert, G. William. 1990. Stock Volatility and the Crash of 87. *The Review of Financial Studies* 3: 77–102. [CrossRef]

Titman, Sheridan, and Roberto Wessels. 1988. The determinants of capital structure choice. *Journal of Finance* 43: 1–19. [CrossRef]

# 4

# Estimation of Effects of Recent Macroprudential Policies in a Sample of Advanced Open Economies

**Ragnar Nymoen [1], Kari Pedersen [2] and Jon Ivar Sjåberg [2,*]**

1 Department of Economics, University of Oslo, 0315 Oslo, Norway; ragnar.nymoen@econ.uio.no
2 The Financial Supervisory Authority of Norway, 0107 Oslo, Norway; Kari.Pedersen@finanstilsynet.no
* Correspondence: Jon.Ivar.Sjaberg@finanstilsynet.no

**Abstract:** We used a time-series cross-section dataset to test several hypotheses pertaining to the role of macroprudential policy instruments in the management of the financial cycle in advanced open economies. The short-run effects are most significant for caps on loan to value and income (LTV and LTI) and risk weights (RW). The long-run coefficients of credit growth with respect to the indicators of amortisation requirements (Amort) and RW are also significant. The estimation results when house price growth is the dependent variable are consistent with these results. Our findings do not support that Basel III type countercyclical buffer (CCyB) has affected credit growth, and we suggest that the variable is mainly a control in our dataset. In that interpretation, it is interesting that the estimated coefficients of the other instruments are robust with respect to exclusion of CCyB from the empirical models. The main results are also robust to controls in the form of impulse indicator saturation (IIS), which we employed as a novel estimation method for macro panels.

**Keywords:** macroprudential policy measures; house prices; credit growth; open economies; cross-section time-series; macro panel; impulse indicator saturation; robust estimation

**JEL Classification:** C23; C44; C58; G28; G38

---

## 1. Introduction

In this paper, we estimate the effects of macroprudential policies on credit growth and housing price changes. The importance of credit and debt for large macroeconomic fluctuations has long been recognised. Irving Fisher's theory of asset price booms and debt-deflation depressions remains an early milestone, and it is interesting to note that, during the first decades after the World War II, leading economists were analysing the increased risk of crisis if and when credit markets again became liberalised (see Anundsen et al. (2014)). In the late 1980s and the early 1990s, boom–busts occurred in Norway, Finland, Sweden and the UK (see Eika and Nymoen (1992), Honkapoja et al. (1996), Honkapoja (2009), and Muellbauer and Murphy (1990)). In the case of Norway, empirical econometric modelling results indicated clearly that both the house price boom, and the ensuing bust, contributed to GDP expansion and recession trough the private saving channel (cf. Brodin and Nymoen (1992) and Eitrheim et al. (2002)).

In recent years, in particular following the global financial crisis that became an income and job crisis, several empirical contributions have recognised the importance of debt and of housing prices in the complex processes that drive economic fluctuations in advanced economies with liberalised credit markets. For example, three studies with consistent findings for the US saving rate dynamics were presented by Carroll et al. (2012), Mian et al. (2013) and Anundsen and Nymoen (2019). Using a dataset with long historical time series for 14 advanced economies, Jordà et al. (2013) concluded that financial factors play an important role in the modern business cycle (see also Anundsen et al. (2016)).

There is a growing consensus about financial crises becoming more serious when credit and house prices have grown sharply in the build-up to the crisis, which it has become custom to include in the calibration of macroprudential stress tests (Anderson et al. (2018)).

Macroprudential policy aims at promoting financial stability partly by, e.g., managing growth in asset prices and credit. Excess growth in these variables over extended periods may be seen as a necessary condition for financial instability (see Borio and Lowe (2002), Reinhardt and Rogoff (2009), Schularick and Taylor (2012), Fahr and Fell (2017) among others). Macroprudential policies however represent a wide menu of policy instruments which has varied in operationalisation both through time and between countries. For example, reserve requirement ratios and limits on foreign currency loans tend to be more used by emerging countries, while caps on loan to value (LTV) have been more used by advanced economies, notably after the financial crisis (see Cerutti et al. (2016)).

To reduce unwanted cross-section heterogeneity, we analysed a time-series cross-section (TSCS) panel dataset consisting of ten advanced and open economies, which are considered to be relatively homogenous in their use of policy measures. The studies that have used (wide) macro panels also indicate that cross section heterogeneity is a factor to be reckoned with. Specifically, the relationship between financial development and macroeconomic activity appears to be stronger in the more advanced open economies (see Chortaes et al. (2015)). This is one reason economies can differ substantially in their response to the various types of policies. In addition to heterogeneity in response, there may be differences in instrument design and operationalisation, meaning that there may be relatively few instances of a given type of instrument even if the cross section dimension is large. Hence, robustness to inclusion of individual countries need careful consideration Kuttner and Shim (2016).

On the other hand, heterogeneity can also give rise to new hypotheses to be tested. For example, Akinci and Olmstead-Rumsey (2017) found evidence that policies directed toward the housing market are driving the results for advanced economies, while non-housing measures matter more for countries that represent emerging markets, and Cerutti et al. (2016) found results supporting that macroprudential measures are less effective for open economies than for relatively closed economies.

The policy measures that we included represent a relatively homogenous set of policy measures in the 10-country sample. The measures are caps (i.e., limits) on loan to value ratios (LTV) and on loan to income ratios (LTI). We also included tools of the type debt service to income (DSTI), risk weights (i.e., in capital requirement regulations of credit institutions, RW) and amortisation requirements (Amort). Again, the idea was that these measures are likely to be sufficiently country-independent to allow time variation in one of the countries to be used (by estimation) to learn about the hypothetical effect of its use in the other countries in the sample.

As a new contribution to the empirical literature on macroprudential policy effects, we included in the panel dataset the level of countercyclical buffer rates (CCyB), as proposed by the Basel Committee on Banking Supervision BCBS (2010a). According to the Basel Committee's multi country study, stronger capital and liquidity buffers can lead to reduced credit, with negative short-term consequences for the economic activity level BCBS (2010b). In modern economies, there is reason to expect that any wide reaching effects of stronger buffer requirements will involve housing markets and prices, and we therefore tested such a hypothesis within the larger model that also takes account of the standard macroprudential measures.

We contribute to the methodology of macroprudential policy effectiveness testing along several dimensions. We note that the custom in the literature, which is to have real credit growth and real house price change as dependent variables, may introduce measurement errors relative to the variable that the policy maker naturally target, which is nominal credit growth specifically. While this measurement error does not necessarily bias the estimates, i.e., if care is taken to use a well specified econometric model equation, it is nevertheless an unnecessary complication that may imply larger than optimal estimated coefficient standard errors. Hence, our main results are for nominal growth rates. However, we also took the custom of the literature into consideration by presenting sensitivity analysis where, e.g., real credit growth is the dependent variable.

Another methodological contribution is that we employed a robust estimator that controls for location breaks in the distribution of the dependent variables. This method was developed for empirical macroeconometric modelling, but has been demonstrated to be useful as a robust estimator of effects of changes in labour market institutions in macro panels (cf. Johansen and Nielsen (2009) and Nymoen and Sparrman (2015)).

In the literature that makes use of macro panels, there is a tendency of including the macroprudential policy measures sequentially, one at a time, to a baseline estimation equation. When the hypotheses are about effectiveness of individual instruments, the obvious problem is that the estimated coefficients estimate joint effects, rather than of intended individual effects (i.e., relative to the specified information set). In our approach, we always included all variables jointly, thus avoiding omitted variable bias and chance positives due to sequential estimation of the effects of macro prudential policy variables.

A final methodological point that we make is that, even though credit growth, housing prices and macroprudential policies are endogenous in a large and complex system, the coefficients of conditional models can nevertheless be relevant parameters of interest when the purpose of the research exercise is the empirical investigation of tangible effects of macroprudential policies.

The remainder of the paper is organised as follows: Section 2 overviews the empirical literature on macroprudential policies most directly related to our own investigation. Section 3 motivates and explains the dataset used, and, in Section 4 several methodological issues relating to model formulation and estimation methods are discussed. Section 5 presents the empirical results for the hypotheses we test: about joint and individual policy instrument significance, differentiation between impact and long-run coefficients, and between credit and housing price effects, as well as several sensitivity tests. Finally, we test the hypothesis that the new Basel III type countercyclical buffer measures has affected credit growth and/or house price change in our sample of advanced open economies. Section 6 concludes.

## 2. The Empirical Literature

During the fist decade of the new millennium, the field of macroprudential policy has come of age (see, e.g., Galati and Moesner (2013) and Anderson et al. (2018)). Already, a sizeable literature has considered the impact and medium term effects of macroprudential policy instruments on measures of credit growth and house price change.

In an important macro panel data study, Kuttner and Shim (2016) found evidence that introduction or reductions of the maximum debt-service-to-income (DSTI) and changes in maximum LTV ratios have been effective for real credit growth. They found that typical DSTI tightening lowered the real credit growth rate by 4–6 per cent over four quarters. The estimation results were considerably weaker for real house prices, both numerically and in terms of statistical significance. The dataset analysed by Kuttner and Shim (2016) consists of 55 countries and quarterly data for the period 1980–2012. The same overall picture emerges from the results of Cerutti et al. (2017), who had an even broader cross-section (119 countries) but much shorter time series dimension (2001–2013). Interestingly, they found that effects are smaller in financially advanced and open economies. Specifically, they mentioned that macroprudential polices may be undermined (circumvented) by cross border banking and other forms of external financing, a reminder that country heterogeneity is a concern.

Stronger evidence for effects on housing prices was found by Akinci and Olmstead-Rumsey (2017), who focused on the imbalances in the housing sector. Carresas et al. (2018) extended the econometric framework used in the literature to cointegration, and found that macroprudential policies can curb house price growth and credit growth also in that econometric model. Dell'Ariccia et al. (2012) presented econometric results which indicate that macroprudential policies can reduce the incidence of credit booms, and reduce the risk of credit booms going wrong (i.e., becoming a banking crisis). In an innovative econometric study, Richter et al. (2018) found that maximum LTV ratios have a duality about them: They affect credit growth and house prices substantially but have relatively modest effects on output and inflation.

Claessens et al. (2013) investigated how changes in maximum LTV and DSTI rates affect individual banks, and found that both asset and leverage growth are reduced. Gambacorta (2017) used registry data from Latin American countries, Canada and the USA. One of their main findings is that macroprudential policies have been quite effective in stabilising credit cycles. In this study, the macroprudential tools have a greater effect on credit growth when reinforced by the use of conventional monetary policy to push in the same direction. In a study of UK banks, Aiyar et al. (2014) found that variation in bank capital requirements during the 1990s and early 2000s became somewhat ineffective due to the lending strategies of branches of foreign banks. It is plausible that similar constellations exist in other advanced open economies, which go some way in explaining the finding about macroprudential policies being less forceful in open than in more closed modern economies.

Compared to the other main macroprudential policy instruments, the literature contains less empirical analysis of changes in countercyclical buffer rates (CCyB), although that is likely to change as central banks develop their operational frameworks for macroprudential stress testing (see Andersen et al. (2019) and the references therein). The work of Akram (2014) is a notable exception. He investigated macro effects of higher bank capital requirements by extending an empirical macroeconometric model for the Norwegian economy (Bårdsen et al. (2005)) and found that increases in capital requirements were primarily transmitted via lending rates to the other variables of the model. The model simulations indicate that, under the recommendations of Basel III, increased buffer rates would have significant effects on house prices and credit, but weaker than in the results reported by BCBS (2010b).

In the studies that make use of macro panels, and which therefore are comparable to our own investigation, there is a tendency of including the macroprudential policy measures sequentially, one at a time, to a baseline estimation equation or constructing a composite indicator and to estimate the effect of that joint macroprudential policy variable. In both practices, the estimated coefficients are interpretable as estimates of joint effects, rather than of individual effects (i.e., relative to the specified information set). Notable exceptions are Kuttner and Shim (2016) and Akinci and Olmstead-Rumsey (2017), who reported results also for model equations where the coefficients of LTV, DSTI and risk weights (RW) are estimated jointly.

In our approach, we always included all variables jointly, thus avoiding omitted variable bias and chance positives due to sequential estimation of the effects of macroprudential policy variables. In several other respects, our approach inherits a lot from Kuttner and Shim (2016), although the list of macroprudential instruments only partly overlap theirs (specifically, in terms of LTV, DSTI and RW). This is a consequence of our choice of a using a relatively homogenous sample, both in terms of economy characteristics and of policies that have been implemented. The motivation was that, with such a sample, the concern that one otherwise has about panel data regression, i.e., the results might be unduly influenced by the inclusion of a single county, is reduced, at least to some extent.

### 3. The Dataset

Our analysis used data from 10 advanced economies that have implemented macroprudential instruments to counter unsustainable household indebtedness and housing price growth since 1998. The instruments included in the analysis are: (i) limits to Loan-to-Value (LTV); (ii) limits to Loan-to-Income (LTI); (iii) limits to Debt-to-Income (DTI); (iv) limits to Debt-Service-to-Income (DSTI); (v) Amortisation requirements (Amort); (vi) tightening of Risk Weights on mortgage loans in the capital adequacy regulation of credit institutions (RW); and (vii) level of Countercyclical Buffer rate (CCyB). To simplify the smorgasbord of instruments in the analysis, DTI was merged in LTI, since these instruments are very similar.[1] Another simplification lies in the definition of DSTI. Here, DSTI included both regulation on the share of income spent on debt servicing (i.e., interests paid, instalments and fees), and imposing on the credit institutions an obligation to carry out debt servicing stress tests to assure that the borrowers are capable to service their mortgages also in the case of a certain interest rate increase.

As mentioned in the Introduction, as a novel trait, the countercyclical buffer rate (CCyB) was included in the set of instruments, even though it is not targeted to impact mortgage loans specifically. However, some claim that, due to increased financing costs, build up of CCyB can dampen credit growth. Applying the same reasoning, all other capital buffer requirements in the Basel III Accord could be included. Unlike the other buffer requirements, however, CCyB is designed to be adjustable over time in order to counteract pro-cyclicality in the financial system. For this reason CCyB is included, and the other buffer requirements are not. Taxes and fees (e.g., regulations on tax deductible interests paid and stamp fees) is another type of instruments which could be included in the analysis. Whether to reckon taxes and fees among the macroprudential instruments or not, seems to differ quite substantially among the countries included in the sample. Lack of consistent and comprehensive data on taxes and fees necessitates omitting this type of instruments from the analysis. Information about the active use of the different measures in the countries in the panel is found in Table 1.

**Table 1.** Use of macroprudential policies in the estimation sample. The array elements indicate in which periods LTV, LTI, DSTI and Amort were used, in which periods RW was elevated, and the current level of CCyB in the various countries. Periods not entered and empty cells represent the numerical value 0.

| | LTV | LTI * | DSTI | Amort | RW | CCyB |
|---|---|---|---|---|---|---|
| Australia | | | 2017(2)-17(2) | 2017(2)-17(2) | 2004(4)-17(2) | |
| Canada | 2008(4)-17(2) | | 2008(4)-17(2) | 2008(4)-17(2) | | |
| Denmark | 2015(4)-17(2) | | 2016(1)-17(2) | | | |
| Finland | 2016(3)-17(2) | | | | | |
| Ireland | 2015(1)-17(2) | 2015(1)-17(2) | 2012(1)-17(2) | | 2007(1)-17(2) | |
| Netherlands | 2013(1)-17(2) | | 2013(1)-17(2) | | | |
| New Zealand | 2013(4)-17(2) | | | | | |
| Norway | 2010(1)-17(2) | 2010(1)-11(4)<br>2017(1)-17(2) | 2011(4)-17(2) | 2015(3)-17(2) | 1998(3)-01(1)<br>2014(1)-17(2) | 2015(3)-16(2), 1%<br>2016(3)-17(2), 1.5% |
| Sweden | 2010(4)-17(2) | | | 2016(2)-17(2) | 2013(2)-17(2) | 2015(4)-16(2), 1%<br>2016(3)-17(1), 1.5%<br>2017(2)-17(2), 2.0% |
| UK | | 2014(4)-17(2) | 2014(2)-17(2) | | | |

Note: *: In Norway, LTI is specifically a DTI-requirement.

Each of the indicators representing the application of the macroprudential instruments LTV, LTI, DSTI and Amort was assigned the numerical value 1 if the instrument has been implemented and activated by the public authorities in the relevant country in the relevant period of time, and 0 otherwise. Risk weights on bank's exposures (explicit or implicit) are inherent in any capital adequacy regulation. Applying the same rule for assigning numerical values to the RW indicator therefore seems little fruitful. Instead, the RW indicator was assigned the numerical value 1 if the risk weight on mortgage loans has been increased in the relevant country in the relevant period of time, and 0 if the risk weight has been lowered. In all periods that the risk weight has been kept unchanged, the RW indicator was assigned the same numerical value as in the previous period. However, the RW indicator is not calibrated to reflect the transition from one generation of Basel Accords to the next.

1 While LTI refers to the ratio between an individual loan to a household's income, DTI refers to the ratio between a household's total debt to income.

The CCyB indicator was assigned numerical value (in per cent) pursuant to the current regulations in the relevant country.

Two special cases need to be commented. In the Netherlands, the market participants established self-regulation prior to the codification into national law in 2013. In accordance with the rules outlined above, self-regulation does not qualify to be assigned the numerical value 1. Hence, LTV and DSTI are assigned the numerical value 1 for the Netherlands only as of first quarter 2013, when the code of conduct was incorporated into national law. As for Canada, macroprudential instruments were implemented and activated well in advance of 2008. The Canadian regulation was in general softened until 2007, and tightened from 2008. This could motivate several different approaches with regard to assigning indicator values. For simplicity, in this analysis, periods in which regulations have been softened were regarded as if there is no instruments activated. Accordingly, LTV, DSTI and Amort were assigned the numerical value 1 for Canada as of fourth quarter 2008.

The data on usage of macroprudential instruments were mostly collected from the International Monetary Fund (IMF), the European Systemic Risk Board (ESRB) and national authorities (financial supervisory authorities and central banks) (see Appendix B for details). To tackle contradictory information provided by the data sources, a set of guiding principles was employed. Closeness between the institution and the data, and to what extent the institution has been utilising the data, were emphasised in the assessment.

There is little doubt that the complete discretisation ("on"/"off") is an oversimplification, and that it is credible that there have been examples of gradualism (tightening and loosening of measures) in macroprudential policies. However, to ensure correct judgements about stricter and less strict policies requires expert knowledge of individual countries that we cannot claim to have. Moreover, it seems plausible that statistically and economically significant response to a change in an indicator variable is a clear sign that also a more refined operational measure of macroprudential policy change will be significant. In any case, we refer to the studies with larger cross-section dimension, a broader definition of non-interest rate policies, but also a shorter sample, for estimated effects of tightening/loosening of policies (e.g., Akinci and Olmstead-Rumsey (2017) and Richter et al. (2018)).

The house price and credit data were retrieved from the Bank of International Settlements (BIS) Statistical Warehouse (see Appendix C.1 for details). All data are seasonally unadjusted and measured on a quarterly basis.

## 4. Method

As noted, there is a new literature on econometric assessment of the effects of macroprudential policy instruments by the use of aggregate panel datasets. There are several and notable differences between the studies, including the operationalisation of the policy variables, the number of time periods and countries included in the sample and preference for estimation method.

However, there is also considerable common ground. All existing studies attempt to estimate the effects on at least two variables, credit growth and housing price change, and by the use of separately estimated equations. The explanatory variables usually belong to three categories: (i) one or more lags of the dependent variable; (ii) economic control variables (e.g., GDP and GNI growth); and (iii) a battery of policy variables. It is custom to include the monetary policy interest rate (i.e., central bank rate) as one of the control variables. This makes sense since it is easy to imagine that the monetary transmission mechanism creates a dependency between the central bank rate and the interest rate that affects housing demand, and hence the evolution of housing price and credit growth.

### 4.1. A Stylised Model Equation

A model that includes the mentioned elements, with a single macroprudential instrument for notational convenience, is:

$$y_t = \varphi_{10} + \varphi_{11} y_{t-1} + \varphi_{12} r_{t-1} + \beta_{10} pol_t + \beta_{11} pol_{t-1} + \gamma_{10} z_t + \varepsilon_{yt} \quad (1)$$

$$r_t = \varphi_{20} + \varphi_{21} y_{t-1} + \varphi_{22} r_{t-1} + \beta_{20} pol_t + \beta_{21} pol_{t-1} + \gamma_{20} z_t + \varepsilon_{rt} \quad (2)$$

where $y_t$ symbolises either credit growth or housing price change in period $t$ (measured as a growth rate or percent change), $r_t$ denotes the central bank rate, $pol_t$ denotes the macroprudential policy indicator and $z_t$ represents the mentioned control variable. In this formulation, we assume that $z_t$ is a valid conditioning variable (to save space there are no lags in this variable).

Equation (1) represents a simplified but typical model equation in the literature. Equation (2) is consistent with the universal treatment of the policy interest rate as an endogenous variable, though no studies actually estimate that equation.

Appendix A contains a derivation of Equations (1) and (2) that commences from a simultaneous equation model (SEM), where not only $y_t$ and $r_t$, but also $pol_t$ are endogenous variables. The aim of the derivation is to clarify whether the endogeneity of $pol_t$ in the system (i.e., SEM or VAR), transfers to the partial model of the system represented by Equations (1) and (2). The answer is "no", because Equations (1) and (2) can be valid conditional models, which implies that $pol_t$ is instantaneously uncorrelated with the disturbance in for example Equation (1). Hence, while $pol_t$ is endogenous in the system, it can be a predetermined variable in the two derived conditional model equations, in Equation (1) specifically, which is our main model equation of interest.

### 4.2. Parameters of Interest

The model equations that we estimated are empirical versions of Equation (1). In the literature, there is some disagreement about parameters of interest. Kuttner and Shim (2016) stated that the individual coefficients in the distributed lag on the policy variables are "of little intrinsic interest"; it is the sum of the coefficients that is of interest. In the notation above, this corresponds to having $(\beta_{10} + \beta_{11})$ as the parameter of interest. However, other studies focus on a single coefficient in the estimated models, cf. Akinci and Olmstead-Rumsey (2017) who estimated models with a single lag in each policy variable (corresponding to setting $\beta_{11}$ as the parameter of interest).

Below, we report baseline model equations for credit growth and house prices, which show point estimates of $\beta_{10}$ and $\beta_{11}$ individually. In the tables that summarise the results, we show $\beta_{10}$, the *Impact* coefficient, together with long-run coefficient, which in the case of Equation (1) is defined as:

$$\text{Long-run} = \frac{(\beta_{10} + \beta_{11})}{1 - \varphi_{11}} \quad (3)$$

noting however that, since the interest rate $r_t$ is endogenous in general, the reported long-run coefficients are only suggestive of the longer-term effects of a policy. Even in our simplified formulation, to represent the full effect, it is required that $\beta_{20} = \beta_{21} = \varphi_{21} = 0$. To assess these conditions requires a more system oriented approach than is usual in the literature, and which goes beyond the scope of the paper.

### 4.3. Estimation Methods

As noted above, the policy variable may be regarded as pre-determined in the conditional model, which corresponds logically to the model equations that we estimate, also when we start from the premise that it is endogenous in the wider economic system. Hence, both the principle of least squares and the principle of method-of-moments estimators (IV methods) give rise to consistent estimators (in the time series dimension) if the model equation is econometrically well specified (i.e., the residuals are approximately Gaussian).

In the context of time-series cross-sectional (TSCS) and panel data, the direct parallel to OLS estimation is least square dummy variable estimation (LSDV), also called the within estimator. The finite $T$ bias of LSDV, which mainly affects the autoregressive parameter $\varphi_{11}$ but which also in principle affects the estimation of coefficients of current and lagged conditioning variables, is known as Hurwicz-bias (Hurwicz (1950)). It is an inevitable consequence of dynamics, since $y_{t-1}$ is a pre-determined variable, not a strictly exogenous variable.

However, in most cases, the magnitude of the Hurwicz-bias of $\hat{\varphi}_{11}$ is not large, and it declines quite rapidly toward zero as $T$ increases. This continues to hold for TSCS and panel data and the LSDV estimator is $T$-consistent. $\hat{\varphi}_{11}$ is asymptotically normally distributed, and the conventional $t$-statistic can be used to test hypotheses, because the t-statistic has a standard normal distribution under the null-hypothesis $\varphi_{11} = 0$. The same property holds for the t-values of the other OLS based estimators of the model equation. Importantly our main parameters of interest are $\beta_{10}$ and the long-run coefficient in Equation (3).

Hence, although the Hurvicz-bias is not alleviated by the cross-sectional dimension of the data (the LSDV estimator is not $N$-consistent), we note that our dataset contains a large number of time series observations, while there are only ten cross section units, and in such sample situations there are few (new) problems raised by estimating model equations of the type in Equation (1) by LSDV (Biorn (2017, Chp. 8.3)). Finally, as we note below, the LSDV estimator can be robustified against the influence of sample variation that the model equation has little to say about, notably structural breaks.

In the random effects model, RE, the inherent equi-correlation damages the predeterminedness of $y_{t-1}$, which may make the feasible RE estimators become both $T$ and $N$ inconsistent (see, e.g., Biorn (2017, Chp. 8.4)). In principle that problem is fixed by the Arellano and Bond GMM estimation method for dynamic macro models (see Arellano and Bond (1991)). In practice, the availability of valid and relevant instrumental variables determines what is gained by panel GMM, if the VAR is relatively well specified in the first place (see Bun and Windmeijer (2010)). It may happen that the fix for a relatively small estimation issue (lack of consistency in the cross-section direction) creates a relatively large cost of inference due to, e.g., an increase in estimated coefficient variance.

However, if we abstract from the dynamic formulation of the model equation, we note that Bell and Jones (2015) pointed out that RE estimation has other features which can make that method attractive for a dataset such as ours, when the purpose is to estimate coefficients that are related to specific effects in the countries in the sample, namely the implementation of macroprudential policies. For this reason, we include the results of RE model estimation in the section on robustness and sensitivity analysis below.

In addition to estimating the effect ($\beta_{10}$) from the introduction of the policy, and the requisite ($\beta_{10} + \beta_{11}$) for long-term effect of unchanged policy, we might be interested in estimating dynamic effects, e.g., four quarters after the introduction, two years after, and so on. These parameters, although well defined in the VAR, cannot in general be efficiently estimated from Equation (1) alone. The required condition is $\varphi_{21} = 0$ in Equation (2), i.e., that the system is characterised by one-way Granger causality.

In practice, the order of dynamics of the VAR must be specified empirically. Underspecification of lag order can imply residual mis-specification, i.e., the assumption about approximate Gaussian VAR disturbances may become untenable, and the statistical inference can become unreliable.

In addition to dynamic specification, the controls are important for securing near white-noise residuals. In this study, the controls took two forms: First, we included economic variables that are likely to be correlated with credit growth and house price changes in open economies: world stock price change, oil price change and growth in international trade. The second class of controls consists of country and period specific indicator variables for breaks in the intercept of the relationship, i.e., temporal location shifts. Because such location breaks often will be correlated with one or more of the regressors, the estimation of the parameters of interest will in general be robustified by the inclusion of significant indicators for breaks (see Hendry and Johansen (2015), Hendry (2018), and Castle et al. (2013)).

The determination of indicators for location shifts was done objectively with the aid of the computer implemented algorithm *Impulse Indicator Saturation (IIS)* in Autometrics (cf. Hendry et al. (2008) and Hendry and Doornik (2014)), using relatively strict significance levels for one country dataset at a time. The significant indicators were then added to the panel dataset and the empirical model equations of Equation (1) were estimated, augmented by the complete set of indicators. These coefficient estimates, following the theoretical developments of Johansen and Nielsen (2009) and the TSCS and panel data application in Nymoen and Sparrman (2015), are reported with the label LSDV-IIS in the section with empirical results.

### 4.4. Nominal or Real House Price and Credit Growth?

Another important decision is the measurement of the dependent variable, $y_t$, above. In the existing literature, the custom has become to model changes in real housing prices and in real credit. However, from a regulator's point of view, the aim is certainly to affect the increase in nominal credit growth, which by itself is an argument for modelling the nominal changes directly. Moreover, as mentioned above, if the information set of the panel data estimation under-specify the data generating process of nominal price level dynamics, the decision to model real growth rates instead of nominal entails a measurement error in the dependent variable.

Interestingly, in a study by Richter et al. (2018), the research question is how macroprudential policies interact with the core objectives to stabilise prices and output. The study focuses on the effects of changes in LTV limits and finds that: "The price response appears to be slightly positive but insignificant [...] and imprecise". The implication seems to be that, unless other macroprudential instruments should happen to be more relevant for price level changes, the custom of modelling real credit and real house price responses lead to mis-measured left-hand side variables. While this type of measurement error does not necessarily bias the estimates (i.e., as long as residual autocorrelation is avoided), it is nevertheless an unnecessary complication which is likely to lead to somewhat inflated estimated coefficient standard errors.

Hence, our main results are for models where the dependent variables were nominal credit and price changes. However, we did take the custom of the literature into account by presenting sensitivity analysis where, e.g., real credit growth was the dependent variable of the estimated model equation.

## 5. Results

As noted above, the number of time periods in our sample is relatively long and covers the 1980s for most countries. This is helpful for the empirical specification of the autoregressive lag structure, which is likely to be of a relatively high order in any historical period. At the same time, it is clear that the information about macroprudential policies comes from the last part of the sample period. This raises the issue about possible sample dependency in the estimated effects of the new policies. However, comparison of the results reported by Kuttner and Shim (2016) (long time series), with the findings of Cerutti et al. (2015) and Akinci and Olmstead-Rumsey (2017) (data start in 2000) does not suggest that sample dependency is a main problem. Another indication of the same is that the authors of the existing papers do not discuss sample selection as a source of over-/underestimation of effects.

### 5.1. Credit Growth

Equation (4) shows a baseline empirical model for nominal credit growth ($\Delta c_t$), estimated by LSDV (dummies for countries), and with robust standard errors. We show the results for the autoregressive part, for the interest rate and for the six macroprudential policy variables. Note that we modelled total credit to households, and not only housing credit.

$$
\begin{aligned}
\Delta c_t = {} & \underset{(0.055)}{0.234}\ \Delta c_{t-1} + \underset{(0.031)}{0.205}\ \Delta c_{t-2} + \underset{(0.077)}{0.121}\ \Delta c_{t-3} + \underset{(0.068)}{0.354}\ \Delta c_{t-4} \\
& - \underset{(0.029)}{0.069}\ r_{t-1} + \underset{(0.028)}{0.039}\ r_{t-2} - \underset{(0.146)}{0.464}\ \mathrm{LTV}_t + \underset{(0.162)}{0.468}\ \mathrm{LTV}_{t-1} \\
& - \underset{(0.131)}{0.232}\ \mathrm{LTI}_t + \underset{(0.198)}{0.3454}\ \mathrm{LTI}_{t-1} - \underset{(0.163)}{0.007}\ \mathrm{DSTI}_t - \underset{(0.149)}{0.089}\ \mathrm{DSTI}_{t-1} \\
& - \underset{(0.226)}{0.722}\ \mathrm{RW}_t + \underset{(0.14)}{0.422}\ \mathrm{RW}_{t-1} + \underset{(0.209)}{0.070}\ \mathrm{Amort}_t - \underset{(0.202)}{0.280}\ \mathrm{Amort}_{t-1} \\
& + \underset{(0.088)}{0.231}\ \mathrm{CCyB}_t + \underset{(0.112)}{0.036}\ \mathrm{CCyB}_{t-1}
\end{aligned} \tag{4}
$$

In the second line in Equation (4), the estimation results for the two lags of the central bank rate, $r_{t-1}$ and $r_{t-2}$, are included. The coefficients give estimated percentage points effects of a unit change in the interest rate. Hence, if the interest rate were increased from two to three per cent in period $t$, Equation (4) implies that nominal credit growth is expected to be reduced by 0.07 per cent in the following quarter (i.e., the point estimate of $r_{t-1}$ in the second line of Equation (4) with two decimals). This estimate is also found in the "memo" part of Table 2, in the column labelled Impact effect in the part of the table with LSDV estimation results.

**Table 2.** Credit growth. Estimated (LSDV and LSDV-IIS) effects for LTV, LTI, DSTI, RW, Amort and CCyB. Results for the central bank rate shown in the memo part of the table. t-values are shown below the estimated impact and long-run effects. Statistical significance (two sided test) is indicated by $**$ (5% level) and $*$ (10% level).

| | **LSDV** | | **LSDV-IIS** | |
|---|---|---|---|---|
| | **Impact** | **Long-Run** | **Impact** | **Long-Run** |
| LTV | −0.46<br>−3.18 ** | 0.05<br>0.06 | −0.42<br>−3.56 ** | 0.30<br>0.52 |
| LTI | −0.23<br>−1.77 * | 1.31<br>1.32 | −0.16<br>−1.12 | 2.11<br>1.98 ** |
| DSTI | −0.01<br>−0.04 | −0.95<br>−1.56 | 0.14<br>1.06 | 0.98<br>1.02 |
| RW | −0.72<br>−3.19 ** | −3.47<br>−1.67 * | −0.62<br>−3.72 ** | −2.36<br>−2.27 ** |
| Amort | 0.07<br>0.033 | −2.43<br>−2.14 ** | −0.02<br>−0.14 | −3.21<br>−2.63 ** |
| CCyB | 0.23<br>2.62 ** | 3.09<br>1.85 ** | 0.23<br>2.31 ** | 3.20<br>3.00 ** |
| Memo: | | | | |
| Interest rate (1 pp increase) | −0.07<br>−2.34 ** | −0.35<br>−2.52 ** | −0.05<br>−2.14 ** | −0.11<br>−1.01 |

While the estimated coefficient of $r_{t-1}$ is negative, the coefficient of $r_{t-2}$ is positive. An estimated sign-change of the interest rate effect is not uncommon in the existing studies, (see, e.g., Kuttner and Shim (2016) and Akinci and Olmstead-Rumsey (2017)). As noted above, despite the sign change, it is not a given thing that the estimated long-run effect is smaller in magnitude than the impact effect. It can go both ways, depending on the estimated sum of the autoregressive coefficients. In Table 2, we see that the long-run effect of a permanent increase in the interest rate on nominal credit growth is estimated to be −0.35 with t-value of −2.52, which is significant at the 1% level.

Turning to the macroprudential policy indicators, Equation (4) and Table 2 show several interesting results. Both LTV and LTI are estimated to have reduced nominal credit growth when they were introduced. The effects are numerically significant: reducing the quarterly growth rate by 0.46 (LTV) and 0.23 (LTI), respectively. These effects are also statistically significant, though strongly so only for LTV. For both indicators the coefficient of the lagged indicator is estimated to be positive. In Table 2, the consequence is that the two long-run coefficients are estimated to be positive, but statistically insignificant.

Equation (4) shows that debt service to income (DSTI) is estimated to have a weak effect on credit growth on impact. Although Table 2, shows that the estimated long-run effect is numerically quite large (−0.95), it is not statistically significant. The results for the two coefficients for the RW policy indicator are quite different, suggesting both a significant impact effect (−0.72 with t-value −3.19), as well as a numerically sizeable long-run effect, estimated to be −3.47 in Table 2.

The estimated impact effect of the Amort policy indicator is statistically insignificant. The long-term effect of Amort is however estimated to be negative, sizeable (−2.43) and statistically significant.

Finally, the countercyclical buffer variable, CCyB, is associated with positive coefficients in this estimation. Hence, there is no support for the view that due to, e.g., increased financing costs, build up of CCyB has dampened credit growth. However, we also remember that the sample information about CCyB comes from only two countries, Sweden and Norway, and one possibility is that CCyB picks up a close correlation between credit growth and introduction of Basel III capital buffer requirements. In that interpretation, where CCyB is a control variable rather than an instrument, it is interesting to note that the results for the remaining five policy indicators are in all important respects unchanged when CCyB is dropped from the empirical model.

We next turn to the results of the robust estimation, using LSDV augmented by indicators for structural breaks as explained above. The results are summarised in the columns of Table 2 labelled LSDV-IIS. The automatic IIS method found 96 indicator variables that were added to the model equation used for the LSDV estimation.

Looking at the Impact-column first, we see that many of the LSDV estimated coefficients are robust. Although there is a tendency towards smaller magnitudes, the impression that LTV, maybe LTI, and definitively RW may have had negative effects when introduced, remains. The columns with the Long-run effects show larger differences between LSDV estimation and LSDV-IIS estimation. However, the estimated coefficients of RW and Amort are numerically and statistically significant also when LSDV-IIS is used.

### 5.2. *Housing Price Growth*

The estimated model in Equation (5) shows a similar specification for nominal house price change ($\Delta p_t$), as we had for credit growth. The only difference, in terms of specification, is that there is a fifth autoregressive term in the house price model (it has t-value of −4.8).

$$
\begin{aligned}
\Delta p_t = {} & \underset{(0.064)}{0.360}\ \Delta p_{t-1} + \underset{(0.028)}{0.012}\ \Delta p_{t-2} + \underset{(0.018)}{0.117}\ \Delta p_{t-3} + \underset{(0.053)}{0.368}\ \Delta p_{t-4} \\
& - \underset{(0.038)}{0.1837}\ \Delta p_{t-5} - \underset{(0.073)}{0.177}\ r_{t-1} + \underset{(0.070)}{0.147}\ r_{t-2} \\
& - \underset{(0.324}{1.04}\ \mathrm{LTV}_t + \underset{(0.316}{0.990}\ \mathrm{LTV}_{t-1} - \underset{(0.472)}{0.300}\ \mathrm{LTI}_t - \underset{(0.316)}{0.04}\ \mathrm{LTI}_{t-1} \\
& - \underset{(0.431)}{0.027}\ \mathrm{DSTI}_t + \underset{(0.562)}{0.268}\ \mathrm{DSTI}_{t-1} - \underset{(0.397)}{0.811}\ \mathrm{RW}_t + \underset{(0.494)}{0.469}\ \mathrm{RW}_{t-1} \\
& - \underset{(0.724)}{0.902}\ \mathrm{Amort}_t + \underset{(0.826)}{0.833}\ \mathrm{Amort}_{t-1} + \underset{(0.386)}{0.384}\ \mathrm{CCyB}_t - \underset{(0.326)}{0.270}\ \mathrm{CCyB}_{t-1}
\end{aligned}
\qquad (5)
$$

In addition, in the house price change equation, the coefficient of the lagged central bank rate is estimated to be negative, and with a numerically larger coefficient than in the credit growth equation (−0.18). In the same way as for credit, there is a sign change for $r_{t-2}$, which is positive and with almost the same magnitude as the coefficient for $r_{t-1}$. Hence, the estimated magnitude of the long-run effect is smaller than the short-run effect (−0.18 and −0.09) in the last row of Table 3.

**Table 3.** House price change. Estimated (LSDV and LSDV-IIS) effects for LTV, LTI, DSTI, RW, Amort and CCyB. Results for the central bank rate shown in the memo part of the table. t-values are shown below the estimated impact and long-run effects. Statistical significance (two sided test) is indicated by ∗∗ (5% level) and ∗ (10% level).

| | LSDV | | LSDV-IIS | |
|---|---|---|---|---|
| | **Impact** | **Long-Run** | **Impact** | **Long-Run** |
| LTV | −1.04<br>−3.22 ** | −0.16<br>−0.48 | −0.98<br>−2.88 ** | −0.28<br>−0.70 |
| LTI | −0.30<br>−0.64 | −0.79<br>−1.25 | −0.18<br>−0.39 | −0.72<br>−1.22 |
| DSTI | −0.03<br>−0.06 | 0.74<br>0.51 | 0.08<br>0.19 | 0.97<br>0.63 |
| RW | −0.811<br>−2.04 ** | −1.05<br>−0.84 | −0.79<br>−2.30 ** | −0.81<br>−0.74 |
| Amort | −0.90<br>−1.25 | −0.21<br>−0.19 | −0.99<br>−1.37 | −0.78<br>−0.64 |
| CCyB | 0.38<br>1.00 | 0.34<br>0.28 | 0.46<br>1.09 | 0.54<br>0.43 |
| Memo: | | | | |
| Interest rate (1 pp increase) | −0.18<br>−2.43 ** | −0.09<br>−2.10 ** | −0.18<br>−2.73 ** | −0.07<br>−1.71 * |

In addition, for the macroprudential policy indicators, Equation (5) and Table 3 show results that are broadly consistent with what we obtained for the credit growth model. In the LSDV estimation, all measures except CCyB get negative impact coefficients, and for LTV and RW the coefficients are sizeable (−0.9 is the average) and statistically significant. The strong results for those two measures also carry over to the LSDV-IIS estimation.

### 5.3. *Tests of Joint Significance and Diagnostic Tests*

Table 4 contains additional tests based on the empirical models that we have considered thus far, i.e., for nominal credit growth and nominal house price change. First, the table shows several tests of joint statistical significance of groups of variables. We see that the dynamic augmentations of the models ("autoregressive terms") are highly significant, and so are the included controls and the policy interest rate. Interestingly, the macroprudential policy indicators are convincingly significant when the joint tests are used. That observation suggests that a certain synchronisation of policies has taken place, and that this may have increased the overall efficiency of macroprudential instrument use.

The second part of the table shows sample size and number of parameters estimated, the multiple correlation coefficient and two standard tests of residual autocorrelation ($AR(1)$ and $AR(2)$). There is indication of significant first order residual autocorrelation in Table 3 (house prices), but not in the robust estimation (moreover the autocorrelation is negative, implying that the t-values of the LSDV estimation may have been underestimated).

**Table 4.** Tests of joint significance and diagnostic tests.

| | | Table 2 | | Table 3 | |
|---|---|---|---|---|---|
| | | LSDV | LSDV-IIS | LSDV | LSDV-IIS |
| *Tests of joint significance:* | | | | | |
| Autoregressive terms | $\chi^2(4)$ | 8221 *** | 3380 *** | | |
| | $\chi^2(5)$ | | | 4362 *** | 789 *** |
| Controls | $\chi^2(6)$ | 90.3 *** | 82.1 *** | 125.4 *** | 171 *** |
| Interest rate | $\chi^2(2)$ | 10.3 *** | 4.75 ** | 8.25 *** | 9.62 *** |
| Macroprudentials | | | | | |
| -All | $\chi^2(12)$ | 992 *** | 307 *** | 145.5 *** | 664.1 *** |
| -Impact: | $\chi^2(6)$ | 20.3 *** | 44.3 *** | 62.5 *** | 109.7 *** |
| -lags: | $\chi^2(6)$ | 86.2 *** | 303.7 *** | 16.0 *** | 14.9 *** |
| *Diagnostics:* | | | | | |
| Number of observations | | 1264 | 1264 | 1589 | 1589 |
| Number of parameters: | | 34 | 130 | 35 | 119 |
| $R^2$ | | 0.68 | 0.82 | 0.39 | 0.58 |
| $AR(1)$-test | | 1.34 | 1.15 | −2.15 ** | −0.15 |
| $AR(2)$-test | | 0.04 | −0.22 | 0.97 | 0.78 |

### 5.4. Comparison with Findings in the Existing Literature

The significant results of the joint tests of the relevance of included policy instruments confirm what appears to have become the consensus view, namely that macroprudential measures can be relied upon to aid the management of the financial cycle. As can be expected, because of data and methodological differences, the results for the individual polices contain both confirmation and departures form the results in the existing empirical literature.

The result about changes in LTV ratios being associated with lower credit growth and lower house price growth sits well with the findings in the existing empirical literature. This instrument is comparable across countries, but it is nevertheless interesting that it stands out also in our sample of advanced open economies. Due to the dynamics of the model equation the implication is that the reduction of the growth rates lasts for several periods, consistent with, e.g., Kuttner and Shim (2016). However, there is no support in our results for a permanent effect on the growth rates of the credit or house price indices, only for a long-term level effect on the two target variables.

The results above also support the view that LTI, RW and Amort are relevant instruments for the management of the financial cycle. There are less consistent findings in the literature about these measures, possibly because they have been difficult to pick up in the studies that use considerably broader cross sections than we do. Although our results show that the coefficient of DSTI has the expected negative sign, there is less strong support for this instrument than in the studies by Kuttner and Shim (2016) and Cerutti et al. (2015).

### 5.5. Sensitivity Analysis

In this section, we first present how the results in Tables 2 and 3 change when the dependent variables are changed from nominal to real growth rates. The results for real credit growth are shown in Table 5. The estimated impact coefficients of LTV, LTI and RW are robust when LSDV is the estimation method. The standard errors of the coefficients are somewhat larger, which affects the magnitude of the t-values. This is consistent with the argument presented in Section 4.4 about induced measurement error. The long-run coefficients of RW and Amort in the LSDV estimation results are only partially robust when the dependent variable is changed from nominal to real credit growth: The coefficient of RW is reduced by one third in magnitude but remains significant, while Amort is reduced even more and becomes statistically insignificant.

**Table 5.** Real credit growth. Estimated (LSDV and LSDV-IIS) effects for LTV, LTI, DSTI, RW, Amort and CCyB . Results for the central bank rate shown in the memo part of the table. t-values are shown below the estimated impact and long-run effects. Statistical significance (two sided test) is indicated by ** (5% level) and * (10% level).

| | LSDV | | LSDV-IIS | |
|---|---|---|---|---|
| | **Impact** | **Long-Run** | **Impact** | **Long-Run** |
| LTV | −0.63<br>−2.13 ** | 0.00<br>0.00 | −0.55<br>−2.01 ** | 0.20<br>0.38 |
| LTI | −0.19<br>−1.07 | 0.29<br>0.66 | −0.13<br>−0.71 | 0.73<br>1.08 |
| DSTI | −0.01<br>−0.03 | −1.65<br>−6.02 ** | 0.13<br>0.90 | −0.66<br>−1.21 |
| RW | −0.68<br>−3.11 ** | −2.53<br>−1.99 ** | −0.58<br>−3.72 ** | −1.91<br>−2.76 ** |
| Amort | 0.60<br>0.033 | −0.60<br>−1.11 | 0.49<br>2.12 ** | −1.31<br>−2.75 ** |
| CCyB | 0.00<br>0.01 | 1.47<br>1.13 | 0.01<br>0.06 | 1.61<br>1.47 |
| Memo: | | | | |
| Interest rate (1 pp increase) | −0.11<br>−2.59 ** | −0.22<br>−2.62 ** | −0.08<br>−1.71 * | −0.08<br>−0.93 |

The results for real house price growth are shown in Table 6. Comparison with Table 3 shows that the estimated impact coefficients of LTV and RW are significant in both tables, and hence can be seen as robust to how the left hand side variable has been measured.

**Table 6.** Real house price change. Estimated (LSDV and LSDV-IIS) effects for LTV, LTI, DSTI, RW, Amort and CCyB . Results for the central bank rate shown in the memo part of the table. t-values are shown below the estimated impact and long-run effects. Statistical significance (two sided test) is indicated by ** (5% level) and * (10% level).

| | LSDV | | LSDV-IIS | |
|---|---|---|---|---|
| | **Impact** | **Long-Run** | **Impact** | **Long-Run** |
| LTV | −1.10<br>−2.16 ** | −0.13<br>−0.34 | −1.06<br>−2.55 ** | −0.25<br>−0.53 |
| LTI | −0.18<br>−0.37 | −0.46<br>−0.72 | −0.07<br>−0.16 | −0.41<br>−0.67 |
| DSTI | 0.02<br>0.06 | 0.38<br>0.99 | 0.13<br>0.29 | 0.62<br>0.41 |
| RW | −0.76<br>−2.22 ** | −0.90<br>−0.87 | −0.71<br>−2.48 ** | −0.67<br>−0.74 |
| Amort | −0.42<br>−0.43 | −0.28<br>−0.24 | −0.53<br>−0.54 | −0.82<br>−0.69 |
| CCyB | 0.10<br>0.20 | 0.07<br>0.06 | 0.17<br>0.52 | 0.25<br>0.23 |
| Memo: | | | | |
| Interest rate (1 pp increase) | −0.22<br>−2.86 ** | −0.19<br>−4.40 ** | −0.24<br>−3.46 ** | −0.18<br>−4.81 ** |

Table 7 shows sensitivity results for the impact coefficients on credit growth along two dimensions: Nominal/real measurement of credit growth, and the use of the fixed effects (LSDV) and random effects (RE) model. As noted in Section 4.3, there are pros and cons of the two estimation methods for a dataset such as ours, where the time series dimension is relatively long, and the cross section dimension is more narrow, a so-called TSCS dataset. Theoretically, RE estimated coefficients are hampered by inconsistency (in the $T$ dimension) when we estimate a dynamic model equation. The fixed effects model and LSDV avoid that type of inconsistency. On the other hand, the sample size is always finite in practice and therefore we know that there is a Hurwicz bias in the LSDV estimation results. In such situations, the more parsimonious RE estimation might benefit from its ability to make better use of between individual country variation. As Table 7 shows, none of the estimation results in Tables 2 and 5 are in any great extent affected by changing from LSDV estimation to RE estimation. We obtained similar results for house price change, and conclude that the results obtained for the impact coefficients are robust with respect to the two types of models of individual heterogeneity.

**Table 7.** Estimated impact coefficients on nominal and real credit growth. Estimated (LSDV, LSDV-ISS, RE, and RE-IIS) effects for LTV, LTI, DSTI, RW, Amort and CCyB. Results for the central bank rate shown in the memo part of the table. t-values are shown below the estimated coefficients. Statistical significance (two sided test) is indicated by ** (5% level) and * (10% level).

| | **LSDV** | | **LSDV-IIS** | | **RE** | | **RE-IIS** | |
|---|---|---|---|---|---|---|---|---|
| | **Nominal** | **Real** | **Nominal** | **Real** | **Nominal** | **Real** | **Nominal** | **Real** |
| LTV | −0.46<br>−3.18 ** | −0.63<br>−2.13 ** | −0.42<br>−3.56 ** | −0.55<br>−2.01 ** | −0.48<br>−1.30 | −0.63<br>−1.46 | −0.42<br>−2.40 ** | −0.55<br>−1.51 |
| LTI | −0.23<br>−1.77 * | −0.19<br>−1.07 | −0.16<br>−1.12 | −0.13<br>−0.71 | −0.20<br>−0.43 | −0.12<br>−0.22 | −0.16<br>−1.12 | −0.10<br>−1.51 |
| DSTI | −0.01<br>−0.04 | −0.01<br>−0.03 | 0.14<br>1.06 | 0.13<br>0.90 | −0.01<br>−0.03 | 0.02<br>0.04 | 0.13<br>1.06 | 0.08<br>0.20 |
| RW | −0.72<br>−3.19 ** | −0.68<br>−3.11 ** | −0.62<br>−3.72 ** | −0.58<br>−3.72 ** | −0.66<br>−1.72 * | −0.56<br>−1.23 | −0.62<br>−3.72 ** | −0.57<br>−1.48 |
| Amort | 0.07<br>0.033 | 0.60<br>2.07 ** | −0.02<br>−0.14 | 0.49<br>2.12 ** | 0.19<br>−0.35 | 0.68<br>1.05 | −0.03<br>−0.14 | 0.61<br>1.14 |
| CCyB | 0.23<br>2.62 ** | 0.00<br>0.01 | 0.23<br>2.31 ** | 0.01<br>0.06 | 0.15<br>0.24 | −0.11<br>−0.14 | 0.20<br>0.42 | −0.06<br>−0.10 |
| Memo: | | | | | | | | |
| Interest rate | −0.07<br>−2.34 ** | −0.11<br>−2.59 ** | −0.05<br>−2.14 ** | −0.08<br>−1.71 * | −0.07<br>−2.43 ** | −0.10<br>−3.29 ** | −0.05<br>−2.14 ** | −0.08<br>−2.79 ** |

## 6. Conclusions

We analysed a quarterly panel dataset consisting of ten advanced open economies, seven European countries as well as Australia, New Zealand and Canada, where macroprudential policy measures have been used since the end of the last millennium. The policy instruments include caps on loan to value and income (LTV and LTI), and debt service to income (DSTI) requirements in particular, but also risk weights (RW), amortisation (Amort) and, less used, countercyclical buffer (CCyB). We estimated dynamic panel data models, which are in line with the pre-existing literature in this field, and which include the central bank rate, and controls for common nominal and real trends.

When the hypothesis of joint significance was tested, the results are convincingly significant for the battery of macroprudential policy instruments. This result applies to both credit growth and housing price change. When it comes to individual policies, we found that some of them have had more potency than others. A main finding is that the estimated short run coefficients of LTV, LTI and RW on credit growth stand out as the most significant. The sizes of these coefficients were economically as well as statistically significant.

For Amort, we were not able to pin down an impact effect. However, the long-run coefficient of total credit growth with respect to Amort was numerically and statistically significant. The policy implication is that amortisation requirements need more time to show its effect on credit growth than LTV, LTI and RW. We found only insignificant short-run and long-run coefficients for the debt service to income indicator (DSTI). As far as we know, our investigation is the first to include countercyclical capital buffer (CCyB) of the Basel III type among the set of macroprudential measures. However, CCyB was estimated to have positive coefficients, which are all statistically insignificant. Hence, any credit dampening effects resulting from the increased financing cost due to capital buffer requirements were not found in our dataset.

The results for housing price change give the same picture, with the loan to value and the risk-weighting variables as the measures with highest statistical significance.

Our findings are not in contradiction with existing econometric panel data studies that used a broader set of countries, but which also have fewer periods with (for example) active LTV-cap and LTI-cap policies. In one respect, our results are stronger about individual policy instrument effects than most of the earlier studies, since we estimated models where all policy variables were included simultaneously from the outset, instead of being added sequentially (estimating the gross effect of one variable at a time).

Methodologically, we show that the estimating equation used in existing studies can be derived as a conditional model to form a multi-equation model where the policy variable is endogenous. Econometrically, there is no requisite to lag the policy variables, in order to mitigate endogeneity problems, and this practice can instead have made it difficult to retrieve relevant policy variables.

We also demonstrate the usefulness of the methodology developed in time series econometrics, which makes use of automatically selected impulse indicators (IIS) to form a robust OLS estimator. Since the panel data LSDV estimator is a weighted sum of OLS estimators for each country, using LSDV with indicators included, is a robust panel data estimator. Empirically, we found that the estimation results of the house price and credit models were consistent, although somewhat stronger for total credit growth than for house price changes. In all main respects, the results were robust with respect to how the dependent variables were measured (nominal or real growth), and with respect to the use of fixed effects or random effects estimation.

**Author Contributions:** Conceptualization, R.N., K.P. and J.I.S.; Data curation, K.P. and J.I.S.; Formal analysis, R.N.; Methodology, R.N.; Writing—original draft, R.N., K.P. and J.I.S.; Writing—review & editing, R.N.

**Funding:** This research received no external funding.

**Acknowledgments:** We are thankful to the editors, and to four reviewers for comments that have contributed to improve the paper considerably. The views expressed are those of the authors and do not necessarily reflect those of The Financial Supervisory Authority of Norway. Thanks to Harald Johansen and Kjersti-Gro Lindquist for comments and discussion of an earlier version.

**Conflicts of Interest:** The authors declare no conflict of interest.

## Appendix A. Endogeniety of Macroprudential Policy Instruments: Consequences for Choice of Estimation Methodology

It is quite common in the literature reviewed above to mention the endogeneity of, for example, LTV as a reason for choosing to estimate by GMM (and instrumental variables estimator). However, neither the term endogenous variable nor its counterpart exogenous variable refers to precise concepts. Depending on that clarification, the need to consider GMM estimation methodology may or may not follow.

To clarify, consider the simultaneous equation model (SEM) with three endogenous variables $y_t$, $r_t$ and $pol_t$ and a single observable exogenous variable $z_t$:

$$\underbrace{\begin{pmatrix} 1 & a_{11} & a_{13} \\ a_{21} & 1 & a_{23} \\ 0 & 0 & 1 \end{pmatrix}}_{A} \begin{pmatrix} y_t \\ r_t \\ pol_t \end{pmatrix} = \underbrace{\begin{pmatrix} b_{11} & b_{12} & b_{13} \\ b_{21} & b_{22} & b_{23} \\ b_{31} & b_{32} & b_{33} \end{pmatrix}}_{B} \begin{pmatrix} y_{t-1} \\ r_{t-1} \\ pol_{t-1} \end{pmatrix} + cz_t + \epsilon_t. \tag{A1}$$

$\boldsymbol{A}$ and $\boldsymbol{B}$ denote the matrices with contemporaneous and lagged coefficients, while $\boldsymbol{c}$ denotes the vector with the three coefficients of $z_t$.

For simplicity, we now regard $pol_t$ as a continuous variable, along with $y_t$ and $r_t$, in which case the linear in parameters formulation is more relevant. Without loss of generality, the vector with SEM disturbances is Gaussian with zero expectation (vector) and diagonal instantaneous covariance matrix.

$pol_t$ is an endogenous variable in Equation (A1), since the $\boldsymbol{B}$ matrix captures that $pol_t$ is Granger caused by $y_t$ and/or $r_t$. The two zeros in the third row of the $\boldsymbol{A}$ matrix captures the idea that endogenous changes in $pol$ in any given quarter is likely to be motivated by past values of credit growth and house price changes (and associated indicators of financial stability), and not by the changes in, e.g., credit growth in the same quarter (decision and implementation lags are usually large enough to make this a reasonable assumption).

The reduced form of Equation (A1) is:

$$\begin{pmatrix} y_t \\ r_t \\ pol_t \end{pmatrix} = \boldsymbol{A}^{-1}\boldsymbol{B} \begin{pmatrix} y_{t-1} \\ r_{t-1} \\ pol_{t-1} \end{pmatrix} + \boldsymbol{A}^{-1} c z_t + \boldsymbol{A}^{-1}\epsilon_t \tag{A2}$$

assuming that the inverse matrix $\boldsymbol{A}^{-1}$ exists. The reduced form residual vector $v_t = \boldsymbol{A}^{-1}\epsilon_t$ is Gaussian with an invertible covariance matrix (not diagonal). Equation (A2) is of course a VAR, and by conditioning on $pol_t$, we can re-parameterise the VAR as a multiple equation model consisting of two conditional equations and one marginal equation, i.e.,

$$y_t = \varphi_{11}y_{t-1} + \varphi_{12}r_{t-1} + \beta_{10}pol_t + \beta_{11}pol_{t-1} + \gamma_{10}z_t + \varepsilon_{yt} \tag{A3}$$

$$r_t = \varphi_{21}y_{t-1} + \varphi_{22}r_{t-1} + \beta_{20}pol_t + \beta_{21}pol_{t-1} + \gamma_{20}z_t + \varepsilon_{rt} \tag{A4}$$

$$pol_t = \phi_{21}y_{t-1} + \phi_{22}r_{t-1} + \phi_{33}pol_{t-1} + \alpha_{20}z_t + v_{polt} \tag{A5}$$

where Equations (A3) and (A4) are the conditional model equations, and Equation (A5) is the marginal model equation (i.e., identical to the third row in Equation (A2)). We see that Equations (A3) and (A4) are identical to Equations (1) and (2) in the main text. They also have the same interpretation, implying that $Cov(\varepsilon_{yt}, v_{polt}) = Cov(\varepsilon_{rt}, v_{polt}) = 0$ as well as $Cov(pol_t, \varepsilon_{yt}) = Cov(pol_t, \varepsilon_{rt}) = 0$. Hence, there is no endogeneity problem due to correlation between $pol_t$ and the disturbance in the model in Equation (1). It follows that IV (or GMM) estimation of Equation (1) should be motivated by other arguments, e.g., the idea that the finite sample bias of OLS estimators for the coefficients in Equation (1) might be alleviated by GMM, which was the original motivation of Arellano and Bond (1991). This estimator addresses the second order issue of finite sample bias of dynamic panel models (see Arellano (2003, Chp. 6.3) and Baltagi (2010, Chp. 8)). However, as mentioned in the main text, empirical models of credit growth and house price changes are likely to include several lags of $y$ from the outset. For model equations of this type, it is unclear how even longer lags of $y$ (than already included) will function as GMM instrumental variables.

## Appendix B. Data Sources

### *Appendix B.1. Housing Prices and Credit*

All data are seasonally unadjusted and are measured on a quarterly basis. The data source was the Bank for International Settlements (BIS) Statistical Warehouse.

Housing price indexes for all countries were retrieved from the BIS Residential Property Price database, and are based on national sources. Further information on the housing prices series are found in https://www.bis.org/statistics/pp_long_documentation.pdf.

Household credit data for all countries were retrieved from the BIS Long Series on Total Credit. The series are based on national sources, and are compiled by data from financial accounts and the balance sheet of domestic banks. Further information can be found in https://www.bis.org/statistics/totcredit/credpriv_doc.pdf.

### *Appendix B.2. Macroprudential Policies in the Sample*

The main sources of the dataset were the European Systemic Risk Board (ESRB), Overview of national macroprudential measures (which can be downloaded from: https://www.esrb.europa.eu/national_policy/html/index.en.html), various reports and publications from the International Monetary Fund (IMF) and national authorities (financial supervisory authorities and central banks). A more detailed note (in Norwegian only) outlining the groundwork for the dataset can be provided on request.

## References

Aiyar, Shekhar, Charles W. Calomiris, and Tomasz Wieladek. 2014. Does macro-prudential regulation leak? Evidence from a UK policy experiment. *Journal of Money Credit and Banking* 46: 181–214. [CrossRef]

Akinci, Ozge, and Jane Olmstead-Rumsey. 2017. How effective are macroprudential policies. *Journal of Financial Intermediation* 33: 33–57. [CrossRef]

Akram, Q. Farooq. 2014. Macro effects of capital requirements and macroprudential policy. *Economic Modelling* 42: 77–93. [CrossRef]

Andersen, Henrik, Karsten R. Gerdrup, Rønnaug M. Johansen, and Tord Krogh. 2019. *A Marcoprudential Stress Testing Framework*. Technical Report. Oslo: Norges Bank.

Anderson, Ron, Jon Danielsson, Chikako Baba, Udaibir S Das, Heedon Kang, and Miguel A. Segoviano Basurto. 2018. *Macroprudential Stress Tests and Policies: Searching for Robust And Implementable Frameworks*. Working Paper 197. Washington, DC: IMF.

Anundsen, André K., Tord S. Krogh, Ragnar Nymoen, and Jon Vislie. 2014. Overdeterminacy and endogenous cycles: Trygve Haavelmo's business cycle model. *Meteroeconomica* 65: 460–86. [CrossRef]

Anundsen, André K., Karsten Gerdrup, Frank Hansen, and Kasper Kragh-Sørensen. 2016. Bubbles and crisis: The role of house prices and credit. *Journal of Applied Econometrics* 31: 1291–311. [CrossRef]

Anundsen, André K., and Ragnar Nymoen. 2019. Testing the empirical relevance of the 'saving for a rainy day' hypothesis in US metro areas. *Oxford Bulletin of Economics and Statistics* forthcoming.

Arellano, Manuel. 2003. *Panel Data Econometrics*. Oxford: Oxford University Press.

Arellano, Manuel, and Stephen Bond. 1991. Some tests of misspecification for panel data: Monte carlo evidence and an application to employment equations. *Review of Economic Statistics* 58: 277–97. [CrossRef]

Baltagi, Badi. 2010. *Econometric Analysis of Panel Data*. New York: Wiley.

Bårdsen, Gunnar, Øyvind Eitrheim, Eilev S. Jansen, and Ragnar Nymoen. 2005. *The Econometrics of Macroeconomic Modelling*. Oxford: Oxford University Press.

BCBS. 2010a. *Guidance for National Authorities Operating the Countercyclical Capital Buffer*. Technical Report. Basel: Bank for International Settlements.

BCBS. 2010b. *Interim Report: Assessing the Macroeconomic Impact of the Transition to Stronger Capital and Liquidity Requirements*. Technical Report. Basel: Bank for International Settlements.

Bell, Andrew, and Kelvyn Jones. 2015. Explaining fixed effects: Random effects modeling of time series cross section data. *Political Science Research and Methods* 3: 133–53. [CrossRef]

Biorn, Erik 2017. *Econometrics of Panel Data*. Oxford: Oxford University Press.

Borio, Claudio E. V., and Philip William Lowe. 2002. *Asset Prices, Financial and Monetary Stability: Exploring the Nexus*. BIS Working Papers 114. Basel: Bank of International Settlements.

Brodin, P. Anders, and Ragnar Nymoen. 1992. Wealth effects and exogeneity: The Norwegian consumption function 1966.1–1989.4. *Oxford Bulletin of Economics and Statistics* 54: 431–54. [CrossRef]

Bun, Maurice J. G., and Frank Windmeijer. 2010. The weak instrument problem of the system GMM estimator in dynamic panel models. *Econometric Journal* 13: 95–126. [CrossRef]

Carresas, Oriol, E. Philip Davis, and Rebecca Piggott. 2018. Assessing macroprudential tools in OECD in a cointegration framework. *Journal of Fiancial Stability* 37: 112–30. [CrossRef]

Carroll, Christopher, Jiri Slacalek, and Martin Sommer. 2012. *Dissecting Saving Dynamics: Measuring Credit, Wealth And Precautionary Effects*. Working Paper 12/219. Washington, DC: IMF.

Castle, Jennifer L., Xiaochuan Qin, and W. Robert Reed. 2013. Using model selection algorithms to obtain reliable coefficient estimates. *Journal of Economic Surveys* 27: 269–96. [CrossRef]

Cerutti, Eugenio, Stijn Claessens, and Luc Laeven. 2015. *The Use and Effectiveness of Macroprudential Policies: New Evidence*. IMF Working Paper 15/61. Washington, DC: International Monetary Fund.

Cerutti, Eugenio, Stijn Claessens, and Luc Laeven. 2017. The use and effectiveness of macroprudential policies: New evidence. *Jounal of Fiancial Stability* 28: 203–24. [CrossRef]

Cerutti, Eugenio, Ricardo Correa, Elisabetta Fiorentino, and Esther Segalla. 2016. *Changes in Prudential Policy Instruments*. IMF Working Paper 16/110. Washington, DC: International Monetary Fund.

Chortaes, Georgios, Georgios Magkonis, Demetrios Moschos, and Theodore Panagiotidis. 2015. Financial development and economic activity in advanced and developing open economies: Evidence from panel cointegration. *Review of Deveopment Economics* 19: 163–77. [CrossRef]

Claessens, Stijn, Swati R. Ghosh, and Roxana Mihet. 2013. Macro-prudential polcies to mitigate financial system vulnerabilities. *Journal of International Monaey and Fiance* 39: 153–85. [CrossRef]

Dell'Ariccia, Giovanni, Deniz Igan, Luc Laeven, Hui Tong, Bas Bakker, and Jérôme Vandenbussche. 2012. *Policies for Macrofinancial Stability. How to Deal With Credti Booms*. IMF Staff Discussion Note 12/06. Washington, DC: International Monetary Fund.

Eika, Kari H., and Ragnar Nymoen. 1992. Finansiell konsolidering som en konjunkturfaktor [Financial consolidation as a business cycle factor]. *Penger og Kreditt* 21: 29–38.

Eitrheim, Øyvind, Eilev Jansen, and Ragnar Nymoen. 2002. Progress from forecast failure: The norwegian consumption function. *Econometrics Journal* 5: 40–64. [CrossRef]

Fahr, Stephan, and John Fell. 2017. Macroprudential policy-Closing the financial stability gap. *Journal of Financial Regulation and Compliance* 25: 334–59. [CrossRef]

Galati, Gabriele, and Richhild Moessner. 2013. Macroprudential polciy—A literature review. *Journal of Economic Surveys* 27: 846–78.

Gambacorta, Leonardo, and Andrés Murcia. 2017. *The Impact of Macroprudential Policies and Their Interaction with Monetary Policy: An Empirical Analysis Using Credit Registry Data*. BIS Working Papers 636. Basel: Bank for International Settlements.

Hendry, David F. 2018. Deciding between alternative approaches in macroeconomics. *International Journal of Forecasting* 34: 119–35. [CrossRef]

Hendry, David F., and Jurgen A. Doornik. 2014. *Empirical Model Discovery and Theory Evaluation. Automatic Selection Methods in Econometrics*. Arne Ryde Memorial Lectures. Cambridge: MIT Press.

Hendry, David F., and S. Johansen. 2015. Model discovery and Trygve Haavelmo's legacy. *Econometric Theory* 31: 93–114. [CrossRef]

Hendry, David F., Søren Johansen, and Carlos Santos. 2008. Automatic selection of indicators in a fully saturated regression. *Computational Statistics* 23: 317–35. [CrossRef]

Honkapoja, Seppo. 2009. *The 1990s Financial Crisies in the Nordic Countries*. Research Discussion Papers 5. Helsinki: Bank of Finland.

Honkapoja, Seppo, Erkki Koskela, and Jouko Paunio. 1996. The depression of the 1990s in Finland: An analytical view. *Finnish Economic Papers* 9: 37–49.

Hurwicz, Leonid 1950. Least squares bias in time series. In *Statistical Inference in Dynamic Economic Models*. Edited by Tjalling Charles Koopmans. Volume 10 of Cowles Commission Monograph, Chapter 15. New York: John Wiley & Sons.

Johansen, Søren, and Bent Nielsen. 2009. Analysis of the indicator saturation estimator as a robust regression estimator. In *The Methodology and Practise of Econometrics*. Edited by Jennifer Castle and Neil Shephard. Oxford: Oxford University Press.

Jordà, Òscar, Moritz Schularick, and Alan M. Taylor. 2013. When credit bites back. *Journal of Money Credit and Banking* 45: 3–28. [CrossRef]

Kuttner, Kenneth N., and Ilhyock Shim. 2016. Can non-interest rate policies stabilise housing markets? evidence from a panel of 57 economies. *Journal of Financial Stability* 26: 31–44. [CrossRef]

Mian, Atif, Kamalesh Rao, and Amir Sufi. 2013. Household balance sheets, consumption, and the economic slump. *Quarterly Journal of Economics* 128: 1687–726. [CrossRef]

Muellbauer, John, and Anthony Murphy. 1990. Is the UK balance of payments sustainable? *Economic Policy* 11: 349–95. [CrossRef]

Nymoen, Ragnar, and Victoria Sparrman. 2015. Equilibrium unemployment dynamics in a panel of oecd countries. *Oxford Bulletin of Economics and Statistics* 77: 164–90. [CrossRef]

Reinhardt, Carmen M., and Kenneth S. Rogoff. 2009. *This Time is Different: Eight Centuries of Financial Folly*. Princeton: Princeton Univeristy Press.

Richter, Björn, Moritz Schularick, and Ilhyock Shim. 2018. *The Macroeconoimic Effects of Macroprudential Policy*. BIS Working Papers 740. Basel: Bank of International Settlements.

Schularick, Moritz, and Alan M. Taylor. 2012. Credit boom gone bust: Monetary policy, leverage cycles and fiancial crisis. *American Economic Review* 102: 1029–61. [CrossRef]

# 5

# Impact of CSR-Relevant News on Stock Prices of Companies Listed in the Austrian Traded Index (ATX)

**Manuela Ender** [1,*] **and Finn Brinckmann** [2]

[1] Campus Urstein, Salzburg University of Applied Sciences, Urstein Süd 1, 5412 Puch/Salzburg, Austria
[2] Biogena Management Holding GmbH, Strubergasse 24, 5020 Salzburg, Austria
* Correspondence: manuela.ender@fh-salzburg.ac.at

**Abstract:** This paper examines the short-term influence of CSR-relevant news on the enterprise value in the form of respective shareholder value, which is represented by the corresponding stock price. This effect is measured using an event study applied to companies in the "Austrian Traded Index" (ATX). Subsequently, the results of the study show that CSR-relevant news in the financial portal finanzen.net trigger statistically significant abnormal returns and average cumulated abnormal returns within a period of five days. Based on these research results, it is stated that CSR-relevant news has a significant impact on the shareholder value of a company represented by its stock price. The hypotheses defined on the basis of the previously conducted studies on this topic were only partially confirmed. In particular, the negative effects of negative CSR-relevant news are insufficiently shown. Based on these findings, it can be deduced that the effects of the news are reinforced by the CSR relevance, although media presence due to the publications is a factor to be explored.

**Keywords:** corporate social responsibility; CSR-relevant news; event study; Austrian Traded Index

**JEL Classification:** G14; G32; Q56

---

## 1. Introduction

People's activities are changing the environment. For example, the exponential growth of humanity has led to the exploitation of groundwater (Smith et al. 2010). Chemicals and plastics are either actively produced or by-products of another production process. They are integrated into the natural cycle and subsequently change it (Jones and Gomes 2014). Companies play a major role in the act of changing the environment because they trigger or intensify such effects through short-term motivated actions. The profit is maximized regardless of the long-term consequences (Smith et al. 2010).

At the same time, companies have the opportunity to reduce these impacts on the environment with comparatively minor changes. The integration of Corporate Social Responsibility (CSR) leads to a focus on measuring, improving and communicating a company's activities, metrics, and developments that protect planet Earth and its inhabitants from damage that can either only be reversed with increased (time-) effort or not at all (White 2009). Businesses are therefore increasingly aware of their responsibility for sustainable development. Thereby the relevance of CSR rises due to the adoption of this concept by organizations in different sectors (Barth and Wolff 2009; Babiak and Trendafilova 2011). This development will continue over the next years as the pressure on society and companies to change the existing system is increased by ongoing climate change (Borowy 2014).

CSR describes a company's contribution to sustainable development beyond the legal requirements (ISO 2010). CSR also means dealing responsibly with those involved in or affected by the value-added process (Vilain 2010). The concept of CSR focuses on the sustainable management of the company, where the concerns of the stakeholders are linked, natural resources are used sparingly and both the ecological and the social environment are protected (Jonker et al. 2011). CSR-relevant news describes published announcements associated with CSR (Oikonomou et al. 2018). In recent years, several papers have provided insights on how CSR-relevant news influences the firm value measured by the stock price. The focus of those studies is mainly on the USA (Cheung 2010; Godfrey et al. 2009; Griffin and Sun 2013; Hamilton 1995; Hannon and Milkovich 1996; Karpoff et al. 2005; Krüger 2015; Ramchander et al. 2012). There are only a few studies on the impact of CSR-relevant news on the stock price in Europe (Cellier and Chollet 2011) and there is not one for companies in Austria. Capelle-Blancard and Petit studied companies worldwide, but a company from Austria was not included (Capelle-Blancard and Petit 2017). However, Austria is an interesting country as the public discussion about CSR started comparatively late, in 2003 (Keinert-Kisin 2015). The reason could be that environmental protection and social standards have been high since the Second World War. As regulations are already relatively high in Austria it is interesting to analyze what the impact of CSR-relevant news on the firm value is. But there is a research gap in the existing literature. There is no discussion of the actual short-term impact on stock prices of Austrian-listed companies. This paper aims to close this research gap. Therefore, the research question is as follows: What short-term effects did CSR-relevant news have on the stock prices of companies listed in the Austrian Traded Index (ATX) within the last three years and how can these findings be used in practice?

The following two hypotheses are examined in a superordinate way:

**Hypothesis 0 ($H_0$).** *CSR-relevant news does not influence the stock price movements of companies in the ATX.*

**Hypothesis 1 ($H_1$).** *CSR-relevant news influences the stock price movements of companies in the ATX.*

The null hypothesis must be refuted in order to accept $H_1$ and, therefore, to confirm a connection between CSR-relevant news and the stock price movements of companies in the ATX. This research is done by calculating the average abnormal return and the cumulated average abnormal return. The price data records are downloaded from finance.yahoo.at[1] and the reports are filtered from the financial platform finanzen.net[2] using a criteria catalog with a focus on CSR.

The remainder of this article is structured as follows: Section 2 gives a short literature review that shows the current state of research. Afterwards, Section 3 illustrates the methodology used by explaining the formulas applied in the calculations. Section 4 describes the sample and the data with a following presentation of the results. This section includes a robustness check. To complement this paper Section 5 discusses the outcomes in a critical way.

## 2. Literature Review

### 2.1. CSR Impact on Firm Value

In the literature, there is still a controversy on the question whether CSR activities have a positive or a negative impact on the market value of companies. The main argument why CSR activities reduce the value is that corporate actions in this area increase costs (Becchetti et al. 2012; Harjoto and Jo 2015). Additional rules narrow the scope of managerial decisions and limit the opportunities. On the other hand, many positive effects are stated in the literature. No wage benefits for employees enhance their productivity. Increasing the intrinsic motivation of the employees can reduce costs as they are more likely to accept lower remuneration (Dhaliwal et al. 2014). Further, CSR activities reduce conflicts with all kinds of stakeholders (Freeman 1984). Suitable CSR actions can improve the company's reputation and reduce the risk of being sued (Lee and Roh 2012; Schiff and Mittelbach-Hörmanseder 2018).

---

1 https://finance.yahoo.com/?guccounter=1.
2 https://www.finanzen.net.

### 2.2. Event Studies on CSR-Relevant News

Given the assumption of efficient capital markets, the stock price of a listed company should promptly reflect the implication of an event. The methodology of an event study reveals the short-term impact of an occasion on the value of a firm (Fama 1991; McWilliams et al. 1999; Mitchell and Netter 1994; Kliger and Gurevich 2014).

The overview of the current state of research is provided by ten event studies in the field of stock reactions to news with CSR content. The hypotheses relevant to our empirical research are derived from the current state of research. McWilliams et al. (1999) compare various event studies from different sources. The comparison of the studies is based on the criteria used in this meta-study. The details of each study are listed in Tables 1–3. The day of the event has the denotation [0]. If the day before the event is examined, [−1] is used as an abbreviation. One day after the event is indicated with [1] and so on. If the event window includes more than one day, the length of the time window is presented as the interval $[t_1, t_2]$, where $t_1$ denotes the start date and $t_2$ denotes the end date of the event window.

**Table 1.** Event studies in the category environment.

| Study | Time Window | Sample Size | Year and Geography | Research Findings |
|---|---|---|---|---|
| Hamilton (1995) | [−1]<br>[0]<br>[0, 5] | 436 | 1989<br>USA | negative abnormal return |
| Karpoff et al. (2005) | [−1, 0] | 487 | 1980–2000<br>USA | negative abnormal return |
| Griffin and Sun (2013) | [−2, 2] | 172 | 2000–2010<br>USA | positive abnormal return |

Source: Own representation based on (McWilliams et al. 1999).

**Table 2.** Event studies in the category society.

| Study | Time Window | Sample Size | Year and Geography | Research Findings |
|---|---|---|---|---|
| Hannon and Milkovich (1996) | [-2, 2] | 290 | 1982–1989<br>USA | Positive abnormal return |
| Godfrey et al. (2009) | [−1, 0] | 187 | 1993–2003<br>USA | Negative abnormal return |
| Krüger (2015) | [−5, 5]<br>[−10, 10] | 2116 | 2001–2007<br>USA | Negative abnormal return |

Source: own representation based on (McWilliams et al. 1999).

**Table 3.** Event studies in the category governance.

| Study | Time Window | Sample Size | Year and Geography | Research Findings |
|---|---|---|---|---|
| Arya and Zhang (2009) | [−1, 1]<br>[−5, 5] | 71 | 1996–2005<br>South Africa | Positive abnormal return |
| Cheung (2010) | [−15, 60] | 177 | 2002–2008<br>USA | Positive and negative abnormal return |
| Ramchander et al. (2012) | [0, 0]<br>[−3, 3]<br>[−1, 3] | 194 | 1990–2007<br>USA | Positive and negative abnormal return |
| Cellier and Chollet (2011) | [−5, 5] | 1588 | 2004–2009<br>Europe | Positive and negative abnormal return |

Source: Own representation based on (McWilliams et al. 1999).

The theoretical model for a clear classification of the scientific studies provides the ESG Rating of MSCI ESG Research. ESG stands for environment, social and governance (MSCI ESG Research 2015). The category environment includes topics such as climate change, renewable energies, and sustainability. The second category, society, covers issues such as human capital, labor management, and social opportunities. As a third and final category, governance includes topics such as corporate governance and conduct in relation to business ethics (MSCI ESG Research 2015).

### 2.3. Environment

Hamilton (1995), Karpoff et al. (2005) and Griffin and Sun (2013) examined studies on pollution and violations of environmental regulations. The details of those studies are shown in Table 1.

Hamilton demonstrated that the publication of toxicological performance indicators by the US Environmental Protection Agency leads to a statistically significant negative abnormal return on the day of disclosure (Hamilton 1995).

Karpoff et al. reported a statistically significant loss of stock prices in the event of a violation of environmental laws (Karpoff et al. 2005). The amount of losses is of a similar magnitude to the legally imposed sanctions (Karpoff et al. 2005).

Griffin and Sun explored voluntary publications through the news portal CSRwire, a leading source of CSR information and events on CSR (Griffin and Sun 2013). As a result of this research, it was described that the publication of news with content about greenhouse gas emissions leads to a positive abnormal return for shareholders (Griffin and Sun 2013).

### 2.4. Society

Hannon and Milkovich (1996), Godfrey et al. (2009), and Krüger (2015) studied stock reactions due to news related to society and various stakeholders. The details of those studies are shown in Table 2.

Hannon and Milkovich examined that being named as one of the best companies for working women leads to a positive abnormal return (Hannon and Milkovich 1996).

Godfrey et al. testified in their study that a negative event results in a negative abnormal return (Godfrey et al. 2009). In addition, it has been confirmed that CSR has an insurance-like effect, as companies dealing with CSR suffer fewer losses of market capitalization compared to companies that do not engage in CSR (Godfrey et al. 2009).

Krüger concluded that negative events lead to strong negative abnormal returns and positive events also to negative abnormal returns but only in a weakened form (Krüger 2015). It has also been shown that news with an increased content of legal and economic information leads to stronger reactions of stock prices (Krüger 2015).

### 2.5. Governance

Arya and Zhang (2009), Cheung (2010), Ramchander et al. (2012), and Cellier and Chollet (2011) review how events related to the strategic implementation and subsequent management of CSR influence the stock prices of respective companies. The details of those studies are shown in Table 3.

Arya and Zhang examined that the publication of CSR initiatives during later phases of institutional reforms lead to a positive development of the stock prices (Arya and Zhang 2009).

Cheung found that inclusion in the Dow Jones Sustainability World Index, a stock index with a composition according to economic, environmental, and social criteria, leads to positive and exclusion to negative abnormal returns (Cheung 2010).

Ramchander et al. investigated the inclusion and exclusion in the Domini Social 400 Index, a social index of 400 US-based companies with an exceptional ESG rating (Ramchander et al. 2012; MSCI Inc. 2018). The result of this study is a positive reaction of the stock price of the announcing company and a negative response to stock prices of competing companies. Removal from the index leads to the opposite reaction (Ramchander et al. 2012).

Cellier and Chollet received significant positive returns two days before and after the release of CSR ratings for European companies (Cellier and Chollet 2011). Additionally, announcements including human rights have a positive effect, announcements including environmental and human resources context have a negative impact on abnormal returns. The topic of contribution to society shows an abnormal return in both directions (Cellier and Chollet 2011).

### *2.6. Hypotheses*

Based on the ten empirical studies presented before on stock reactions to CSR-relevant events, the hypotheses presented in Table 4 can be derived. The hypotheses $H_2$, $H_6$, and $H_{10}$ state that the publication of positive CSR-relevant news leads to significant positive average abnormal returns. According to $H_3$, $H_7$, and $H_{11}$ announcements with a positive tendency lead to significant positive cumulated average abnormal returns in the reviewed time window. The hypotheses $H_4$, $H_8$, and $H_{12}$ state that the publication of negative CSR-relevant news leads to significant negative abnormal returns. $H_5$, $H_9$, and $H_{13}$ connect the announcements with a negative tendency to significant negative cumulated average abnormal returns. The respective null hypotheses indicate that the publication of CSR-relevant news shows no significant or significant contrary results. The hypotheses do not distinguish between the three subcategories environment, society, and governance but differences in the results will be examined.

**Table 4.** Hypotheses derived from the literature review.

| Tendency of Announcements | Hypotheses Derived | |
|---|---|---|
| positive | $H_2, H_6, H_{10}$: | AAR > 0 |
| | $H_0$: | AAR ≤ 0 |
| | $H_3, H_7, H_{11}$: | CAAR > 0 |
| | $H_0$: | CAAR ≤ 0 |
| negative | $H_4, H_8, H_{12}$: | AAR < 0 |
| | $H_0$: | AAR ≥ 0 |
| | $H_5, H_9, H_{13}$: | CAAR < 0 |
| | $H_0$: | CAAR ≥ 0 |

Source: Own representation.

## 3. Methodology

In the entire process of empirical research, objectivity is ensured as all stock prices are assessed according to the same pattern. Their reliability is ensured by an optimal balanced selection of the sample. In order to achieve validity, the evaluation scheme is directly aligned with the research question (Schnell et al. 2013).

Execution and evaluation follow Bowman's phase model of event studies. In total, five steps are performed, which are shown in Table 5 (Bowman 1983). After selecting the events to be explored in step one and establishing the hypotheses in step two, the abnormal returns are calculated in step three and cumulated in step four. The analysis of the research results is carried out as step five (Bowman 1983).

**Table 5.** Phase model for the systemic execution of an event study.

| Step | Content |
|---|---|
| 1 | Select event |
| 2 | Establish hypotheses |
| 3 | Calculate abnormal returns |
| 4 | Calculate the cumulated abnormal returns |
| 5 | Analyze the results |

Source: Own representation based on (Bowman 1983).

The time window investigated ranges from two days before the event indicated by [−2] to two days thereafter indicated by [2]. The time window of the event study and its descriptions are shown in Figure 1.

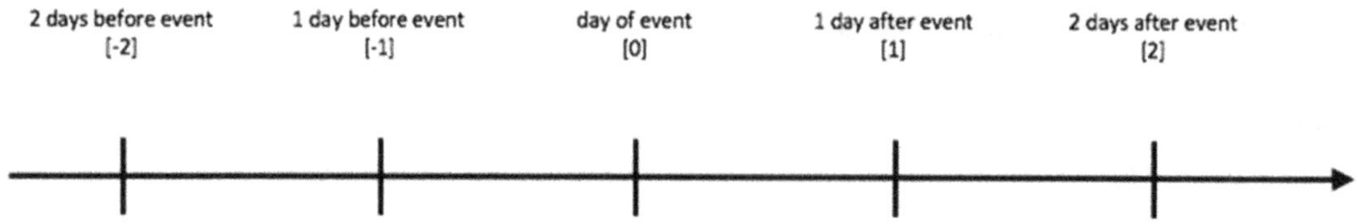


**Figure 1.** Time window of the event study. Source: own representation based on (McWilliams et al. 1999).

The qualitative data is evaluated using the approach of Mayring (2016). The methodology is chosen according to previous empirical studies in order to allow a comparison of results.

The following four key figures are calculated within the time window of 5 days [−2, 2] set around the moment of the announcement on finanzen.net (Kliger and Gurevich 2014):

- Abnormal return *AR*
- Cumulated abnormal return *CAR*
- Average abnormal return *AAR*
- Cumulated average abnormal return *CAAR*

The abnormal return AR of a stock $i$ at a certain point of time $t$ is calculated as the difference between the observed return $R$ and the expected return $K$ (Kliger and Gurevich 2014):

$$AR_{it} = R_{it} - K_{it}. \tag{1}$$

The expected return $K$ is calculated using the market model, which compares the return of a stock with a reference market. This role is played by the ATX, which is a price index developed by the Vienna Stock Exchange and that is representing the price movements of the 20 largest Austrian listed companies (Wiener Börse 2019a) The expected return of stock $i$ is the intersection $\alpha_i$ of the regression line plus the product of the slope of the regression line $\beta_i$ with the observed return $R$ of the reference market $m$ at time $t$ (Kliger and Gurevich 2014):

$$AR_{it} = R_{it} - (\propto_i + \beta_i \times R_{mt}) \tag{2}$$

The expected return $K$ is based on the observed returns of the 252 trading days before the time window examined. Thus, the observed returns from the last calendar year are included in the calculation (Morris 2014). The $t$-test is used to calculate the significance of the results. For this, the $t$-value of the previous outcome is determined by dividing the abnormal return by the standard deviation $\sigma$ of the values of the regression. Subsequently, the significance of the value is identified using the $t$-table with a notice that this test is two-tailed. Therefore, the value does not have to be divided by two (Kothari and Warner 2008):

$$t - value_{AR} = \frac{AR_{it}}{\sigma} \tag{3}$$

Furthermore, the average abnormal return *AAR* is calculated. For this purpose, the total abnormal returns are summed up on a uniform day $t$ of the time window and then divided by the quantity of the sample size $N$ (Kliger and Gurevich 2014):

$$AAR = \frac{1}{N} \sum_{i=1}^{N} AR_{it}\,. \tag{4}$$

This result is also checked for significance using the *t*-test. The root of the number of observed events is multiplied by the result of the average abnormal return *AAR* divided by its standard deviation $\sigma_{AAR}$ (Kothari and Warner 2008):

$$t - value_{AAR} = \sqrt{N} \_\_ \frac{AAR}{\sigma_{AAR}}. \quad (5)$$

Subsequently, the cumulated abnormal returns *CAR* are calculated, which is the sum of the five individual abnormal returns *AR* of the respective time window (Godfrey et al. 2009):

$$CAR\ (t_{-2},\ t_2) = \sum_{t=t_{-2}}^{t_2} AR_{it}\ . \quad (6)$$

As stated earlier, the period examined ranges from two days before the event $t_{-2}$ until two days afterward $t_2$. The significance of the cumulated abnormal return *CAR* was determined using the *t*-test. For this purpose, the value of the cumulated abnormal return *CAR* was divided by the result obtained by multiplying the root of the variance of the cumulated abnormal return with the length of the examined time window *L* (Kothari and Warner 2008):

$$t - value_{CAR} = \frac{CAR(t_{-2}, t_2)}{\sqrt{L \times \sigma_{CAR}{}^2}}. \quad (7)$$

The last measure is the cumulated average abnormal return *CAAR*. This outcome is calculated as the sum of all cumulated abnormal returns of an examined category divided by their number (Kliger and Gurevich 2014):

$$CAAR = \frac{1}{N} \sum_{i=1}^{N} CAR(t_{-2}, t_2). \quad (8)$$

The last *t*-value is calculated by dividing the result of the cumulated average abnormal return *CAAR* by its standard deviation $\sigma_{CAAR}$. This value is multiplied by the root of the sample number that gives the *t*-value (Kothari and Warner 2008):

$$t - value_{CAAR} = \sqrt{N} \times \frac{CAAR}{\sigma_{CAAR}}. \quad (9)$$

## 4. Empirical Analysis

### *4.1. Sample and Data*

Since different markets respond unequally to information, the empirical research is limited to the geographic area of the ATX in order to correct the effects of market differences and obtain results with an increased informative value (Chan et al. 2000). For the sample of the event study, all announcements on the platform finanzen.net of companies listed on the ATX were examined within a three-year period between 1 September 2015 and 31 August 2018. The platform finanzen.net was chosen because the quality, completeness, and overview of the respective announcements on individual companies are leading for the German-speaking countries compared to other competing providers.

The relevance of CSR was examined and filtered using a catalog of criteria based on the ESG rating. The criteria for categorization are presented in Table 6 and serve the purpose of achieving the best objectivity possible and ensuring complete transparency of the overall research design (MSCI ESG Research 2015). For each event, its influence regarding the three categories in form of a specific act, behavior or error of the respective company was challenged. In addition, it categorizes whether the announcement is to be considered as positive or negative for the company.

**Table 6.** Catalog of criteria for CSR-relevant news.

| Category | Topics | Key Terms |
|---|---|---|
| Environment | Climate change | Sustainability report<br>Release of carbon |
| | Natural resources | Use of resources<br>Environmental destruction<br>Environmental protection |
| | Environmental pollution | Discharge of dangerous substances<br>Waste management |
| | Ecological opportunities | Driving the energy transition<br>Use of ecological opportunities<br>Building environmentally friendly infrastructure |
| Society | Human capital | Innovation<br>Increase human capital |
| | Labor force | Appreciation of the employees<br>Establishing jobs |
| | Product liability | Responsible investment |
| | Social opportunities | Charitable activities<br>Building infrastructure for society<br>Development of society |
| Governance | Corporate management | Rating based on ESG<br>Fulfillment of laws |
| | Company's behavior | Business ethics<br>Quality of relationships with stakeholders<br>Strengthening trust/peace<br>Charges/arguments/convictions<br>Corruption |

Source: Own representation based on (MSCI ESG Research 2015).

The price data of the companies listed on ATX was imported from Yahoo Finance. The adjusted closing prices of the individual days were taken since this represents the last price of the stock on a day, adjusted to the price effects of stock splits and dividends in the considered period. Thus, a uniform and distortion-free calculation of abnormal returns is possible.

In the period relevant to the study, the ATX was not published on eleven days due to public holidays. These days are listed in Table A1 in the Appendix A. The sample was adjusted for these days. On 31 August 2018, the last day of the investigation, the ATX consisted of the companies listed below (Wiener Börse 2018).

- Andritz AG
- AT & S Austria
- BAWAG Group AG
- CA Immobilien Anlagen AG
- Erste Group Bank AG
- FACC AG
- Immofinanz AG
- Lenzing AG
- Österreichische Post AG
- OMV AG
- PORR AG
- Raiffeisen Bank International AG

- S IMMO AG
- Schoeller-Bleckmann Oilfield Equipment AG
- Telekom Austria AG
- Uniqa Insurance Group AG
- Verbund AG
- Vienna Insurance Group AG
- Voestalpine AG
- Wienerberger AG

Out of the 20 companies listed above, the following five do not have any CSR-relevant news on the platform over the period studied. Therefore, those five companies have no direct impact on the research results. Since they are all active in different industries, no conclusions can be drawn from this aspect.

- AT & S Austria
- CA Immobilien Anlagen AG
- Erste Group Bank AG
- Schoeller-Bleckmann Oilfield Equipment AG
- Uniqa Insurance Group AG

Due to the IPO[3] in October 2017, there is insufficient price data for BAWAG AG to calculate the expected return. Therefore, the sample does not include any CSR-relevant news from this company (Wiener Börse 2019b). Finally, the sample researched in the event study consists of 85 positive and 44 negative announcements (Table 7) with CSR context from a total of 14 companies.

**Table 7.** Sample size.

| Category | Positive | Negative |
|---|---|---|
| Environment | 33 | 6 |
| Society | 44 | 6 |
| Governance | 8 | 32 |
| Total | 85 | 44 |

Source: Own representation.

In order to gain an understanding of the results of the research and for the announcements contained in the sample, Table 8 gives an example for each category.

In total, 129 announcements remained after the filtering process based on the catalog of criteria and were therefore suitable for the event study. Of these 129 news, 118 defined the day of the message as $t_0$ of the investigated time window, while at eleven days $t_0$ was adjusted. Five notifications were published on days when the stock market was not opened for trading. Table A2 in the Appendix A provides an overview of these five reports. As a substitute for $t_0$ of these days, the next possible exchange trading day has been chosen. This way the reactions of the market triggered by the messages fall within the period of $t_0$. The remaining six reports were published after the announcement of the ATX was finished for that day. This is the case if the news was published on the original $t_0$ but between 17:31 and 23:59 of that day. These outliers were handled in a similar way as the publications on non-trading days. Instead of the original $t_0$ of the announcement, the next possible trading day has been selected, in order to exclude the reactions of the market at $t_{-1}$ and then include them at $t_0$. Table A3 in the Appendix A provides a clear overview of these six reports. Thus, the sample of the

[3] Initial Public Offering.

empirical research has been designed uniformly so that the reactions of the market are not included in $t_{-1}$, but in $t_0$. According to our research this is the most appropriate to deal with these anomalies. The dataset needed was imported into Microsoft Excel, where the formulas described were calculated in order to extract the results as the last step.

**Table 8.** Examples of CSR-relevant reports.

| Category | Tendency of Report | Company | Headline of Report |
|---|---|---|---|
| Environment | positive | Lenzing AG | 100 million Euro for sustainability * |
| | negative | OMV AG | Greenpeace protests in front of OMV headquarters against Arctic drilling * |
| Society | positive | Voestalpine AG | Voestalpine supports hurricane sufferers in Texas with 350,000 USD in emergency funding * |
| | negative | Wienerberger AG | End of April: Wienerberger closes plant in Fürstenfeld * |
| Governance | positive | Immofinanz AG | Immofinanz wins 'Asset Management Company of the Year' |
| | negative | Telekom Austria AG | Corruption at Telekom Austria: OGH confirms guilty statements * |

Source: Own representation. * translated.

## 4.2. Empirical Results

This section is structured according to the categories of hypotheses. The components relate to the aspect's environment, society, and governance in line with the ESG rating and are additionally divided into positive and negative announcements.

### 4.2.1. Environment—Positive

A total of 33 announcements were assigned to this category. The average abnormal return *AAR* was negative on the day before and on the day of the event. On the day before, the day after, and two days after the event, the average abnormal return was in the positive range. A significant positive return was recorded the day before the announcement and a highly significant one on the day after it (Table 9). The cumulated average abnormal return *CAAR* has a significant positive value, as shown in Table 9.

**Table 9.** Results of event studies.

| Category | Tendency of Reports | Hypotheses Established | AAR | CAAR |
|---|---|---|---|---|
| Environment | positive | $H_2$: AAR > 0 c<br>$H_3$: CAAR > 0 c | $t_{-1}$ 0.0107 *<br>$t_1$ 0.0113 **** | 0.0107 ** |
| | negative | $H_4$: AAR < 0<br>$H_5$: CAAR < 0 | $t_0$ 0.0138 *** | 0.0199 |
| Society | positive | $H_6$: AAR > 0 c<br>$H_7$: CAAR > 0 c | $t_{-2}$ 0.0057 ***<br>$t_1$ 0.0062 *** | 0.0148 *** |
| | negative | $H_8$: AAR < 0<br>$H_9$: CAAR < 0 | $t_{-1}$ 0.0217 *** | 0.0076 |
| Governance | positive | $H_{10}$: AAR > 0 c<br>$H_{11}$: CAAR > 0 | $t_{-1}$ 0.0248 *** | 0.0316 |
| | negative | $H_{12}$: AAR < 0 c<br>$H_{13}$: CAAR < 0 | $t_{-1}$ 0.0038 *<br>$t_0$ −0.0073 *<br>$t_1$ 0.0045 **<br>$t_2$ 0.0079 *** | 0.0113 ** |

c hypotheses confirmed; **** 1%, *** 5%, ** 10%, * 15% level of significance. Source: Own representation.

These results confirm $H_2$ that the announcement of a positive CSR-relevant news with environmental context leads to significant positive average abnormal returns in the time window investigated. Also, the results confirm $H_3$ that these conditions lead to a significant positive cumulated average abnormal return. Therefore, the null hypothesis is rejected in each case.

#### 4.2.2. Environment—Negative

A total of six announcements were assigned to this category. Positive average abnormal returns were observed in the period of two days prior to reporting until one day later. This was determined in a negative form two days after the event. The only significant average abnormal return was detected on the day of the announcement as a positive value (Table 9). The cumulated average abnormal return was not significant, as shown in Table 9.

These results do not confirm $H_4$—that the announcement of negative CSR-relevant news with environmental context leads to significant negative average abnormal returns in the time window investigated. Additionally, the results do not confirm $H_5$ that these conditions lead to a significant negative cumulated average abnormal return. Therefore, the null hypothesis cannot be rejected in each case.

#### 4.2.3. Society—Positive

Forty-four messages have been assigned to this category. Positive average abnormal returns were observed on all five days of the time window studied, with significance being detected only two days before and on the day after the event (Table 9). The result of the cumulated average abnormal return has a significant positive value.

These results confirm $H_6$ that the announcement of positive CSR-relevant news with societal context leads to significant positive average abnormal returns in the time window investigated. Also, the results confirm $H_7$ that these conditions lead to a significant positive cumulated average abnormal return. Therefore, the null hypothesis is rejected in each case.

#### 4.2.4. Society—Negative

Six announcements have been assigned to this section. Events from this category resulted in negative average abnormal returns on four days, two days before, on the day of the event and on the two following days. The only positive value and the only significant one was shown on the day before the announcement. Table 9 shows that a cumulated average abnormal return in the positive range was found in the time window, which has no significance.

These results do not confirm $H_8$ that the announcement of negative CSR-relevant news with societal context leads to significant negative average abnormal returns in the time window investigated. Also, the results do not confirm $H_9$ that these conditions lead to a significant negative cumulated average abnormal return. Therefore, the null hypotheses cannot be rejected in each case.

#### 4.2.5. Governance—Positive

A total of eight announcements have been assigned to this section. The average abnormal returns were positive on the two days before and the two days after the report. The only negative average abnormal return was detected on the day of the report. The only significant observation was positive on the day before the event. The cumulated average abnormal return is positive, but the value is not statistically significant from zero as shown in Table 9.

These results confirm $H_{10}$ that the announcement of positive CSR-relevant news with governance context leads to significant positive average abnormal returns in the time window investigated. The results do not confirm $H_{11}$ that these conditions lead to a significant positive cumulated average abnormal return. Therefore, the null hypothesis is rejected for $H_{10}$, but not for $H_{11}$.

4.2.6. Governance—Negative

Thirty-two announcements in this category led to an observation of a significant average abnormal return on four out of five days (Table 9). On the day before the event and the two following days, the values were positive. The only negative value was observed on the day of the announcement. The result of the cumulated average abnormal return is a positive and a significant value (Table 9).

These results confirm $H_{12}$ that the announcement of negative CSR-relevant news with governance context leads to significant negative average abnormal returns in the time window investigated. These results do not confirm $H_{13}$ that these conditions lead to a significant negative cumulated average abnormal return. Therefore, the null hypothesis is rejected for $H_{12}$, but not for $H_{13}$.

Based on the significant empirical results presented so far, it can be concluded that the null hypothesis $H_0$ can be rejected and $H_1$ can, thus, be assumed.

### *4.3. Robustness Check*

To test the robustness of our event study, we performed the same study with a change in the observed trading days prior to the window we examined. We have changed the number from 252 to 126 or 63 days, with the expected return not based on the last year, but on the last six months or three months before the event, respectively. The results of this robustness test confirm the trends and conclusions of the original event study. The results of the robustness test for 126 days are shown in Table A4 in Appendix A. The results for 63 days show the same pattern and are therefore not presented separately.

In accordance with the described methodology, we used the market model to estimate abnormal returns. This is the most common model used in event studies where more advanced models do not necessarily improve the goodness of fit (Becchetti et al. 2012; Cable and Holland 1999). The distribution of $R^2$ is shown in Figure 2. The goodness of fit of the regression is within the usual limits and appropriate for the purpose.

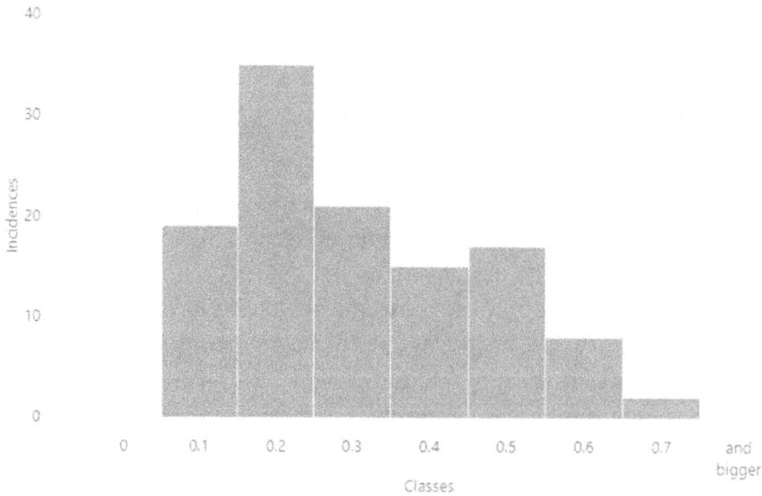


**Figure 2.** Distribution of $R^2$. Source: Own representation.

## 5. Discussion of the Results

### *5.1. Summary*

The average abnormal returns examining the possible effects of CSR-related news on stock prices in the time window confirm the theory only partly. Out of a total of 30 days studied, eleven had statistically significant results. Out of these eleven significant abnormal returns, ten were positive and only one negative. The trend expected out of the theory was confirmed in only six cases but refuted in five.

A positive cumulated average abnormal return was found in all six categories studied, whereas only three were significant. These were observed in the sections Environment—Positive, Society—Positive, and Governance—Negative. The theory expects a positive result for positive reports, and vice versa. While the results in the first two significant results confirm the expectations from the literature, the third result mentioned had a development in the opposite direction, like the theoretically expected negative result. Empirical evidence did not confirm this expectation of negative cumulated average returns in a single case.

Based on these results, it is reasonable to state that any company announcement in the CSR area trigger a positive effect in the form of cumulated average abnormal returns and that negative effects can only be observed within the short-term period of a day. On the one hand, these results partially confirm the expectations of the theory while, on the other hand, they refute them. The research suggests that the positive cumulated average abnormal returns are less related to content, but more to the company's short-term media presence.

### 5.2. Critical Acclaim

Event studies examine only short-term effects of published information on stock prices (Chan et al. 2000). An assessment of long-term development due to individual management actions is not optimally reflected (McWilliams et al. 1999; Jeng 2015). With a sample size of 129 this study is below the optimal size of 170–200 taken from the ten studies compared in the literature review. An extension of the research from 3 to 5 to 10 years will, therefore, have a positive effect on the result's relevance (Chan et al. 2000; Zhang 2014). Although the selection and classification of the CSR-relevant events examined was as objective as possible and carried out according to fixed criteria, the subjectivity it contains leaves a possible bias.

The current empirical research is mainly based on the results of the *t*-tests. This is the first step of the analysis to examine the impact of CSR news. The next step is to conduct a regression analysis with CAR, AAR and CAAR as dependent variables to measure the effects of other factors that could have an influence on the return.

In addition, only news from the platform finanzen.net was analyzed for the composition of the sample. Although the market leader serves as a source, a possible error rate remains to be accepted in terms of completeness (Schmidt 1982; Jennings and Starks 1985). Another point of criticism is the danger that a market does not optimally assess the observed event and thus over- or underestimates the corresponding announcement (Klassen and McLaughlin 1996). In this respect, a comparison with other markets is helpful as there is a different level of market efficiency and liquidity that could impact the results (Jennings and Starks 1985; Chan et al. 2000). In the future, it will be necessary to further investigate to what extent the proven effects can be attributed to the topic of CSR and not merely to the naming of the company in the media (Mumford 2016). The corresponding follow-up study would aim to find statistical evidence that assign the elements of the reactions to each of the two possible factors.

### 5.3. Implications

The result of the study is that positive CSR-relevant news in the areas of environment and society have a significant positive impact on stock prices in the short-term. From these results, the recommendation can be derived for companies to integrate CSR in order to obtain an additional tool for the company's management to influence the stock price in short-term for a specific cause. For companies, this study proves that the integration of CSR not only opens up numerous opportunities in the fields of economic, environmental and social affairs but that CSR can also be used as an element for controlling the stock price (Barth and Wolff 2009). Furthermore, the research findings have identified a way to measure the success of CSR and thereby increased the monetary incentive for the integration of CSR (Brejning 2016).

Now that the companies listed in the ATX have been provided with additional tools and space for actions, it is up to the organizations to implement these tools in practice and to unlock new potentials. In theory, the possibilities of applying stock price control lie in the aimed increase of the market value of the company, the associated marketing for the target group of the investors and improvement of the company's seal of quality (Lechler 2003). In addition, the aimed increase in the stock price provides possible protection against external takeovers and the possibilities of action of the company's management is widened by reducing the involvement of the shareholders in the business (Schäfer 1999; Lechler 2003). Opportunities are being created to prepare the stock price specifically for the implementation of capital measures and, thus, to optimize its overall process (Hermanns 2006).

As a result, it is possible to derive the exact recommendation for companies to integrate CSR into the company and, subsequently, to regularly publish CSR-relevant news via the platform finanzen.net in order to obtain a short-term improvement of the individual stock price and, therefore, to benefit from the added opportunities.

## 6. Conclusions

The event study concluded that both positive and negative CSR-related events over the last three years had a positive overall effect on ATX stocks in the form of accumulated average abnormal returns. However, only half of the cumulated average abnormal returns were significant. These were the positive reports related to the environmental category, the positive ones related to the category society and the negative ones to the category governance. Thus, although the impact of CSR-related reports on stock prices was confirmed, a negative cumulated average abnormal return was never observed. Therefore, the expected trend, whether positive or negative, has not been shown to play a decisive role. The event study conducted confirms the hypothesis that CSR-relevant reports lead to abnormal returns in the time window studied.

The tendency expected from the other hypotheses, positive or negative, was only confirmed in selected cases. Ten out of eleven significant abnormal returns in the event window were positive, only one was negative. Thus, the theory of a clearly visible tendency in both directions is only partially confirmed. The results of the research can, thus, be interpreted as meaning that CSR-relevant news leads to changes in stock prices, although these are only partially due to the content. Presumably, the media presence initiated with the announcement is an influential factor. In order to verify this statement, a follow-up study is necessary.

For companies, these research results are important as it shows that CSR-relevant events can be used to influence the stock price according to individual needs. These include a wanted increase in the market value of the company, marketing for investors or strengthening the individual brand. Based on the research findings demonstrating a positive effect of CSR-related news, an increase in the relevance of CSR in companies is to be expected, as the shareholder value is profiting from that. Thus, the integration of CSR not only creates measurable added value for the shareholder but also for the environment and society.

**Author Contributions:** Conceptualization, F.B. and M.E.; methodology, F.B.; validation, F.B. and M.E.; formal analysis, F.B.; resources, F.B. and M.E.; data curation, F.B.; writing—original draft preparation, F.B.; writing—review and editing, M.E.; visualization, F.B.; supervision, M.E.; project administration, M.E.

**Funding:** This research received no external funding.

**Acknowledgments:** We thank for the administrative and technical support of Eva-Maria Eder.

**Conflicts of Interest:** The authors declare no conflict of interest.

## Appendix A

**Table A1.** Days when the ATX was not published.

| | Date | Reason |
|---|---|---|
| 1 | 31 May 2018 | Corpus Christi |
| 2 | 21 May 2018 | Whit Monday |
| 3 | 10 May 2018 | Ascension of Christ |
| 4 | 8 December 2017 | Mary's conception |
| 5 | 1 November 2017 | All Saints' Day |
| 6 | 26 October 2017 | National holiday |
| 7 | 15 June 2017 | Corpus Christi |
| 8 | 25 May 2017 | Ascension of Christ |
| 9 | 2 January 2017 | No data on finance.yahoo.com |
| 10 | 16 January 2015 | No data on finance.yahoo.com |
| 11 | 24 December 2014 | Christmas eve |

Source: Own representation based on Yahoo Finance.

**Table A2.** CSR-relevant notifications on non-trading days.

| | $t_0$ Report | Reason | $t_0$ Used |
|---|---|---|---|
| 1 | 14 July 2018 | Sunday | 16 July 2018 |
| 2 | 9 April 2018 | No data on finance.yahoo.com | 10 April 2018 |
| 3 | 11 February 2018 | Sunday | 12 February 2018 |
| 4 | 19 August 2017 | Saturday | 21 August 2017 |
| 5 | 25 May 2017 | Ascension of Christ | 26 May 2017 |

Source: own representation based on Yahoo Finance.

**Table A3.** CSR-relevant messages between 17:31h and 23:59h.

| | $t_0$ Report | Time of Announcement | $t_0$ Used |
|---|---|---|---|
| 1 | 20 April 2018 | 19:07 h | 23 April 2018 |
| 2 | 9 October 2017 | 17:51 h | 10 October 2017 |
| 3 | 12 September 2017 | 18:52 h | 13 September 2017 |
| 4 | 19 April 2017 | 18:13 h | 20 April 2017 |
| 5 | 19 January 2016 | 23:13 h | 20 January 2016 |
| 6 | 26 November 2015 | 18:01 h | 27 January 2015 |

Source: own representation based on Yahoo Finance.

**Table A4.** Results of robustness check (126 days).

| Category | Tendency of Reports | Hypotheses Established | AAR | CAAR |
|---|---|---|---|---|
| Environment | positive | $H_2$: AAR > 0 c<br>$H_3$: CAAR > 0 c | $t_{-1}$ 0.0048 *<br>$t_1$ 0.0112 **** | 0.0101 ** |
| | negative | $H_4$: AAR < 0<br>$H_5$: CAAR < 0 | $t_0$ 0.0127 *** | 0.0171 |
| Society | positive | $H_6$: AAR > 0 c<br>$H_7$: CAAR > 0 c | $t_{-2}$ 0.0057 ***<br>$t_1$ 0.0064 *** | 0.0150 *** |
| | negative | $H_8$: AAR < 0<br>$H_9$: CAAR < 0 | $t_{-1}$ 0.0250 *** | 0.0093 |
| Governance | positive | $H_{10}$: AAR > 0 c<br>$H_{11}$: CAAR > 0 | $t_{-1}$ 0.0259 *** | 0.0351 |
| | negative | $H_{12}$: AAR < 0 c<br>$H_{13}$: CAAR < 0 | $t_0$ −0.0075 *<br>$t_1$ 0.0045 **<br>$t_2$ 0.0078 *** | 0.0105 ** |

c hypotheses confirmed; **** 1%, *** 5%, ** 10%, * 15% level of significance. Source: own representation.

## References


Arya, Bindu, and Gaiyan Zhang. 2009. Institutional Reforms and Investor Reactions to CSR Announcements. Evidence from an Emerging Economy. *Journal of Management Studies* 46: 1089–112. [CrossRef]

Babiak, Kathy, and Sylvia Trendafilova. 2011. CSR and Environmental Responsibility. Motives and Pressures to Adopt Green Management Practices. *Corporate Social Responsibility and Environmental Management* 18: 11–24. [CrossRef]

Barth, Regine, and Franziska Wolff. 2009. Corporate Social Responsibility and sustainability impact: Opening up the arena. In *Corporate Social Responsibility in Europe. Rhetoric and Realities*. Edited by Regine Barth and Franziska Wolff. Cheltenham: Edward Elgar, pp. 3–25.

Becchetti, Leonardo, Rocco Ciciretti, Iftekhar Hasan, and Nada Kobeissi. 2012. Corporate Social Responsibility and Shareholder's Value. *Journal of Business Research* 65: 1628–35. [CrossRef]

Borowy, Iris. 2014. *Defining Sustainable Development for Our Common Future. A History of the World Commission on Environment and Development (Brundtland Commission)*. London: Routledge.

Bowman, Robert. 1983. Understanding and Conducting Event Studies. *Journal of Business Finance & Accounting* 10: 561–84.

Brejning, Jeanette. 2016. *Corporate Social Responsibility and the Welfare State. The Historical and Contemporary Role of CSR in the Mixed Economy of Welfare*. London: Routledge.

Cable, John, and Kevin Michael Holland. 1999. Modelling normal returns in event studies: A model-selection approach and pilot study. *The European Journal of Finance* 5: 331–41. [CrossRef]

Capelle-Blancard, Gunther, and Aurélien Petit. 2017. Every little helps? ESG news and stock market reaction. *Journal of Business Ethics* 157: 543–65. [CrossRef]

Cellier, Alexis, and Pierre Chollet. 2011. The Impact of Corporate Social Responsibility Rating Announcement on Stock Prices: An Event Study on European Markets. Paper presented at International Conference of the French Finance Association (AFFI), Montpellier, France, May 11–13; pp. 1–33.

Chan, Kalok, Allaudeen Hameed, and Wilson Tong. 2000. Profitability of momentum strategies in the international equity markets. *Journal of Financial and Quantitative Analysis* 2: 153–72. [CrossRef]

Cheung, Adrian. 2010. Do Stock Investors Value Corporate Sustainability? Evidence from an Event Study. *Journal of Business Ethics* 2: 145–65.

Dhaliwal, Dan, Oliver Zhen Li, Albert Tsang, and Yong Georg Yang. 2014. Corporate social responsibility disclosure and the cost of equity capital: The roles of stakeholder orientation and financial transparency. *Journal of Accounting and Public Policy* 33: 328–55. [CrossRef]

Fama, Eugene Francis. 1991. Efficient Capital Markets: II. *The Journal of Finance* 46: 1575–617. [CrossRef]

Freeman, Robert Edward. 1984. *Strategic Management: A Stakeholder Approach*. Boston: Pitman.

Godfrey, Paul, Craig Merril, and Jared Hansen. 2009. The relationship between corporate social responsibility and shareholder value. An empirical test of the risk management hypothesis. *Strategic Management Journal* 30: 425–45. [CrossRef]

Griffin, Paul, and Yuan Sun. 2013. Going green. Market reaction to CSR newswire releases. *Journal of Accounting and Public Policy* 32: 93–113. [CrossRef]

Hamilton, James. 1995. Pollution as News. Media and Stock Market Reactions to the Toxics Release Inventory Data. *Journal of Environmental Economics and Management* 28: 98–113. [CrossRef]

Hannon, John, and George Milkovich. 1996. The Effect of Human Resource Reputation Signals on Share Prices. An Event Study. *Human Resource Management* 3: 405–24. [CrossRef]

Harjoto, Maretno Agus, and Hoje Jo. 2015. Legal vs. normative CSR: Differential impact on analyst dispersion, stock return volatility, cost of capital, and firm value. *Journal of Business Ethics* 128: 1–20. [CrossRef]

Hermanns, Julia. 2006. *Optimale Kapitalstruktur und Market Timing. Empirische Analyse Börsennotierter Deutscher Unternehmen*. Wiesbaden: GWV.

ISO. 2010. *ISO 26000. Guidance on Social Responsibility*. Geneva: ISO.

Jeng, Jau-Lian. 2015. *Analyzing Event Statistics in Corporate Finance. Methodologies, Evidences, and Critiques*. New York: Palgrave Macmillan.

Jennings, Robert, and Laura Starks. 1985. Information content and the speed of stock price adjustment. *Journal of Accounting Research* 1: 336–50. [CrossRef]

Jones, Oliver, and Rachel Louise Gomes. 2014. Chemical Pollution of the Aquatic Environment by Priority Pollutants and its Control. In *Pollution. Causes, Effects and Control*. Edited by R. Harrison. Cambridge: The Royal Society of Chemistry, pp. 1–31.

Jonker, Jan, Wolfgang Stark, and Stefan Tewes. 2011. *Corporate Social Responsibility und Nachhaltige Entwicklung. Einführung, Strategie und Glossar*. Berlin/Heidelberg: Springer.

Karpoff, Jonathan, John Lott, and Eric Wehrly. 2005. The reputational penalties for environmental violations. Empirical evidence. *Journal of Law and Economics* 48: 653–75. [CrossRef]

Keinert-Kisin, Christina. 2015. CSR in Austria: Exemplary Social and Environmental Practice or Compliance-Driven Corporate Responsibility? *Corporate Social Responsibility in Europe*, 137–51. [CrossRef]

Klassen, Robert, and Curtis McLaughlin. 1996. The Impact of Environmental Management on Firm Performance. *Management Science* 8: 1199–214. [CrossRef]

Kliger, Doron, and Gregory Gurevich. 2014. *Event Studies for Financial Research. A Comprehensive Guide*. New York: Palgrave Macmillan.

Kothari, S. P., and Jerold Warner. 2008. Econometrics of Event Studies. In *Handbook of Corporate Finance. Empirical Corporate Finance*. Edited by B. Espen Eckbo. Amsterdam: North Holland, Elsevier, vol. 1, pp. 3–36.

Krüger, Philipp. 2015. Corporate Goodness and Shareholder Wealth. *Journal of Financial Economics* 115: 304–29. [CrossRef]

Lechler, Jörg. 2003. Investor Marketing aus Sicht eines Emissionshauses. In *Investor Marketing. Aktionäre erfolgreich gewinnen. Investoren langfristig binden. Börsenkurse nachhaltig steigern*. Edited by Bernhard Ebel and Markus Hofer. Wiesbaden: Gabler, pp. 79–94.

Lee, Jooh, and James Jungbae Roh. 2012. Revisiting corporate reputation and firm performance link. *Benchmarking. An International Journal* 4: 649–64. [CrossRef]

Mayring, Philipp. 2016. *Einführung in die qualitative Sozialforschung. Eine Anleitung zu qualitativem Denken*. Weinheim: Beltz.

McWilliams, Abagail, Donald Siegel, and Siew Hong Teoh. 1999. Issues in the Use of the Event Study Methodology. A Critical Analysis of Corporate Social Responsibility Studies. *Organizational Research Methods* 2: 340–65. [CrossRef]

Mitchell, Mark, and Jeffry Netter. 1994. The Role of Financial Economics in Securities Fraud Cases. Applications at the Securities and Exchange Commission. *The Business Lawyer* 2: 545–90.

Morris, Gregory. 2014. *Investing with the Trend. A Rules-based Approach to Money Management*. Hoboken: John Wiley & Sons.

MSCI ESG Research. 2015. *MSCI ESG Rating Methodology. Executive Summary*. New York: MSCI Inc.

MSCI Inc. 2018. MSCI KLD 400 Social Index (USD). Available online: https://www.msci.com/documents/10199/904492e6-527e-4d64-9904-c710bf1533c6 (accessed on 6 February 2019).

Mumford, Paul. 2016. *The Stock Picker. A Financial History from the Sharp End*. Petersfield: Harriman House.

Oikonomou, Ioannis, Aspasia Pastra, and Ilias Visvikis. 2018. A Financial Business Case for Corporate Social Responsibility. In *Corporate Social Responsibility in the Maritime Industry*. Edited by Lisa Loloma Froholdt. Cham: Springer, pp. 219–36.

Ramchander, Sanjay, Robert Schwebach, and KIM Staking. 2012. The Informational Relevance of Corporate Social Responsibility. Evidence from DS400 Index Reconstitutions. *Strategic Management Journal* 33: 303–14. [CrossRef]

Schäfer, Frank. 1999. Zulässigkeiten und Grenzen der Kurspflege. *WM*, 1345–52.

Schiff, Felix, and Stéphanie Mittelbach-Hörmanseder. 2018. Verpflichtende Nachhaltigkeitsberichterstattung. Ein Überblick. *RWZ* 1: 34–7.

Schmidt, Reinhard. 1982. Rechnungslegung als Informationsproduktion auf nahezu effizienten Kapitalmärkten. *Schmalenbach Zeitschrift für betriebswirtschaftliche Forschung* 34: 728–48.

Schnell, Rainer, Paul Hill, and Elke Esser. 2013. *Methoden der Empirischen Sozialforschung*. Munich: Oldenbourg.

Smith, Michael, Karlson James Hargroves, and Cheryl Julia Kiran Desha. 2010. *Cents and Sustainability. Securing Our Common Future by Decoupling Economic Growth from Environmental Pressures*. London: Routledge.

Vilain, Michael. 2010. Meine Firma, meine Mitarbeiter, meine Heimat. Merkmale unternehmerischen Engagement im deutschen Mittelstand. In *Gesellschaftliches Engagement von Unternehmen. Der deutsche Weg im internationalen Kontext*. Edited by Sebastian Braun. Wiesbaden: Vs, pp. 106–39.

White, Gwendolen. 2009. *Sustainability Reporting. Managing for Wealth and Corporate Health*. New York: Business Expert Press.

Wiener Börse. 2018. Zusammensetzung ATX. Available online: https://www.wienerborse.at/indizes/aktuelle-indexwertezusammensetzung/?ID_NOTATION=92866&ISIN=AT0000999982 (accessed on 31 August 2018).

Wiener Börse. 2019a. Definition ATX. Available online: https://www.wienerborse.at/wissen/boersenlexikon/buchstabe-a/atx/ (accessed on 7 February 2019).

Wiener Börse. 2019b. Österreichs größter Börsengang: BAWAG Group AG im PRIME market der Wiener Börse gelistet. Available online: https://www.wienerborse.at/news/wiener-boerse-news/news/borsengang-bawag-group/ (accessed on 7 February 2019).

Zhang, Ying. 2014. *Stock Message Boards. A Quantitative Approach to Measuring Investor Sentiment*. New York: Palgrave Macmillan.

# 6

# An Empirical Investigation of the Performance of Japanese Mutual Funds: Skill or Luck?

**Keith Pilbeam [1,*] and Hamish Preston [2]**

1 Department of Economics, City, University of London, Northampton Square, London EC1V 0HB, UK
2 S&P Dow Jones Indices, 55 Water Street, New York, NY 1004, USA; hamish.preston@spglobal.com
* Correspondence: k.s.pilbeam@city.ac.uk

**Abstract:** This paper assesses the performance of 355 actively managed Japanese Equity Mutual Funds between April 2011 and April 2016. The equal weight portfolio and Jensen's alpha measures of active management provide strong evidence that Japanese Mutual Funds fail to outperform the benchmark four-factor capital asset pricing model. When it comes to market timing, the Treynor and Mazuy measure shows that 33 funds have significant positive market timing ability which is largely offset by 31 funds with significant negative timing ability. To ensure the statistical inference is robust to the non-normality found in 33 funds we employ Fama and French's cross-sectional bootstrap. The results show that a large proportion of funds fail to outperform a hypothetical world with no skill. On the persistence of skill we find that there is stronger persistence for poor performing funds than for strong performing funds.

**Keywords:** mutual fund performance; bootstrap; Jensen's alpha; Fama and French model

**JEL Classification:** C15; G11

---

## 1. Introduction

Mutual funds allow investors to benefit from diversified portfolios by grouping investments together and these investment groupings typically differ according to investment style. Owing to the purported skill involved in actively managing investors' money, active mutual funds typically charge higher fees than exchange-traded funds (ETFs) that seek to mimic the market returns. Despite a plethora of literature being available for US mutual funds, relatively little focus has been given to Japanese mutual funds[1].

This paper contributes to the literature by using popular performance measures to infer the active managers' skill level in Japan[2] by analyzing Japanese mutual fund performance over the period April 2011 and April 2016, This paper considers gross returns that include trading costs, management fees, and expenses, therefore the tests of skill enables us to determine if fund managers had sufficient skill to beat passive, diversified benchmarks.

The equal weight (EW) measure[3] of fund performance provides an analysis of the average fund returns and gives an indication of the abnormal performance of the Japanese mutual fund market

---

1 For clarity, Japanese mutual funds are defined as unit trusts on Datastream owing to the different legal structure in place. However, this difference does not materially impact the objective of active managers therefore we refer to the Japanese unit trusts as Japanese mutual funds for the remainder of the paper.

2 Some research has been done into Japanese mutual fund performance, notably Cai et al. (1997), but such papers focus on returns from earlier periods and do not use some of the performance tests in this paper.

3 All the performance measures, except the persistence measure, use $t$-statistics to discern between performance driven by luck or skill.

relative to the stated benchmark.[4] The measure is also useful for understanding the factors driving cross-sectional returns, thus establishing the four-factor CAPM model as a valid benchmark.

This paper adds to the existing literature by discussing the interaction between stock-picking and market timing abilities. The stock picking ability of each fund is analyzed using the Jensen's alpha measure, defined as the "average incremental rate of return on the portfolio per unit of time which is solely due to the managers' ability to forecast future security prices" Jensen (1968). Forecasting security prices is analogous to stock picking since managers would not buy stocks if they forecast them to perform poorly. If a fund's alpha is positive (negative) this implies that managers exhibit good (poor) stock selection ability. The greater granularity of this measure compared to EW also means the distribution of funds' alphas can be examined.

To measure the market timing ability of funds we use the Treynor and Mazuy (1966) test on each fund; excess fund returns are expected to be a convex function of the market's excess returns if a fund manager has timing ability. The rationale for this follows from Bollen and Busse (2001) definition:

> Market timing refers to the dynamic allocation of capital among broad classes of investments, often restricted to equities and short-term government debt. The successful market timer increases portfolio weight on equities prior to a rise in the market and decreases the weight prior to a fall in the market.

An additional contribution to the existing literature on the performance measures is the use of Fama and French (2010) cross-sectional bootstrap. No studies to our knowledge have thus far used this method to assess Japanese funds. This methodology is used because the *t*-statistics in the aforementioned tests rely on the regression residuals being normally distributed. There are many reasons why this assumption fails for mutual fund returns; Kosowski et al. (2006) offer several explanations such as many fund managers holding large positions in specific stocks/sectors use dynamic risk strategies in response to a change in their relative rankings. Fund managers' incentive to change risk is dependent on their year-to-date returns. In their well-known study, Chevalier and Ellison (1997) provide strong evidence of non-normality, it is for this reason that we employ the Royston (1982) version of the Shapiro and Wilk (1965) test for normality.

Analyzing the persistence of fund returns enables one to draw conclusions about whether skill can be identified based on prior returns. This is important because investors may believe they can overcome a scarcity in active managers' skill levels if they are able to identify the best skilled managers based on previous performance and also avoid poor performance if there is persistence in poor performing funds. We focus on the extreme 60 funds (the 30 best and 30 worst performing by Jensen's alpha measure) across different formation periods.[5]

The rest of this paper is structured as follows: Section 2 provides a literature review, Section 3 outlines the dataset used in this study and Section 4 looks at the key equal weight regression analysis employed in our empirical research. Section 5 looks at Jensen's alpha and Section 6 looks at the Treynor and Mazuy measure for market timing. In Section 7 we undertake tests for normality while in Section 8 the Fama and French (2010) bootstrap method is outlined along with the associated results for our selection of Japanese funds. Section 9 looks at the issue of persistence in fund performance and Section 10 concludes.

## 2. Literature Review

Jensen (1968) created the Jensen's alpha measure to determine whether active managers had skill in forecasting security prices. In his study, the average returns of 115 mutual funds between 1955

---

[4] Throughout this paper, abnormal performance and alpha are used interchangeably.

[5] One might question why the paper departs from using *t*-statistics. The reason is the underlying non-normality in many funds' residuals makes inferences from *t*-statistics potentially misleading, whereas the parameter estimates themselves do not depend upon normality to be unbiased and consistent.

and 1964 showed no such skill, although this result may be impacted by survivorship bias. Jensen also concluded that there was little evidence of any individual fund being able to do significantly better than the random buy-and-hold the market strategy.

Building on the market timing test methodology developed by Treynor (1965), Treynor and Mazuy (1966) analyzed a sample of 57 mutual funds between 1953 and 1962. The authors found that that only one fund had the desired convex curvature in characteristic lines consistent with market timing; the other 56 fund managers appeared to have no market timing ability. Whilst Treynor and Mazuy mention that this does not rule out managers delivering positive abnormal performance, their results indicate that this performance derives from forecasting security prices rather than timing the market. The results from Treynor and Mazuy (1966) are robust to the time period studied and the test used. Henriksson (1984) used the market timing measure of Henriksson and Merton (1981) to show only 3 funds out of 116 exhibited significant positive market timing between 1968 and 1980. Similarly, Graham and Harvey (1996) used the suggested allocations between cash and equity from 326 distinct funds' investment newsletters and found no significant evidence of timing ability over the period 1983 to 1995.

A more recent development involves increasing the frequency of the data used in the tests. Goetzmann et al. (2000) explain that monthly data may not capture market timing ability because decisions on market exposure are likely made over shorter horizons for many funds. Bollen and Busse (2001) show that the use of daily data reveals that more funds exhibit timing ability, raising concerns about the aforementioned papers' market timing results, all of which used monthly (or annual) data.

Another issue for the research on market timing is that the estimation techniques did not allow for variation in mutual funds' risks and risk premia. Jensen et al. (1972) recognized this and examined changes to intercept and slope parameters over several different sub-periods. Such studies, including Grant (1977), interpreted any changes in parameter estimates as reflecting superior information or market timing ability. Ferson and Schadt (1996) question this assessment; they argue that alpha pertaining to an active portfolio strategy that can be replicated using readily available public information should not be interpreted as superior performance. By incorporating conditional models into the analysis of mutual fund performance and timing ability for 67 mutual funds between 1968 and 1990, Ferson and Schadt (1996) find that the perverse market timing evidence was removed and the average abnormal performance became centered around zero rather than negative.

With respect to Japanese mutual fund performance, Cai et al. (1997) show that Jensen's alpha results are not sensitive to the use of conditional factor models (or to the choice of benchmark). Their results show that funds' alpha remained negative and significant in all cases over the period 1981–1992. Whilst this underperformance of the average active manager supports the equilibrium accounting discussed in Fama and French (2010), which in turn is based on Sharpe (1991), some evidence does exist of outperformance. Otten and Bams (2002) use both conditional and unconditional four-factor models to assess the net returns of 506 mutual funds from the five largest European countries covering 85% of European mutual fund assets. They find evidence of outperformance in their survivorship bias free study in four of the countries namely, France, the UK, Netherlands, and Italy and a negative alpha only in the case of Germany.

More recently, Fama and French (2010) and Kosowski et al. (2006) have raised concerns that all inferences arising from the significance of parameter estimates rely on the assumption of normality. With many return profiles failing the normality assumption, a bootstrapping methodology has been developed to assess whether skilled funds exist without identifying the particular funds. This ensures an ex-ante distribution is not imposed on the returns distribution. A further development has been to allow parameter estimates to change over time; by incorporating such changes in the Fama and French (2010) bootstrap methodology. Ercolani et al. (2018) find substantial evidence of time variation in US mutual funds' parameter estimates and their results reveal little evidence of performance differing from the benchmark.

Some researchers have highlighted the need to be cautious when using test statistics, simulated or otherwise. Cuthbertson et al. (2012) analyze the false discovery rate (FDR) of UK funds based upon the significance of alpha. They find that a large percentage of the outperforming funds delivered significant performance by chance. By correcting for so-called 'false positives' their method provides another way to assess the mutual fund industry as a whole.

An additional assessment of active management incorporates the persistence of funds' abnormal returns relative to their peers; if there is low persistence then abnormal returns are likely driven by luck than skill. Whilst the majority of evidence shows past relative performance is a poor predictor of future fund performance, Carhart (1997) found evidence of return persistence in US mutual funds. In light of the general poor predictability of returns, many academics have concluded this supports market efficiency, see for example, Malkiel (1995). That many investors continue using active management, when skill appears to be scarce and unpredictable, remains largely unexplained. One possible set of explanations relies upon behavioral issues of investors outlined by Kahneman and Riepe (1998) and Cuthbertson et al. (2016).

### 3. The Data

The fund returns in this paper are derived from the monthly adjusted-close prices (in US dollars) between April 2011 and April 2016 on Japanese Mutual Funds from the DataStream mutual fund database. The use of adjusted-close prices ensures the returns include management fees and trading costs, and the returns account for splits and/or mergers of funds across our sample period. Hence, we are able to directly determine if managers' skill is sufficient to outperform the stated benchmark without having taken into account the impact of each fund's fee structures on performance relative to the benchmark—Fama and French (2010) point out that trading cost estimates may be subject to large errors owing to the time variation in costs.

The data is restricted to those funds that are based in Japan and invest primarily in Japanese equity markets.[6] To ensure we focus on active funds whose objective it is to outperform the Japanese equity market, tracker funds are removed from our study. Failing to remove these funds would skew our results towards not finding significant outperformance.[7]

One of the issues with the DataStream database is survivorship bias; funds that cease to exist during the sample period are not included in the dataset. To ensure this paper's results are not distorted by funds with small returns histories, all funds contained in the dataset are alive for the entire sample period of 61 months. This left us with 355 funds to analyze[8].

The four-factor capital asset pricing model (CAPM) is used as the benchmark because including Fama and French (1993) size and book-to-market, along with Carhart (1997) momentum factors have been shown to capture a large fraction of Sharpe's (1964) single-factor CAPM anomalies. Using a four-factor model ensures fund performance does not arise from fund managers exploiting these well-known anomalies.[9] The monthly returns (in US dollars) on this benchmark are constructed from the Japanese data on Kenneth French's online factor library; details of which can be found on the factor library website.

For those concerned that tests of performance are sensitive to the chosen benchmark, as found in papers such as Grinblatt and Titman (1992), it should be noted that Cai et al. (1997) results on Japanese mutual fund performance were robust to the choice of benchmark.

---

6 Datastream defines equity funds as those with more than 50% of its assets invested in equities.

7 To remove such funds, names including "Index", "IDX", "ETF", "tracker fund" and any other permutations are highlighted. A search of these funds' objectives was run to verify their omission from the dataset.

8 Another possible issue is incubation bias, which arises from how funds may be "created" prior to opening a fund for public investment. The funds with the best returns are the ones most likely to be made available to the public. Despite the returns profile seeming impressive compared to a benchmark, there is a good chance that the performance arose from luck rather than skill. As Fama and French (2010) find only trivial effects of incubation bias and recent papers such as Barras et al. (2010) and Cuthbertson et al. (2008) make no particular adjustment for it we do not make an adjustment either.

9 As Bollen and Busse (2001) point out, an alternative method to deal with the issue of benchmark efficiency would be to use the stochastic discount factors as in Chen and Knez (1996); Dahlquist and Söderlind (1999); and Farnsworth et al. (2002). We leave it to future research to determine if using this alternative method leads to a material difference in the results.

## 4. The Equal Weight Portfolio

The first measure to assess the performance of Japanese mutual funds relative to the four-factor benchmark is the equal weight (EW) portfolio. The EW portfolio returns are calculated by averaging the 355 fund returns in each month and subtracting the corresponding one-month US T-bill rate.[10] This yields the average fund return in excess of the (US) risk free rate in each month, *t*.

The following time series regression was run:

$$R_t = \alpha + b(R_{Mt} - R_{ft}) + s(SMB_t) + h(HML_t) + m(MOM_t) + \varepsilon_t$$

In each month, *t*, $R_t$ is the EW average excess return; $R_{Mt}$ - $R_{ft}$ is the excess market return; and $SMB_t$ and $HML_t$ are the Japanese size and value factors, respectively, calculated from Fama and French (1993). $MOM_t$ is the Japanese momentum factor from Carhart (1997). Finally, $\alpha$ is the average fund return that is left unexplained by the benchmark model. $\varepsilon_t$ is the regression residual. The alpha or intercept in the above regression is assumed to be constant which is consistent with the model of manager skill developed by Berk and Green (2004).

An explanation of the three factors we use in our regression is as follows: Small minus big (SMB)—this factor is also referred to as the "small firm effect," or the "size effect," where size is based on a company's market capitalization. In other words, if a portfolio has more small-cap companies in it, it should outperform the market over the long run. High minus low (HML)—'high' refers to companies with a high book value to market value ratio while 'low' refers to companies with a low book value to market value ratio. This factor is also referred to as the "value factor" or the "value versus growth factor" because companies with a high book to market ratio are typically considered value while companies with a low market to book value are typically growth stocks. Research has shown that value stocks tend to outperform growth stocks in the long run. So, over the long run, a portfolio with a large proportion of value stocks should outperform one with a large proportion of growth stocks. Momentum (MOM)—refers to funds with strong past performance continue to outperform funds with poor past performance in the next period. It is calculated by taking the average return on the two high prior return portfolios minus the average return on the two low prior return portfolios when the portfolios have been divided up into 6 portfolios based upon prior 12 month returns.

Following other papers assessing Japanese mutual fund performance, such as Cai et al. (1997), it is expected that the b coefficient will be positive; investors are rewarded for the non-diversifiable systematic risk they hold. Research into the interaction between momentum and value in Japan by Asness (2011) and Fama and French (2012) suggests that *m* will be negative and *h* will be positive; historically momentum has not been rewarded in Japan and there exists an historical negative correlation between momentum and value. It is also expected that *s* will be negative given that Fama and French (2010) find the value premia in average stock returns increase with size in Japan. If these results should materialize, it indicates that the average fund excess return is positively driven by the market and value premia but is negatively influenced by the momentum anomaly and the size factor. This outcome could suggest there were more managers employing value and reversal strategies, along with those strategies based on market risk premia, and that fund managers tended to invest in large companies compared to smaller ones.

There is debate over whether the average SMB, HML, and MOM returns at each time period exist as rewards for risk or mispricing, we do not take a view on this matter. As in Fama and French (2010), the interpretation of the four-factor returns included on the right-hand side of the regression is that they represent returns from diversified portfolios that capture the patterns of average returns between April 2011 and April 2016.

---

[10] The monthly US T-bill rate is also taken from Kenneth French's factor library.

To determine good or bad performance this paper invokes Dybvig and Ross (1985) analysis. Theorem 5 in their paper states that if $\alpha$ is positive (negative), a portfolio that places a positive (negative) weight on the benchmark portfolio of funds along with a positive weight on the passive benchmark portfolios will generate returns with a higher Sharpe ratio than simply having a positive weighting on the portfolios of benchmark returns. Since the Sharpe ratio discounts excess returns by the non-diversifiable risk taken by an investor in achieving those excess returns, $\alpha$ therefore indicates if the equal weight portfolio, on average, produces risk-adjusted returns different from what would be expected by simply having exposure to the benchmark portfolios. Table 1 reports the results over the entire sample period; the constant term refers to $\alpha$.

**Table 1.** Summary statistics for equal weight regression.

| | $R_M$-$R_f$ | *SMB* | *HML* | *MOM* | *Constant* |
|---|---|---|---|---|---|
| Coefficient | 0.5936 | 0.2646 | −0.4059 | −0.2910 | −0.0028 |
| t-statistic | 8.55 | 2.18 | −2.77 | −3.08 | −1.12 |
| Adjusted R-squared | 0.5418 | | | | |
| F-test statistic | 18.74 | | | | |

Of the four-factors in the benchmark model, all are significant at the 5% level,[11] with the market excess return factor being especially significant with a *t*-statistic of 8.55. All the factor coefficients have the expected sign, indicating that the average excess returns are driven as in other papers. The fact the F-test statistic is significant at all levels indicates that the four-factor model is reasonable at describing the average excess fund returns in our sample period.

The negative alpha indicates that the EW portfolio has delivered average monthly excess returns below what was obtained from the benchmark portfolios. As the corresponding *t*-statistic is not significant, the performance of the EW portfolio did not differ significantly from the four-factor model in the sample. This result is similar to that of Cai et al. (1997); their EW regressions always delivered a negative alpha, although the estimated alphas in their paper were always significant and the adjusted $R^2$ reported for their EW regressions between 1981 and 1992 were higher. The similarities in the results suggests that the average fund performance still delivered monthly returns below what could be achieved from the benchmark portfolios. The difference in significance on the alphas may suggest that the portfolio of funds became slightly better in delivering average excess returns, which were not statistically different from the benchmark.

## 5. Jensen's Alpha Measure

As outlined by Jensen (1968), the setup is very similar to the EW portfolio. For each fund $i$, the following regression is run over the entire 61 months, correcting the residuals for the observed heteroskedasticity[12]

$$R_{it} = \alpha_i + b_i(R_{Mt} - R_{ft}) + s_i(SMB_t) + h_i(HML_t) + m_i(MOM_t) + \varepsilon_{it}$$

$R_{it}$ is the excess return for fund $i$ at time $t$. The factors remain the same as in the EW portfolio regression; the subscripts on the parameter estimates reflect the 355 sets of estimates that are obtained. Since Jensen's alpha assesses each fund separately, the interpretation of $\alpha$ becomes whether fund managers have an ability to forecast security prices. Of the 355 estimates for alpha, 53 are positive and 302 are negative. Table 2 below shows the distribution of these alphas, along with how many alpha estimates are significant for each range of alpha estimates.

---

11 The 5% level is based on conducting five separate two-tail tests on whether each coefficient is equal to zero.

12 Calculating robust standard errors is necessary since 23 of 355 funds' residuals exhibit heteroskedasticity at the 5% level across the entire sample period. These results come from undertaking a Breusch-Pagan test for heteroskedasticity.

**Table 2.** Distribution of Jensen's alpha estimates across 355 funds between April 2011 and April 2016.

| Estimated Alpha | Frequency | Number of Significant Alpha Estimates by Category |
|---|---|---|
| $\alpha \leq -0.024$ | 0 | 0 |
| $-0.024 < \alpha \leq -0.022$ | 1 | 1 |
| $-0.022 < \alpha \leq -0.020$ | 1 | 1 |
| $-0.020 < \alpha \leq -0.018$ | 1 | 1 |
| $-0.018 < \alpha \leq -0.016$ | 3 | 3 |
| $-0.016 < \alpha \leq -0.014$ | 6 | 4 |
| $-0.014 < \alpha \leq -0.012$ | 10 | 7 |
| $-0.012 < \alpha \leq -0.010$ | 6 | 4 |
| $-0.010 < \alpha \leq -0.08$ | 8 | 2 |
| $-0.08 < \alpha \leq -0.06$ | 19 | 2 |
| $-0.06 < \alpha \leq -0.04$ | 34 | 2 |
| $-0.04 < \alpha \leq -0.02$ | 117 | 0 |
| $-0.02 < \alpha \leq 0.00$ | 96 | 0 |
| $0.00 < \alpha \leq 0.02$ | 35 | 0 |
| $0.02 < \alpha \leq 0.04$ | 12 | 0 |
| $\alpha > 0.04$ | 6 | 0 |
| **Total** | **355** | **27** |

This indicates that funds were more likely to deliver negative than a positive alpha in monthly returns. To ascertain if these alphas differ significantly from the returns offered by the benchmark portfolios, we turn to the heteroskedastic-adjusted *t*-statistics on the 355 alpha estimates.

Only 27 funds' alphas are significant at the 5% level and all of these funds have negative alpha estimates.[13] 328 alpha estimates (and all of the positive abnormal performance) are not statistically different from zero, meaning the returns from these funds are very similar to the returns from the diversified portfolio. Our results show that there is strong evidence that funds were more likely to underperform the benchmark model than to beat it.

The asymmetry in the fund alpha supports the results from the EW section; the non-significant alpha estimate for EW portfolio manifests itself in the non-significant alpha of many individual fund alphas. The added insight from the Jensen's alpha measure is that statistically significant fund returns correspond entirely to underperformance of the benchmark model.

For an investor contemplating using active mutual funds the results are worrisome; any positive abnormal performance relative to the benchmark model is not discernable from luck whereas there appears to be evidence of statistically significant bad skill. This outcome arises even with the presence of survivorship bias, where the results are likely to be skewed in favor of finding funds that outperform the benchmark. Given previous papers such as Carhart (1997) have found that US mutual funds with poor past performance are more likely to perish or remain poorly performing funds than successful funds are likely to remain successful, the above results arguably represent an upper-bound for managers' true skill.[14]

The results are even worse from a practical perspective because active fund managers charge higher fees than passive alternatives. Given the inability of funds to generate significant outperformance in a manner conducive to the presence of skill in forecasting security prices, there is little evidence from this dataset to support paying higher fees in order to beat the benchmark model. Paying such fees appears to be accepting performance that is mainly very similar to the benchmark model, or significantly underperforms the benchmark.

---

[13] The 5% significance is based on undertaking a two-tail test of a particular fund's alpha being different from zero against the null hypothesis that alpha for the same fund is zero.

[14] This assumes the forces driving the dynamic found in Carhart (1997) apply to Japanese funds, or that the funds excluded from the analysis were more likely to have performed poorly than been successful over the sample period.

## 6. Treynor and Mazuy Measure for Market Timing

The method we use to test for market timing is based upon the Treynor and Mazuy (1966) paper.[15] In their paper, the following regression was used

$$r_{p,t} = \alpha_p + \beta_p r_{m,t} + \gamma_p r_{m,t}^2 + \varepsilon_{p,t}$$

At time $t$, $r_{p,t}$ is the excess return on the portfolio, $r_{m,t}$ is the excess return on the market and $\gamma_p$ measures timing ability. If managers have timing ability, we would expect $\gamma_p$ to be positive and for the portfolio's return to be a convex function of the market's return. The change in this paper, as performed by Bollen and Busse (2001), is to include the four-factor model in the setup so as to not reward managers for exploiting well-known anomalous returns. Hence, the regression becomes

$$r_{p,t} = \alpha_p + \sum_{i=1}^{4} \beta_{p,i} r_{i,t} + \gamma_p r_{m,t}^2 + \varepsilon_{p,t}$$

Each portfolio, $p$, describes a particular fund's returns. The betas in the summation term are the four-factors in the benchmark model, with the corresponding returns to these factors being given by the $r_{i,t}$. As in the Jensen's alpha section, the regression for each fund is run over the entire 61 months and corrects for the observed heteroskedasticity in the residuals. Of the 355 gamma estimates, 259 are negative and 96 are positive. Table 3 shows the distribution of these estimates.

**Table 3.** Distribution of market timing ability for each of the 355 funds between April 2011 and April 2016.

| Estimated Gamma $\gamma$ | Frequency of Gamma | Number of Significant Gamma Estimates |
|---|---|---|
| $-8 \leq \gamma$ | 2 | 2 |
| $-8 < \gamma \leq -7$ | 8 | 7 |
| $-7 < \gamma \leq -6$ | 5 | 4 |
| $-6 < \gamma \leq -5$ | 8 | 6 |
| $-5 < \gamma \leq -4$ | 12 | 7 |
| $-4 < \gamma \leq -3$ | 11 | 2 |
| $-3 < \gamma \leq -2$ | 40 | 1 |
| $-2 < \gamma \leq -1$ | 104 | 2 |
| $-1 < \gamma \leq 0$ | 69 | 0 |
| $0 < \gamma \leq 1$ | 38 | 0 |
| $1 < \gamma \leq 2$ | 21 | 5 |
| $2 < \gamma \leq 3$ | 34 | 26 |
| $3 < \gamma \leq 4$ | 1 | 1 |
| $\gamma > 4$ | 2 | 0 |
| **Total** | **355** | **63** |

The results indicate that 73.2% of the funds exhibit no market timing ability; the remaining 26.8% of funds show some timing ability.[16] The heteroskedastic-adjusted $t$-statistics show that 31 of the 259 negative gamma estimates are significant whereas 32 of the 96 positive gamma estimates are significant both at the 5% significance level.[17] As a result, any significant market-timing ability is as likely to be good as it is bad.

15 Another approach to market timing is the study of Jagannathan and Korajczyk (1986).

16 These percentages are calculated as follows (2 + 8 + 5 + 8 + 12 + 11 + 40 + 104 + 69)/355 and (38 + 21 + 34 + 1 + 2)/355 from Table 3.

17 The two-tail test carried out is based on the null hypothesis that a particular fund's gamma equals zero against the alternative hypothesis that the same fund's gamma differs from zero.

It is perhaps unsurprising that many mutual fund returns exhibit no significant timing ability. Bollen and Busse (2001) point out that mutual fund managers can often be constrained by the investment objectives of the fund and are also restricted in their use of leverage and derivatives by regulators.

In addition, the momentum factor returns being included within the benchmark may be a driving force behind many funds failing to exhibit timing ability. Intuitively, market timing is similar to a momentum strategy because timing involves buying the market portfolio when market returns increase; the momentum factor returns involves buying stocks whose price has increased recently. Given the significance of the momentum factor in explaining the cross-sectional fund returns, it is reasonable to suppose that our method underestimates the true market timing ability of fund managers because much of this ability is encapsulated by the momentum factor returns.

Exacerbating this issue is the use of monthly data in returns. Goetzmann et al. (2000) explain that monthly frequency may fail to capture a manager's timing abilities because timing decisions are likely made on a much more frequent basis.[18] Given that Bollen and Busse (2001) found the power of timing tests to be higher for daily data than monthly data, our results likely provide a lower bound for the number of managers with true timing ability. Such a lower bound in timing ability makes the bad-skill in security selection more worrying; if more managers have timing ability yet the stock picking assessment is robust to data frequency, there is likely to be more fund managers who can identify market trends but fail to select securities to deliver significant positive returns thereafter. To illustrate this point, only 6 of the 33 funds with a positive, significant gamma estimate have a positive Jensen's alpha estimate. The other 27 funds have negative alpha estimates and none of these alphas is significant at the 5% level. This suggests that investors should be wary of paying active managers for market timing ability because this ability is unlikely to be transmitted through higher abnormal returns.

Our results also indicate that negative timing ability is associated with poor stock picking ability; only 10 of the 31 funds that possess significant negative timing ability (referred to as bad skill) have a positive (but not significant) alpha. The remaining 21 funds delivered negative alpha, with only one alpha estimate being significant at the 5% level. Consequently, bad skill appears to be transferable, which suggests investors should have been cautious of thinking active managers could overcome bad market timing ability with good stock picking skill.

One potential explanation for the above dynamic is that some managers were too confident in their ability to select securities based on forecasting prices (even when there is no evidence of significant skill) and as such they were reluctant to change their investments as market trends evolved, resulting in significant negative timing ability. Another possible interpretation is that of Braun et al. (2012) who, in the context of open-end life settlement funds, argue that it is possible that fund managers are only interested in collecting fees and not really in the fund's long-term performance, this is especially the case when fees are paid upfront and there can be penalties for early redemption

## 7. Testing for Normality

We use the Shapiro and Wilk (1965) test to carry out a test of normality. Whilst alternative tests are available, such as the Anderson and Darling (1952); Lilliefors (1967); and Kolmogorov–Smirnov (Massey 1951) tests, it has been shown via Monte Carlo simulation that the Shapiro–Wilk test has the highest power for a given significance level, see Razali and Wah (2011). Using the following hypotheses:

Hypothesis H0: The distribution is normal.

Hypothesis H1: The distribution is not normal.

---

18 For those concerned of a frequency issue in the results from the Jensen's alpha section, standard tests relating to selection ability are theoretically robust to observation frequency because the estimate is more a function of sample length. See Goetzmann et al. (2000) for more details.

A regression is carried out of each fund on the benchmark four-factor model over the 61 months, calculating robust residuals in each case. Each funds' residuals are saved and ordered from smallest to largest. The test statistic is given by

$$W = \frac{\left(\sum_{i-1}^{61} a_i x_{(i)}\right)^2}{\sum_{i-1}^{61} (x_i - \overline{x})^2}$$

where $x_i$ is the saved residual for a particular fund in a month and $x_{(i)}$ is the $i$th order statistic

$$a' = (a_1, \ldots, a_{61}) = m'V^{-1} / (m'V^{-1}V^{-1}m)^{1/2}$$

where $m' = (m_1, \ldots, m_{61})$ is the expected values of the residuals, assuming they have been sampled from a standard normal distribution, and $V$ is the variance–covariance matrix of the saved residuals (i.e., the observed residuals not the expected value of the residuals). As there are 61 months of data for each fund, and Shapiro–Wilk's 1965 test is valid up to 50 observations (months), the Royston (1982) adjustment has been used. This ensures $W$ is equal to the squared correlation coefficient and lies between 0 and 1.

The results from this test are omitted for conciseness but in 33 of the 355 test statistics are critical at the 5% level. Given 9.2% of the funds in the dataset exhibit non-normally distributed residuals, the analysis based on the significance of $t$-statistics has the potential to be misleading. The attention of this paper now turns to analyzing fund performance without imposing the ex-ante assumption of normality onto our regression.

### 8. The Fama and French (2010) Bootstrap

In the Fama and French (2010) bootstrap, the objective is to draw inferences from the cross-section of true alpha for active funds. The focus is particularly on whether the cross-section of actual alpha estimates differs sufficiently from the corresponding cross-section of a hypothetical world with no skill. For the purposes of extreme performance relative to the four-factor benchmark, the tails of the distribution are important for determining if managers have skill (or bad skill) when it comes to beating the benchmark model.

To have something with which to compare the bootstrap, for each fund $i$, the following regression is run over the entire 61 months

$$R_{it} = \alpha_i + b_i(R_{Mt} - R_{ft}) + s_i(SMB_t) + h_i(HML_t) + m_i(MOM_t) + \varepsilon_{it}$$

The components of the regression are identical to those of the 355 Jensen's alpha regressions. The 355 sets of parameter and residual estimates are saved for each fund. The $t$-statistics on the alphas—referred to as '$t$-alpha' are also saved to ensure we have a distribution of the "true" precision-adjusted abnormal performance of funds.

To create the hypothetical world without managerial fund skill, each fund's estimated alpha is subtracted from the corresponding fund's observed excess returns in all 61 months. This gives the benchmark-adjusted fund return across all 355 funds and the results are saved in a 61 by 355 matrix (in row 1 will be the adjusted returns for month 1 for fund $i$ in column j). If we add to this matrix four columns corresponding to the four-factor returns for each of the 61 months, it is possible to run the 10,000 simulations.

Each simulation involves sampling (with replacement) 61 months across the 61 months in the dataset. Each fund's benchmark-adjusted returns are then regressed on the corresponding month's four-factor returns; the resampling method ensures that the four-factor returns correspond to the same sequence of months as for the funds. This gives 355 estimates of $t$-alpha per simulation.

This method of resampling has an important advantage. Indeed, Fama and French (2010) point out that because each simulation run is the same random sample of months for all funds, the simulations capture the cross-correlation of fund returns and its effects on the distribution of $t$-alpha. Since the method also jointly samples fund returns and explanatory returns, any correlated heteroskedasticity of the four-factor returns and disturbances of the benchmark model are captured.[19]

The results from the 10,000 simulation runs are given in Table 4. The actual column represents the distribution of $t$-alpha from the initial 355 regressions in this section. The Sim column gives the average value of $t$-alpha at selected percentiles from across the entire simulations. The Percent < Actual column shows the percent of simulation runs that delivered $t$-alpha less than the actual $t$-alpha for a given percentile.

Table 4 makes grim reading from an active management perspective; evidence of active funds beating the four-factor benchmark model requires a relatively small proportion of simulation runs delivering $t$-alpha more than the actual $t$-alpha. Given only 14% of simulated $t$-alpha are less than actual $t$-alpha at the 99% percentile, there is strong evidence that active managers did exhibit much skill in beating the returns of the benchmark model.

Making this result even more emphatic is some oversampling of fund returns owing to all the funds being alive for 8 or more months (a restriction imposed by Fama and French in their 2010 paper). Hence, the $t$-alpha distribution from the simulation runs tends to have more degrees of freedom and thinner tails than the estimates for actual fund returns; even when we are more likely to find evidence of outperformance by funds compared to a world with no skill, the results contradict this overwhelmingly.

On the negative fund performance, active funds appeared to do significantly better; over half of the simulation runs delivered $t$-alpha less than actual counterparts at the 1% level. Whilst this may be due to active managers being proficient at not underperforming the benchmark model, survivorship bias may play a role in distorting the results; funds with highly significant negative $t$-alpha may be more likely to perish than other funds. Future research may look to apply the bootstrap to a dataset free of survivorship bias.

Our results suggest that funds were relatively successful at not achieving extremely poor results but were also rather bad at delivering extremely good performance. This somewhat supports the lack of significance in the majority of the Jensen's alpha estimates; active management failed resoundingly to deliver significantly positive alpha regardless of whether we impose the normality restriction in the regressions.

Fama and French (2010) provide some further drawbacks to this bootstrap method. First, randomly sampling months means the effects of serial autocorrelation are lost, although following on from the research into autocorrelation in US stock returns by Fama (1965), it is suggested this is a minor issue. Additionally, any effects of time variation of parameter estimates are lost by randomly sampling months. Ercolani et al. (2018) have implemented the bootstrapping methodology whilst allowing for time varying parameters. It is left to future research to extend their analysis of US mutual funds to Japanese Mutual Funds.[20]

---

19 It is for this reason that the initial regressions in this section did not correct for the heteroscedasticity.

20 As outlined in the 2018 paper, previous research has found parameter estimates change over five-year cycles. Hence, to extend this analysis, future research may have to extend the returns history of this dataset.

**Table 4.** Comparison of the actual and simulated $t$-alpha for Japanese Mutual Funds using the $t$-alpha Fama and French (2010) bootstrap method.

| Percentage | Simulated | Actual | Percent < Actual |
|---|---|---|---|
| 1% | −4.8246 | −4.4872 | 53% |
| 2% | −4.1366 | −3.8401 | 54% |
| 3% | −3.5866 | −3.1627 | 66% |
| 4% | −3.2047 | −2.4852 | 81% |
| 5% | −2.9171 | −2.2832 | 85% |
| 6% | −2.6953 | −2.1936 | 77% |
| 7% | −2.5401 | −2.0443 | 77% |
| 8% | −2.4016 | −1.7890 | 82% |
| 9% | −2.2734 | −1.7021 | 82% |
| 10% | −2.1739 | −1.6254 | 78% |
| 20% | −1.5219 | −1.0662 | 73% |
| 30% | −1.1299 | −0.7645 | 68% |
| 40% | −0.8356 | −0.6476 | 58% |
| 50% | −0.5803 | −0.5149 | 51% |
| 60% | −0.3414 | −0.4217 | 46% |
| 70% | −0.0826 | −0.2249 | 47% |
| 80% | 0.2335 | −0.0242 | 37% |
| 90% | 0.7003 | 0.2688 | 24% |
| 91% | 0.7596 | 0.3235 | 22% |
| 92% | 0.8296 | 0.3627 | 21% |
| 93% | 0.9023 | 0.4546 | 24% |
| 94% | 0.9839 | 0.5468 | 26% |
| 95% | 1.0726 | 0.6307 | 24.% |
| 96% | 1.2024 | 0.7389 | 23% |
| 97% | 1.3614 | 0.8488 | 21% |
| 98% | 1.5688 | 0.9300 | 15% |
| 99% | 1.8594 | 1.1557 | 14% |

An alternative issue for further research would be to use Kosowski et al. (2006) bootstrap technique to determine if there are any changes to the inferences; their paper finds more evidence of fund manager skill than Fama and French (2010). The technique involves running independent simulations for each fund, which has the benefit of ensuring the number of months a fund is in the simulation exactly matches the number of months of returns for that fund.

## 9. Persistence in Relative Skill

The method for identifying the persistence of skill is as follows: for a one year formation period a regression is run of each fund's excess returns on the four-factor model to estimate the particular fund's alpha for a given year. Each fund alpha is then ranked relative to the alphas of other funds for the corresponding year; this yields five distinct rankings, one for each year. The persistence is then calculated as the percentage of the top (bottom) 30 performing funds that remain in the top (bottom) 30 over the following few years. The percentages for each year after the formation period are averaged over the number of available portfolios; a one-year formation period for year 3 would only have two years of data after the formation period. The results are given Table 5.

Table 5 indicates that a poorly performing fund was more likely to remain a poorly performing fund, relative to its peers, than a good performing fund was to remain successful. This is not surprising in light of research into US mutual funds; Carhart (1997) find that the probability of a loser remaining a loser was higher than the probability of a winner remaining a winner. In their study Busse et al. (2014) also find little evidence of persistence in performance covering 27 countries. Our results suggest an asymmetry in the persistence of relative skill, even in the presence of survivorship bias.

**Table 5.** Persistence in the extreme 60 Japanese mutual funds, according to each fund's alpha over rolling one-year formation periods

| | Years after Formation Period | | | |
|---|---|---|---|---|
| | **Year 1** | **Year 2** | **Year 3** | **Year 4** |
| Percentage that remain in top 30 | 8.33% | 13.33% | 10.00% | 3.33% |
| Percentage that remain in bottom 30 | 18.33% | 31.67% | 45.00% | 23.33% |

Combined with the fact the persistence in the top 30 funds is rather small, the results suggest it is difficult for an investor to isolate skilled funds by ranking them based on prior abnormal performance. This fits in with the previous sections; if there had been strong abnormal return persistence, we would have expected it to show up in the significance of alpha or the Fama and French (2010) bootstrap. To further highlight this point, Table 6 shows the reversal in relative abnormal performance; after each formation period, the percentage of top (bottom) 30 funds who become bottom (top) 30 funds is calculated.

**Table 6.** Reversal in the alpha of the extreme 60 Japanese mutual funds

| | Years after Formation Period | | | |
|---|---|---|---|---|
| | **Year 1** | **Year 2** | **Year 3** | **Year 4** |
| Percentage of top 30 that become bottom 30 | 16.67% | 10.00% | 3.33% | 16.67% |
| Percentage of bottom 30 that become top 30 | 21.67% | 6.67% | 10.00% | 3.33% |

Given the large reversal in fortunes for both the top and bottom 30 funds, there appears to be little evidence of skill persistence. One could argue this shows luck plays a significant role in determining fund performance relative to its peers. Alternatively, the relationship could suggest that active managers are poor at adapting to different investment landscapes. Should various investment styles work better at different times, and if there were sufficient differences in investment styles across funds, the reversal in funds' fortunes relative to their peers would be unsurprising.[21] The results could also illustrate that Japanese equity markets are extremely efficient, therefore it is extremely difficult to use active management to beat the benchmark in a significant way. The large degree of luck in generating abnormal returns is then illustrated by the low persistence (and some strong reversal) in extreme alpha rankings.

Alongside inferences of significant absolute benchmark underperformance from previous sections, the asymmetry in relative skill persistence made fund selection a difficult task for investors; skill was relatively scarce and extreme skill was more likely to remain bad than remain good. A large portion of luck therefore accompanied successful selection of ex-post successful funds by investors. In summary, the prevalence and persistence of active mutual funds' skill did not appear sufficient to justify using active management to outperform the benchmark when passive alternatives were available.

## 10. Conclusions

This paper has analyzed the skill of active managers in 355 Japanese mutual funds. Compared to the four-factor benchmark model, the results indicate that managers had little ability to outperform the benchmark in a significant manner. The average excess return was not statistically different from the benchmark.

---

21 It is left to further research to determine if funds fail to adapt their investment approach, such as through risk management, asset class selection and security selection, sufficiently in order to capture the reversal.

Even when managers had market timing ability, few were able to translate this skill into delivering significant positive abnormal returns to investors. These results are robust to the normality assumption since the bootstrap technique showed that only 14% of funds would have been expected to outperform a world with no manager skill. This suggests that any outperformance was largely luck-based rather than indicative of the average manager's investment approach. Allowing for parameter estimates to adjust over time would ensure this statement could be made with more certainty, especially in light of the differences uncovered in US mutual funds by Ercolani et al. (2018) compared to Fama and French (2010). The frequency of the data may be cause for concern in the market timing tests; monthly data will fail to capture managers updating their market exposure more regular than once a month. Hence, our results may have understated market timing ability. This is particularly the case given the returns to market timing may have been subsumed by the momentum factor returns in the benchmark model. However, since Jensen's alpha is robust to data frequency, investors may not concern themselves with this issue if managers with timing ability are unable to deliver statistically significant positive Jensen's alpha. Consequently, investors may want to better understand the skills their fees are rewarding, especially in light of our results indicating the transferability of bad skill between stock picking and market timing.

The results are somewhat contradictory regarding underperformance; the bootstrap method suggests active funds did considerably better at not underperforming than would be expected in a hypothetical no-skill world, whereas Jensen's alpha indicated significant performance is entirely negative. An issue with such a result is survivorship bias in the dataset; it seems likely that many of the funds were similar to the benchmark because it was these funds that were the best placed to survive over an extended period of time.

On the persistence side, our results show that there was an asymmetry in funds' relative success; poorly performing funds were more likely to remain poorly performing funds than successful funds were to remain successful. The persistence levels were also relatively low—under 50% for both types of funds across all years. Our overall results highlight the difficulty, historically, in using active mutual funds in Japan to beat the benchmark model. A possible avenue for future research is the approach employed by Pouliot (2016) using a $U$-statistic process to construct two statistics each devised to test different hypotheses regarding a one-time change in either the alpha or betas of the regression model. One statistic is devised to test jointly for a change in the intercept or slope while the second tests for a one-time change in slope that is robust to a change in the intercept.

**Author Contributions:** Conceptualization, K.P. and H.P.; methodology, K.P. and H.P.; formal analysis, K.P. and H.P.; writing—review and editing, K.P. and H.P.

**Funding:** This research received no external funding.

**Acknowledgments:** We are extremely grateful to the two referees for their extensive set of comments that led to significant improvements in the paper. The usual caveat applies.

**Disclaimer:** The views expressed in the paper are attributed entirely to the authors and do not necessarily reflect the views of the places at which they work.

**Conflicts of Interest:** The authors declare no conflict of interest.

## References

Anderson, Theodore W., and Donald A. Darling. 1952. Asymptotic Theory of Certain 'Goodness of Fit' Criteria Based on Stochastic Processes. *Annals of Mathematical Statistics* 23: 193–212. [CrossRef]

Asness, Clifford. 2011. Momentum in Japan: The Exception that Proves the Rule. *Journal of Portfolio Management* 3: 67–75. [CrossRef]

Barras, Laurent, Olivier Scaillet, and Russ Wermers. 2010. False Discoveries in Mutual Fund Performance: Measuring Luck in Estimated Alphas. *The Journal of Finance* 65: 179–216. [CrossRef]

Berk, Jonathan B., and Richard C. Green. 2004. Mutual Fund Flows in Rational Markets. *Journal of Political Economy* 112: 1269–95. [CrossRef]

Bollen, Nicolas P. B., and Jeffrey A. Busse. 2001. On the Timing Ability of Mutual Fund Managers. *The Journal of Finance* 56: 1075–94. [CrossRef]

Braun, Alexander, Nadine Gatzert, and Hato Schmeiser. 2012. Performance and Risks of Open-End Life Settlement Funds. *The Journal of Risk and Insurance* 79: 193–230. [CrossRef]

Busse, Jeffrey A., Amit Goyal, and Sunil Wahal. 2014. Investing in a Global World. *Review of Finance* 18: 561–90. [CrossRef]

Cai, Jun, Kalok C. Chan, and Takeshi Yamada. 1997. The Performance of Japanese Mutual Funds. *The Review of Financial Studies* 10: 237–74. [CrossRef]

Carhart, Mark M. 1997. On Persistence in Mutual Fund Performance. *The Journal of Finance* 52: 57–82. [CrossRef]

Chen, Zhiwu, and Peter J. Knez. 1996. Portfolio Performance Measurement: Theory and Applications. *The Review of Financial Studies* 9: 511–55. [CrossRef]

Chevalier, Judith, and Glenn Ellison. 1997. Risk Taking by Mutual Funds as a Response to Incentives. *Journal of Political Economy* 105: 1167–200. [CrossRef]

Cuthbertson, Keith, Dirk Nitzsche, and Niall O'Sullivan. 2016. A Review of Behavioural and Management Effects in Mutual Fund Performance. *International Review of Financial Analysis* 44: 162–76. [CrossRef]

Cuthbertson, Keith, Dirk Nitzsche, and Niall O'Sullivan. 2008. UK Mutual Fund Performance: Skill or Luck? *Journal of Empirical Finance* 15: 613–34. [CrossRef]

Cuthbertson, Keith, Dirk Nitzsche, and Niall O'Sullivan. 2012. False Discoveries in UK Mutual Fund Performance. *European Financial Management* 18: 444–63. [CrossRef]

Dahlquist, Magnus, and Paul Söderlind. 1999. Evaluating Portfolio Performance with Stochastic Discount Factors. *The Journal of Business* 72: 347–83. [CrossRef]

Dybvig, Philip H., and Stephen A. Ross. 1985. The Analytics of Performance Measurement Using a Security Market Line. *The Journal of Finance* 40: 401–16. [CrossRef]

Ercolani, Marco G., William Pouliot, and Joanne S. Ercolani. 2018. Luck Versus Skill Over Time: Time Varying Performance in the Cross-Section of Mutual Fund Returns. *Applied Economics* 50: 3686–701. [CrossRef]

Fama, Eugene F. 1965. The Behavior of Stock-Market Prices. *The Journal of Business* 38: 34–105. [CrossRef]

Fama, Eugene F., and Kenneth R. French. 1993. Common Risk Factors in the Returns on Stocks and Bonds. *Journal of Financial Economics* 33: 3–56. [CrossRef]

Fama, Eugene F., and Kenneth R. French. 2010. Luck Versus Skill in the Cross-Section of Mutual Fund Returns. *The Journal of Finance* 65: 1915–47. [CrossRef]

Fama, Eugene F., and Kenneth R. French. 2012. Size, Value, and Momentum in International Stock Returns. *Journal of Financial Economics* 105: 457–72. [CrossRef]

Farnsworth, Heber, Wayne E. Ferson, David Jackson, and Steven Todd. 2002. *Performance Evaluation with Stochastic Discount Factors.* NBER Working Paper No. 8791. Cambridge, MA, USA: National Bureau of Economic Research.

Ferson, Wayne E., and Rudi W. Schadt. 1996. Measuring Fund Strategy and Performance in Changing Economic Conditions. *The Journal of Finance* 51: 425–61. [CrossRef]

Goetzmann, William N., Jonathan Ingersoll Jr., and Zoran Ivković. 2000. Monthly Measurement of Daily Timers. *The Journal of Financial and Quantitative Analysis* 35: 257–90. [CrossRef]

Graham, John R., and Campbell R. Harvey. 1996. Market Timing Ability and Volatility Implied in Investment Newsletters' Asset Allocation Recommendations. *Journal of Financial Economics* 42: 397–421. [CrossRef]

Grant, Dwight. 1977. Portfolio Performance and the Cost of Timing Decisions. *The Journal of Finance* 32: 837–846.

Grinblatt, Mark, and Sheridan Titman. 1992. Performance Persistence in Mutual Funds. *The Journal of Finance* 47: 1977–84. [CrossRef]

Henriksson, Roy D. 1984. Market Timing and Mutual Fund Performance: An Empirical Investigation. *Journal of Business* 57: 73–96. [CrossRef]

Henriksson, Roy D., and Robert C. Merton. 1981. On Market Timing and Investment Performance. II. Statistical Procedures for Evaluating Forecasting Skills. *Journal of Business* 54: 513–33. [CrossRef]

Jagannathan, Ravi, and Robert A. Korajczyk. 1986. Assessing the Market Timing Performance of Managed Portfolios. *Journal of Business* 59: 217–35. [CrossRef]

Jensen, Michael C. 1968. The Performance of Mutual Funds in the Period 1945–1964. *The Journal of Finance* 23: 389–416. [CrossRef]

Jensen, Michael C., Fischer Black, and Myron S. Scholes. 1972. *The Capital Asset Pricing Model: Some Empirical Tests.* Studies in the Theory of Capital Markets. Santa Barbara: Praeger Publishers Inc.

Kahneman, Daniel, and Mark W. Riepe. 1998. Aspects of Investor Psychology. *The Journal of Portfolio Management* 24: 52–65. [CrossRef]

Kosowski, Robert, Allan Timmermann, Russ Wermers, and Hal White. 2006. Can Mutual Fund Stars Really Pick Stocks? New Evidence from a Bootstrap Analysis. *The Journal of Finance* 61: 2551–95. [CrossRef]

Lilliefors, Hubert W. 1967. On the Kolmogorov-Smirnov Test for Normality with Mean and Variance Unknown. *Journal of American Statistical Association* 62: 399–402. [CrossRef]

Malkiel, Burton G. 1995. Returns from Investing in Equity Mutual Funds 1971 to 1991. *The Journal of Finance* 50: 549–72. [CrossRef]

Massey, Frank J. 1951. The Kolmogorov-Smirnov Test for Goodness of Fit. *Journal of the American Statistical Association* 46: 68–78. [CrossRef]

Otten, Roger, and Dennis Bams. 2002. European Mutual Fund Performance. *European Financial Management* 8: 75–101. [CrossRef]

Pouliot, William. 2016. Robust Tests for Change in Intercept and Slope in Linear Regression Models with Application to Manager Performance in the Mutual Fund Industry. *Economic Modelling* 58: 523–34. [CrossRef]

Razali, Nornadiah Mohd, and Yap Bee Wah. 2011. Power Comparisons of Shapiro–Wilk, Kolmogorov-Smirnov, Lilliefors and Anderson-Darling Tests. *Journal of Statistical Modeling and Analytics* 2: 21–33.

Royston, J. Patrick. 1982. An Extension of Shapiro and Wilk's W Test for Normality to Large Samples. *Journal of the Royal Statistical Society. Series C (Applied Statistics)* 31: 115–24. [CrossRef]

Shapiro, Samuel Sanford, and Martin B. Wilk. 1965. An Analysis of Variance Test for Normality (Complete Samples). *Biometrika* 52: 591–611. [CrossRef]

Sharpe, William F. 1991. The Arithmetic of Active Management. *Financial Analysts Journal* 47: 7–9. [CrossRef]

Treynor, Jack L. 1965. How to Rate Management of Investment Funds. *Harvard Business Review* 43: 63–75.

Treynor, Jack, and Kay Mazuy. 1966. Can Mutual Funds Outguess the Market? *Harvard Business Review* 44: 131–36.

# 7

# The Turn of the Month Effect on CEE Stock Markets

**Peter Arendas * and Jana Kotlebova**

Department of Banking and International Finance, Faculty of National Economy, University of Economics in Bratislava, 852 35 Bratislava, Slovakia; jana.kotlebova@euba.sk

* Correspondence: peter.arendas@euba.sk

**Abstract:** The Turn of the month effect is one of the better-known calendar anomalies. If a stock market is affected by the Turn of the month effect, it records significantly higher returns during a relatively short time period around the end of the old month and the beginning of the new one, than during the remainder of the month. This paper investigates the presence of the Turn of the month effect in the stock markets of 11 Central and Eastern European (CEE) countries. We focused not only on the anomaly in returns, but also on the anomaly in price volatility. The results show that, during a 20-year period (1999–2018), a statistically significant Turn of the month effect was present in the stock markets of seven out of 11 investigated countries. However, the anomaly affected only the stock market returns, not price volatility.

**Keywords:** turn of the month effect; calendar anomaly; stock market; CEE; G01; G14; G15

---

## 1. Introduction

The Central and Eastern European (CEE) stock markets, with the exception of Turkey, are relatively young. They were established during the 1990s, after the collapse of the centrally planned economies and transition to market economy. Although they keep on evolving, they still face various issues. Especially, their liquidity tends to be lower in comparison to the developed stock markets of Western Europe and North America. In recent years, numerous authors paid attention to various issues that were related to the CEE stock markets as a group, or to some individual countries.

In this paper, we aim to extend the current state of knowledge regarding the CEE stock markets. More specifically, we focus on the investigation of presence of the Turn of the month effect on the stock markets of 11 CEE region countries.

The Turn of the month effect is one of the calendar anomalies that have been identified over the recent decades. Multiple studies confirm that various calendar anomalies can be found in stock (but also bond and commodity) markets around the world (Lakonishok and Smidt 1988; Milonas 1991; Giovanis 2009; Borowski 2015). According to Bouman and Jacobsen (2002), one of them, the Halloween effect, can be tracked back to the late 17th century. Although the strength of the calendar anomalies changes over time, several studies confirm that, in the long-term, they can be exploited to generate abnormal returns (Kunkel and Compton 1998; Andrade et al. 2013; Dichtl and Drobetz 2015).

The main feature of the Turn of the month effect is an uneven distribution of stock market returns during the month. More specifically, if the Turn of the month effect is present in a particular stock market, the majority of returns are concentrated in the turn of the month period, which can be defined as several days at the end of the old month and the beginning of the new one. Some studies even conclude that almost all of the positive stock market returns are concentrated in a short period of several days around the turn of the month (Lakonishok and Smidt 1988; McConnell and Xu 2008).

In this paper, we investigate the presence of the Turn of the month effect on stock markets of 11 CEE region countries, during the time period that spans from January 1999 to December 2018.

However, we focus not only on the presence of the Turn of the month effect in the stock market returns, but also on its presence in stock market volatilities. As the vast majority of studies focuses only on returns, we believe that the analysis of the relation of the Turn of the month effect and the stock market volatilities might be an important addition to the current state of knowledge. Moreover, the presence of the Turn of the month effect in the CEE region may confirm the lack of efficiency of these markets (as defined by Fama 1965), as the calendar anomalies can often be used in the investment process to generate abnormal returns.

## 2. Literature Review

The Turn of the month effect is one of the better known calendar anomalies that impact the stock markets, such as the Day of the week effect, the Halloween effect, the January effect, the Holiday effect, etc.

The Day of the Week effect was studied by Aggarwal and Schatzberg (1997), Philpot and Peterson (2011) or Brusa and Liu (2004). This calendar anomaly is based on the tendency of the stock market to record significantly better or worse returns during a particular day of the week. The returns usually tend to be higher on Fridays and lower on Mondays.

The Halloween effect is a calendar anomaly that assumes that the stock market returns tend to be significantly higher during the winter half of year (November–April) than during the summer half of year (May–October). Moreover, as this anomaly was first observed back in the 19th century, it is relatively easily exploitable in an investment strategy, and numerous authors paid attention to it. Authors, such as Bouman and Jacobsen (2002), Andrade et al. (2013), Arendas (2017), Arendas and Chovancova (2016), Arendas et al. (2018) or Burakov and Freidin (2018), Burakov et al. (2018) investigated the presence of the Halloween effect on stock, commodity, and bond markets.

The January effect is based on the premise that the stock market returns recorded during the month of January tend to be significantly higher than the stock market returns that were recorded over the other months. This calendar anomaly was investigated by numerous authors, for example by Wachtel (1942), Keim (1983), or Moller and Zilca (2008).

Additionally, the Holiday effect is one of the better known calendar anomalies. This anomaly is based on the observation that abnormally high stock market returns tend to be recorded during the last trading day before a holiday. Lakonishok and Smidt (1988) or Ariel (1990) investigated this anomaly.

The calendar anomalies are often investigated in relation to the Efficient markets theory, as formulated by Fama (1965). According to Fama, on an efficient market, the share price always reflects all of the important information, which means that the shares always trade at their fair value, thus investors cannot use technical analysis or market timing to beat the general market performance. The presence of a statistically significant calendar anomaly disrupts the "random walk" of stock prices and it can often be used to generate abnormal returns, which means that a market affected by a calendar anomaly cannot be regarded as efficient. Roberts (1967) introduced three forms of market efficiency: the weak form (the share prices reflect all historically known information), the semi-strong form (the share prices instantly reflect all publicly known information), and strong form (the share prices always reflect all, even yet unknown information). Lo (2004) later introduced the Adaptive markets hypothesis that assumes that the stock prices reflect as much information as dictated by the combination of environmental conditions and the number and nature of market participants.

Probably, the first author who paid attention to the Turn of the month effect was Ariel (1987). He came to a conclusion that, during the 1963–1981 period, on average, positive returns were only generated during the turn of the month period, while during the remainder of the month, the returns were close to zero.

Lakonishok and Smidt (1988), who investigated the Dow Jones Industrial Average returns over the 1897–1986 period, confirmed the findings of Ariel. They concluded that, during a four-day period consisting of the last trading day of the old month and first three trading days of the new month, the majority of all positive stock market returns was recorded.

Additionally, McConnell and Xu (2008) analyzed the Dow Jones Industrial Average returns, but over a longer time period, spanning from 1897 to 2015. They came to the conclusion that, on average, all of the positive returns were concentrated into a time period of the last trading day and first three trading days of a month.

While McConnell and Xu focused on the Dow Jones Industrial Average, Liu (2013) paid attention to another major U.S. stock index, S&P 500. He found out that, during the 2001–2011 time period, the stock prices had the tendency to bottom on the fifth or sixth trading day before the end of the month and to peak on the first or second trading day of the month. He also concluded that the Turn of the month effect is the strongest during the last four trading days of an old month and first two trading days of a new month.

Various authors also investigated the presence of the Turn of the month effect on other than U.S. stock markets. Cadsby and Ratner (1992) discovered a significant Turn of the month effect in Canada, the United Kingdom, Australia, Switzerland, and former West Germany. Agrawal and Tandon (1994) investigated stock markets of 18 different countries during the 1971–1987 period, concluding that, in six of them, more than 70% of the average monthly returns were generated during a five-day turn of the month period. Kunkel et al. (2003) investigated the 1988–2000 time period and confirmed the presence of the Turn of the month effect in 16 out of 19 investigated countries. They concluded that, on average, 87% of monthly returns were generated over a four-day turn of the month period. While, in the USA, they accounted for 66% of monthly returns, in Japan, it was 139% of monthly returns. They also concluded that the Turn of the month effect in various countries around the world is not only a spillover from the U.S. stock market.

From the more recent studies, Giovanis (2014) discovered the Turn of the month effect in 19 out of 20 investigated countries. Kayacetin and Lekpek (2016) confirmed the presence of a strong Turn of the month effect on the Turkish stock market during the 1988–2015 period. According to them, the average daily return was 0.46% during a period including the last trading day of an old month and first two trading days of a new month, and only 0.09% during the remaining days. Arendas and Bukoven (2017) identified the Turn of the month effect in the Czech stock market. Aziz and Ansari (2017) discovered the Turn of the month effect in 11 out of 12 stock markets of the Asia-Pacific region, during the 2000–2015 period. Caporale and Plastun (2017) investigated the presence of various calendar anomalies on the Ukrainian stock market; however, they have not discovered the presence of the Turn of the month effect. Chen et al. (2018) focused on the New Zealand stock market between 2001 and 2017. They discovered a significant Turn of the month effect; moreover, they concluded that it is not driven by company characteristics and that the dividend effect, price pressure, and window dressing are not satisfactory explanations for its existence.

The Turn of the month effect is a relatively well-documented calendar anomaly, yet, its origin is still unknown. Ogden (1990) was of the opinion that the Turn of the month effect is related by the standardization of payments, which leads to a notable increase of liquidity and stock returns at the end of every calendar month. This theory was further supplemented by Burnett (2017), who added a behavioral insight to Ogden's hypothesis. According to Burnett, the effect is stronger, especially when investors' confidence is at a high level. According to a theory that was presented by Nikkinen et al. (2009), who believed that the Turn of the month effect is related to the U.S. macroeconomic news, the majority of the news is announced during the time period around the turn of the month. This theory is slightly in line with Burnett's theory, as positive macroeconomic news should also lead to higher investors' confidence. A completely different standpoint was taken by Maher and Parikh (2013), who believed that the Turn of the month effect was initiated by the increased activity of institutional investors that occurs at the end of each month.

Although the origins of the Turn of the month effect are unknown, this calendar anomaly is strong enough to be used as a part of investment strategies. Kunkel and Compton (1998) developed an investment strategy that was based on investing in stocks during the turn of the month periods and investing in money market assets during the remainder of each month. On average, this strategy was able to outperform a passive "buy & hold" investment strategy by 2.1 percentage points per year. Vasileiou (2018) tested a similar strategy, where investor's funds were invested in the stock market during the turn of the month period and they were held on a bank account that provides no interest at all during the remainder of the month. Even in this case, the Turn of the month effect-based investment strategy was able to outperform the buy & hold investment strategy.

As can be seen, the majority of authors focus on the Turn of the month effect on developed stock markets. Although various authors paid attention to various aspects of the emerging stock markets, (the CEE region stock markets included) in recent years (Ferreira 2018; Horvath et al. 2018; Vychytilova 2018; Zaremba 2019, etc.), only little attention was paid to the investigation of presence of calendar anomalies on these stock markets. This paper aims to partially fill this gap and it focuses on the emerging stock markets of the Central and Eastern Europe (CEE). Moreover, it not only investigates whether the Turn of the month effect affects the stock market returns, but also the stock market volatility. As a result, the main aim of this paper is to investigate the presence of the Turn of the month effect in returns and volatility of the CEE stock markets.

## 3. Data and Methodology

In this paper, 11 CEE region stock markets are investigated for the presence of the Turn of the month effect. The stock markets are represented by the benchmark stock indices (Bulgaria—SOFIX, Czech Republic—PX, Estonia—OMXT, Hungary—BUX, Latvia—OMXR, Lithuania—OMXV, Poland—WIG 20, Romania—BET, Russia—RTS, Slovakia—SAX, and Turkey—XU 100). The data were provided by the Stooq database. The investigated time period includes 20 years from January 1999 to December 2018. However, in several cases, the investigated time periods are slightly shorter, as some of the stock indices were established later than in 1999. Table 1 displays the exact investigated time periods, as well as other basic descriptive statistics.

**Table 1.** Daily returns of analyzed stock indices—descriptive statistics.

| Stock Index | Investigated Time Period | Number of Observations | Minimum | Maximum | Average | Standard Deviation |
|---|---|---|---|---|---|---|
| BET | I.2001—XII.2018 | 4481 | −11.220803% | 15.692382% | 0.069648% | 1.513504% |
| BUX | I.1999—XII.2018 | 4995 | −11.881658% | 14.084531% | 0.048107% | 1.521051% |
| OMXR | I.2000—XII.2018 | 4784 | −13.675108% | 12.295415% | 0.055334% | 1.388776% |
| OMXT | I.2000—XII.2018 | 4792 | −6.803389% | 12.856257% | 0.049475% | 1.051448% |
| OMXV | I.2000—XII.2018 | 4768 | −11.252746% | 11.629430% | 0.043117% | 0.993942% |
| PX | I.1999—XII.2018 | 5018 | −14.943519% | 13.160903% | 0.027363% | 1.346030% |
| RTS | I.1999—XII.2018 | 5001 | −19.103064% | 22.389596% | 0.083270% | 2.250214% |
| SAX | I.1999—XII.2018 | 4884 | −13.765592% | 12.614764% | 0.033568% | 1.238184% |
| SOFIX | I.2002—XII.2018 | 4192 | −10.738496% | 7.564913% | 0.046038% | 1.230003% |
| WIG 20 | I.1999—XII.2018 | 5006 | −9.247392% | 8.496571% | 0.023472% | 1.506484% |
| XU 100 | I.1999—XII.2018 | 5005 | −18.109327% | 19.450967% | 0.095103% | 2.194097% |

The presence of the Turn of the month effect is investigated not only for the stock index returns, but also for the volatility of the stock indices. However, due to the lack of available data, the analysis of volatility is only performed in the case of BUX, RTS, WIG 20, and XU 100. The process of data analysis is based on the following steps:

1. The trading days are divided into two groups, depending on whether they belong to the turn of the month window (ToM) or to the rest of the month (RoM). The former authors investigated the Turn of the month effect while using different lengths of the turn of the month window. For

example, Ariel (1987) used a window consisting of the last trading day of an old month and first eight trading days of a new month, Lakonishok and Smidt (1988) and McConnell and Xu (2008) used the last trading day of an old month and the first three trading days of a new month, Liu (2013) used the last and the first four trading days, Kayacetin and Lekpek (2016) used the last two and first four trading days of each month, etc. We investigate three alternatives of the turn of the month window, which cover the last and the first trading days of a month evenly. The first one includes the first and the last trading day of each month (1+1), the second one includes the first two and the last two trading days of each month (2+2), and the third one includes the first three trading days and the last three trading days of each month (3+3).

2. The daily returns are calculated while using the following formula, where $R_X$ is return generated on day X, $P_X$ stands for the closing price on day X and $P_{X-1}$ stands for the closing price on the day preceding day X:

$$R_X = (P_X - P_{X-1})/P_{X-1} \tag{1}$$

3. The statistical significance of differences in daily returns recorded during the ToM and the RoM period is evaluated, while using the parametric two-sample *t*-test as well as the non-parametric Wilcoxon rank-sum test.
4. Two alternatives of daily volatilities are calculated. The first one uses the following formula, where $V_X$ is volatility recorded on day X, $PH_X$ is the highest price reached on day X, $PL_X$ is the lowest price recorded on day X, and $P_X$ is the closing price on day X.

$$V_X = (PH_X - PL_X)/P_X \tag{2}$$

The second alternative of the daily volatility is the Garman Klass volatility that was calculated using the methodology that was presented by Molnar (2012). The following formulas are used:

$$c = \ln(P_X) - \ln(PO_X) \tag{3}$$

$$h = \ln(PH_X) - \ln(PO_X) \tag{4}$$

$$l = \ln(PL_X) - \ln(PO_X) \tag{5}$$

$$V_X = 0.5 \times (h - l)^2 - (2\ln 2 - 1) \times c^2 \tag{6}$$

where $P_X$ stands for the closing price on day X, $PO_X$ stands for the opening price on day X, $PL_X$ is the lowest price recorded on day X, and $PH_X$ is the highest price recorded on day X.

5. The statistical significance of differences in daily volatilities recorded during the ToM and the RoM period is evaluated, while using the parametric two-sample *t*-test as well as the non-parametric Wilcoxon rank-sum test.

The following hypotheses are evaluated:

**Hypothesis 1.** *The Turn of the month effect is present on stock markets of the CEE region countries, as the returns recorded during the ToM periods are statistically significantly higher compared to returns recorded during the RoM periods.*

**Hypothesis 2.** *On investigated stock markets, the statistically significantly higher returns recorded over the ToM periods are accompanied by volatilities that are statistically significantly higher compared to volatilities recorded over the RoM periods.*

## 4. Results

As stated in chapter "Data and Methodology", the data analysis is based on comparing the daily returns that were recorded over the turn of the month windows (T-o-M) to the daily returns that were recorded over the remaining days (R-o-M).

Figure 1 shows the comparison of average daily returns recorded during the (1+1) turn of the month windows and returns recorded over the remaining days. As can be seen, in the majority of cases, the average daily returns recorded over the turn of the month periods are notably higher. The biggest differences can be seen in the case of the Romanian BET index (0.382 percentage points), Turkish XU 100 (0.316 percentage points), and Polish WIG 20 (0.226 percentage points). On the other hand, the smallest differences could be observed in the case Lithuanian OMXV (0.045 percentage points) and Latvian OMXR (0.047 percentage points).

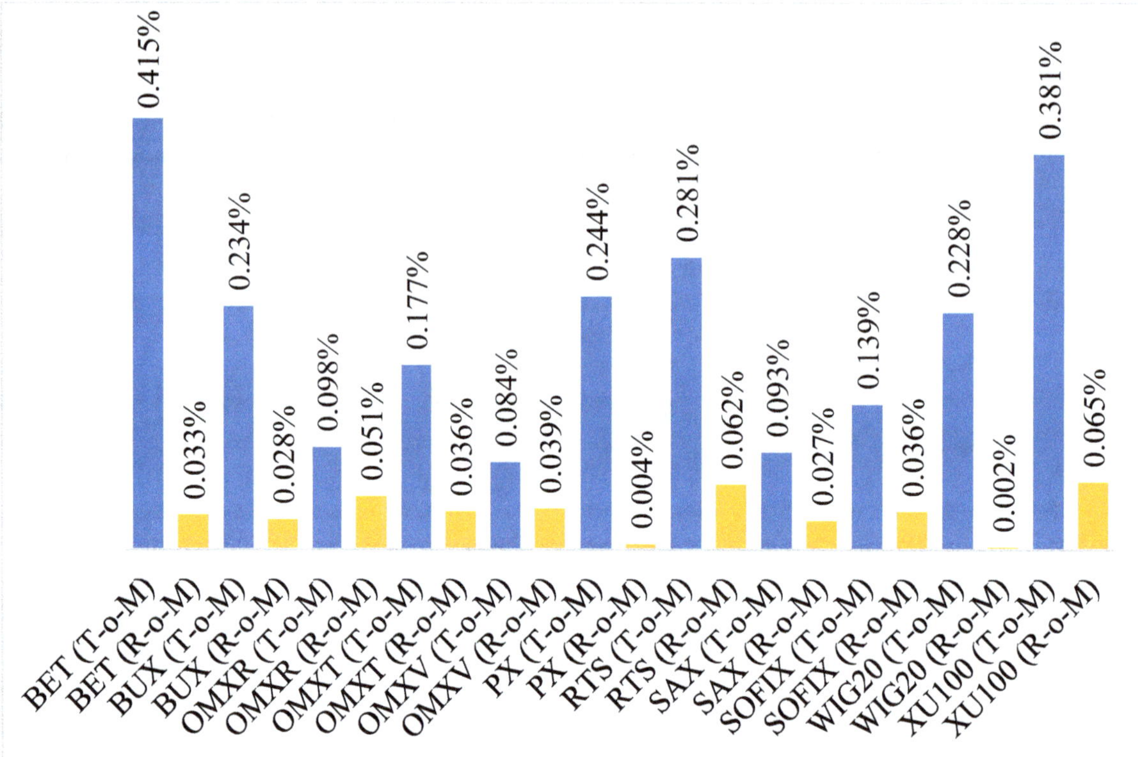


**Figure 1.** Comparison of average daily returns—Turn of the month window (1+1).

Table 2 shows the results of statistical significance tests for the turn of the month window (1+1). Parametric two-sample *t*-test and non-parametric Wilcoxon rank-sum test are both included. However, according to the Jarque-Bera test (Appendix A—Table A1), all of the data analyzed return series are non-normally distributed, which means that the non-parametric Wilcoxon rank-sum test should be more robust (histograms for selected data series can be found in Appendix B—Figures A1 and A2). This applies for all of the analyzed alternatives of the turn of the month window. However, given the large size of analyzed data samples, and given the existence of the central limit theorem, the results of the parametric two-sample *t*-test should also have some informative value. Moreover, as shown in Tables 2–4, there are only two cases when the two-sample *t*-test and the Wilcoxon rank-sum test provide meaningfully different results (OMXV and WIG 20 for the Turn of the month window (3+3)). At a significance level of $\alpha = 0.01$, the Turn of the month effect for the (1+1) T-o-M window is statistically significant in six cases (BET, BUX, OMXT, PX, WIG 20, XU 100). At $\alpha = 0.1$, it is statistically significant in two more cases (OMXV, RTS).

**Table 2.** Results of the statistical significance tests—Turn of the month window (1+1).

| Stock Index | Two-Sample *t*-Test | | Wilcoxon Rank-Sum Test | |
|---|---|---|---|---|
| | Value | Probability | Value | Probability |
| BET | 5.0075 | 0.0000 | 4.7009 | 0.0000 |
| BUX | 2.8218 | 0.0048 | 2.9203 | 0.0035 |
| OMXR | 0.6914 | 0.4894 | 1.2858 | 0.1985 |
| OMXT | 2.7320 | 0.0063 | 3.2043 | 0.0014 |
| OMXV | 0.9192 | 0.3580 | 1.6835 | 0.0923 |
| PX | 3.7095 | 0.0002 | 3.9504 | 0.0001 |
| RTS | 2.0277 | 0.0426 | 1.9458 | 0.0517 |
| SAX | 1.1144 | 0.2652 | 0.9631 | 0.3355 |
| SOFIX | 1.6155 | 0.1063 | 1.4379 | 0.1505 |
| WIG 20 | 3.1376 | 0.0017 | 2.9476 | 0.0032 |
| XU 100 | 3.0067 | 0.0027 | 3.4600 | 0.0005 |

**Table 3.** Results of the statistical significance tests—Turn of the month window (2+2).

| Stock Index | Two-Sample *t*-Test | | Wilcoxon Rank-Sum Test | |
|---|---|---|---|---|
| | Value | Probability | Value | Probability |
| BET | 4.5216 | 0.0000 | 4.8144 | 0.0000 |
| BUX | 2.6798 | 0.0074 | 2.3977 | 0.0165 |
| OMXR | −0.3000 | 0.7642 | 0.3289 | 0.7422 |
| OMXT | 2.9295 | 0.0034 | 3.3269 | 0.0009 |
| OMXV | 0.7973 | 0.4253 | 1.5144 | 0.1299 |
| PX | 2.8653 | 0.0042 | 3.2157 | 0.0013 |
| RTS | 1.9552 | 0.0506 | 1.6707 | 0.0948 |
| SAX | −0.0090 | 0.9928 | 0.5046 | 0.6139 |
| SOFIX | 2.9379 | 0.0033 | 2.8998 | 0.0037 |
| WIG 20 | 1.5027 | 0.1330 | 1.3383 | 0.1808 |
| XU 100 | 3.2330 | 0.0012 | 3.6999 | 0.0002 |

**Table 4.** Results of the statistical significance tests—Turn of the month window (3+3).

| Stock Index | Two-Sample *t*-Test | | Wilcoxon Rank-Sum Test | |
|---|---|---|---|---|
| | Value | Probability | Value | Probability |
| BET | 3.0611 | 0.0022 | 3.0191 | 0.0025 |
| BUX | 3.9972 | 0.0001 | 3.5453 | 0.0004 |
| OMXR | −0.9506 | 0.3418 | 0.1356 | 0.8921 |
| OMXT | 2.0334 | 0.0421 | 2.1110 | 0.0348 |
| OMXV | 1.5939 | 0.1110 | 2.0261 | 0.0428 |
| PX | 2.6007 | 0.0093 | 2.4169 | 0.0157 |
| RTS | 1.6586 | 0.0972 | 1.0553 | 0.2913 |
| SAX | −0.3582 | 0.7202 | 0.3137 | 0.7538 |
| SOFIX | 2.5412 | 0.0111 | 2.9812 | 0.0029 |
| WIG 20 | 1.8293 | 0.0674 | 1.5956 | 0.1106 |
| XU 100 | 3.1812 | 0.0015 | 3.3532 | 0.0008 |

After expanding the turn of the month window to first two and last two trading days of a month (2+2), the results are still very interesting, although the difference in average returns is lower when compared to the (1+1) window. As shown in Figure 2, in this case, the biggest difference in returns was recorded by Romanian BET (0.258 percentage points) and Turkish XU 100. In both of the cases, the average T-o-M returns were higher than the R-o-M returns. However, there were also two stock markets (Latvian—OMR and Slovak—SAX), where the average R-o-M returns were higher than the average T-o-M returns.

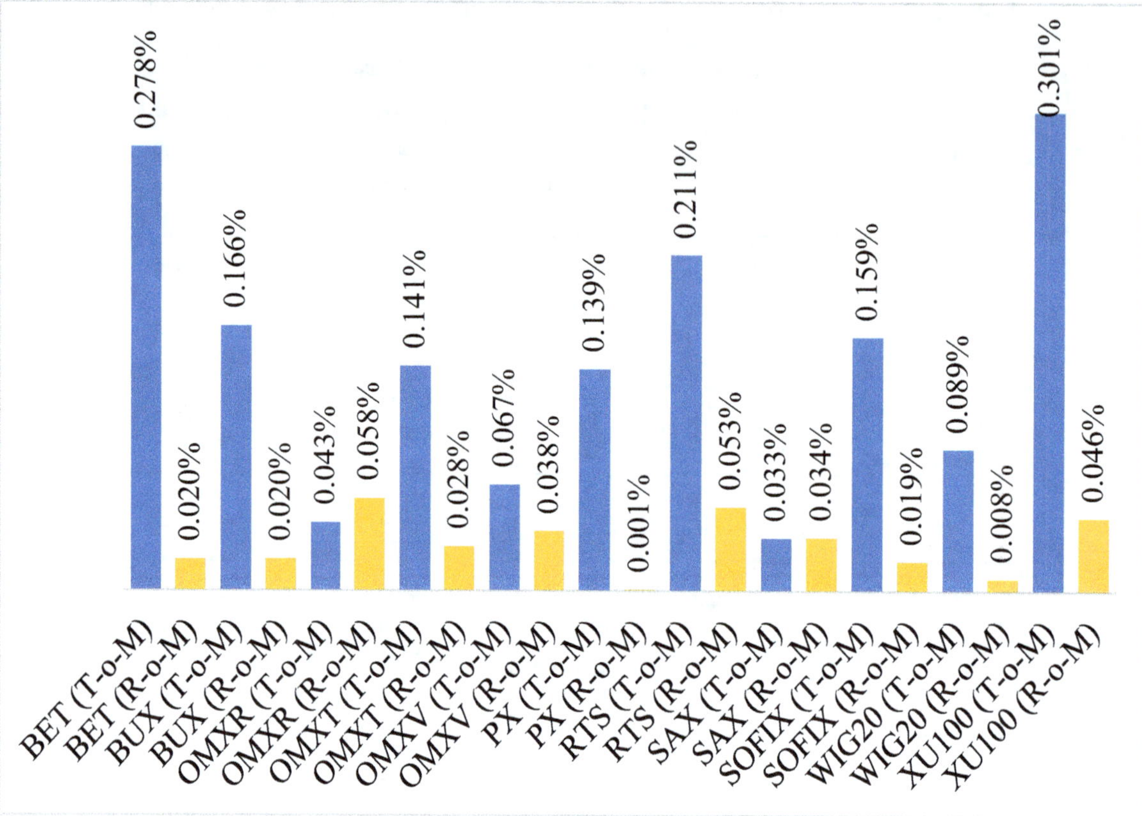


**Figure 2.** Comparison of average daily returns—Turn of the month window (2+2).

Table 3 presents the results of the statistical significance tests for the (2+2) turn of the month window. A very strong Turn of the month effect that is statistically significant at $\alpha = 0.01$ is confirmed in five cases (BET, OMXT, PX, SOFIX, XU 100). At $\alpha = 0.05$, a statistically significant Turn of the month was also observed in the case of BUX and at $\alpha = 0.1$ in the case of RTS.

Figure 3 shows the results for the third alternative of the turn of the month window. In this case, the window consists of the first three and last three trading days of a month (3+3). As can be seen, the differences in returns are lower than in the previous two cases. The biggest difference was recorded by Turkish XU 100 (0.223 percentage points) and Romanian BUX (0.176 percentage points). On the Latvian (OMXR) and Slovak (SAX) stock markets, the average T-o-M returns were lower than the average R-o-M returns again.

As shown in Table 4, for the turn of the month window (3+3), the differences between the daily T-o-M returns and R-o-M returns were statistically significant in four cases (BET, BUX, SOFIX, XU 100) at $\alpha = 0.01$ and in three more cases (OMXT, OMXV, PX) at $\alpha = 0.05$.

Figure 4 shows the differences in average daily volatilities (alternative 1) calculated as the difference between the highest and lowest trading price recorded during a trading day, divided by the closing price of that trading day. As can be seen, in the case of all four investigated stock markets, the differences between the volatilities recorded over the T-o-M days and volatilities recorded over the R-o-M days is negligible. Moreover, in all of the cases, the R-o-M volatility tends to be slightly higher when compared to the T-o-M volatility. This finding is valid for all three alternatives of the turn of the month window. This finding is surprising, according to the generally accepted theory, higher returns should be connected with higher risk. It means that the stock markets behave counterintuitively, as even on stock markets where a statistically significant Turn of the month effect is present in returns, it is not present in volatility.

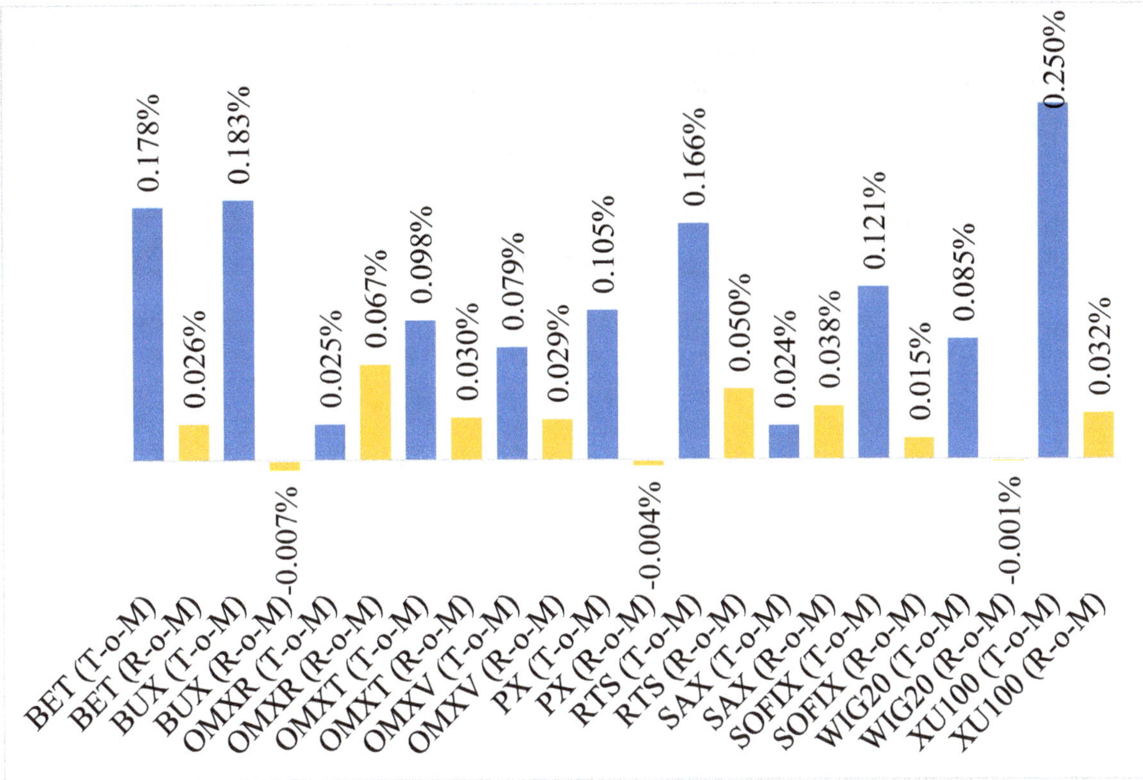


**Figure 3.** Comparison of average daily returns—Turn of the month window (3+3).

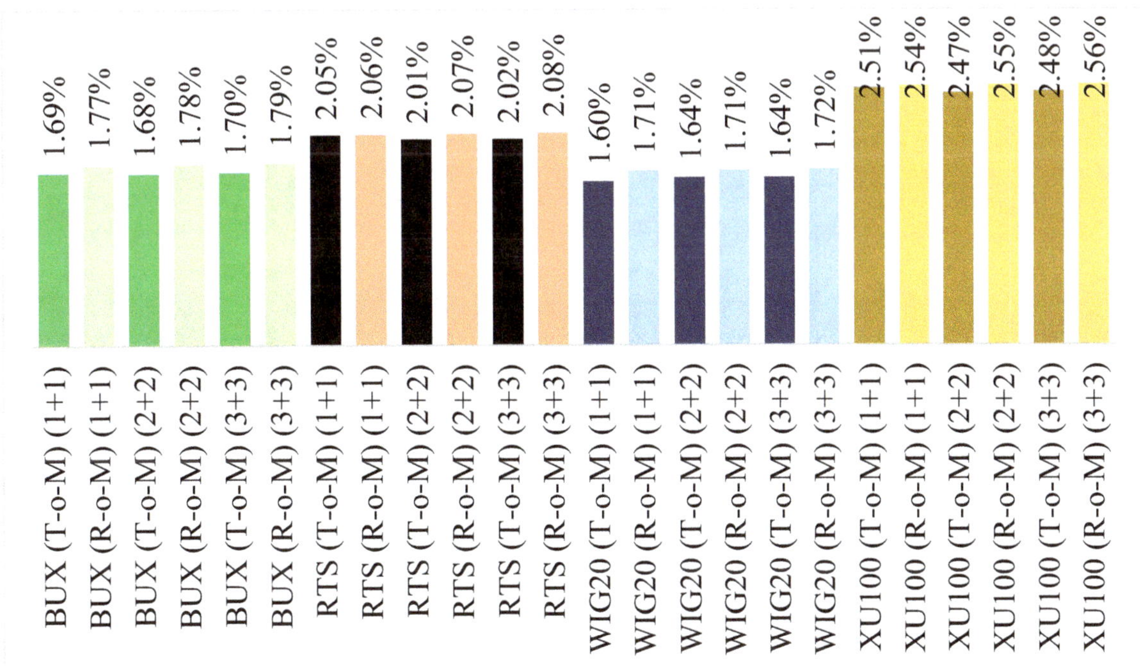


**Figure 4.** Comparison of average daily volatilities (alternative 1).

Data that are presented in Figure 4 are also confirmed by the statistical significance tests results that are presented in Table 5. Additionally, for all of the volatility data series applies that they have a non-normal distribution (Appendix A—Table A2), which means that the results of the non-parametric Wilcoxon rank-sum test should be more robust. As can be seen, the difference between the T-o-M and R-o-M daily volatilities is only statistically significant in the case of Hungarian stock index BUX and turn of the month windows (2+2) and (3+3). However, in both cases, the average volatility that was recorded over the T-o-M period is lower than average volatility recorded over the R-o-M period. In other words, the assumption that the statistically significantly higher T-o-M returns should be accompanied by statistically significantly higher T-o-M volatility was not confirmed.

**Table 5.** Results of the statistical significance tests—Daily volatilities (alternative 1).

| Stock Index | Two-Sample *t*-Test | | Wilcoxon Rank-Sum Test | |
|---|---|---|---|---|
| | Value | Probability | Value | Probability |
| BUX (1+1) | −1.5274 | 0.1267 | 0.7620 | 0.4461 |
| BUX (2+2) | −2.4648 | 0.0137 | 1.9642 | 0.0495 |
| BUX (3+3) | −2.7387 | 0.0062 | 1.7878 | 0.0738 |
| RTS (1+1) | −0.1291 | 0.8973 | 0.0683 | 0.9455 |
| RTS (2+2) | −1.0619 | 0.2883 | 0.5688 | 0.5695 |
| RTS (3+3) | −1.2893 | 0.1974 | 0.3038 | 0.7613 |
| WIG 20 (1+1) | −2.2743 | 0.0230 | 1.6083 | 0.1078 |
| WIG 20 (2+2) | −1.9763 | 0.0482 | 1.1131 | 0.2657 |
| WIG 20 (3+3) | −2.5958 | 0.0095 | 1.5381 | 0.1240 |
| XU 100 (1+1) | −0.3010 | 0.7635 | 0.1625 | 0.8709 |
| XU 100 (2+2) | −1.2753 | 0.2023 | 0.7782 | 0.4365 |
| XU 100 (3+3) | −1.346556 | 0.1782 | 0.936922 | 0.3488 |

Figure 5 presents the data for daily Garman-Klass volatilities (alternative 2). As can be seen, although the differences between the T-o-M and R-o-M levels of volatility are more noticeable when compared to the first alternative of volatility, the results are consistent and in all of the cases, the average daily volatility was slightly higher during the R-o-M periods.

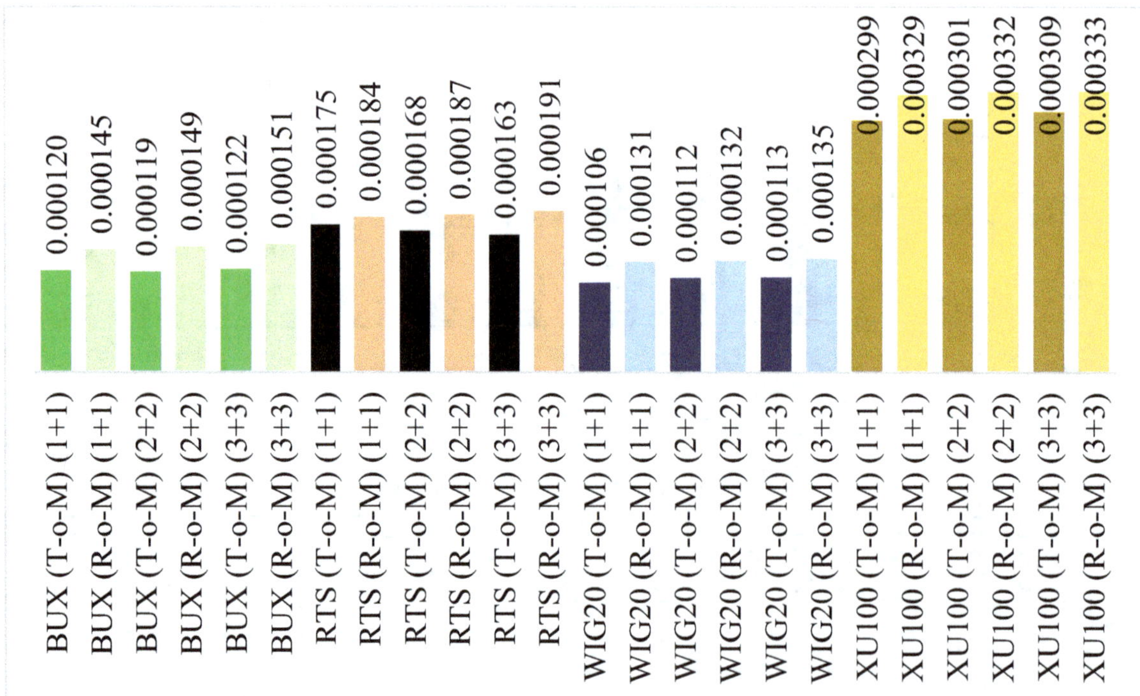


**Figure 5.** Comparison of average daily volatilities (alternative 2).

The results of the statistical significance tests for the Garman-Klass volatilities show that statistically significant differences can be seen in the case of BUX (2+2), BUX (3+3), WIG 20 (1+1), and WIG 20 (3+3). What is important, the results of the analysis of Garman-Klass volatility are in line with results of the first alternative of volatility. In the case of all four stock indices and all three turn of the month windows, the average daily volatility is higher during the R-o-M periods. However, the differences are mostly not statistically significant (Table 6).

**Table 6.** Results of the statistical significance tests—Daily volatilities (alternative 2).

| Stock Index | Two-Sample *t*-Test | | Wilcoxon Rank-Sum Test | |
|---|---|---|---|---|
| | Value | Probability | Value | Probability |
| BUX (1+1) | −1.5856 | 0.1129 | 0.8511 | 0.3947 |
| BUX (2+2) | −2.5354 | 0.0113 | 2.4960 | 0.0126 |
| BUX (3+3) | −2.8672 | 0.0042 | 2.0788 | 0.0376 |
| RTS (1+1) | −0.3193 | 0.7495 | 0.0829 | 0.9339 |
| RTS (2+2) | −0.9501 | 0.3421 | 0.7559 | 0.4497 |
| RTS (3+3) | −1.6359 | 0.1019 | 0.6900 | 0.4902 |
| WIG 20 (1+1) | −2.2770 | 0.0228 | 2.1693 | 0.0301 |
| WIG 20 (2+2) | −2.5556 | 0.0106 | 1.5430 | 0.1228 |
| WIG 20 (3+3) | −3.1614 | 0.0016 | 1.7917 | 0.0732 |
| XU 100 (1+1) | −0.9517 | 0.3413 | 0.2275 | 0.8200 |
| XU 100 (2+2) | −1.3281 | 0.1842 | 1.1773 | 0.2391 |
| XU 100 (3+3) | −1.155565 | 0.2479 | 1.084122 | 0.2783 |

## 5. Discussion

The results presented in the previous chapter show that a statistically significant Turn of the month effect could be found on the CEE region stock markets. However, there are several exemptions, as our results did not confirm the presence of a statistically significant Turn of the month effect on the Slovak (SAX) and Latvian (OMXR) stock markets. As a result, Hypothesis 1 (The Turn of the month effect is present on stock markets of the CEE region countries, as the returns recorded during the ToM periods are statistically significantly higher when compared to returns recorded during the RoM periods.) can be confirmed for nine out of 11 investigated stock markets.

These results are in line with some previous studies that concluded the presence of the Turn of the month effect on some of the CEE region stock markets (Heininen and Vesa 2008; Kayacetin and Lekpek 2016; Arendas and Bukoven 2017). According to Heininen and Puttonen, in Croatia, Hungary, Poland, Romania, Russia, and Slovenia, 85% of monthly returns were recorded during the turn of the month period, between January 1997 and February 2008. Kayacetin and Lekpek confirmed a strong Turn of the month effect on the Turkish stock market, during the 1988–2014 time period. Their turn of the month window included the last and the first two trading days of each month, with an average daily return of 0.46%. Over the remaining days, a return of only 0.09% was recorded. Arendas and Bukoven discovered a strong Turn of the month effect on the Czech stock market during the 1997–2016 period.

While on all the other stock markets, even in the case that the differences were not statistically significant, the average T-o-M returns were higher than the average R-o-M returns for all three alternatives of turn of the month windows, the (2+2) and (3+3) windows for OMXR and the (3+3) window for SAX recorded average R-o-M returns higher when compared to the average T-o-M returns. The tendency of the Slovak stock market to behave differently in comparison to the majority of stock markets in the CEE region was confirmed by numerous researchers, including (Arendas and Chovancova 2016; Olbrys and Majewska 2016; Carausu et al. 2018). This fact is often explained by its lower level of development, insufficient liquidity, and very low market capitalization.

It is also possible to observe an unusual behavior of the Turn of the month effect on the Bulgarian stock market that is represented by SOFIX. While for all of the other stock indices, the p-values tended to increase (or at least stagnate) along expanding turn of the month window, SOFIX behaved in an exactly opposite way. While for the (1+1) window, the differences between the T-o-M and R-o-M windows were not statistically significant, with a p-value of 0.1505, for the (2+2) window the $p$-value was 0.0037, and for the (3+3) window it was 0.0029. However, the explanation of this behavior will take a more detailed study that directly focuses on specifics of the Bulgarian stock market.

The results also show that, in some of the cases, the differences in T-o-M and R-o-M returns are significant enough to be exploited by an investment strategy. Vasileiou (2018) proposed an investment strategy of holding stocks during the T-o-M windows and keeping the money on a bank account that provides no interest during the rest of the month. During the investigated time periods, this very simple investment strategy would be able to beat a buy & hold investment strategy in the case of the (3+3) T-o-M windows on the Hungarian, Czech, and Polish stock market, as these markets recorded negative average daily returns during the R-o-M periods. Kunkel and Compton (1998) developed a similar strategy, based on switching between the stock market (during the T-o-M periods) and the money market (during the R-o-M periods). Obviously, this investment strategy would also be able to beat the market performance in the case of the Hungarian, Czech, and Polish stock market, due to negative R-o-M returns. Moreover, this strategy provides some potential to also outperform on other markets, especially those with low R-o-M returns (for example, Romania and Bulgaria). However, probably not in the current environment of extremely low interest rates that suppress the money market returns significantly.

It is also possible to note that the observed results are in a contradiction to the efficient markets theory (Fama 1965), according to which the stock prices always reflect all of the important information, thus it is impossible to outperform the market while using technical analysis and market timing. As a result, the presence of an exploitable calendar anomaly, in this case the Turn of the month effect means that the impacted stock market cannot be regarded as efficient.

The most surprising results are related to the testing of the Turn of the month effect in stock market volatilities. In all of the four investigated cases (BUX, RTS, WIG 20, XU 100), although a statistically significant Turn of the month effect in returns was confirmed, the volatility recorded over the T-o-M periods was not statistically significantly higher than the volatility recorded over the R-o-M periods. The average daily volatilities were similar and in all of the cases slightly higher during the R-o-M periods. As a result, Hypothesis 2 (on investigated stock markets, the statistically significantly higher returns recorded over the ToM periods are accompanied by volatilities that are statistically significantly higher when compared to volatilities recorded over the RoM periods) can be completely rejected. This is a very interesting finding, as it is in a direct contradiction to the generally accepted financial markets rule that higher returns are accompanied by higher risk.

**Author Contributions:** Conceptualization, P.A.; formal analysis, P.A. and J.K.; investigation, P.A. and J.K.; methodology, P.A.; validation, J.K.; writing—original draft preparation, P.A.; writing—review and editing, J.K.

**Funding:** This paper is an outcome of the science project VEGA (1/0257/18), VEGA (1/0009/17) and VEGA (1/0613/18).

**Conflicts of Interest:** The authors declare no conflict of interest.

## Appendix A

**Table A1.** Descriptive statistics—returns.

| Data | Observ. | Max. | Min. | Average | Jarque-Bera | Prob. |
|---|---|---|---|---|---|---|
| BET (1+1) R-o-M | 4049 | 0.1569 | −0.1122 | 0.0003 | 26,166.14 | 0 |
| BET (1+1) T-o-M | 432 | 0.0950 | −0.0421 | 0.0042 | 569.33 | 0 |
| BET (2+2) R-o-M | 3617 | 0.1569 | −0.1122 | 0.0002 | 25,263.62 | 0 |
| BET (2+2) T-o-M | 864 | 0.0950 | −0.0776 | 0.0028 | 1248.52 | 0 |
| BET (3+3) R-o-M | 3185 | 0.1569 | −0.1122 | 0.0003 | 22,517.77 | 0 |
| BET (3+3) T-o-M | 1296 | 0.0950 | −0.1068 | 0.0018 | 2940.94 | 0 |
| BUX (1+1) R-o-M | 4515 | 0.1408 | −0.1188 | 0.0003 | 8716.05 | 0 |
| BUX (1+1) T-o-M | 480 | 0.0573 | −0.0452 | 0.0023 | 45.81 | 0 |
| BUX (2+2) R-o-M | 4035 | 0.1408 | −0.1188 | 0.0002 | 8653.64 | 0 |

**Table A1.** *Cont.*

| Data | Observ. | Max. | Min. | Average | Jarque-Bera | Prob. |
|---|---|---|---|---|---|---|
| BUX (2+2) T-o-M | 960 | 0.0738 | −0.0477 | 0.0017 | 159.50 | 0 |
| BUX (3+3) R-o-M | 3555 | 0.1126 | −0.1188 | −0.0001 | 5660.66 | 0 |
| BUX (3+3) T-o-M | 1440 | 0.1408 | −0.0477 | 0.0018 | 3082.05 | 0 |
| OMXR (1+1) R-o-M | 4328 | 0.1230 | −0.1368 | 0.0005 | 45,093.82 | 0 |
| OMXR (1+1) T-o-M | 456 | 0.0759 | −0.1220 | 0.0010 | 7250.06 | 0 |
| OMXR (2+2) R-o-M | 3872 | 0.1230 | −0.1368 | 0.0006 | 43,322.12 | 0 |
| OMXR (2+2) T-o-M | 912 | 0.0776 | −0.1220 | 0.0004 | 9489.82 | 0 |
| OMXR (3+3) R-o-M | 3416 | 0.1230 | −0.1368 | 0.0007 | 38,782.96 | 0 |
| OMXR (3+3) T-o-M | 1368 | 0.0776 | −0.1220 | 0.0003 | 14,224.45 | 0 |
| OMXT (1+1) R-o-M | 4336 | 0.1286 | −0.0680 | 0.0004 | 23,743.65 | 0 |
| OMXT (1+1) T-o-M | 456 | 0.0501 | −0.0422 | 0.0018 | 362.79 | 0 |
| OMXT (2+2) R-o-M | 3880 | 0.1286 | −0.0680 | 0.0003 | 23,604.25 | 0 |
| OMXT (2+2) T-o-M | 912 | 0.0501 | −0.0558 | 0.0014 | 928.31 | 0 |
| OMXT (3+3) R-o-M | 3424 | 0.1286 | −0.0680 | 0.0003 | 23,011.80 | 0 |
| OMXT (3+3) T-o-M | 1368 | 0.0501 | −0.0558 | 0.0010 | 1221.10 | 0 |
| OMXV (1+1) R-o-M | 4312 | 0.1163 | −0.1125 | 0.0004 | 100,522.60 | 0 |
| OMXV (1+1) T-o-M | 456 | 0.0304 | −0.0601 | 0.0008 | 739.34 | 0 |
| OMXV (2+2) R-o-M | 3856 | 0.1163 | −0.1125 | 0.0004 | 93,131.35 | 0 |
| OMXV (2+2) T-o-M | 912 | 0.0501 | −0.0971 | 0.0007 | 8146.88 | 0 |
| OMXV (3+3) R-o-M | 3400 | 0.1163 | −0.1125 | 0.0003 | 91,128.62 | 0 |
| OMXV (3+3) T-o-M | 1368 | 0.0501 | −0.0971 | 0.0008 | 9452.05 | 0 |
| PX (1+1) R-o-M | 4538 | 0.1316 | −0.1494 | 0.0000 | 31,730.44 | 0 |
| PX (1+1) T-o-M | 480 | 0.0620 | −0.0409 | 0.0024 | 106.10 | 0 |
| PX (2+2) R-o-M | 4058 | 0.1316 | −0.1494 | 0.0000 | 31,518.89 | 0 |
| PX (2+2) T-o-M | 960 | 0.0917 | −0.0541 | 0.0014 | 897.24 | 0 |
| PX (3+3) R-o-M | 3578 | 0.1173 | −0.1494 | 0.0000 | 24,076.20 | 0 |
| PX (3+3) T-o-M | 1440 | 0.1316 | −0.0541 | 0.0011 | 6998.43 | 0 |
| RTS (1+1) R-o-M | 4521 | 0.2239 | −0.1910 | 0.0006 | 13,164.68 | 0 |
| RTS (1+1) T-o-M | 480 | 0.1683 | −0.1201 | 0.0028 | 2111.88 | 0 |
| RTS (2+2) R-o-M | 4041 | 0.2239 | −0.1910 | 0.0005 | 11,089.39 | 0 |
| RTS (2+2) T-o-M | 960 | 0.1781 | −0.1201 | 0.0021 | 4454.55 | 0 |
| RTS (3+3) R-o-M | 1440 | 0.1781 | −0.1201 | 0.0017 | 4252.29 | 0 |
| RTS (3+3) T-o-M | 3561 | 0.2239 | −0.1910 | 0.0005 | 10,915.61 | 0 |
| SAX (1+1) R-o-M | 4404 | 0.1261 | −0.1377 | 0.0003 | 33,200.63 | 0 |
| SAX (1+1) T-o-M | 480 | 0.0511 | −0.0844 | 0.0009 | 1422.10 | 0 |
| SAX (2+2) R-o-M | 3924 | 0.0955 | −0.1377 | 0.0003 | 24,408.79 | 0 |
| SAX (2+2) T-o-M | 960 | 0.1261 | −0.0913 | 0.0003 | 8045.54 | 0 |
| SAX (3+3) R-o-M | 3444 | 0.0955 | −0.1085 | 0.0004 | 11,268.57 | 0 |
| SAX (3+3) T-o-M | 1440 | 0.1261 | −0.1377 | 0.0002 | 19,033.62 | 0 |
| SOFIX (1+1) R-o-M | 3784 | 0.0756 | −0.1074 | 0.0004 | 14,788.46 | 0 |
| SOFIX (1+1) T-o-M | 408 | 0.0875 | −0.0679 | 0.0014 | 1821.45 | 0 |
| SOFIX (2+2) R-o-M | 3376 | 0.0756 | −0.1074 | 0.0002 | 14,517.77 | 0 |
| SOFIX (2+2) T-o-M | 816 | 0.0875 | −0.0679 | 0.0016 | 2195.79 | 0 |
| SOFIX (3+3) R-o-M | 2968 | 0.0756 | −0.1074 | 0.0002 | 13,287.55 | 0 |
| SOFIX (3+3) T-o-M | 1224 | 0.0875 | −0.0791 | 0.0012 | 3294.55 | 0 |
| WIG20 (1+1) R-o-M | 4526 | 0.0850 | −0.0925 | 0.0000 | 1509.32 | 0 |
| WIG20 (1+1) T-o-M | 480 | 0.0635 | −0.0511 | 0.0023 | 57.14 | 0 |
| WIG20 (2+2) R-o-M | 4046 | 0.0850 | −0.0925 | 0.0001 | 1428.46 | 0 |
| WIG20 (2+2) T-o-M | 960 | 0.0695 | −0.0660 | 0.0009 | 155.12 | 0 |
| WIG20 (3+3) R-o-M | 3566 | 0.0850 | −0.0925 | 0.0000 | 1214.28 | 0 |
| WIG20 (3+3) T-o-M | 1440 | 0.0773 | −0.0660 | 0.0008 | 358.03 | 0 |
| XU100 (1+1) R-o-M | 4525 | 0.1945 | −0.1811 | 0.0006 | 10,682.99 | 0 |
| XU100 (1+1) T-o-M | 480 | 0.1515 | −0.1249 | 0.0038 | 1202.94 | 0 |
| XU100 (2+2) R-o-M | 4045 | 0.1945 | −0.1811 | 0.0005 | 10,032.85 | 0 |
| XU100 (2+2) T-o-M | 960 | 0.1515 | −0.1249 | 0.0030 | 1990.83 | 0 |
| XU100 (3+3) R-o-M | 3565 | 0.1864 | −0.1811 | 0.0003 | 6590.06 | 0 |
| XU100 (3+3) T-o-M | 1440 | 0.1945 | −0.1249 | 0.0025 | 5335.24 | 0 |

**Table A2.** Descriptive statistics—volatilities.

| Data | Observ. | Max. | Min. | Average | Jarque-Bera | Prob. |
|---|---|---|---|---|---|---|
| BUX (1+1) R-o-M (HL) | 4515 | 0.1766 | 0.0000 | 0.0177 | 128,075.60 | 0 |
| BUX (1+1) T-o-M (HL) | 480 | 0.0645 | 0.0041 | 0.0169 | 590.34 | 0 |
| BUX (2+2) R-o-M (HL) | 4035 | 0.1766 | 0.0000 | 0.0178 | 122,576.80 | 0 |
| BUX (2+2) T-o-M (HL) | 960 | 0.0645 | 0.0041 | 0.0168 | 1191.09 | 0 |
| BUX (3+3) R-o-M (HL) | 3555 | 0.1766 | 0.0000 | 0.0179 | 112,319.30 | 0 |
| BUX (3+3) T-o-M (HL) | 1440 | 0.0810 | 0.0041 | 0.0170 | 3390.14 | 0 |
| RTS (1+1) R-o-M (HL) | 4521 | 0.2767 | 0.0000 | 0.0206 | 231,355.50 | 0 |
| RTS (1+1) T-o-M (HL) | 480 | 0.1427 | 0.0006 | 0.0205 | 6054.83 | 0 |
| RTS (2+2) R-o-M (HL) | 4041 | 0.2767 | 0.0000 | 0.0207 | 213,977.40 | 0 |
| RTS (2+2) T-o-M (HL) | 960 | 0.1573 | 0.0006 | 0.0201 | 15,253.23 | 0 |
| RTS (3+3) R-o-M (HL) | 3561 | 0.2767 | 0.0000 | 0.0208 | 200,790.60 | 0 |
| RTS (3+3) T-o-M (HL) | 1440 | 0.1573 | 0.0006 | 0.0202 | 16,600.13 | 0 |
| WIG20 (1+1) R-o-M (HL) | 4526 | 0.1403 | 0.0035 | 0.0171 | 41,457.13 | 0 |
| WIG20 (1+1) T-o-M (HL) | 480 | 0.0538 | 0.0048 | 0.0160 | 355.79 | 0 |
| WIG20 (2+2) R-o-M (HL) | 4046 | 0.1403 | 0.0035 | 0.0171 | 40,513.95 | 0 |
| WIG20 (2+2) T-o-M (HL) | 960 | 0.0612 | 0.0037 | 0.0164 | 843.59 | 0 |
| WIG20 (3+3) R-o-M (HL) | 3566 | 0.1403 | 0.0035 | 0.0172 | 38,170.42 | 0 |
| WIG20 (3+3) T-o-M (HL) | 1440 | 0.0612 | 0.0037 | 0.0164 | 1200.64 | 0 |
| XU100 (1+1) R-o-M (HL) | 4525 | 0.2233 | 0.0000 | 0.0254 | 41,770.67 | 0 |
| XU100 (1+1) T-o-M (HL) | 480 | 0.1494 | 0.0000 | 0.0251 | 4625.07 | 0 |
| XU100 (2+2) R-o-M (HL) | 4045 | 0.2233 | 0.0000 | 0.0255 | 37,845.86 | 0 |
| XU100 (2+2) T-o-M (HL) | 960 | 0.1494 | 0.0000 | 0.0247 | 8374.23 | 0 |
| XU100 (3+3) R-o-M (HL) | 3565 | 0.2233 | 0.0000 | 0.0256 | 31,016.39 | 0 |
| XU100 (3+3) T-o-M (HL) | 1440 | 0.1796 | 0.0000 | 0.0248 | 15,708.37 | 0 |
| BUX (1+1) R-o-M (GK) | 4515 | 0.0139 | 0.0000 | 0.0001 | 93,778,956.00 | 0 |
| BUX (1+1) T-o-M (GK) | 480 | 0.0010 | 0.0000 | 0.0001 | 2981.27 | 0 |
| BUX (2+2) R-o-M (GK) | 4035 | 0.0139 | 0.0000 | 0.0001 | 72,960,991.00 | 0 |
| BUX (2+2) T-o-M (GK) | 960 | 0.0015 | 0.0000 | 0.0001 | 22,038.93 | 0 |
| BUX (3+3) R-o-M (GK) | 3555 | 0.0139 | 0.0000 | 0.0002 | 55,999,012.00 | 0 |
| BUX (3+3) T-o-M (GK) | 1440 | 0.0019 | 0.0000 | 0.0001 | 89,751.11 | 0 |
| RTS (1+1) R-o-M (GK) | 4521 | 0.0299 | 0.0000 | 0.0002 | 571,000,000.00 | 0 |

**Table A2.** *Cont.*

| Data | Observ. | Max. | Min. | Average | Jarque-Bera | Prob. |
|---|---|---|---|---|---|---|
| RTS (1+1) T-o-M (GK) | 480 | 0.0042 | 0.0000 | 0.0002 | 95,374.30 | 0 |
| RTS (2+2) R-o-M (GK) | 4041 | 0.0299 | 0.0000 | 0.0002 | 464,000,000.00 | 0 |
| RTS (2+2) T-o-M (GK) | 960 | 0.0042 | 0.0000 | 0.0002 | 221,552.20 | 0 |
| RTS (3+3) R-o-M (GK) | 1440 | 0.0042 | 0.0000 | 0.0002 | 331,714.90 | 0 |
| RTS (3+3) T-o-M (GK) | 3561 | 0.0299 | 0.0000 | 0.0002 | 341,000,000.00 | 0 |
| WIG20 (1+1) R-o-M (GK) | 4526 | 0.0054 | 0.0000 | 0.0001 | 4,591,646.00 | 0 |
| WIG20 (1+1) T-o-M (GK) | 480 | 0.0010 | 0.0000 | 0.0001 | 3590.90 | 0 |
| WIG20 (2+2) R-o-M (GK) | 4046 | 0.0054 | 0.0000 | 0.0001 | 3,771,200.00 | 0 |
| WIG20 (2+2) T-o-M (GK) | 960 | 0.0011 | 0.0000 | 0.0001 | 8880.60 | 0 |
| WIG20 (3+3) R-o-M (GK) | 1440 | 0.0012 | 0.0000 | 0.0001 | 16,561.43 | 0 |
| WIG20 (3+3) T-o-M (GK) | 3566 | 0.0054 | 0.0000 | 0.0001 | 2,997,413.00 | 0 |
| XU100 (1+1) R-o-M (GK) | 4525 | 0.0179 | 0.0000 | 0.0003 | 4,427,421.00 | 0 |
| XU100 (1+1) T-o-M (GK) | 480 | 0.0066 | 0.0000 | 0.0003 | 49,526.45 | 0 |
| XU100 (2+2) R-o-M (GK) | 4045 | 0.0179 | 0.0000 | 0.0003 | 4,357,226.00 | 0 |
| XU100 (2+2) T-o-M (GK) | 960 | 0.0071 | 0.0000 | 0.0003 | 107,348.80 | 0 |
| XU100 (3+3) R-o-M (GK) | 3565 | 0.0179 | 0.0000 | 0.0003 | 4,254,954.00 | 0 |
| XU100 (3+3) T-o-M (GK) | 1440 | 0.0108 | 0.0000 | 0.0003 | 418,241.10 | 0 |

## Appendix B

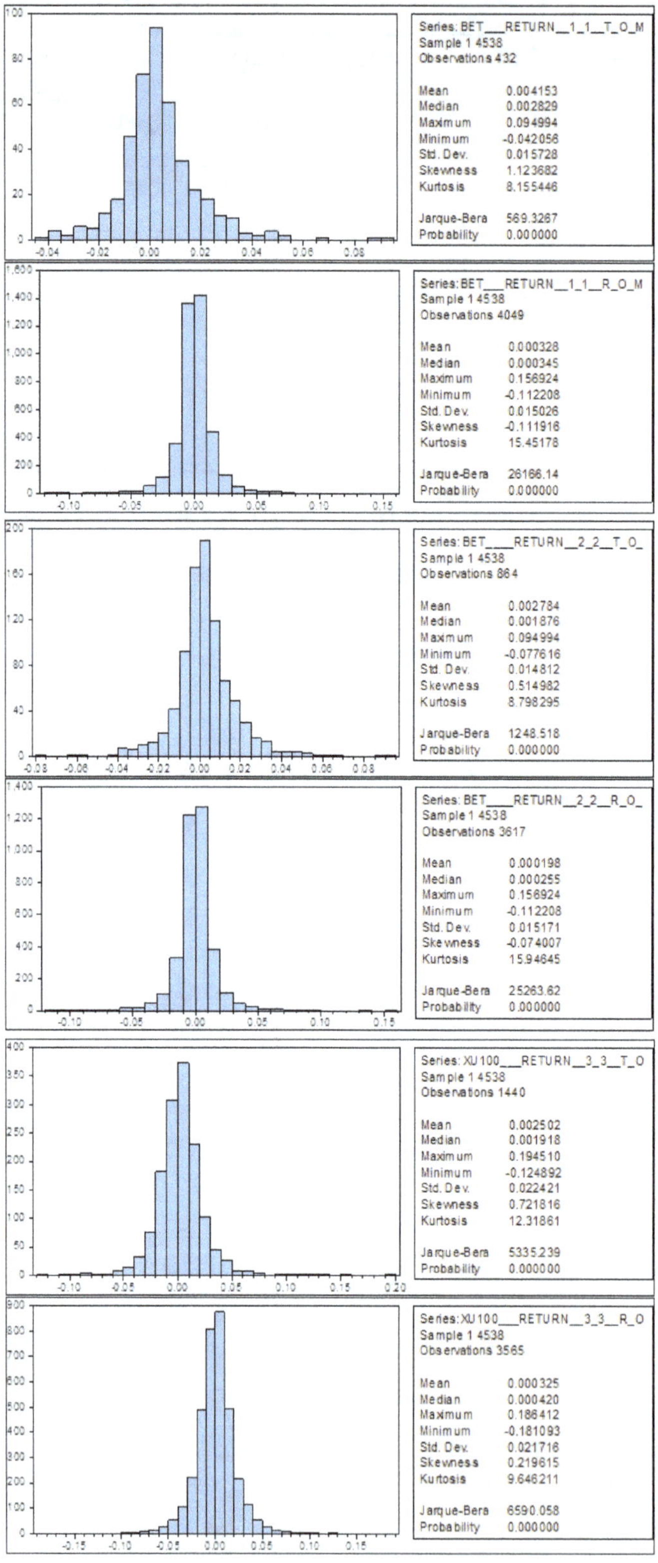


**Figure A1.** Histograms and descriptive statistics for data samples with highest difference between average T-o-M and R-o-M returns.

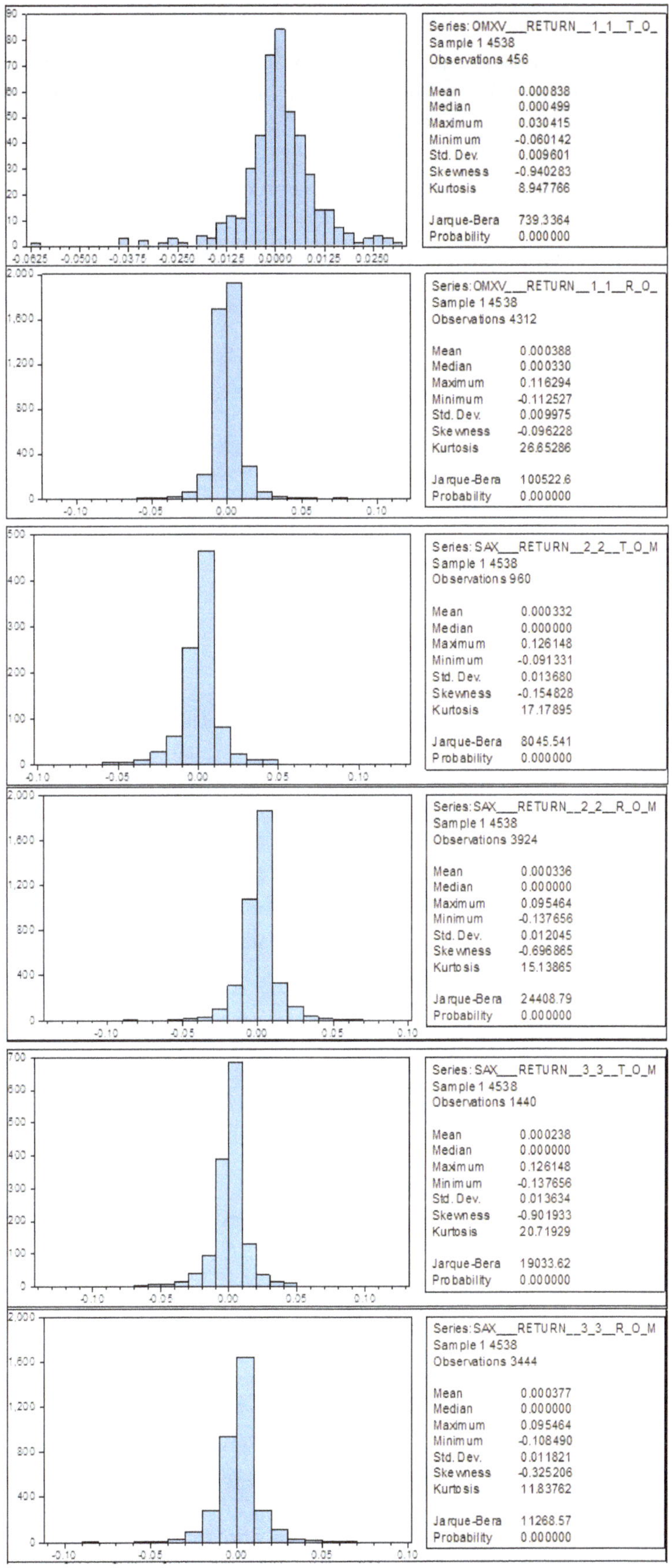


**Figure A2.** Histograms and descriptive statistics for data samples with lowest difference between average T-o-M and R-o-M returns References.

## References


Aggarwal, Raj, and John D. Schatzberg. 1997. Day of the week effects, information seasonality, and higher moments of security returns. *Journal of Economics and Business* 49: 1–20. [CrossRef]

Agrawal, Anup, and Kishore Tandon. 1994. Anomalies or illusions? Evidence from stock markets in eighteen countries. *Journal of International Money and Finance* 13: 83–106. [CrossRef]

Andrade, Sandro C., Vidhi Chhaochharia, and Michael E. Fuerst. 2013. "Sell in May and Go Away" Just Won't Go Away. *Financial Analysts Journal* 69: 94–105. [CrossRef]

Arendas, Peter. 2017. The Halloween Effect on the Agricultural Commodities Markets. *Agricultural Economics* 63: 441–48. [CrossRef]

Arendas, Peter, and Jan Bukoven. 2017. Turn of the month effect on the Prague stock exchange. Paper presented at the 8th International Scientific Conference, Finance and Performance of Firms in Science, Education and Practice, Zlin, Czech Republic, April 26–27.

Arendas, Peter, and Bozena Chovancova. 2016. Central and Eastern European Share Markets and the Halloween Effect. *Montenegrin Journal of Economics* 12: 61–71. [CrossRef]

Arendas, Peter, Viera Malacka, and Maria Schwarzova. 2018. A Closer Look at the Halloween Effect: The Case of the Dow Jones Industrial Average. *International Journal of Financial Studies* 6: 42. [CrossRef]

Ariel, Robert A. 1987. A Monthly Effect in Stock Returns. *Journal of Financial Economics* 18: 621–28. [CrossRef]

Ariel, Robert A. 1990. High Stock Returns before Holidays: Existence and Evidence on Possible Causes. *The Journal of Finance* 45: 1611–26. [CrossRef]

Aziz, Tariq, and Valeed A. Ansari. 2017. The Turn of the Month Effect in Asia-Pacific Markets: New Evidence. *Global Business Review* 19: 214–26. [CrossRef]

Borowski, Krzysztof. 2015. Analysis of selected seasonality effects in market of barley, canola, rough rice, soybean oil and soybean meal future contracts. *Journal of Economics and Management* 21: 73–89.

Bouman, Sven, and Ben Jacobsen. 2002. The Halloween indicator, "sell in May and go away": Another puzzle. *American Economic Review* 92: 1618–35. [CrossRef]

Brusa, Jorge, and Pu Liu. 2004. The Day-of-the-Week and the Week-of-the-Month Effects: An Analysis of Investors' Trading Activities. *Review of Quantitative Finance and Accounting* 23: 19–30. [CrossRef]

Burakov, Dmitry, and Max Freidin. 2018. Is the Halloween Effect Present on the Markets for Agricultural Commodities? *Agris on-line Papers in Economics and Informatics* 10: 23–32. [CrossRef]

Burakov, Dmitry, Max Freidin, and Yuriy Solovyev. 2018. The halloween effect on energy markets: An empirical study. *International Journal of Energy Economics and Policy* 8: 121–26. [CrossRef]

Burnett, John E. 2017. Liquidity and investor confidence in the turn-of-the-month regularity. *Applied Economics Letters* 24: 273–78. [CrossRef]

Cadsby, Charles, and Mitchell Ratner. 1992. Turn-of-month and pre-holiday effects on stock returns: Some international evidence. *Journal of Banking & Finance* 16: 497–509. [CrossRef]

Caporale, Guglielmo M., and Alex Plastun. 2017. Calendar anomalies in the Ukrainian stock market. *Investment Management and Financial Innovations* 14: 104–14. [CrossRef]

Carausu, Dimitru N., Bogdan F. Filip, Elena Cigu, and Carmen Toderascu. 2018. Contagion of Capital Markets in CEE Countries: Evidence from Wavelet Analysis. *Emerging Markets Finance & Trade* 54: 618–41. [CrossRef]

Chen, Jun, Bart Frijns, Ivan Indriawan, and Haodong Ren. 2018. Turn of the Month effect in the New Zealand stock market. *New Zealand Economic Papers*, 1–19. [CrossRef]

Dichtl, Hubert, and Wolfgang Drobetz. 2015. Sell in May and Go Away: Still Good Advice for Investors? *International Review of Financial Analysis* 38: 29–43. [CrossRef]

Fama, Eugene F. 1965. Random Walks in Stock Market Prices. *Financial Analysts Journal* 21: 55–59. [CrossRef]

Ferreira, Paulo. 2018. What guides Central and Eastern European stock markets? A view from detrended methodologies. *Post-Communist Economies* 30: 1–15. [CrossRef]

Giovanis, Eleftherios. 2009. Calendar Effects in Fifty-five Stock Market Indices. *Global Journal of Finance and Management* 1: 75–98.

Giovanis, Eleftherios. 2014. The Turn-of-the-Month-Effect: Evidence from Periodic Generalized Autoregressive Conditional Heteroskedasticity (PGARCH) Model. *International Journal of Economic Sciences and Applied Research* 7: 43–61. [CrossRef]

Heininen, Polina, and Puttonen Vesa. 2008. Stock Market Efficiency In The Transition Economies Through The Lens Of Calendar Anomalies. Paper presented at EACES 10th Bi-Annual Conference Patterns of Transition and New Approaches to Comparative Eoconomics, Higher School of Economics, Moscow, Russia, August 28–30.

Horvath, Roman, Stefan Lyocsa, and Eduard Baumohl. 2018. Stock market contagion in Central and Eastern Europe: Unexpected volatility and extreme co-exceedance. *The European Journal of Finance* 24: 391–412. [CrossRef]

Kayacetin, Volkan, and Senad Lekpek. 2016. Turn-of-the-month effect: New evidence from an emerging stock market. *Finance Research Letters* 18: 142–57. [CrossRef]

Keim, Donald B. 1983. Size-Related Anomalies and Stock Return Seasonality: Further Empirical Evidence. *Journal of Financial Economics* 12: 13–32. [CrossRef]

Kunkel, Robert A., and William S. Compton. 1998. A tax-free exploitation of the turn-of-the-month effect: C.R.E.F. *Financial Services Review* 7: 11–23. [CrossRef]

Kunkel, Robert, William S. Compton, and Scott B. Beyer. 2003. The turn-of-the-month effect still lives: The international evidence. *International Review of Financial Analysis* 12: 207–21. [CrossRef]

Lakonishok, Josef, and Seymour Smidt. 1988. Are Seasonal Anomalies Real? A Ninety-Year Perspective. *The Review of Financial Studies* 1: 403–25. [CrossRef]

Liu, Lan. 2013. The Turn-Of-The-Month Effect In The S&P 500 (2001–2011). *Journal of Business & Economics Research* 11: 269–76. [CrossRef]

Lo, Andrew W. 2004. The Adaptive Markets Hypothesis: Market Efficiency from an Evolutionary Perspective. *Journal of Portfolio Management* 30: 15–29. [CrossRef]

Maher, Daniela, and Anokhi Parikh. 2013. The turn of the month effect in India: A case of large institutional trading patterns as a source of higher liquidity. *International Review of Financial Analysis* 28: 57–69. [CrossRef]

McConnell, John J., and Wei Xu. 2008. Equity Returns at the Turn of the Month. *Financial Analysts Journal* 64: 49–64. [CrossRef]

Milonas, Nikolaos T. 1991. Measuring Seasonalities in Commodity Markets and the Half-Month Effect. *The Journal of Futures Markets* 11: 331–45. [CrossRef]

Moller, Nicholas, and Shlomo Zilca. 2008. The evolution of the January effect. *Journal of Banking & Finance* 32: 447–57. [CrossRef]

Molnar, Peter. 2012. Properties of range-based volatility estimators. *International Review of Financial Analysis* 23: 20–29. [CrossRef]

Nikkinen, Jussi, Sahlstrom Petri, Takko Karri, and Janne Aijo. 2009. Turn-of-the-month and Intramonth Anomalies and U.S. Macroeconomic News Announcements on the Thinly Traded Finnish Stock Market. *International Journal of Economics and Finance* 1: 3–11. [CrossRef]

Ogden, Joseph P. 1990. Turn-of-Month Evaluations of Liquid Profits and Stock Returns: A Common Explanation for the Monthly and January Effects. *The Journal of Finance* 45: 1259–72. [CrossRef]

Olbrys, Joanna, and Elzbieta Majewska. 2016. Crisis periods and contagion effects in the CEE stock markets: The influence of the 2007 US subprime crisis. *International Journal of Computational Economics and Econometrics* 6: 124–37. [CrossRef]

Philpot, James, and Craig A. Peterson. 2011. A brief history and recent developments in day-of-the-week effect literature. *Managerial Finance* 37: 808–16. [CrossRef]

Roberts, Harry. 1967. *Statistical Versus Clinical Prediction of the Stock Market*. Chicago: CRSP University of Chicago.

Vasileiou, Evangelos. 2018. Is the turn of the month effect an "abnormal normality"? Controversial findings, new patterns and... hidden signs(?). *Research in International Business and Finance* 44: 153–75. [CrossRef]

Vychytilova, Jana. 2018. Stock market development beyond the GFC: The case of V4 countries. *Journal of Competitiveness* 10: 149–63. [CrossRef]

Wachtel, Sidney B. 1942. Certain Observations on Seasonal Movements in Stock Prices. *The Journal of Business of the University of Chicago* 15: 184–93. [CrossRef]

Zaremba, Adam. 2019. Trading costs, short sale constraints, and the performance of stock market anomalies in Emerging Europe. *Economic Research-Ekonomska Istrazivanja* 32: 403–22. [CrossRef]

# Investor Attention and Stock Market Activities: New Evidence from Panel Data

**Chaiyuth Padungsaksawasdi [1,*], Sirimon Treepongkaruna [2] and Robert Brooks [3]**

[1] Thammasat Business School, Department of Finance, Thammasat University, Bangkok 10200, Thailand
[2] University of Western Australia Business School, Accounting and Finance, The University of Western Australia, 6009 Perth, Australia; sirimon.treepongkaruna@uwa.edu.au
[3] Monash Business School, Department of Econometrics and Business Statistics, Monash University, Clayton VIC 3800, Australia; robert.brooks@monash.edu
* Correspondence: chaiyuth@tbs.tu.ac.th

**Abstract:** Using the panel vector autoregression (VAR) method, this paper documents relationships between investor attention and stock market activities; i.e., return, volatility, and trading volume, respectively. In sum, bidirectional dynamic interdependence of the SVI–stock market activities relationship exists, in which the SVI–trading volume relationship shows the strongest evidence. This is consistent with prior literature using trading volume as a proxy of investor attention. However, the relationships in the developed and developing markets are statistically significantly different. The stock markets in the developed markets over-react more to the search volume than those in the developing markets. We postulate that investor attention is one of the key elements in asset pricing in stock markets.

**Keywords:** investor attention; Google SVI; panel VAR; stock index activities; Pacific-basin countries

**JEL Classification:** G400; G14; G15

---

## 1. Introduction

Differences in cross-sectional and time-varying investor attention are important components for improving the quality of investment decision-making, as well as for supporting the economic aggregates (Jacobs 2015), though attention is a scarce cognitive resource (Kahneman 1973). Investors have attention constraints that limit their ability to analyze all available information arriving to equity markets, thus they focus only on information of their immediate interests. This in turn suggests that investor attention should be related to activities in the markets. For example, DellaVigna and Pollet (2009) show the Friday inattention effect, in which stock prices on Friday earnings announcements show a larger drift and a slower response than the other days. Seminal works on investor attention at the country level show that investor attention measured by the Google SVI[1] influences stock market activities such as return (Da et al. 2011 and Tantaopas et al. 2016), volatility (Dimpfl and Jank 2016; and Andrei and Hasler 2015), trading volume (Takeda and Wakao 2014), and liquidity (Ding and Hou 2015), respectively.[2] These findings provide support for a potential of interrelations between investor

---

[1] The survey study in New Zealand of Tourani-Rad and Kirkby (2005) shows that almost half of the respondents actively uses the internet as a source of information for making decision in the investment, which is subject to the psychological bias (investor socialization). Recently, Laksomya et al. (2018) show an impact of message board posted on internet on price manipulation in the stock exchange of Thailand.

[2] It should also be noted that the Google SVI has also been used to capture retail investor attention in other markets such as foreign exchange and real estate markets. For example, Yung and Nafar (2017) document high search-intensity REITs possess

attention and stock market activities, including predictability. However, at present, there exists no empirical evidence to demonstrate whether investor attention causes stock market returns, stock market volatility, and stock market trading volume, respectively, or vice versa in a cross-country analysis.

Even though prior literature shows the attention-stock market activities association in a number of countries,[3] Tantaopas et al. (2016) note that the level of investor attention is potentially affected by the shareholder base, culture, ownership structure, legal protection, law enforcement, and financial education, respectively. These characteristics are unique for an individual country. Thus, from a bird's eye view, studying on an individual country basis might not show comprehensive findings on the attention effect in stock markets. It is likely that each fixed effect factor in each country influences the attention-market activities relationship differently. We question whether prior findings in each country are driven by an influence of these unobservable fixed effects. This research aims to fill the gap in this regard.

This paper contributes to prior literature in four main areas shedding light on the role of investor attention in stock markets. First, this study is the first to examine the dynamic attention-stock market activities relationship using the panel vector autoregression (VAR) model. Studies of the attention effect on time series data of an individual stock market potentially lead to conclusions that are subject to a selected country. Thus, the panel VAR is superior to other methodologies by taking into account of the effect of both cross-section (i.e., unobservable fixed effect factors) and time series. Second, we add to existing literature by directly comparing and discussing our results in terms of potential differences in the attention-stock market activities relationships between developed and developing countries. Investors in each country might react differently due to a limited attention. Third, our results highlight the significant role of investor attention in financial markets by documenting the relationship of the level of attention and stock market activities at the aggregate level (panel data) and the predictive power of these activities. Last, we reaffirm that the attention effect is an international phenomenon that is not evidenced in a particular country.

As in Grossmann et al. (2014), we apply the panel VAR for our cross-country analysis. Some beneficial issues of using panel VAR distinguish our paper from prior studies. First, the concept of VAR is an appropriate technique for a general setup, such as the relationship of investor attention and stock market activities as presented in this paper. Second, both fixed and time-varying effects are taken into consideration under the panel VAR specification. Thus, our results are not biased from a time-invariant unobserved heterogeneous factor as well as a time-varying unobservable factor. Last, we can apply the panel VAR with a relatively short data period. The panel VAR technique takes both cross-sectional and intertemporal data in the computation, which increases the number of observations and subsequently helps improve the quality of parameter estimations.

We employ the panel VAR to investigate the relationship between the Google SVI and stock market activities. Throughout the study, we separate our analyses into three categories, the full sample, the developed countries, and the developing countries, respectively. The data includes ten countries in the Asia-Pacific region as in Tantaopas et al. (2016) because we would like to show, compare, and contrast our results on panel data with the results of individual country analyses. Our results in this study strengthen the importance of archival finance research in the Asia-Pacific Basin suggested by Benson et al. (2014). Mostly, two-way panel Granger causality dynamic relationships between the investor attention and each stock market activity exist, especially for the attention-trading volume relationship that we observe in all categories. We conjecture that investor attention, as a behavioral factor, is one of the key determinants in stock markets regardless of the effects of unique

high expected returns and the search query is important, especially for small stocks, high book-to-market stocks, and less informative stocks. In foreign exchange markets, Goddard et al. (2015), show the co-movement between the Google search intensity and volatilities in major currencies, and conjecture that investor attention is a risk factor in the FOREX markets.

3 For example, see Aouadi et al. (2013) for France, Bank et al. (2011) for Germany, Ying et al. (2015) for China, Takeda and Wakao (2014) for Japan, Tantaopas et al. (2016) for the Asia-Pacific countries, and Da et al. (2011) for the U.S.

characteristics (fixed effect) in each country sample, showing that limited investor attention violates the efficient market hypothesis. However, among three attention-stock market activity relationships, only the attention-trading volume relationship is statistically significant for the developing markets. We postulate that search by individuals causes excessive trading volumes in stock markets and vice versa, though the impact of the volume to the investor attention seems to be less. This evidence supports that attention is primarily related to abnormal trading volume and is consistent with prominent literature using trading volume as a proxy of attention[4] (Barber and Odean 2008 and Gervais et al. 2001), We infer that the correlation between trading volume and attention should be notably high. It is interesting to note that we observe a one-way causality relationship of the investor attention in the full sample and weak impacts of the volume to the investor attention in the developed and developing countries. In general, people might gather information before they trade. However, when trading volume is high, investors do not gather more information to trade on fundamentals, rather herd behavior is dominant. Focusing on the results of the other two relationships in the developing countries, we find that investors in these countries do not search for information when they trade stocks.

For the panel VAR estimations, most results are in general consistent with the panel Granger causality. The attention-return relationship is significantly negative with the effect of the return on the SVI stronger than the other way around. Negative events catch more attention than positive ones, implying that investors concern more on the downside risk (Ang et al. 2006). In contrast, the attention-volatility relationship is positive and significant. The impact of the volatility on the SVI is shorter-lived and greater in magnitude than that of the SVI on the volatility. Swing movements in the market catch more attention. Dimpfl and Jank (2016) support our findings by showing the co-movement of the DJIA search keyword and its realized volatility during July 2006 to December 2011. They find that the search query is higher than the average during the turbulent period. Thus, searching behavior is time-varying. In addition, we cannot neglect the important role of trading volume on the higher moments of the stock return distribution as suggested by Do et al. (2014). In the study the attention-abnormal trading volume relationship has the strongest results with relatively higher numbers of statistically significant coefficients for all samples in our analysis. However, the impact of the trading volume is mixed, as the sign shows both negative and positive relationships. We find that the relationship between SVI and abnormal trading volume is negative for a window of the previous two weeks, but reverses to be positive for a window of the past week. The intuition of the positive relationship is straightforward; when investors pay attention to stocks, they are likely to trade them. The higher the investor attention, the larger the trading volume, and vice versa. Our findings seem to make intuitive sense in that information in the further past (e.g., previous two weeks) is already priced, as such investors do not search for any information. However, information asymmetry in a more recent past (e.g., previous one week) is relatively high, leading to an increase in search volume.

All orthogonalized impulse response functions depict similar patterns to the panel VAR results. A comparison of the attention effect between the developing and developed markets indicates significant differences between the two groups. We conclude that the investor attention is common in equity markets, albeit the impact (both the magnitude and number of statistically significant coefficients) is larger in the developed markets. A possible explanation of these differences is that the equity markets in the developed countries over-react more to the level of investor attention than are those in the developing countries. The under-reaction in the developing markets is explained by the frog-in-the-pan hypothesis (Da et al. 2014), stating that investors under-react when small amounts of information arrive to the market relative to large amounts of information arrival. These findings reconfirm the arguments proposed in Tantaopas et al. (2016) that the level of investor attention could

4 Barber and Odean (2008) argue that without investor attention, trading volume cannot happen. Thus, trading volume is a consequence of actual attention.

be impacted by the shareholder base, culture, ownership structure, legal protection, law enforcement, and financial education.

## 2. Relevant Literature

The efficient market hypothesis shows when information arrives in the market, investors can receive, analyze, and decide to trade securities without limited time, limited processing resources, and limited attention. Thus, asset prices change immediately and appropriately, driving to rational trading. However, psychological research[5] suggests that investors have limited attention that they can utilize and so focus on information of their interests within a given period. Investor attention and stock markets then co-move over time (Peng et al. 2007). Investor attention is traditionally proxied by either news and headlines, trading volume, advertising expenses, or ceiling price, however each of these measures has drawbacks. Recently, research on the impact of investor attention in financial markets[6] has gained interests from scholars and the Google SVI is widely used as a reliable and direct proxy of retail investor attention. This is consistent to Benson et al. (2014), who conjecture that behavioral explanation in stock market activities have gained popularity in Asia-Pacific Basin journals.

Merton (1987) shows that investors will trade a stock as far as they recognize it. Consequently, Huberman and Regev (2001) and Barber and Odean (2008) suggest when information arrives in the market, only attention from investors causes changes in prices, implying that investor attention is a necessary condition of stock trading. Thus, investor attention is the key of investors' decision-making. This is consistent with Da et al. (2011), documenting that investor attention influences stock movement and is not constant over time. High and low levels of investor attention affect the reaction of the stock market differently.[7] A high level of investor attention causes a pressure to stock prices and drives the prices to be efficient, while investors under-react when they pay less attention. In fact, researchers provide evidence of the relationship of investor attention and financial market activities in terms of both individual securities and the aggregate market level. Recently, Tsukioka et al. (2017) using textual analysis to extract related investor sentiment words, show that high levels of investor attention and investor sentiment help explain IPO puzzles in the Japanese market. Another example of the effect of internet message boards on price manipulation in the Thai stock market is investigated by Laksomya et al. (2018). In general, the results of the firm-level data are not qualitatively different from those of the market-wide level in that there exists a relationship between investor attention and stock market activities. For example, Bijl et al. (2016) document the negative return predictability of the Google SVI in the S&P 500 companies, which contradicts Da et al. (2011) and Joseph et al. (2011), who suggest a positive predictive power of the Google SVI on stock returns. In sum, we cannot avoid the effect of the internet's power in financial markets.

However, Vozlyublennaia (2014) and Tantaopas et al. (2016) document that the Google SVI should be tested with a country-wide investment. We thus limit our discussion in this section only on existing evidence of the aggregate level, which is consistent with the aim and the scope of this study. Importantly, not many studies conduct research on the aggregate level of stock performance, stock volatility, and stock trading volume in a single study. Our research thus provides such additional evidence.

Evidence regarding investor attention has remained mixed, as to whether it strengthens or worsens market efficiency. On the supporting side, Vozlyublennaia (2014) shows the dynamic interrelationship of investor attention and aggregate market activities in several asset classes in the U.S. markets. Moreover, the presence of investor attention helps improve return efficiency. An increase in attention

---

5 Two other popular behavioral factors influencing stock market activities include investor mood (Harding and He 2016) and investor sentiment (Piccoli et al. 2018 and Johnman et al. 2018).

6 The study of the attention effect is not limited only in stock markets and the results in other markets largely confirm the findings in stock markets. See, for example, Goddard et al. (2015) for foreign exchange markets, Li et al. (2015) for energy markets, and Rochdi and Dietzel (2015) and Braun (2016) for real estate markets.

7 An asymmetric impact of the investor attention is similar to that of the investor sentiment. Tsai (2017) demonstrates that pessimistic investor sentiment spreads over more than optimistic investor sentiment, confirming the asymmetry.

reveals information to asset prices.[8] Hamid and Heiden (2015) confirm this in terms of volatility predictability, and document that investor attention drives the Dow Jones equity index to be more efficient both in- and out-of-sample and especially in the high volatile state. Moreover, Tantaopas et al. (2016) extend prior studies by examining the investor attention effect both in developing and developed countries. The attention diminishes return and volatility predictability, consistent with the information discovery hypothesis. However, they do find an ceffect on trading volume predictability.

On the opposing side, Dimpfl and Jank (2016) find the contemporaneous co-movement between the Dow Jones' search volume intensity and realized volatility. Moreover, search volume increases the volatility predictability, consistent with the noise trader hypothesis. Keyword search by retail investors is considered as uninformed noise traders and causes the market to become more volatile.

In summary, existing literature is largely based on evidence on individual countries in advanced economies, especially in the U.S. markets and the results are still inconclusive. This paper fills a considerable gap in this field providing new evidence on the cross-country analysis based on an international perspective, considering developing countries, and developed countries, respectively.

## 3. Data

### 3.1. *Google Search Intensity*

We analyzed selected search keywords obtained by Google Trends[9] in this study following the approach adopted by Tantaopas et al. (2016). Our sample for analysis consisted of ten countries categorized into two subsamples, developing (China,[10] India, Malaysia, and Thailand) and developed markets (Australia, Hong Kong, Japan, Korea, New Zealand, and Singapore). We decided to employ the same country sample for a direct comparison. Moreover, we shed light on additional evidence of the index performances rather than on individual stocks as suggested by Vozlyublennaia (2014). The search keywords employed in this study are shown in the Appendix A.[11] Other stock markets data were from DataStream. Our sample spanned the time period from January 2004 to December 2014.

### 3.2. *Stock Market Return, Volatility, and Abnormal Trading Volume*

In this study Google's weekly SVI starts on Sundays and is shown in terms of a natural logarithm. Weekly stock index returns ($R$) in each country are calculated as the natural logarithm of closing stock market index price changes on Mondays and Fridays during the same week. Weekly stock index return volatility ($\sigma^2$) in each country is the weekly squared return from Mondays to Fridays during the same

---

8 Storms et al. (2015) also document the efficiency-improving role of investor attention in individual stocks in the European and the U.S. markets. The efficiency improvement is more pronounced during bullish markets. Aouadi et al. (2013) find the same evidence in the French stock market.

9 From the Google Trends' website, we select the "global region" in order to capture the "true" investor attention around the globe.

10 Even though some employ the Baidu search engine rather than Google search engine in the mainland Chinese stock market due to the exit of the Google on March 23, 2010, we prefer using the Google SVI for a few reasons. First, uses of the same international search engine for all countries make the data consistent and comparable. Our approach is similar to Gao et al. (2016), who study the Google sentiment on stock markets in a cross country analysis around the globe, including mainland China. Second, though Google search is prohibited in the mainland China, foreign retail investors are still able to use Google to search information and decide to trade in the Chinese stock markets or local investor can use the virtual private networks (VPNs) to access the Google website (Wang et al. 2017). Thus, Google search intensity for the Chinese stock market is valid.

11 The search keywords are in the English language. There are some working papers that use the local language for the search queries. For example, Storms et al. (2015) rely on the search keywords in local languages for stocks in European countries. However, they show that the local search keywords are highly correlated with the English search keywords. Thus, the search keyword is not biased from the choice of the languages. The results are similar to the findings of Al-Eroud et al. (2011), who study the language preferences for searching Google queries for Arab countries. The internet users in these countries favor to use English language rather than their own local languages to Google search. Thus, our use of English search keywords in the study is in line with other literature.

week. We follow Takeda and Wakao (2014) to define abnormal trading volume (*ATV*) in each stock market *i* as below.

$$ATV_{i,t} = \frac{TV_{i,t} - \overline{TV_i}}{\overline{TV_i}} \quad (1)$$

where $TV_{i,t}$ is natural logarithm of trading volume of the stock market *i* during week *t*. $\overline{TV_i}$ is the average trading volume of stock market *i* over the entire sample period.

## 4. Panel Vector Autoregression

Prior literature shows that SVI and other markets variables possess dynamic interrelationships. In a reduced form, the VAR for panel data is presented as:

$$\begin{bmatrix} SVI_{i,t} \\ Y_{i,t} \end{bmatrix} = \begin{bmatrix} a_{11} & b_{11} \\ a_{21} & b_{21} \end{bmatrix} \begin{bmatrix} SVI_{i,t-1} \\ Y_{i,t-1} \end{bmatrix} + \begin{bmatrix} a_{12} & b_{12} \\ a_{22} & b_{22} \end{bmatrix} \begin{bmatrix} SVI_{i,t-2} \\ Y_{i,t-2} \end{bmatrix} + \cdots + \begin{bmatrix} a_{1p} & b_{1p} \\ a_{2p} & b_{2p} \end{bmatrix} \begin{bmatrix} SVI_{i,t-p} \\ Y_{i,t-p} \end{bmatrix} + \begin{bmatrix} f_{1i} \\ f_{2i} \end{bmatrix} + \begin{bmatrix} e_{1i,t} \\ e_{2i,t} \end{bmatrix} \quad (2)$$

where $SVI_{i,t}$ is the appropriate selected keyword of the stock market index in country *i* in week *t*. *Y* represents the stock market variables; namely stock market index return, stock market return volatility, and stock market abnormal trading volume. *i* represents ten countries, which are divided into two groups, developing markets (China, India, Malaysia, and Thailand) and developed markets (Australia, Hong Kong, Japan, Korea, New Zealand, and Singapore). *p* is the optimal lag length suggested by Andrews and Lu (2001), which is equal to one in the SVI–return relationship and two in the SVI–volatility, and the SVI–abnormal trading volume relationships, respectively. Andrews and Lu (2001) developed a new methodology for the model selection procedures known as the consistent model and moment selection criteria (MMSC), which is based on GMM estimation. Their proposed technique is similar, but superior, to maximum likelihood estimation used in the Akaike information criteria (AIC), the Bayesian information (BIC), and Hannan–Quinn information criteria (HQIC), respectively. A consensus of the minimum lag length of MMSC-AIC, MMSC-BIC, and MMSC-HQIC was the criterion for the model selection in this study.

In panel data, we might encounter some individual heterogeneity. $f_i$ represents a fixed effect in the model, thus unobservable factors in each country are not time-variant. It is common and essential to control for the country's fixed effect in a panel analysis. However, incorporating unobservable country's fixed effect variables in the model induces a correlation among independent variables because of the lagged values of the dependent variables. A common use of first-differencing procedure for solving this problem yields biased and inconsistent estimated coefficients. This might cause more missing data in an unbalanced panel. We alleviated this potential problem by taking a forward mean-differencing procedure known as the Helmert transformation procedure or forward orthogonal deviation (Arellano and Bover 1995). This procedure eliminates the fixed effect of the model by transforming all variables in terms of differences from forward means, subsequently reducing missing data. Hayakawa (2009) addresses the choice of transformation that is of concern in GMM estimation of a finite sample for empirics and shows that the first difference transformation method is inferior to the forward orthogonal deviation transformation method. Thus, a new panel VAR model after Helmert transformation (*H*) is:

$$\begin{bmatrix} SVI^H_{i,t} \\ Y^H_{i,t} \end{bmatrix} = \begin{bmatrix} a_{11} & b_{11} \\ a_{21} & b_{21} \end{bmatrix} \begin{bmatrix} SVI^H_{i,t-1} \\ Y^H_{i,t-1} \end{bmatrix} + \begin{bmatrix} a_{12} & b_{12} \\ a_{22} & b_{22} \end{bmatrix} \begin{bmatrix} SVI^H_{i,t-2} \\ Y^H_{i,t-2} \end{bmatrix} + \cdots + \begin{bmatrix} a_{1p} & b_{1p} \\ a_{2p} & b_{2p} \end{bmatrix} \begin{bmatrix} SVI^H_{i,t-p} \\ Y^H_{i,t-p} \end{bmatrix} + \begin{bmatrix} v_{1i,t} \\ v_{2i,t} \end{bmatrix} \quad (3)$$

Because of dynamic interrelationships among the SVI, stock market variables, and the fixed effect, the estimation of the least squares dummy variable procedure (LSDV) yields biased estimated coefficients (Rousseau and Wachtel 2000). A new panel VAR model using GMM estimation was a more appropriate technique in this study for the causality relationships (see for example, Love and Zicchino 2006 and Grossmann et al. 2014). We follow the GMM estimation proposed by Holtz-Eakin et al. (1988).

For our panel VAR analysis, we ran pairwise relationships between the SVI and stock market index return, the SVI and stock market volatility, and the SVI and stock market abnormal trading volume, respectively.

**5. Empirical Results**

The stationarity for all variables for panel data was confirmed by using Fisher-type unit root test based on Augmented Dickey Fuller (ADF) and Philips–Perron (PP) statistics as suggested by Choi (2001).[12] For all analyses, we present our results in three panels, i.e., Panel A for the relationship between the SVI and stock market index return (SVI–return), Panel B for the relationship between the SVI and stock market volatility (SVI–volatility), and Panel C for the relationship between the SVI and stock market abnormal trading volume (SVI–volume). Moreover, we separated our sample into three categories for in-depth analyses: (i) full sample, (ii) developed markets (Australia, Hong Kong, Japan, Korea, New Zealand, and Singapore), and (iii) developing markets (China, India, Malaysia, and Thailand). Overall, we present, compare, and discuss our results both in terms of types of the relationships and those of market developments.

*5.1. Panel Granger Causality*

Table 1 shows the panel Granger causality tests for the SVI–return, the SVI–volatility, and the SVI–abnormal trading volume. Overall, two-way relationships existed in most cases.[13] This was consistent with the information discovery hypothesis, indicating that the SVI and each market activity hold interdependence relationships. However, evidence in the developing markets was weakest, such that we did not find any causality relationship of the SVI–return and the SVI–volatility. This was consistent with Tsai (2017), who finds mostly no Granger causality relationship between the Kumar and Lee (2006) sentiment index of different types of institutional traders and stock market returns in the Taiwanese stock exchange. Our findings on broad market activity contradict the results of the experimental design by Boduroglu et al. (2009) that Westerners allocate their attention in a narrower manner than East Asians. Interestingly, the evidence of two-way interdependence relationships was very strong; significant SVI–volume relationships existed in all cases. This finding is consistent with Miller (1977) and Gervais et al. (2001), who document that trading volume attracts investor attention and encourage markets participants to buy stocks. Thus, the larger the trading volume, the higher the investor attention. In general, our results are consistent with Tantaopas et al. (2016), who investigate the attention effect in individual countries. However, our evidence in the developing countries appears weaker.

*5.2. Panel Vector Autoregression*

In this section, we assess the causal relationships through panel VAR using GMM estimation as presented in Table 2. We confirmed our model identification by employing Hansen's *J*-statistic test. The null hypothesis of the test was not rejected; hence, the model estimation was valid. Overall, the results were consistent with our findings from the panel Granger causality analysis. Panel A of Table 2 shows the two-way relationship for the full sample and the one-way SVI–return relationship for the developed markets. In general, the relationship was negative and the effect of the return on the SVI was greater than that of the SVI on the return. For the full sample, the magnitude of negative lagged

---

12 The null hypothesis is that panels are unit roots. The Z statistic is presented as $Z = \frac{1}{\sqrt{N}} \sum_{i=1}^{N} \Phi^{-1}(p_i)$, where $p_i$ is the $i$th panel and $\Phi^{-1}$ is the inverse of the standard normal cumulative distribution function. $Z$ is normally distributed with zero mean and unity variance. The results are available upon request.

13 It is interesting to note that one-way relationships are detected in the SVI–volatility relationship of the developed markets and the SVI–volume relationship of the full sample. SVI Granger causes stock market volatility and abnormal trading volume, but not the other way around. When people search more they are making the market more volatile or executing more trade orders. Thus, Google search intensity is a good proxy of retail investor attention.

returns on the current SVI (1.8397) was larger than the impact of the negative lagged SVI on the current returns (0.0035). However, only negative lagged returns influenced the current SVI for the developed markets. We argue that people searched more for information after a crash in equity markets in those countries. Interestingly, we did not observe this relationship for the developing markets. We propose possible explanations as follows. First, investors in the developing markets do not search information via search engines. The number of non-users internet relative to the population in developing countries is much greater than that of developed countries.[14] Alternatively, technological advance in developing countries is less than that of developed countries. Second, Nisbett et al. (2001) show that Asians are less analytic, less rational, and more holistic than Westerners, the considerable social differences affect people's belief and cognitive processes. Chang et al. (2000) show that herd behavior is strongly apparent in developing markets, but not in developed markets. Moreover, herd behavior in developing markets is more asymmetric than in developed markets, especially in up markets (Chiang and Zheng 2010).

**Table 1.** Panel Granger causality.

| | Chi-Square | *p*-Value |
|---|---|---|
| Panel A: SVI and Return | | |
| Full Sample | | |
| SVI does not Granger cause return | 3.847 ** | 0.050 |
| Return does not Granger cause SVI | 6.312 ** | 0.012 |
| Developed markets | | |
| SVI does not Granger cause return | 3.092 * | 0.079 |
| Return does not Granger cause SVI | 5.35 ** | 0.021 |
| Developing markets | | |
| SVI does not Granger cause return | 0.004 | 0.947 |
| Return does not Granger cause SVI | 0.992 | 0.319 |
| Panel B: SVI and Volatility | | |
| Full Sample | | |
| SVI does not Granger cause volatility | 7.674 ** | 0.022 |
| Volatility does not Granger cause SVI | 4.901 * | 0.086 |
| Developed markets | | |
| SVI does not Granger cause volatility | 15.695 *** | 0.000 |
| Volatility does not Granger cause SVI | 1.249 | 0.536 |
| Developing markets | | |
| SVI does not Granger cause volatility | 2.201 | 0.333 |
| Volatility does not Granger cause SVI | 2.954 | 0.228 |
| Panel C: SVI and Abnormal Trading Volume | | |
| Full Sample | | |
| SVI does not Granger cause volume | 414.089 *** | 0.000 |
| Volume does not Granger cause SVI | 1.362 | 0.506 |
| Developed markets | | |
| SVI does not Granger cause volume | 28.301 *** | 0.000 |
| Volume does not Granger cause SVI | 5.222 * | 0.073 |
| Developing markets | | |
| SVI does not Granger cause volume | 268.509 *** | 0.000 |
| Volume does not Granger cause SVI | 4.648 * | 0.098 |

Table 1 shows the results of the panel Granger causality test for three relationships. Panels A to C show the results for the SVI–return, the SVI–volatility, and the SVI–abnormal trading volume, respectively. *, ** and *** denote the 10%, 5%, and 1% significance levels, respectively.

---

14 http://www.internetlivestats.com/internet-users-by-country/.

**Table 2.** Panel vector autoregression (VAR) estimations.

| | | | | | | |
|---|---|---|---|---|---|---|
| | | | **Panel A: SVI and Return.** | | | |
| | **Full Sample** | | **Developed Markets** | | **Developing Markets** | |
| | $SVI_t$ | $R_t$ | $SVI_t$ | $R_t$ | $SVI_t$ | $R_t$ |
| $SVI_{t-1}$ | 0.7512 *** | −0.0035 *** | 0.8790 *** | −0.0041 | 0.6753 *** | −0.0026 |
| | (0.0588) | (0.0014) | (0.0583) | (0.0018) | (0.0872) | (0.0026) |
| $R_{t-1}$ | −1.8397 *** | −0.0534 ** | −2.0877 * | −0.0411 | −0.0701 | −0.0493 |
| | (0.9379) | (0.0224) | (1.1872) | (0.0352) | (1.0598) | (0.0496) |
| Hansen $J$ Test | 0.168 | | 0.127 | | 0.990 | |
| | | | **Panel B: SVI and Volatility.** | | | |
| | **Full Sample** | | **Developed Markets** | | **Developing Markets** | |
| | $SVI_t$ | $\sigma_t^2$ | $SVI_t$ | $\sigma_t^2$ | $SVI_t$ | $\sigma_t^2$ |
| $SVI_{t-1}$ | 0.5861 *** | 0.0000 | 0.7683 *** | 0.0000 | 0.5299 *** | −0.0000 |
| | (0.0624) | (0.0001) | (0.0769) | (0.0001) | (0.0817) | (0.0001) |
| $SVI_{t-2}$ | 0.2436 *** | 0.0002 ** | 0.1643 ** | 0.0001 | 0.1726 ** | 0.0002* |
| | (0.0610) | (0.0001) | (0.0693) | (0.0001) | (0.0797) | (0.0001) |
| $\sigma_{t-1}^2$ | 28.6188 * | 0.4334 *** | 49.8386 *** | 0.5011 *** | −9.2805 | 0.3144 *** |
| | (17.0147) | (0.0817) | (17.1577) | (0.0852) | (6.6255) | (0.1016) |
| $\sigma_{t-2}^2$ | 8.7659 | 0.2885 *** | 9.4705 | 0.1961 *** | 3.5395 | 0.1244 ** |
| | (9.3922) | (0.0548) | (9.2032) | (0.0535) | (16.8600) | (0.0494) |
| Hansen $J$ Test | 0.888 | | 0.584 | | 0.998 | |
| | | | **Panel C: SVI and Abnormal Trading Volume.** | | | |
| | **Full Sample** | | **Developed Markets** | | **Developing Markets** | |
| | $SVI_t$ | $ATV_t$ | $SVI_t$ | $SVI_t$ | $ATV_t$ | $SVI_t$ |
| $SVI_{t-1}$ | 0.5687 *** | 0.0022 | 0.5632 *** | −0.0023 | 0.5938 *** | 0.0001 |
| | (0.0419) | (0.0021) | (0.0580) | (0.0019) | (0.0529) | (0.0020) |
| $SVI_{t-2}$ | 0.2178 *** | 0.0001 | 0.2887 *** | 0.0037 ** | 0.1695 *** | 0.0034 ** |
| | (0.0392) | (0.0017) | (0.0558) | (0.0016) | (0.0503) | (0.0016) |
| $ATV_{t-1}$ | 2.5403 *** | 0.7262 *** | 4.4586 *** | 1.2674 *** | 0.5779 *** | 0.5282 *** |
| | (0.2191) | (0.0514) | (0.8500) | (0.0784) | (0.1134) | (0.0660) |
| $ATV_{t-2}$ | −0.5859 *** | 0.2207 *** | −3.9262 *** | −0.2962 *** | 1.1878 *** | 0.4054 *** |
| | (0.0845) | (0.0449) | (0.7693) | (0.0694) | (0.1898) | (0.0636) |
| Hansen $J$ Test | 0.631 | | 0.931 | | 0.637 | |

Panels A to C of Table 2 show the panel VAR estimations of relationships between the SVI and stock market indices, the SVI and stock market volatilities, and the SVI and market abnormal trading volumes, respectively. The minimum consenting MMSC-AIC, MMSC-BIC, and MMSC-HQIC optimal lag length, which is equal to one for the SVI–return relationship and two for the SVI–volatility and the SVI–abnormal volume relationships. Hansen $J$ test tells about over-identification restrictions of the GMM estimation. Standard errors are shown in parentheses. *, ** and *** denote the 10%, 5%, and 1% significance levels, respectively.

Panel B of Table 2 presents the results of the full sample for the SVI–volatility relationship. As in the SVI–return relationship, we find lagged volatilities had impacts on the current SVI and vice versa.[15] Again, the impact of the volatility was larger than that of SVI, but the relationship between the SVI and volatility was positive. The search intensity was one of the key determinants of market volatility. Interestingly, past volatilities of the market called for market-wide attention in the developed markets, but not vice versa. This confirms that investors are more concerned about large price movements due to heightened uncertainty. Surprisingly, the volatility effect did not play a role in the developing markets, but the search intensities did. The higher the search intensity in the past, the more volatile the market. Searching information by retail investors caused noises to the market. Again, we did not

[15] Examples of a linkage between information and volatility in FX markets include Treepongkaruna and Gray (2009) and Treepongkaruna et al. (2012).

observe a strong SVI–volatility relationship in the developing markets. The difference in results of the relationships between the developed and developing markets could be explained as follows. Similar to the argument put forward in the SVI–return relationship, we argue that Asians are less analytic, less rational, and more holistic than Westerners (Nisbett et al. 2001).

For developing countries, investing in stock markets is more likely to be a gamble than investment. Thus, they do not care about the variability in the stock markets. Kumar (2009), studying the tendency to gamble and trading decisions supports this statement. Low-income investors (i.e., retail investors in developing markets) prefer trading in lottery-type stocks and the level of investing in lottery-type stock is higher in markets in which traders like to trade them. Finally, developing markets have different market microstructures compared to developed markets (Madhavan 2000).

Compared with the other relationships, Panel C of Table 2 indicates somewhat different results for the SVI–volume analyses. A weak relationship was noted for the full sample, where only abnormal trading volumes in the past influenced the current SVI. In contrast, strong evidence was observed in both developed and developing countries, where abnormal trading volumes had impacts on the current SVI and vice versa. Moreover, the effects of abnormal trading volume dominated those of SVI in all cases. It seemed that trading volume showed a strong connection with the SVI. This was consistent with the prior literature (Barber and Odean 2008 and Gervais et al. 2001) that uses the trading volumes as a proxy of investor attention. A logical explanation is that investors pay more attention on their interesting stocks and have a large tendency to trade them. Thus, the trading volume is more closely related to attention. In other words, without attention, trading volumes cannot emerge.

In sum, the dynamic interrelationships between investor attention and stock market activities were more prominent in the developed countries than in the developing countries. Our findings were attributed to behavioral biases, for instance Hou et al. (2009) document that over-reaction is the result of the attention. Without attention, investors cannot process and over-react to available information. Weak evidence on the developing countries showed that people do not search for information before they decide to trade, in contrast to the suggestion of Merton (1987).

Additionally, we present the impulse response functions for the three models employed in this study in Figure 1. As usual, Panels A to C depict the impulse responses of the SVI–return, the SVI–volatility, and the SVI–volume relationships, respectively. The impulse response function was estimated by employing the Cholesky decomposition (Sim 1980). The 5% error bands were created by using 500 repetitions of a Monte Carlo simulation. In general, the impulse responses were consistent with the panel VAR estimated coefficients and most of them showed pulse-like lines, which tended to reverse within five weeks for the return relationship and within ten weeks for the volatility and trading volume. Shocks in returns seemed to have a lower effect than the other two cases. Thus, stock markets were more efficient in terms of return than volatility and trading volumes. The responses of the SVI to return and those of the return to SVI were negative for all cases as depicted in Panel A. This was consistent with the prior literature that shows a dynamic interdependence relationship between the SVI and stock market index returns. However, a different pattern was present in the relationship between the SVI and stock index volatility as depicted in Panel B and the SVI and abnormal trading volume as depicted in Panel C, respectively. The impulse responses of the SVI to volatility and those of the volatility to SVI were positive, hence a shock in the SVI (volatility) increased the stock market index volatility (SVI). This pattern was similar to the SVI–abnormal trading volume relationship. Thus, a shock in SVI increased trading volumes and vice versa, which supports prior studies (Barber and Odean 2008 and Gervais et al. 2001) using trading volume a proxy of investor attention.

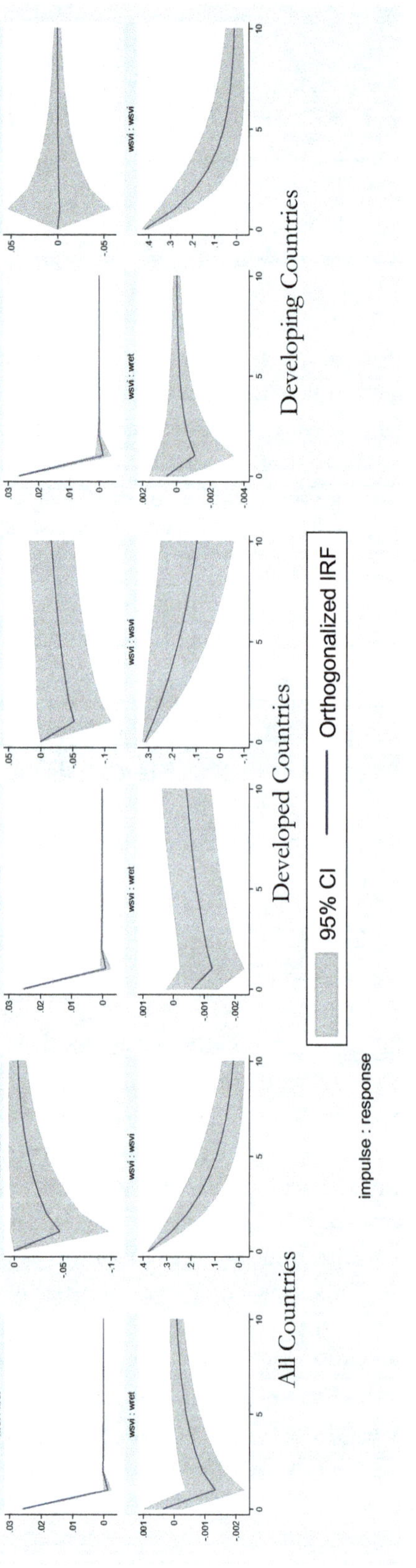


(A) SVI and Return.

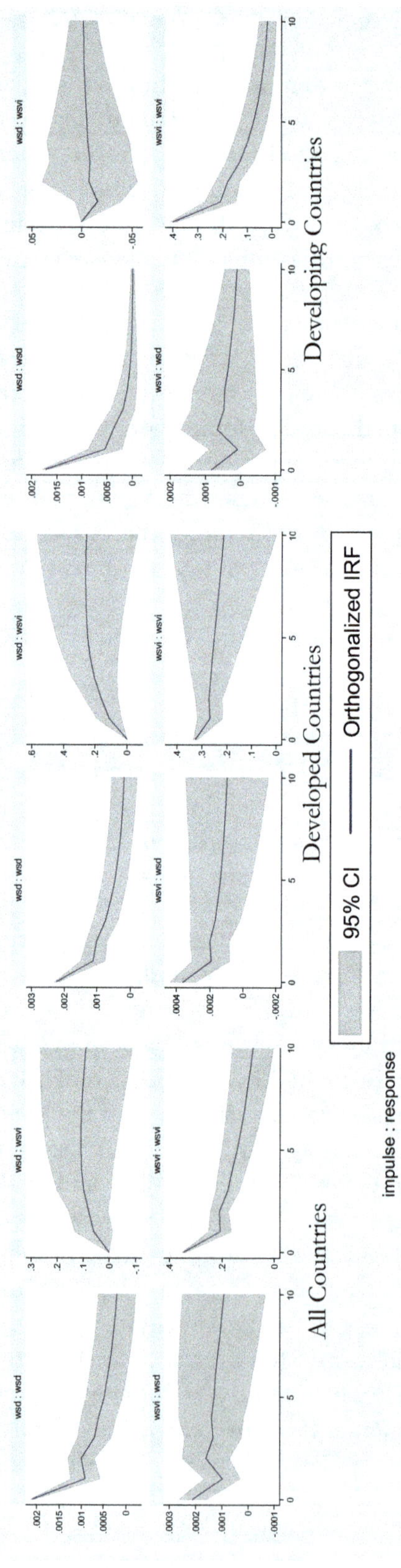


(B) SVI and Volatility.

**Figure 1.** *Cont.*

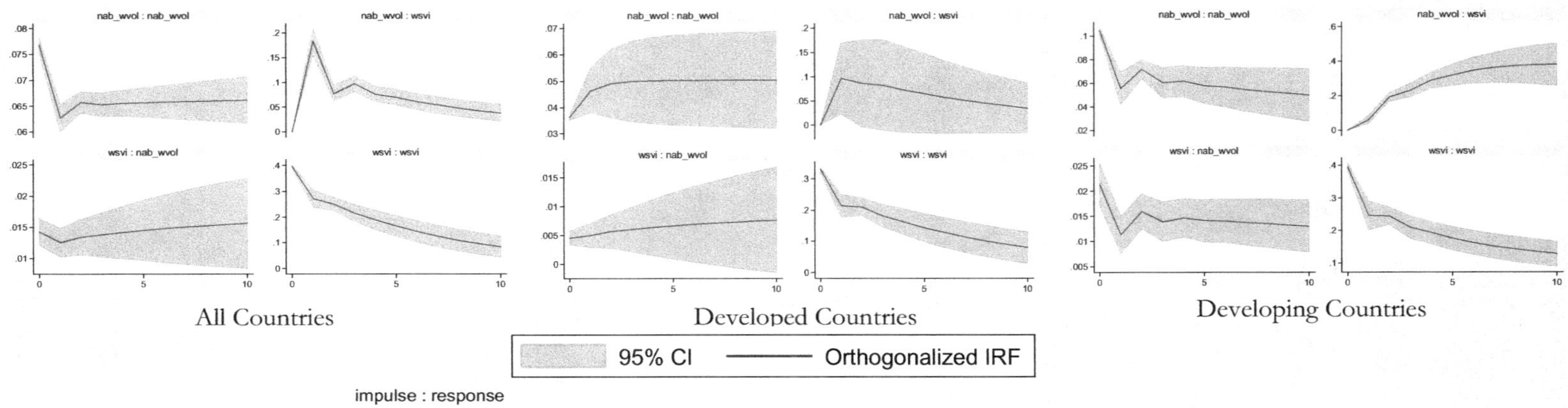


(C) SVI and Abnormal Volume.

**Figure 1.** Orthogonalized impulse responses for the SVI relationships. Figure 1 depicts the impulse responses for the SVI–return (**A**), the SVI–volatility (**B**), and the SVI–abnormal trading volumes (**C**), respectively. From the left to right, each figure represents the impulse responses of the full sample, developed countries, and developing countries. The 95% confidence interval (CI) is created by the Monte Carlo simulation with 500 repetitions.

*5.3. Variance Decomposition*

A variance decomposition showed the accumulated impact of the shock on one variable to the proportion of variation in a given variable. Table 3 presents the forecast-error variance decomposition for all relationships in the three cases. Panel A reports the variance decomposition of the SVI–return relationship. We found that returns explain the variation in SVI approximately to be 1.33% for the full sample and 2.00% for developed countries of total variations for ten periods ahead, respectively. The effect in the developing countries was very small, which is consistent with our finding on the non-existent SVI–return relationship. Moreover, the effects of the SVI on the return variation were small for all cases. The effects of the volatility on the shock in the SVI were more pronounced than that in the SVI–return relationship, as shown in Panel A. This was true for the cases of the developed and developing countries. The effects of the abnormal trading volume on the shock in the SVI were the largest, accounting for almost 50% variation. Again, the trading volume was a good proxy of investor attention and showed interdependence relationship.

**Table 3.** Variance decomposition.

**Panel A: SVI and Return.**

| Response | Forecast | Impulse Variable | | | | | |
|---|---|---|---|---|---|---|---|
| Variable | Horizon | Full Sample | | Developed Countries | | Developing Countries | |
| | | SVI | Return | SVI | Return | SVI | Return |
| SVI | 1 | 1.0000 | 0.0000 | 1.0000 | 0.0000 | 1.0000 | 0.0000 |
| | 2 | 0.9901 | 0.0099 | 0.9848 | 0.0152 | 1.0000 | 0.0000 |
| | 3 | 0.9878 | 0.0122 | 0.9809 | 0.0191 | 1.0000 | 0.0000 |
| | 4 | 0.9868 | 0.0132 | 0.9789 | 0.0211 | 1.0000 | 0.0000 |
| | 5 | 0.9863 | 0.0137 | 0.9778 | 0.0222 | 1.0000 | 0.0000 |
| | 6 | 0.9860 | 0.0140 | 0.9771 | 0.0229 | 1.0000 | 0.0000 |
| | 7 | 0.9859 | 0.0141 | 0.9766 | 0.0234 | 1.0000 | 0.0000 |
| | 8 | 0.9858 | 0.0142 | 0.9762 | 0.0238 | 1.0000 | 0.0000 |
| | 9 | 0.9857 | 0.0143 | 0.9760 | 0.0240 | 1.0000 | 0.0000 |
| | 10 | 0.9857 | 0.0143 | 0.9758 | 0.0242 | 1.0000 | 0.0000 |
| Return | 1 | 0.0002 | 0.9998 | 0.0006 | 0.9994 | 0.0004 | 0.9996 |
| | 2 | 0.0029 | 0.9971 | 0.0031 | 0.9969 | 0.0022 | 0.9978 |
| | 3 | 0.0041 | 0.9959 | 0.0049 | 0.9951 | 0.0028 | 0.9972 |
| | 4 | 0.0049 | 0.9951 | 0.0064 | 0.9936 | 0.0031 | 0.9969 |
| | 5 | 0.0053 | 0.9947 | 0.0075 | 0.9925 | 0.0033 | 0.9967 |
| | 6 | 0.0056 | 0.9944 | 0.0084 | 0.9916 | 0.0033 | 0.9967 |
| | 7 | 0.0057 | 0.9943 | 0.0091 | 0.9909 | 0.0034 | 0.9966 |
| | 8 | 0.0058 | 0.9942 | 0.0097 | 0.9903 | 0.0034 | 0.9966 |
| | 9 | 0.0058 | 0.9942 | 0.0101 | 0.9899 | 0.0034 | 0.9966 |
| | 10 | 0.0059 | 0.9941 | 0.0105 | 0.9895 | 0.0034 | 0.9966 |

**Panel B: SVI and Volatility.**

| Response | Forecast | Impulse Variable | | | | | |
|---|---|---|---|---|---|---|---|
| Variable | Horizon | Full Sample | | Developed Countries | | Developing Countries | |
| | | SVI | Volatility | SVI | Volatility | SVI | Volatility |
| SVI | 1 | 1.0000 | 0.0000 | 1.0000 | 0.0000 | 1.0000 | 0.0000 |
| | 2 | 0.9785 | 0.0215 | 0.9350 | 0.0650 | 0.9987 | 0.0013 |
| | 3 | 0.9546 | 0.0454 | 0.8669 | 0.1331 | 0.9987 | 0.0013 |
| | 4 | 0.9252 | 0.0748 | 0.8009 | 0.1991 | 0.9985 | 0.0015 |
| | 5 | 0.8972 | 0.1028 | 0.7458 | 0.2542 | 0.9984 | 0.0016 |
| | 6 | 0.8713 | 0.1287 | 0.7010 | 0.2990 | 0.9984 | 0.0016 |
| | 7 | 0.8485 | 0.1516 | 0.6650 | 0.3350 | 0.9983 | 0.0017 |
| | 8 | 0.8288 | 0.1712 | 0.6360 | 0.3640 | 0.9983 | 0.0017 |
| | 9 | 0.8120 | 0.1880 | 0.6125 | 0.3875 | 0.9983 | 0.0017 |

**Table 3.** *Cont.*

| Panel A: SVI and Return. | | | | | | | |
|---|---|---|---|---|---|---|---|
| **Response** | **Forecast** | **Impulse Variable** | | | | | |
| **Variable** | **Horizon** | **Full Sample** | | **Developed Countries** | | **Developing Countries** | |
| | 10 | 0.7980 | 0.2020 | 0.5934 | 0.4066 | 0.9983 | 0.0017 |
| Volatility | 1 | 0.0101 | 0.9899 | 0.0252 | 0.9748 | 0.0023 | 0.9977 |
| | 2 | 0.0103 | 0.9897 | 0.0259 | 0.9741 | 0.0021 | 0.9979 |
| | 3 | 0.0128 | 0.9872 | 0.0275 | 0.9725 | 0.0033 | 0.9967 |
| | 4 | 0.0145 | 0.9855 | 0.0290 | 0.9710 | 0.0039 | 0.9961 |
| | 5 | 0.0165 | 0.9835 | 0.0305 | 0.9695 | 0.0045 | 0.9955 |
| | 6 | 0.0182 | 0.9818 | 0.0318 | 0.9682 | 0.0048 | 0.9952 |
| | 7 | 0.0199 | 0.9801 | 0.0330 | 0.9670 | 0.0051 | 0.9949 |
| | 8 | 0.0213 | 0.9787 | 0.0341 | 0.9659 | 0.0052 | 0.9948 |
| | 9 | 0.0226 | 0.9774 | 0.0352 | 0.9649 | 0.0053 | 0.9947 |
| | 10 | 0.0237 | 0.9763 | 0.0361 | 0.9639 | 0.0054 | 0.9946 |

| Panel C: SVI and Abnormal Trading Volume. | | | | | | | |
|---|---|---|---|---|---|---|---|
| **Response** | **Forecast** | **Impulse Variable** | | | | | |
| **Variable** | **Horizon** | **Full Sample** | | **Developed Countries** | | **Developing Countries** | |
| | | **SVI** | **Volume** | **SVI** | **Volume** | **SVI** | **Volume** |
| SVI | 1 | 1.0000 | 0.0000 | 1.0000 | 0.0000 | 1.0000 | 0.0000 |
| | 2 | 0.8716 | 0.1284 | 0.9288 | 0.0712 | 0.9834 | 0.0166 |
| | 3 | 0.8054 | 0.1946 | 0.8994 | 0.1006 | 0.8719 | 0.1281 |
| | 4 | 0.7175 | 0.2825 | 0.8726 | 0.1274 | 0.7728 | 0.2272 |
| | 5 | 0.6427 | 0.3573 | 0.8532 | 0.1468 | 0.6672 | 0.3328 |
| | 6 | 0.5766 | 0.4234 | 0.8368 | 0.1632 | 0.5809 | 0.4191 |
| | 7 | 0.5210 | 0.4790 | 0.8228 | 0.1772 | 0.5094 | 0.4906 |
| | 8 | 0.4744 | 0.5256 | 0.8104 | 0.1896 | 0.4524 | 0.5476 |
| | 9 | 0.4355 | 0.5645 | 0.7992 | 0.2008 | 0.4067 | 0.5933 |
| | 10 | 0.4029 | 0.5971 | 0.7890 | 0.2110 | 0.3700 | 0.6300 |
| Volume | 1 | 0.0515 | 0.9485 | 0.0298 | 0.9702 | 0.0396 | 0.9604 |
| | 2 | 0.0539 | 0.9461 | 0.0252 | 0.9748 | 0.0397 | 0.9604 |
| | 3 | 0.0558 | 0.9442 | 0.0264 | 0.9736 | 0.0417 | 0.9583 |
| | 4 | 0.0575 | 0.9425 | 0.0282 | 0.9718 | 0.0430 | 0.9570 |
| | 5 | 0.0589 | 0.9411 | 0.0304 | 0.9696 | 0.0446 | 0.9554 |
| | 6 | 0.0603 | 0.9397 | 0.0326 | 0.9674 | 0.0459 | 0.9541 |
| | 7 | 0.0615 | 0.9385 | 0.0349 | 0.9651 | 0.0471 | 0.9529 |
| | 8 | 0.0626 | 0.9374 | 0.0371 | 0.9629 | 0.0482 | 0.9518 |
| | 9 | 0.0636 | 0.9364 | 0.0392 | 0.9608 | 0.0491 | 0.9509 |
| | 10 | 0.0644 | 0.9356 | 0.0412 | 0.9588 | 0.0500 | 0.9500 |

Table 3 shows the variance decompositions of the relationships. Panels A to C show the proportion of the response variable explained by the shock of the impulse variable of the relationships between the SVI and stock market indices, the SVI and stock market volatilities, and the SVI and market abnormal trading volumes, respectively, in the next 10 periods.

### 5.4. *Developing and Developed Countries*

In order to investigate the difference in the SVI–return, the SVI–volatility, and the SVI–volume relationships between the developed and developing countries, we followed Love and Zicchino (2006) and Grossmann et al. (2014) by taking the difference in impulse responses of these two groups. Figure 2 depicts the impulse responses of the difference between developed and developing markets of all relationships. The significance of the difference in impulse responses was greater than 5%. These findings confirm differences detected in developed and developing countries reported from our panel VAR analyses.

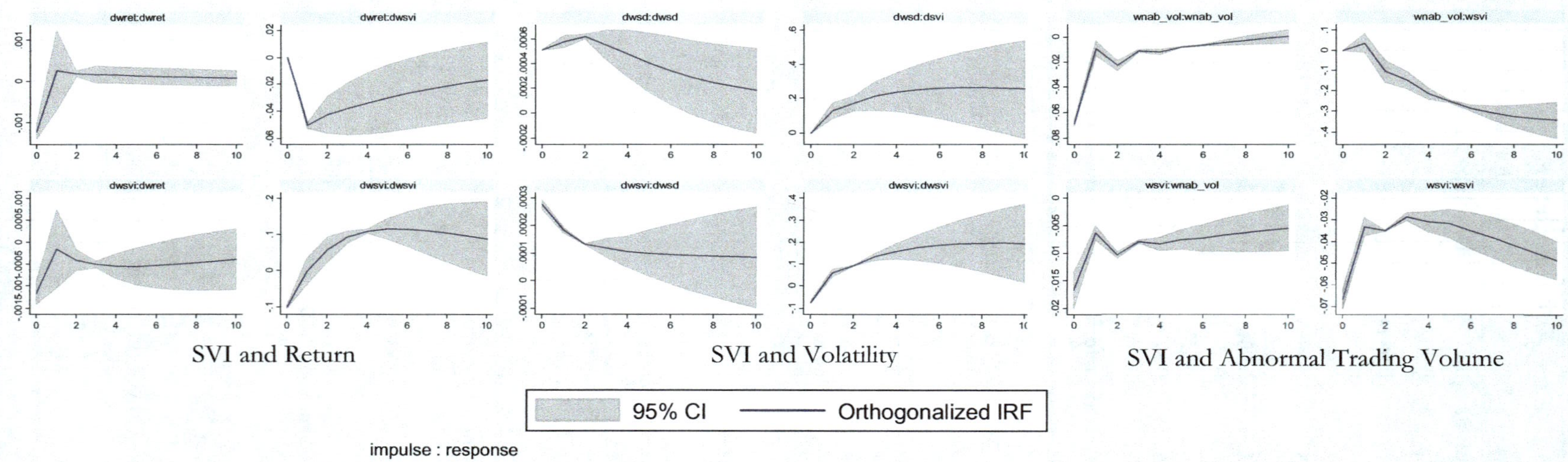


**Figure 2.** Orthogonalized impulse response for the difference between developed and developing markets. Figure 2 depicts the impulse response function of the difference between the developed and developing markets in three relationships.

## 6. Conclusions

In this study, we examine the role of investor attention in stock markets. Google SVI is chosen as a proxy of retail investor attention with stock market activities, i.e., market return, market volatility, and market abnormal trading volume. We apply a new methodology, the panel vector autoregressive model, to investigate these relationships. This technique is superior to other techniques commonly employed in the existing literature, as it takes into account of both the fixed and the time-varying effects. Employing panel VAR addresses concerns raised in Tantaopas et al. (2016) that attention behavior might be different in each country due to differences the shareholder base, culture, ownership structure, legal protection, law enforcement, and financial education.

After controlling for both fixed and time-varying effects, we find general support for prior evidence that investor attention is related to the returns, volatility, and trading volume. However, our results shed a new light on multi-country analyses as follows. We observe mostly two-way panel Granger causality in all relationships, though the weakest relationship is detected in the developing countries. These findings are reconfirmed by the panel VAR analyses, indicating dynamic and interdependent relationships. However, for both SVI–return and SVI–volatility relationships, we find the negative impact on the SVI is greater than that of the SVI on return or volatility. The investor attention–abnormal trading volume relationship is mixed but statistically significant in all cases. To investigate the different level of investor attention between developing and developed markets, we employ and take the difference of the impulse response functions between these two groups and find that the attention is statistically significantly different. Thus, we conclude that investor attention is necessary for equity markets, but the effect is different between developed and developing countries. An interrelation among all stock market activities and investor attention is left for future research.

**Author Contributions:** The contribution to this article is distributed as follows: C.P. 65%, S.T. 20% and R.B. 15%.

**Funding:** Chaiyuth Padungsaksawasdi acknowledges financial support from the Business Research Center of the Thammasat Business School.

**Acknowledgments:** We thank the editor and the anonymous referee for their suggestion. We benefit from the discussants and the seminar participants at the Finance Research Workshop, Department of Finance, Thammasat Business School, the 2016 Paris Financial Management Conference, and the 24th annual conference of the Multinational Finance Society, Bucharest, Romania. We are grateful to Tatre Jantarakolica for support and comment. We thank Phenpimol Boonbundanrit, Jutamas Wongkantarakorn, and Phasin Wanidwaranan for their excellent research assistance.

**Conflicts of Interest:** The author declares no conflict of interest.

## Appendix A

**Table A1.** Google search keywords for stock market indices.

| Country | Google Search Keyword |
|---|---|
| Developing countries | |
| China | shanghai_stock_exchange |
| India | bse |
| Malaysia | klse |
| Thailand | set_50 |
| Developed countries | |
| Australia | asx_200 |
| Hong Kong | hsi |
| Japan | nikkei |
| Korea | kospi |
| New Zealand | nzx |
| Singapore | straits_times |

## References


Al-Eroud, Ahmed F., Mohammad A. Al-Ramahi, Mohammad N. Al-Kabi, Izzat M. Alsmadi, and Emad M. Al-Shawakfa. 2011. Evaluating Google queries based on language preferences. *Journal of Information Science* 37: 282–92. [CrossRef]

Andrei, Daniel, and Michael Hasler. 2015. Investor attention and stock market volatility. *The Review of Financial Studies* 28: 33–72. [CrossRef]

Andrews, Donald W. K., and Biao Lu. 2001. Consistent model and moment selection procedures for GMM estimation with application to dynamic panel data models. *Journal of Econometrics* 101: 123–64. [CrossRef]

Ang, Andrew, Joseph Chen, and Yuhang Xing. 2006. Downside risk. *The Review of Financial Studies* 19: 1191–239. [CrossRef]

Aouadi, Amal, Mohamed Arouri, and Frédéric Teulon. 2013. Investor attention and stock market activity: Evidence from France. *Economic Modelling* 35: 674–81. [CrossRef]

Arellano, Manuel, and Olympia Bover. 1995. Another look at the instrumental variable estimation of error-components models. *Journal of Econometrics* 68: 29–51. [CrossRef]

Bank, Matthias, Martin Larch, and Georg Perter. 2011. Google search volume and its influence on liquidity and returns of German stocks. *Financial Market Portfolio Management* 25: 239–64. [CrossRef]

Barber, Brad M., and Terrance Odean. 2008. All that glitters: the effect of attention of attention and news on the buying behavior of individual and institutional investors. *The Review of Financial Studies* 21: 785–818. [CrossRef]

Benson, Karen, Robert Faff, and Tom Smith. 2014. Fifty years of finance research in the Asia Pacific Basin. *Accounting & Finance* 54: 335–63.

Bijl, Laurens, Glenn Kringhaug, Polar Molnár, and Eirik Sandvik. 2016. Google searches and stock returns. *International Review of Financial Analysis* 45: 150–56. [CrossRef]

Boduroglu, Aysecan, Priti Shah, and Richard E. Nisbett. 2009. Cultural differences in allocation of attention in visual information processing. *Journal of Cross Cultural Psychology* 40: 349–60. [CrossRef] [PubMed]

Braun, Nicole. 2016. Google search volume sentiment and its impact on REIT market movements. *Journal of Property Investment & Finance* 34: 249–62.

Chang, Eric C., Joseph W. Cheng, and Ajay Khorana. 2000. An examination of herd behavior in equity markets: An international perspective. *Journal of Banking and Finance* 24: 1651–79. [CrossRef]

Chiang, Thomas C., and Dazhi Zheng. 2010. An empirical analysis of herd behavior in global stock markets. *Journal of Banking & Finance* 34: 1911–21.

Choi, In. 2001. Unit root tests for panel data. *Journal of International Money and Finance* 20: 249–72. [CrossRef]

Da, Zhi, Joseph Engelberg, and Pengjie Gao. 2011. In search of attention. *The Journal of Finance* 66: 1461–99. [CrossRef]

Da, Zhi, Umit G. Gurun, and Mitch Warachka. 2014. Frog in the pan: continuous information and momentum. *The Review of Financial Studies* 27: 2171–218. [CrossRef]

DellaVigna, Stefano, and Joshua M. Pollet. 2009. Investor inattention and Friday earnings announcements. *The Journal of Finance* 64: 709–49. [CrossRef]

Dimpfl, Thomas, and Stephan Jank. 2016. Can Internet Search Queries Help to Predict Stock Market Volatility? *European Financial Management* 22: 171–92. [CrossRef]

Ding, Rong, and Wenxuan Hou. 2015. Retail investor attention and stock liquidity. *Journal of International Financial Markets, Institutions & Money* 37: 12–26.

Do, Hung Xuan, Robert Brooks, Sirimon Treepongkaruna, and Eliza Wu. 2014. How does trading volume affect financial return distributions? *International Review of Financial Analysis* 35: 190–206. [CrossRef]

Gao, Zhenyu, Haohan Ren, and Bohui Zhang. 2016. Googling Investor Sentiment around the World. *Journal of Financial and Quantitative Analysis*, 1–66. [CrossRef]

Gervais, Simon, Ron Kaniel, and Dan H. Mingelgrin. 2001. The high-volume return premium. *The Journal of Finance* 61: 877–919. [CrossRef]

Goddard, John, Arben Kita, and Qingwei Wang. 2015. Investor attention and FX market volatility. *Journal of International Financial Markets & Institutions & Money* 38: 79–96.

Grossmann, Axel, Inessa Love, and Alexei G. Orlov. 2014. The dynamics of exchange rate volatility: A panel VAR approach. *Journal of International Financial Markets, Institutions & Money* 33: 1–27.

Hamid, Alain, and Moritz Heiden. 2015. Forecasting volatility with empirical similarity and Google trends. *Journal of Economic Behavior & Organization* 117: 62–81.

Harding, Noel, and Wen He. 2016. Investor mood and the determinants of stock prices: An experimental analysis. *Accounting & Finance* 56: 445–78.

Hayakawa, Kazuhiko. 2009. First difference or forward orthogonal deviation-which transformation should be used in dynamic panel data models? A simulation study. *Economics Bulletin* 29: 2008–17.

Holtz-Eakin, Douglas, Whitney Newey, and Harvey S. Rosen. 1988. Estimated vector autoregressions with panel data. *Econometrica* 56: 1371–95. [CrossRef]

Hou, Kewei, Wei Xiong, and Lin Peng. 2009. *A Tale of Two Anomalies: The Implications of Investor Attention for Price and Earnings Momentum*. SSRN Working Paper. Amsterdam: Elsevier.

Huberman, Gur, and Tomer Regev. 2001. Contagious speculation and a cure for cancer: A nonevent that made stock prices soar. *The Journal of Finance* 56: 387–96. [CrossRef]

Jacobs, Heiko. 2015. The role of attention constraints for investor behavior and economic aggregates: What have we learnt so far? *Management Review Quarterly* 65: 217–37. [CrossRef]

Johnman, Mark, Bruce James Vanstone, and Adrian Gepp. 2018. Predicting FTSE 100 returns and volatility using sentimental analysis. *Accounting & Finance* 58: 253–74.

Joseph, Kissan, M. Babajide Wintoki, and Zelin Zhang. 2011. Forecasting abnormal stock returns and trading volume using investor sentiment: Evidence from online search. *International Journal of Forecasting* 27: 1116–27. [CrossRef]

Kahneman, Daniel. 1973. *Attention and Effort*. Englewood Cliffs: Princeton Hall.

Kumar, Alok. 2009. Who Gambles in the Stock Market? *The Journal of Finance* 64: 1889–933. [CrossRef]

Kumar, Alok, and Charles M. C. Lee. 2006. Retail Investor Sentiment and Return Comovements. *The Journal of Finance* 61: 2451–86. [CrossRef]

Laksomya, Nattapong, John G. Powell, Suparatana Tanthanongsakkun, and Sirimon Treepongkaruna. 2018. Are Internet message boards used to facilitate stock price manipulation? evidence from an emerging market, Thailand. *Accounting & Finance* 58: 275–309.

Li, Xin, Jian Ma, Shouyang Wang, and Xun Zhang. 2015. How does Google search affect trader positions and crude oil prices? *Economic Modelling* 49: 162–71. [CrossRef]

Love, Inessa, and Lea Zicchino. 2006. Financial development and dynamic investment behavior: Evidence from panel VAR. *The Quarterly Review of Economics and Finance* 46: 190–210. [CrossRef]

Madhavan, Ananth. 2000. Market microstructure: A survey. *Journal of Financial Markets* 3: 205–58. [CrossRef]

Merton, Robert C. 1987. A simple model of capital market equilibrium with incomplete information. *The Journal of Finance* 42: 483–510. [CrossRef]

Miller, Edward M. 1977. Risk, uncertainty, and divergence of opinion. *The Journal of Finance* 32: 1151–68. [CrossRef]

Nisbett, Richard E., Kaiping Peng, Incheol Choi, and Ara Norenzayan. 2001. Culture and systems of thought: holistic versus analytic cognition. *Psychological Review* 108: 291–310. [CrossRef] [PubMed]

Peng, Lin, Wei Xiong, and Tim Bollerslev. 2007. Investor attention and time-varying comovements. *European Financial Management* 13: 394–422. [CrossRef]

Piccoli, Pedro, Newton C. A. da Costa Jr., Wesley Vieira da Silva, and June A. W. Cruz. 2018. Investor sentiment and the risk-return tradeoff in the Brazilian market. *Accounting & Finance* 58: 599–618.

Rochdi, Karim, and Marian Dietzel. 2015. Outperforming the benchmark: Online information demand and REIT market performance. *Journal of Property Investment & Finance* 33: 169–95.

Rousseau, P. L., and P. Wachtel. 2000. Equity markets and growth: Cross-country evidence on timing and outcomes, 1980–1995. *Journal of Banking and Finance* 24: 1933–57. [CrossRef]

Sim, Christopher A. 1980. Macroeconomics and reality. *Econometrica* 48: 1–48.

Storms, Konstantin, Julia Kapraun, and Markus Rudolf. 2015. *Can Retail Investor Attention Enhance Market Efficiency? Insights from Search Engine Data*. SSRN Working Paper. Amsterdam: Elsevier.

Takeda, Fumiko, and Takumi Wakao. 2014. Google search intensity and its relationship with returns and trading volume of Japanese stocks. *Pacific-Basin Finance Journal* 27: 1–18. [CrossRef]

Tantaopas, Parkpoom, Chaiyuth Padungsaksawasdi, and Sirimon Treepongkaruna. 2016. Attention effect via internet search intensity in Asia-Pacific stock markets. *Pacific-Basin Finance Journal* 38: 107–24. [CrossRef]

Tourani-Rad, Alireza, and Stephen Kirkby. 2005. Investigation of investors' overconfidence, familiarity and socialization. *Accounting & Finance* 45: 283–300.

Treepongkaruna, Sirimon, and Stephen Gray. 2009. Information and volatility links in the foreign exchange market. *Accounting & Finance* 49: 385–405.

Treepongkaruna, Sirimon, Robert Brooks, and Stephen Gray. 2012. Do trading hours affect volatility links in the foreign exchange market? *Australian Journal of Management* 37: 7–27. [CrossRef]

Tsai, I.-Chun. 2017. Diffusion of optimistic and pessimistic investor sentiment: An empirical study of an emerging market. *International Review of Economics and Finance* 47: 22–34. [CrossRef]

Tsukioka, Yasutomo, Junya Yanagi, and Teruko Takada. 2017. Investor sentiment extracted from internet stock message boards and IPO puzzles. *International Review of Economics and Finance* 56: 205–17. [CrossRef]

Vozlyublennaia, Nadia. 2014. Investor attention, index performance, and return predictability. *Journal of Banking and Finance* 41: 17–35. [CrossRef]

Wang, Kemin, Xiaoyun Yu, and Bohui Zhang. 2017. The Power of the Passive Information Intermediary: Evidence from Google's China Exit. Working Paper. Available online: http://english.ckgsb.edu.cn/sites/default/files/files/GoogleChina%202017%209%204%20cleaned_Xiaoyun%20Yu.pdf (accessed on 4 September 2017).

Ying, Qianwei, Dongmin Kong, and Danglun Luo. 2015. Investor attention, institutional ownership, and stock return: empirical evidence from China. *Emerging Markets Finance and Trade* 51: 672–85. [CrossRef]

Yung, Kenneth, and Nadia Nafar. 2017. Investor attention and the expected returns of reits. *International Review of Economics and Finance* 48: 423–39. [CrossRef]

# 9

# Time Varying Spillovers between the Online Search Volume and Stock Returns: Case of CESEE Markets

**Tihana Škrinjarić**

Faculty of Economics and Business, University of Zagreb, 10000 Zagreb, Croatia; tskrinjar@net.efzg.hr

**Abstract:** This research observes a time varying relationship between stock returns, volatilities and the online search volume in regard to selected CESEE (Central, Eastern and South-Eastern European) stock markets. The main hypothesis of the research assumes that a feedback relationship exists between stock returns, volatilities and the investor's attention variable (captured by the online search volume). Moreover, the relationship is assumed to be time varying due to changing market conditions. Previous research does not deal with the time-varying multi-directional relationship. Thus, the contribution to existing research consists of estimating the aforementioned relationship between return, volatility and the search volume series for selected CESEE countries by using a novel approach of spillover indices within the VAR (Vector AutoRegression) model framework. The results indicate that the Google search volume affects the risk series more than the return series on the selected markets.

**Keywords:** investor attention; Google search volume; spillover index; VAR; stock returns; realized volatility

**JEL Classification:** C32; G10; G12

## 1. Introduction

The efficient market hypothesis (EMH, Fama 1965, 1970) has been challenged ever since its formation. This research belongs to the group of papers that challenge the EMH by observing the investor's attention and how it affects stock pricing. Namely, the investor's attention was defined in Da et al. (2011) via the online search volume regarding a specific stock or stock index. Although the investor recognition hypothesis[1] was defined by Merton (1987) in the late 1980s, the majority of empirical research has appeared only in the last decade. The reason for that lies in the fact that measuring the investor's attention is now much more convenient since there is free and easy access to the online search volume regarding specific stocks and stock indices.

The investor recognition hypothesis (Merton 1987) describes the relationship between investor recognition of stock and its return. If the investor is aware of only a certain group of stocks, those of which he is unaware of should earn higher future returns. This is due to the incomplete information on stock markets and imperfect diversification. In the early 2010s, this was rediscovered in the work of Mondria et al. (2010) and Da et al. (2011) as investor's attention (hypothesis). Since then, an increasing number of researches can be found, which include the online search engine volume as a measure of investor's attention to stock price, volume and volatility prediction: See Da et al. (2010), Li and Yu (2012), Bank et al. (2011), Smith (2012) and Kim et al. (2019), as well as some earlier works.

[1] For details, please see Lehavy and Sloan (2008).

However, the majority of existing research utilizes two common approaches: The first one being that the online search volume is being used as a predictor in a combination of ARIMA-GARCH[2] model of stock return and/or volatility series; and the second one is using the VAR[3] framework in order to identify the Granger causality test results. However, Vozlyublennaia (2014) and Hamid and Heiden (2015) have shown that there exists a bi-directional relationship between investor's attention and stock returns. Moreover, Bijl et al. (2016) introduced dynamics by calculating rolling returns and stock betas with the investor's attention included in the model. The authors have shown that the attention variable improves the return forecasting on a rolling basis. Thus, the analysis should include the possibility of the feedback relationship between variables of interest, as well as enable time varying parameters in the study, due to ongoing changes in stock markets.

The novelty and contribution of this research, compared to existing ones, is that here we allow for a feedback relationship between stock returns, volatilities and investor's attention by utilizing a VAR model; and more importantly, the VAR framework is extended via the Diebold and Yilmaz (2009, 2012) spillover index calculation. The spillover index estimates total spillovers of shocks between all of the variables in the VAR model. Besides the total spillover index, we calculate the rolling spillover index and in that way, we enable time varying effects between the variables in the model. Finally, we calculate the net spillover indices in order to obtain information on which variable is the net emitter or net receiver of shocks in the system. The contribution to the literature is to be found in estimating the spillover indices, which are rarely present in related research (as will be seen in the literature review section). For the empirical analysis, we have selected several Central and Eastern European (CEE) and South and Eastern European (SEE) stock markets: Hungary, Croatia, Slovenia, Slovakia, Serbia, Bosnia and Herzegovina, Bulgaria, Ukraine, Poland and the Czech Republic. The aforementioned countries were selected due to data availability and the fact that the existing research mostly focuses on more developed stock markets. However, it is important for (potential) investors to know if predictability of returns, volatilities and/or investor's attention is possible on the aforementioned markets in order to obtain extra profits and if the EMH is violated in that sense. Finally, this research will give a comprehensive study of the effects of investor's attention on stock returns and volatilities, in order to obtain insights into the relationship between those variables on the emerging markets.

Thus, the rest of the paper is structured as follows. Section 2 reviews the previous related research while the methodology description is given in Section 3. Section 4 deals with empirical analysis and the discussion with conclusions is given in Section 5.

## 2. Related Research

Research that focuses on including the online search volume in financial modeling has been rapidly growing in the last couple of years. Thus, the focus will be on those papers that are most closely linked to this study. Interested readers can look up the following research in which the online search volume is used to model and/or predict other economic variables. These include tourism demand forecasting (Havranek and Zeynalov 2018; Dergiades et al. 2018; Önder 2017); economic state and recession forecasting (Bortoli and Combes 2015; Tkacz 2013); cinema tickets sales (Goel et al. 2010); total consumer demand (Vosen and Schmidt 2011; Woo and Owen 2019); gasoline prices (Molnár and Bašta 2017); Bitcoin trading activity (Aalborg et al. 2019); foreign exchange markets (Goddard et al. 2015); etc. Other applications over the years (more than 650 papers in total) can be found summarized in Jun et al. (2018). The majority of studies related to this one include modeling via the ARMA-GARCH, VAR models and sometimes panel models. Short-term models and forecasting are utilized due to the nature of stock markets and turbulences that occur on them. The research is relatively new compared to other areas of stock market modeling, due to data available from online

---

2 Autoregressive integrated moving average—generalized autoregressive conditional heteroskedasticity.
3 Vector auto regression.

search engines. At the end of this section we give conclusions based on existing research in order to put in perspective the contributions in this research compared to the existing ones.

Early work includes Mondria et al. (2010) and Da et al. (2010, 2011) in which the AOL (America Online) database was used, as well as news searches for the construction of the FEARS index so that future stock returns and volatilities could be forecasted. Since the Google search volume itself did not have a sufficient length of the time series, authors opted to construct their own variables. Fang and Peress (2009) used newspaper articles and, on a sample of randomly selected 500 companies quoted on NYSE (period: January 1993–December 2002), they showed that stocks that had a smaller coverage in news earned a higher return (no-media premium as the authors call it). Other earlier work also focuses on news media coverage (see Grullon et al. 2004; Frieder and Subrahmanyam 2005; Barber and Odean 2007; Joseph et al. 2011; Preis et al. 2010, 2013, etc.).

Recent research includes the following findings. Chen (2017) utilized regression, panel regression and VAR models for 67 countries all over the world to observe the relationship between stock return and the Google search volume. This research included different markets, both the developing ones and the most developed, for the period from January 2004 to December 2014. The results indicate that a decrease of returns is followed by an increase of investor's attention. Padungsaksawasdi et al. (2019) applied panel VAR on nine Asian and Australian markets to focus on return, volatility, trading volume and investor's attention variable. The sample included both developed and developing markets and authors found statistically significant results that differ between the two groups of markets. More developed markets react more strongly to the search volume, which should be taken into consideration in asset pricing models. Tantaopas et al. (2016) observed Asia-Pacific stock markets as well (period: January 2004–December 2014), and observed pairwise Granger causality tests between the return, volatility, trading volume and Google search volume, with the extension of using quantile regression models. Results in this study indicate that the investor's attention contributes to the market efficiency. Different results for each country are explained as due to differences in the shareholder base, culture, legislative, financial education and other factors.

Tan and Tas (2019) focused on the Turkish stock market from April 2013 to September 2017 and calculated an abnormal search volume for all shares, which constitute the BIST index. The sample included 481 stocks. Thus, the authors could form portfolios based on size and value which is why the analysis was similar to the usual asset pricing model's approach. The results show that portfolio sorting based on investor's attention levels and trading with long positions in high attention and short positions in low investor's attention leads to significant returns. Chen et al. (2019) aggregated different attention proxies in order to predict future market returns. Thus, the Google search volume is a part of the whole picture, due to authors using the partial LS (least squares) method by combining seven major individual attention proxies on the NYSE. The authors have shown that their hybrid index can predict stock market movements better than some of the individual indices, with possible economic gains in asset allocation. Han et al. (2017) focused on 15 developed stock markets, for the period from January 2004 to October 2015, and accounted for business cycles on those markets. The results indicate that the predictive power of the asymmetric effects of investor's attention measured by the Google search volume index is short lived, with greater values when pessimism is more pronounced.

Vozlyublennaia (2014) applied a VAR model for the DJIA, S&P 500 and NASDAQ indices (January 2004–December 2012), i.e., their return and volatility series with the Google volume search index. The author examined the vector approach due to findings that not only the investor's attention causes return and risk series, but a bi-directional relationship is found in this research. Hamid and Heiden (2015) also focused on the DJIA index by utilizing the VAR, ARMA (AutoRegressive Moving Average) and HAR (heterogeneous AR) models, with a focus on risk forecasting. Again, the reciprocal causality was found here as well (time span: January 2004–October 2013). Dimpfl and Jank (2016) also focus on the DJIA index with ARMA and VAR as used methodologies. Search volume was found to Granger cause the DJIA volatility and better forecasts are made by including the search volume variable in modeling volatility. Bijl et al. (2016) also looked at the American stock market (S&P 500 index, from 2008–2013), by using the daily data (a rare approach, usually due to data unavailability) and calculated rolling betas within the asset pricing modeling and regression analysis approach. Results in this study have shown that an increase of search volume leads to a decrease of return series, which is in accordance with the investor recognition hypothesis and other empirical work. Škrinjarić (2018a) observed the Croatian market (for the period January 2004–September 2018) as a rare example of a small developing stock market. Here, the author uses univariate modeling and compares benchmark models (ARMA-GARCH) where investor's attention is not included with models where the search volume variable is included. Results have shown that the forecast error was lowered by including the Google search volume in selected models. Additionally, the author has simulated several investing strategies based on the aforementioned models. Even with included transaction costs, the strategies based on including the search volume variable have provided the investor with higher portfolio values. This additional utilization of estimation results is rarely found in existing research. Other related research, again, is mostly focused on developed countries such as Habibah et al. (2017) on the American market, Kim et al. (2019) on the Norwegian, Bank et al. (2011) on German, Dzielinski (2012) also selected developed markets (American, Australian, Canadian, UK, German and Japanese), Zhang Wei et al. (2013) chose Shanghai, Takeda and Wakao (2014) the Japanese market, Yang et al. (2019) and Zhang et al. (2018) the Chinese one, etc.

Finally, several conclusions can be made by observing previous related empirical literature. First, the majority of research focuses on the American stock market, followed by other more developed markets as well. Developing stock markets are sometimes included if the analysis includes many countries in its sample. Thus, it is interesting to expand the research to less developed stock markets in order to obtain information about what is happening there; i.e., does the investor's attention affect stock returns and/or risks; or what are the consequences for the asset pricing models and the EMH. Therefore, this research fills the gap in the literature by focusing (for some markets for the first time) on selected CEE and SEE markets, which have not yet been examined in such a fashion. Second, there is a lack of research that allows for all of the variables to be endogenous in the model. In other words, the investor's attention variable is mostly used as only an explanatory variable. Recent papers have shown that a reciprocal relationship exists between stock market variables and the search volume. This is another contribution in this research, where we allow for shock spillovers between variables to be dynamic. Third, the majority of research has a starting date of January 2004. This is because of the data availability of the Google trends search volume, which is publicly and freely available from the aforementioned date. For some countries, Google correlate data is available on a weekly basis, however the majority of research uses monthly data. Since this paper deals with countries for which only monthly data is available, we make the best of the given sample.

## 3. Methodology Description

Since the VAR methodology is widely known, we only briefly described the basic terms in the VAR model in order to define the spillover index. Details can be found in Diebold and Yilmaz (2009, 2011, 2012), Koop et al. (1996), Pesaran and Shin (1998), Urbina (2013), Lütkepohl (1993, 2006, 2010) and Demirer et al. (2018). We observed a stabile VAR($p$) model for $N$ variables in a compact form $\boldsymbol{Y}_t = \boldsymbol{a} + \boldsymbol{A}\boldsymbol{Y}_{t-1} + \boldsymbol{\varepsilon}_t$, where $\boldsymbol{Y}_t$ is the vector containing vectors $y$ of variables of the system, $\boldsymbol{a} = [v\ 0 \ldots\ 0]'$, $\boldsymbol{A} = \begin{bmatrix} \boldsymbol{A}_1 & \boldsymbol{A}_2 & \cdots & \boldsymbol{A}_{p-1} & \boldsymbol{A}_p \\ I_N & 0 & \cdots & 0 & 0 \\ 0 & I_N & & \vdots & \vdots \\ \vdots & & \ddots & \vdots & \vdots \\ 0 & 0 & \cdots & I_N & 0 \end{bmatrix}$ and $\varepsilon_t = \begin{bmatrix} \boldsymbol{\varepsilon}_t & \boldsymbol{0} & \cdots & \boldsymbol{0} \end{bmatrix}'$, where $\boldsymbol{\varepsilon}_t$ is the innovation vector for which it holds that $E(\boldsymbol{\varepsilon}_t) = 0$, $E(\boldsymbol{\varepsilon}_t\ \boldsymbol{\varepsilon}_t') = \Sigma_\varepsilon < \infty$ and $E(\boldsymbol{\varepsilon}_t\ \boldsymbol{\varepsilon}_s') = 0$ when $t \neq s$. The impulse response function is calculated based on the MA($\infty$) representation of the VAR model as follows: $Y_t = (I_{Np} - A)^{-1}a + \sum_{i=1}^{\infty} A^i\varepsilon_{t-i}$, with its polynomial form given as:

$$Y_t = \Phi(L)\varepsilon_t, \tag{1}$$

with $\Phi(L)$ denoting polynomial of the lag operator $L$. Values in $\Phi(L)$ are the impulse response coefficients, which are usually graphed on figures in the empirical analysis. Now, since the innovations in $\varepsilon_t$ are correlated, their variance–covariance matrix is orthogonalized by the Choleski decomposition. Another approach is to calculate the generalized forecast error variance decomposition (GFEVD), which does not depend on variable ordering. Thus, we utilize the GFEVD approach.

Forecast error for $h$ steps ahead is calculated by detracting the expected values from the real ones, as follows: $e_{t+h} = Y_{t+h} - E(Y_{t+h})$; and then the mean squared error for the variance is calculated for every element in $e_{t+h}$ as $E(y_{j,t+h} - E(y_{j,t+h}))^2$. Then, every variance is decomposed to shares of every variable in the VAR model, $\omega_{jk,h}$, due to shocks in the individual variables as follows:

$$\omega_{jk,h} = \frac{\sigma_j^{-1}\sum_{i=0}^{h-1}\left(e_j'\Phi_i\Sigma_\varepsilon e_k\right)^2}{e_j'\Phi_i\Sigma_\varepsilon\Phi_i' e_j}, \tag{2}$$

where values $\omega_{jk,h}$ are interpreted as shares of the variance of variable $j$ in the VAR model in the forecast step $h$ caused by the shock in variable $k$. $e_j$ and $e_k$ are the unit vectors from matrix $I_{Np}$. The numerator is the contribution of shock in variable $k$ to variance of variable $j$ for $h$ steps, whilst the denominator is the variance of forecasted values of variable $j$.

In the Diebold and Yilmaz (2009, 2011, 2012) it is defined as the following ratio:

$$S = \frac{\sum_{\substack{j,k=1 \\ j\neq k}}^{N} \omega_{jk,h}}{\sum_{i=0}^{h-1}\sum_{j,k=1}^{N} \omega_{jk,h}} 100\%, \tag{3}$$

where it is obvious that the numerator is the sum of all shares in variances of all variables due to shocks in every variable in the model, while the denominator is the total forecast variance. The "from" and "to" indices are calculated as well, in order to obtain information on which variable is the net emitter of shocks in the system and which is the net receiver. These indices are calculated as $S_{\cdot j,h} = \frac{1}{N}\sum_{\substack{k=1 \\ j\neq k}}^{N} \omega_{kj,h} 100\%$ (the "from" index) and $S_{j\cdot,h} = \frac{1}{N}\sum_{\substack{k=1 \\ j\neq k}}^{N} \omega_{jk,h} 100\%$ ("to" index). Now, the net index is calculated as the difference between the two mentioned indices.

Finally, in order to allow for time varying spillovers and to introduce dynamics to the VAR model, the rolling indices can be calculated.

## 4. Results

This section presents the main results for every country individually. First, we show information on the data for which the main calculations were made afterwards.

### *4.1. Data Description*

From the website Investing Data Website (2019) we obtained the daily data on stock indices for the following countries: Hungary, Croatia, Slovenia, Slovakia, Serbia, Bosnia and Herzegovina,

Bulgaria, Ukraine, Poland and the Czech Republic. Main indices of each country were used for the rest of the study (names are given in Table 1, which are the search terms within Google trends data as well, in the category of finance). Names of indices were used as search terms, due to observing national indices in the study, as previous research has this approach as well: Hamid and Heiden (2015) use term "dow" for the DOW index; "dow", "S&P 500" and "NASDAQ" were used for the same indices in Vozlyublennaia (2014); "crobex" for CROBEX in Škrinjarić (2018a); "dax" for DAX in Škrinjarić and Čižmešija (2019); terms regarding names of following markets in Padungsaksawasdi et al. (2019): Chinese, Indian, Malaysian, Thailand, Australian, Hong Kong, Japanese, Korean, New Zealand and Singaporean; and 67 country index names in Chen (2017), etc.[4]. Since we used the names of the indices, this means that we were observing noise-traders (or retail investors), due to explanations given in Peng and Xiong (2006), Da et al. (2011), Odean (1998), Grinblatt and Keloharju (2000), Black (1986) and De Long Bradford et al. (1990): Retail investors are more likely to use Internet searches for the comparisons of investment opportunities, due to not being able to process as much information as professional investors do. Thus, noise investors opt to focus on broader indices compared to specific stocks. That is why some models (Black 1986; De Long Bradford et al. 1990) forecast that such behavior from noise traders leads to increases of volatility.

**Table 1.** Data time span by country.

| Country | Initial Date | $N$ | Index Name |
|---|---|---|---|
| Hungary | March 2011 | 100 | BUX |
| Croatia | January 2004 | 186 | CROBEX |
| Ukraine | January 2004 | 186 | PFTS |
| Slovenia | April 2006 | 159 | SBITOP |
| Poland | March 2011 | 100 | WIG |
| Bosnia and Herzegovina | December 2012 | 79 | BIRS |
| Czech Republic | January 2012 | 90 | PX |
| Slovakia | August 2011 | 95 | SAX |
| Bulgaria | August 2011 | 95 | SOFIX |
| Serbia | December 2012 | 79 | BELEX |

Source: Investing Data Website (2019). Note: End date for every country is June 2019. Index name represents the name of the used index returns, as well as the Google trends data search terms.

Based on daily values, the daily return series were calculated and were then converted to a monthly basis by calculating monthly average returns. Moreover, for the risk series we calculated the realized volatility, by following Andersen and Bollerslev (1998) and Barndorff-Nielsen and Shephard (2002): $RV_\tau = \sqrt{\sum_{t=1}^{\tau} r_t^2}$, where $r_t$ is the daily return series within a month. Finally, for the variable of investor's attention, we used the standardized values of Google Trends Data (2019) on the search volume for every index name in each country. The search engine Google was used due to it representing the greatest majority of the online search volume (see Netmarketshare 2019; over 75% since 2016). Detailed reasoning can be found in Da et al. (2011), such as it being an exact query, the search volume on Google is becoming larger every day and can capture sentiment, i.e., attention of both individual and institutional investors, especially individual ones (Peng and Xiong 2006). The search volume from Google trends data is a relative measure, ranging from 0 to 100, due to its representing total searches of the geography and time range so that the popularity of an expression is expressed relatively. The reasoning why we calculated monthly return and volatility series is that Google trends data for the observed countries was available only on a monthly basis, i.e., the search terms regarding names of the stock market indices within the finance category of Google trends data were available on a monthly

[4] Individual company names are utilized in studies, which observe those company returns series, as in Preis et al. (2010); Bijl et al. (2016); Tan and Tas (2019) and Khan and Ahmad (2018).

basis. Index name (last column of Table 1) was used as a search term. Time span for every country differs, which can be seen in Table 1. Most data was available for Croatia and Ukraine and least amount for Bosnia and Herzegovina and Serbia (N column).

Before the analysis, all of the variables were tested for unit roots, with detailed results shown in Appendix A in Table A1. All of the variables were found to be stationary, thus we proceeded with VAR modeling. Moreover, Figures A1–A10 depict monthly time series of excess return, realized volatility and Google search volume (GSV from now on) for every country.

### 4.2. VAR Results

The adequate lag length for VAR models was checked by calculating the usual information criteria. Then, the model was estimated by going from the smallest number of lag until there was no problem of multivariate autocorrelation and heteroskedasticity found. Optimal lag lengths are shown in Table 2. Detailed results on mentioned tests of autocorrelation and heteroskedasticity for lag lengths in Table 2 are shown in Appendix A in Table A2. Thus, the rest of the analysis was continued with lag lengths from Table 2.

**Table 2.** VAR ($p$) model details, by country.

| Country | $p$ (Length) |
|---|---|
| Hungary | 2 |
| Croatia | 6 |
| Ukraine | 3 |
| Slovenia | 4 |
| Poland | 1 |
| Bosnia and Herzegovina | 1 |
| Czech Republic | 2 |
| Slovakia | 1 |
| Bulgaria | 2 |
| Serbia | 1 |

Granger causality tests have been conducted in every VAR model. Results are given in Table 3. Here, each value by column depicts the partial F test value for the null hypothesis that the series in that column does not Granger cause the other two series in the VAR model. It could be seen that the GSV variable Granger causes the other two variables for only the Hungarian, Croatian, Ukrainian, Serbian and Slovenian markets. This indicates that the investor's attention variable could affect return and volatility series on the mentioned markets to some extent. Interesting results are in the column denoted RV, where it was seen that the variable RV Granger causes the other two variables. Finally, the excess return Granger causes the other two variables only on the Croatian, Hungarian and Slovenian markets. The Bosnian market was the only one with significant results regarding excess return causing other variables in the model (on 10%). The other markets seemed not to be having causal effects between any of the variables. The reason for such results could be in the small sample size due to unavailability of data. However, since the Granger test did not indicate the sign of the found effects in each variable, we continued to the impulse response functions.

All of the impulse response functions were graphed in Figures A11–A20 in Appendix A, with confidence intervals being constructed by bootstrapping them with 1000 replications. We could comment on the relevant results. Firstly, no effects on any of the variables were found for the Ukrainian, Bosnian, Czech and Slovakian markets. This was in line with the results in Table 3. Next, the majority of the significant results were found for Hungarian, Croatian, Slovenian and Polish markets. On the Hungarian market, RV shocks affected GSV series in the first three months, by increasing the search volume. Shocks in GSV negatively affected the return series at lags 3 and 5. Next, on the Croatian market, shocks in GSV caused a decrease of return series in the first two months and a RV increase in the first two months as well. Shocks in the volatility series led to an increase of GSV in the first month. The Polish market was characterized by an increase of GSV in the first 2 months as a result of shocks in RV. On the Slovenian market, the results indicate that shocks in return series led to an increase of GSV in months 1 and 6. The return series were increased in the first 2 months as a result of shocks in GSV, whereas the RV series also rose in the first 2 months after a GSV shock. Moreover, GSV increased in the first 2 months as a result of shocks in RV. Some marginal results were found on the Polish market (shocks in RV led to an increase of GSV until the second month); Serbian (RV increased in first 2 months as a result of a shock in GSV) and Bulgarian (lagged effects of shocks in GSV on RV series, from third month onwards).

**Table 3.** Granger causality tests.

| Country/Cause in the Granger Test | Excess Return | RV | GSV |
|---|---|---|---|
| Hungary | 1.148 (0.334) | 3.809 (0.005) *** | 2.169 (0.073) * |
| Croatia | 0.506 (0.911) | 3.808 (0.000) *** | 3.559 (0.000) *** |
| Ukraine | 1.393 (0.215) | 1.114 (0.341) | 1.111 (0.355) |
| Slovenia | 0.926 (0.495) | 6.881 (0.000) *** | 4.075 (0.000) *** |
| Poland | 0.027 (0.973) | 0.084 (0.919) | 0.517 (0.597) |
| Bosnia and Herzegovina | 2.607 (0.076) * | 0.374 (0.688) | 0.010 (0.989) |
| Czech Republic | 0.759 (0.553) | 0.709 (0.587) | 0.778 (0.540) |
| Slovakia | 0.403 (0.669) | 0.111 (0.895) | 0.410 (0.664) |
| Bulgaria | 1.590 (0.177) | 1.285 (0.276) | 3.175 (0.014) ** |
| Serbia | 0.454 (0.636) | 2.014 (0.136) | 2.655 (0.073) * |

Note: Test values of the partial $F$ test are given with respective $p$-values in brackets. *, ** and *** denote statistical significance on 10%, 5% and 1% respectively. The null hypothesis of each test (based on columns) assumes that the variable does not Granger cause other variables in the model.

The results in which shocks in GSV led to negative values of return series was in line with Dimpfl and Jank (2016); as well as the increase of GSV caused by shocks in volatility series being in line with Vozlyublennaia (2014). By comparing the mentioned results, it could be said that the investor's attention hypothesis could be confirmed only on the Hungarian and Croatian markets. Other markets did not experience such predictability. The results for other markets are in line with Chen et al. (2002) where a positive relationship was found between stock return and investor recognition (breadth of ownership). Thus, mixed results were found here, as in the previous literature, which could be explained by differences in the (tax related) legislation, depth of the markets, macroeconomic fundamentals, financial exposure, etc. This was in line with explanations given in Sibley et al. (2016), where the investor sentiment variable was strongly related to economic fundamentals, which in turn are important in asset pricing models.

### 4.3. *Spillover Indices Results*

Next, we moved forward to the estimation of the total spillovers within every VAR model for the entire sample. Tables 4–13 depict the total spillover indices (bolded values in the bottom left corner) and all of the directional indices, based on the forecast horizon $h = 12$ (as in Antonakakais et al. 2016). E.g., by focusing on Table 4, the total variability of return series on the Serbian market was explained by shocks in the return series in the amount of 95.34%; by shocks in RV in the amount of 2.30% and GSV 2.36%. Total spillover in the observed period between all of the variables was small and was equal to 6.42%. Similar interpretations could be made for every other following table. The smallest spillovers were found for the aforementioned Serbian market, as well as Bosnian, Ukrainian, Czech, Bulgarian and Slovakian markets. The greatest spillovers were found on the Hungarian, Croatian, Slovenian and Polish markets. These tables are useful for (potential) investors in order to estimate the amount of volatility of a variable caused by other variables in the system and to which extent the lead values of some variables can cause future values of other variables. If one focuses on the columns labeled GSV, it can be seen that the shocks in Google search volume explain a greater percentage of risk series (RV) when compared to return series in the majority of cases. This is especially true for the markets where the greatest total spillovers are found. This result is in line with Andrei and Andrei and Hasler (2014) and Vlastakis and Markellos (2012), where greater volatility predictability over return predictability is found by using GSV.

**Table 4.** Total spillover, Serbia.

| | Excess Return | RV | GSV | From |
|---|---|---|---|---|
| Excess Return | 95.34 | 2.30 | 2.36 | 1.55 |
| RV | 2.23 | 91.85 | 5.92 | 2.72 |
| GSV | 2.01 | 4.43 | 93.56 | 2.15 |
| TO | 1.41 | 2.24 | 2.76 | **6.42** |

**Table 5.** Total spillover, Hungary.

| | Excess Return | RV | GSV | From |
|---|---|---|---|---|
| Excess Return | 91.45 | 7.23 | 1.32 | 2.85 |
| RV | 3.56 | 68.65 | 27.79 | 10.45 |
| GSV | 3.31 | 31.16 | 65.53 | 11.49 |
| TO | 2.29 | 12.80 | 9.70 | **24.79** |

**Table 6.** Total spillover, Croatia.

| | Excess Return | RV | GSV | From |
|---|---|---|---|---|
| Excess Return | 70.55 | 16.03 | 13.42 | 9.82 |
| Std dev | 1.26 | 66.04 | 32.69 | 11.32 |
| GSV | 3.52 | 17.60 | 78.89 | 7.04 |
| TO | 1.59 | 11.21 | 15.37 | **28.17** |

**Table 7.** Total spillover, Ukraine.

| | Excess Return | RV | GSV | From |
|---|---|---|---|---|
| Excess Return | 98.28 | 1.48 | 0.24 | 0.57 |
| Std dev | 0.55 | 89.86 | 9.59 | 3.38 |
| GSV | 2.18 | 2.79 | 95.03 | 1.66 |
| TO | 0.91 | 1.42 | 3.28 | **5.61** |

**Table 8.** Total spillover, Bosnia and Herzegovina.

| | Excess Return | RV | GSV | From |
|---|---|---|---|---|
| Excess Return | 98.41 | 1.36 | 0.23 | 0.53 |
| RV | 3.15 | 93.76 | 3.09 | 2.08 |
| GSV | 3.31 | 3.01 | 93.68 | 2.11 |
| TO | 2.15 | 1.46 | 1.11 | **4.72** |

**Table 9.** Total spillover, Czech Republic.

| | Excess Return | RV | GSV | From |
|---|---|---|---|---|
| Excess Return | 98.17 | 1.36 | 0.47 | 0.61 |
| RV | 2.65 | 92.08 | 5.27 | 2.64 |
| GSV | 0.32 | 8.65 | 91.03 | 2.99 |
| TO | 0.99 | 3.34 | 1.91 | **6.24** |

**Table 10.** Total spillover, Slovakia.

| | Excess Return | RV | GSV | From |
|---|---|---|---|---|
| **Excess Return** | 96.28 | 0.63 | 3.09 | 1.24 |
| **RV** | 1.48 | 97.22 | 1.30 | 0.93 |
| **GSV** | 2.82 | 0.79 | 96.93 | 1.20 |
| **TO** | 1.43 | 0.47 | 1.46 | **3.37** |

**Table 11.** Total spillover, Slovenia.

| | Excess Return | RV | GSV | From |
|---|---|---|---|---|
| **Excess Return** | 74.92 | 17.19 | 7.89 | 8.36 |
| **RV** | 3.39 | 79.74 | 16.33 | 6.75 |
| **GSV** | 11.03 | 6.86 | 82.11 | 5.96 |
| **TO** | 4.99 | 8.02 | 8.07 | **21.07** |

**Table 12.** Total spillover, Bulgaria.

| | Excess Return | RV | GSV | From |
|---|---|---|---|---|
| **Excess Return** | 99.17 | 0.11 | 0.72 | 0.28 |
| **RV** | 3.70 | 80.04 | 26.26 | 6.65 |
| **GSV** | 3.13 | 4.78 | 92.09 | 2.64 |
| **TO** | 2.28 | 1.63 | 5.66 | **9.57** |

**Table 13.** Total spillover, Poland.

| | Excess Return | RV | GSV | From |
|---|---|---|---|---|
| **Excess Return** | 97.86 | 0.83 | 1.31 | 0.71 |
| **RV** | 0.24 | 61.54 | 38.22 | 12.82 |
| **GSV** | 0.11 | 36.87 | 63.02 | 12.33 |
| **TO** | 0.12 | 12.57 | 13.17 | **25.86** |

In order to account for the dynamics over time, we calculated rolling spillover indices, with a 30 month rolling window length (as in Antonakakais et al. 2016). Thus, the dynamics could be commented on. The rolling spillover indices are shown in Figures 1 and 2. This could help to forecast when the spillovers between variables in the model would increase or decrease in order to tailor specific international portfolio strategies. When an investor expects an increase of total spillover between the return, volatility and search volume variables, he can better forecast all of the variables and thus either buy or sell on individual markets, depending on forecasts and investor's preferences. The greatest spillovers over time were found for the Hungarian, Croatian, Slovenian and Ukrainian markets. Thus, these markets had the potential to violate the EMH. This is in line with Andries et al. (2018) and Škrinjarić (2018c), and the lack of spillovers for the Polish market is in line with Ferreira (2018).

Moreover, detailed insights are provided on Figures 3–12, where the net indices for every variable are shown. Now, an investor could obtain information on which variable gives shocks to others in the system, and in which period. This contributes to the literature by looking at which variable is the net emitter of shocks in different market conditions. Positive values of each index indicate that that variable was the net emitter of shocks. Net values were smaller for those countries in which the total spillover index was smaller as well, and the opposite was true for those countries with greater spillover values in Tables 4–12. In the Hungarian case, the RV and GSV variables were, for the majority of the time, net givers of shocks. In Croatia, the financial crisis of 2008 shows that the GSV was the net emitter of shocks (similar was true for 2017, when a local crisis caused by the Agrokor concern was happening, for details please see Škrinjarić (2018b) and Škrinjarić and Orlović (2019)). In the rest of the observed period, there was an interchangeability of net emitters and receivers of shocks. On the

Ukrainian market, the RV variable was the net emitter of shocks in the last 3 years; Serbian market was characterized by the GSV being the net emitter most of the time and this was true for the variable RV in the middle of the observed period on the Bosnian market. All three variables were sometimes receivers and sometimes emitters of shocks on the Slovakian and Slovenian markets, with GSV being the net receiver on the Bulgarian market. Finally, the GSV was the net giver of shocks in almost the entire observed period on the Polish market.

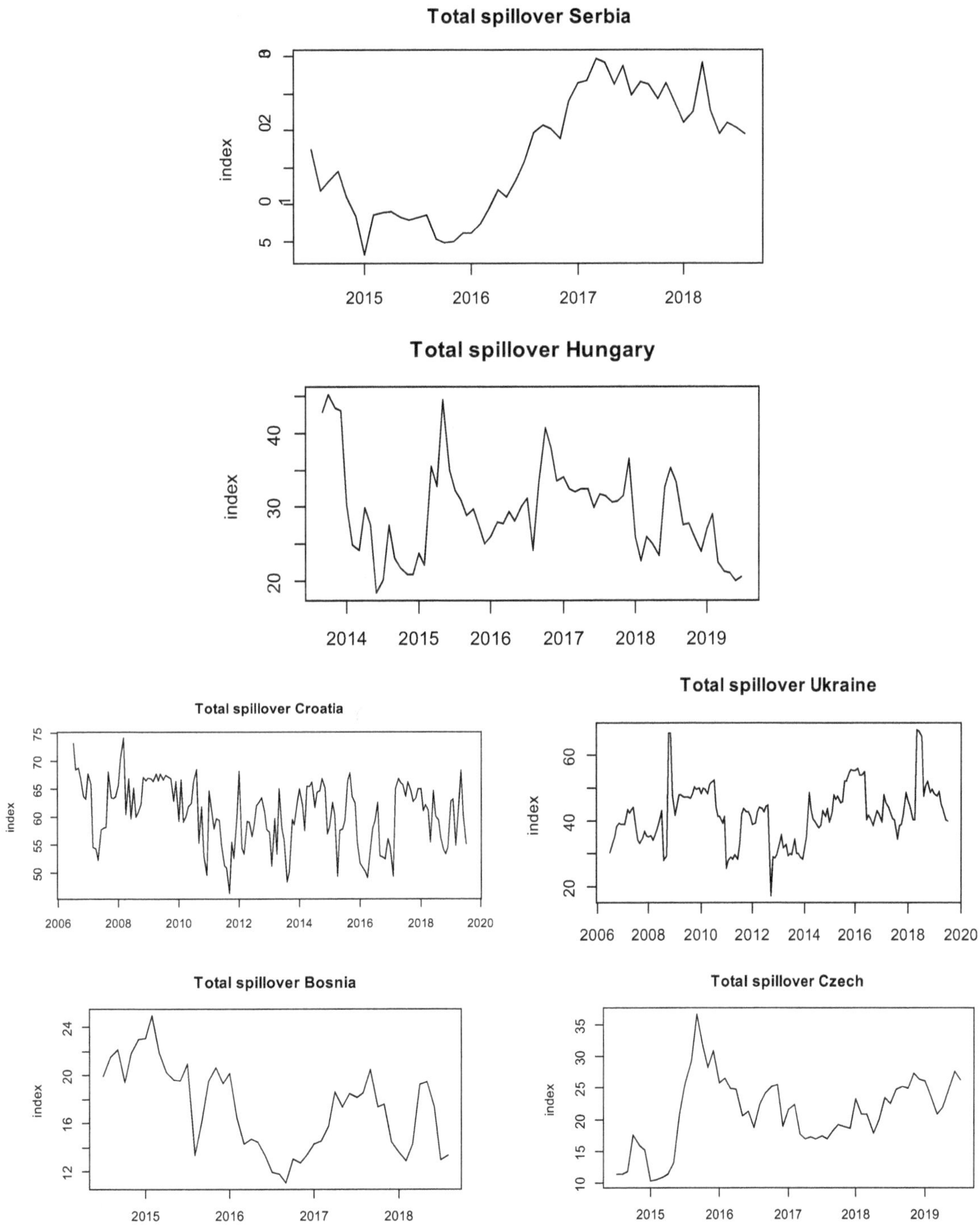


**Figure 1.** Total spillover indices (from top to bottom, left to right): Serbia, Hungary, Croatia, Ukraine, Bosnia and Herzegovina and Czech Republic.

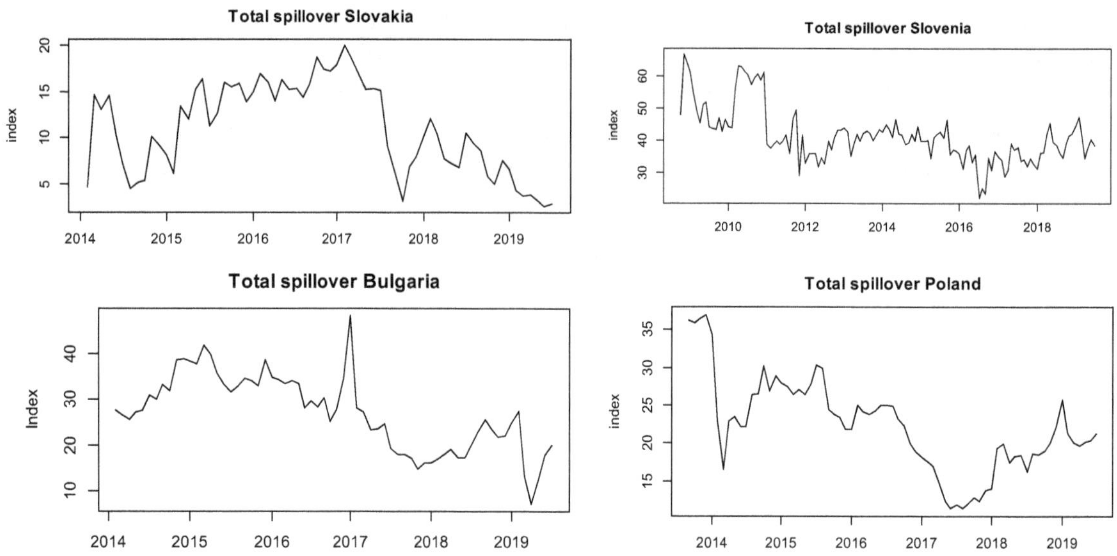


**Figure 2.** Total spillover indices (from top to bottom, left to right): Slovakia, Slovenia, Bulgaria and Poland.

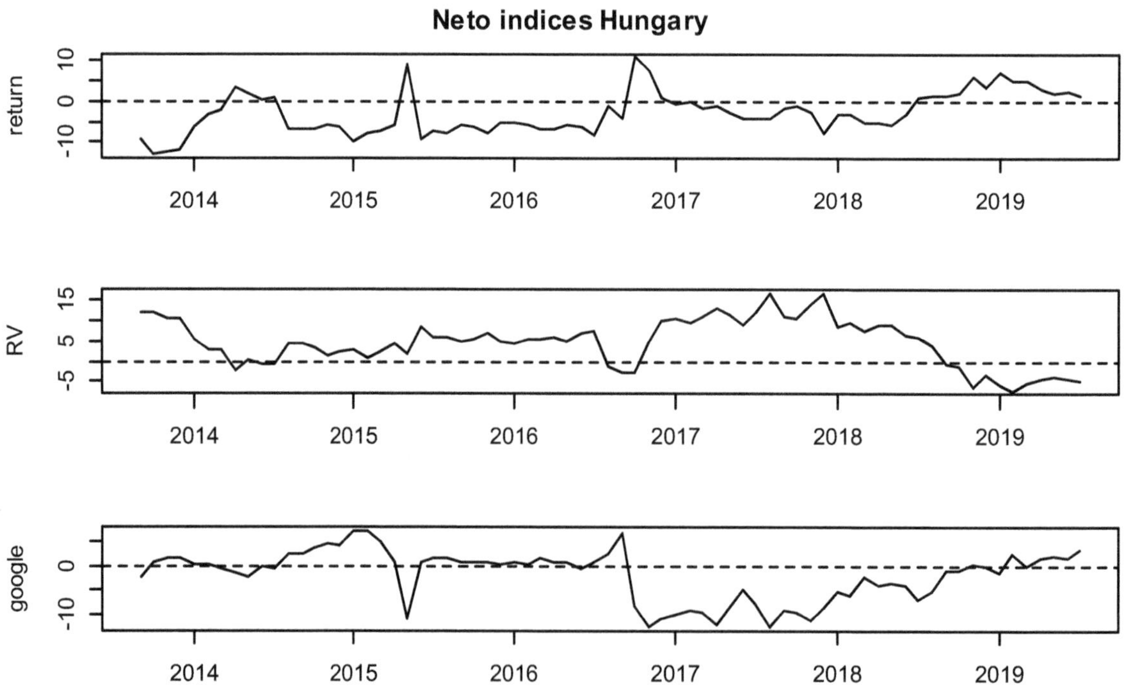


**Figure 3.** Net rolling indices, Hungary.

These findings indicate that some dynamics should be observed in such modeling. The differences of increasing and decreasing spillovers over time between markets, of course, exist. These could be due to political, economic, social and other intra-country events, which are specific to that country alone. However, the results that were found to be significant could be explained by non-efficiencies of the observed markets, which is in line with Necula and Radu (2012)[5] and Baele et al. (2015)[6].

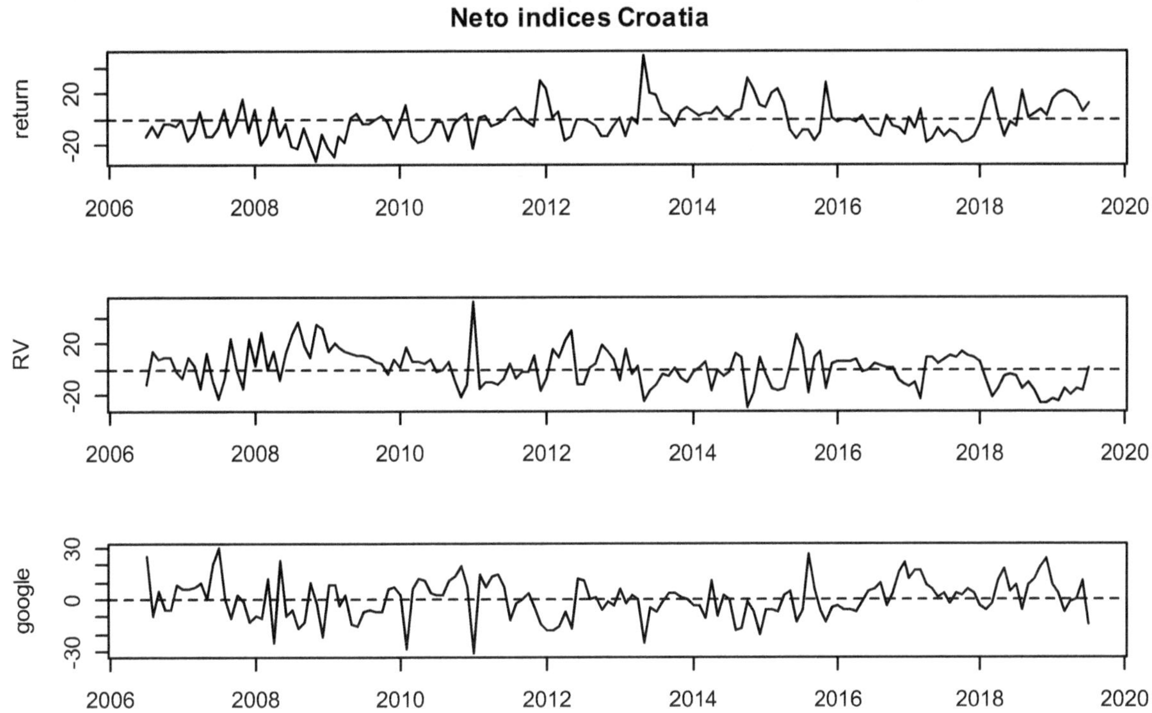


**Figure 4.** Net rolling indices, Croatia.

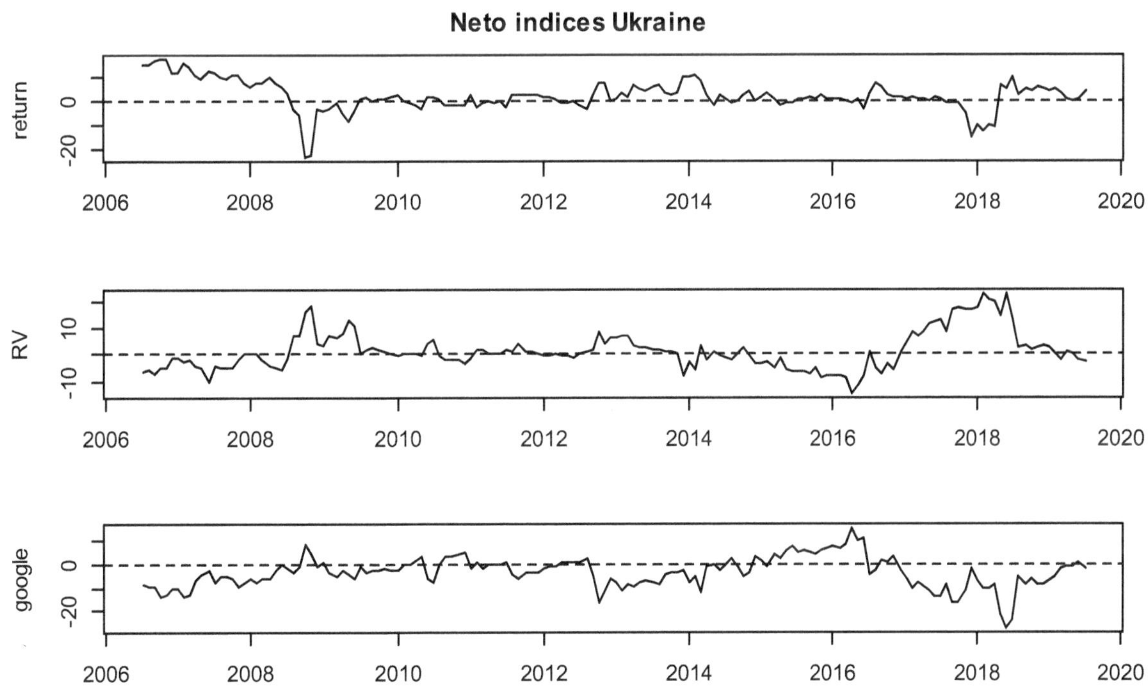


**Figure 5.** Net rolling indices, Ukraine.

---

5 Authors observed Romania, Hungary, Czech Republic, Poland, Slovenia, Bulgaria, Slovakia and Croatia and found inefficiencies of the stock markets by using the fractional differencing approach.

6 Authors compared CEE stock markets by using a variety of measures regarding growth, development, concentration, etc. Although these countries faced a similar past regarding the economic system, their stock markets today have somewhat great differences in terms of market concentration, liquidity, etc.

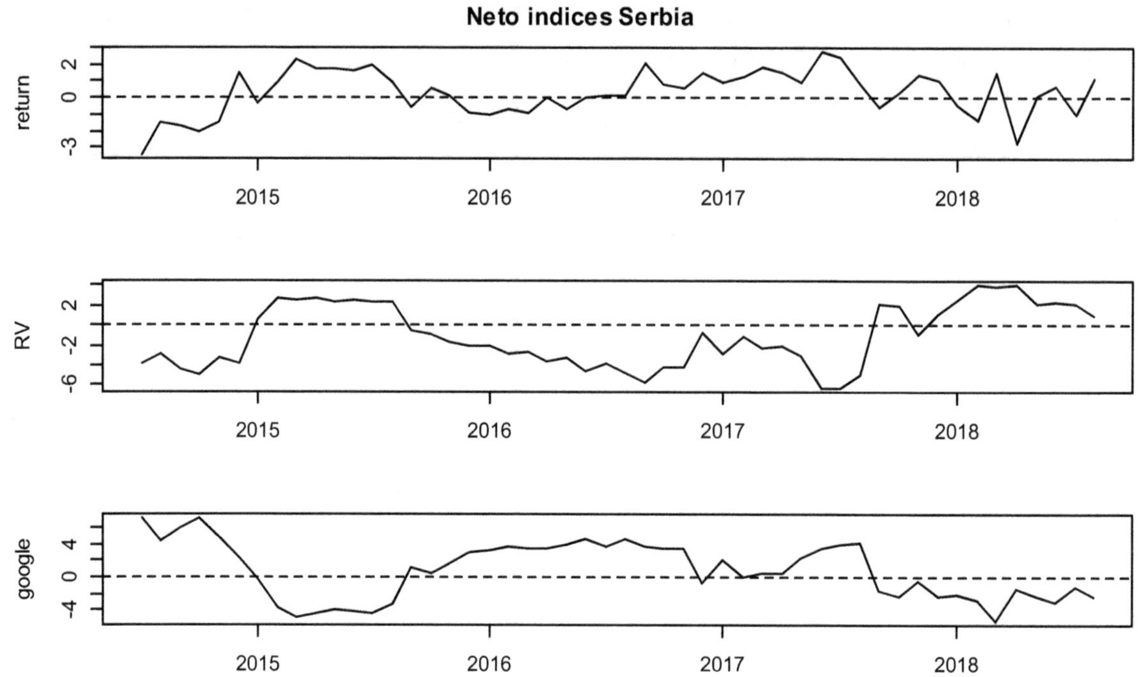


**Figure 6.** Net rolling indices, Serbia.

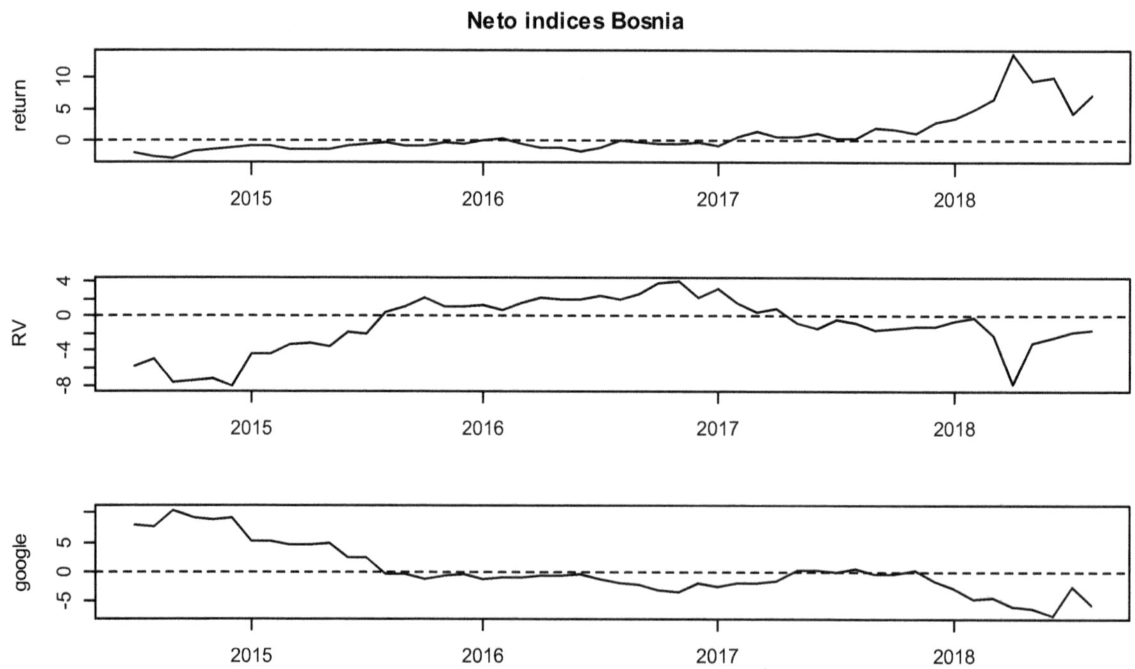


**Figure 7.** Net rolling indices, Bosnia and Herzegovina.

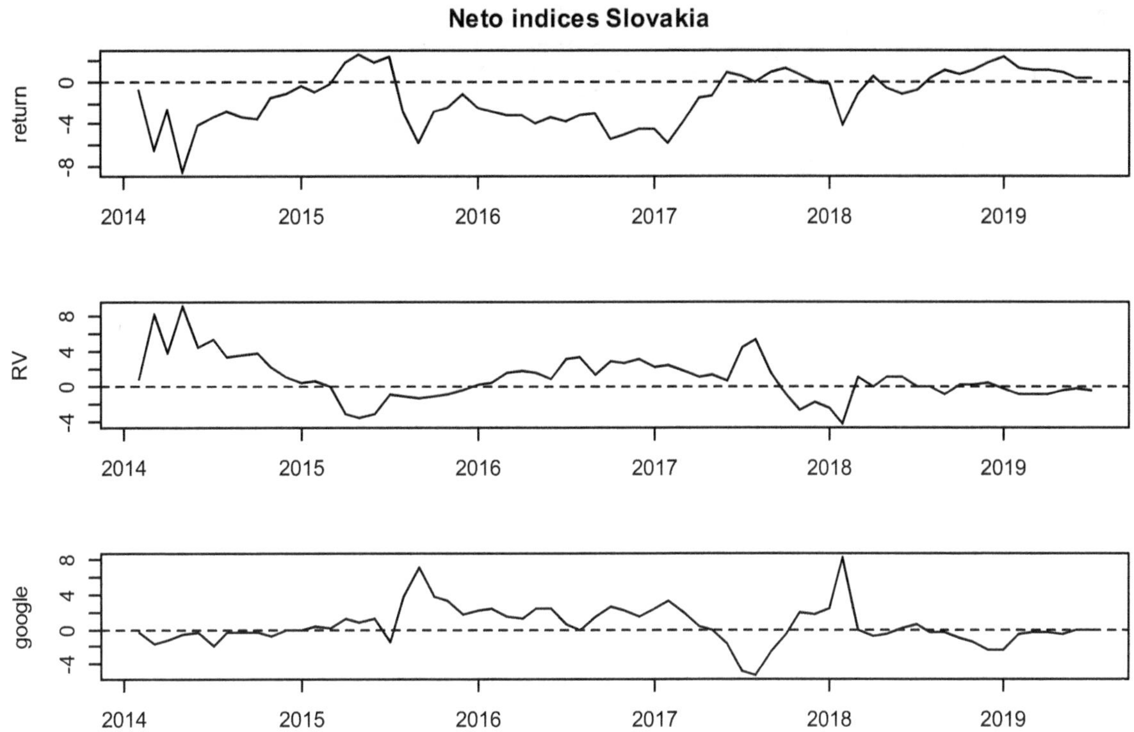


**Figure 8.** Net rolling indices, Slovakia.

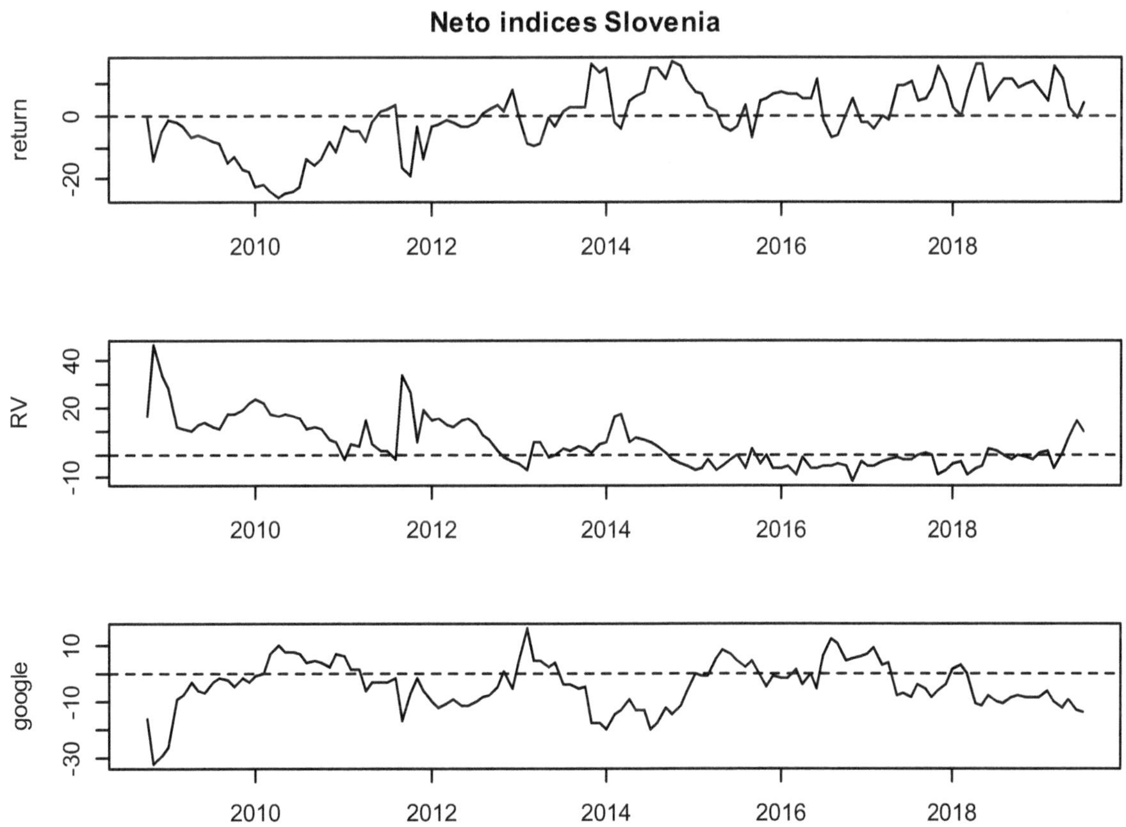


**Figure 9.** Net rolling indices, Slovenia.

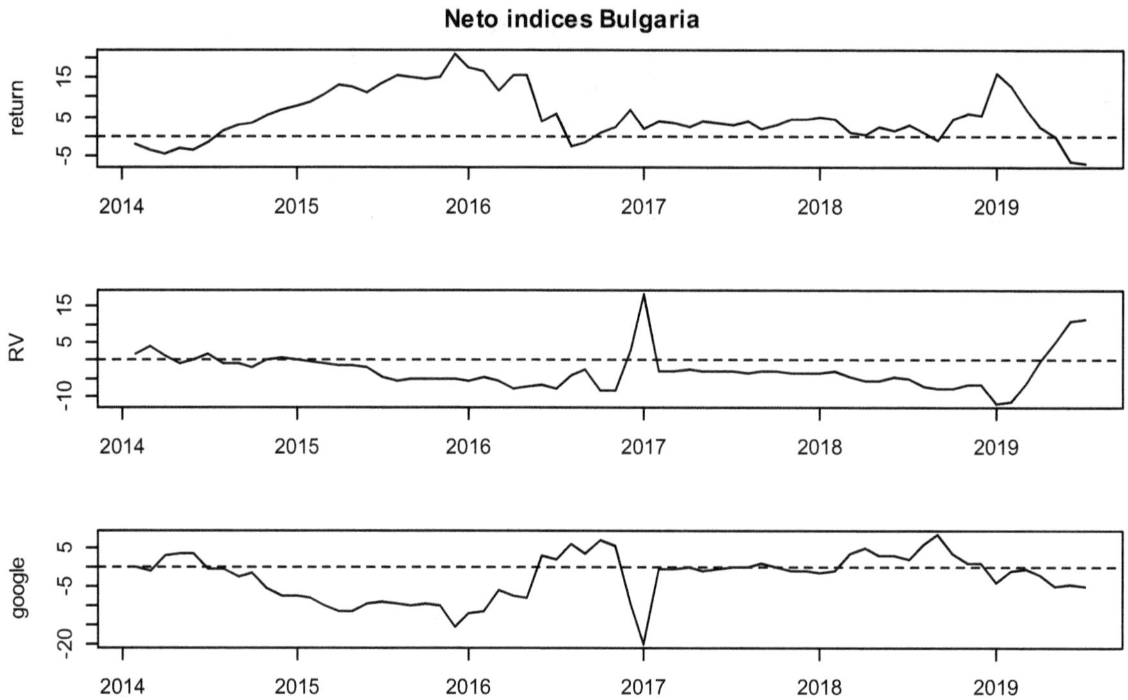


**Figure 10.** Net rolling indices, Bulgaria.

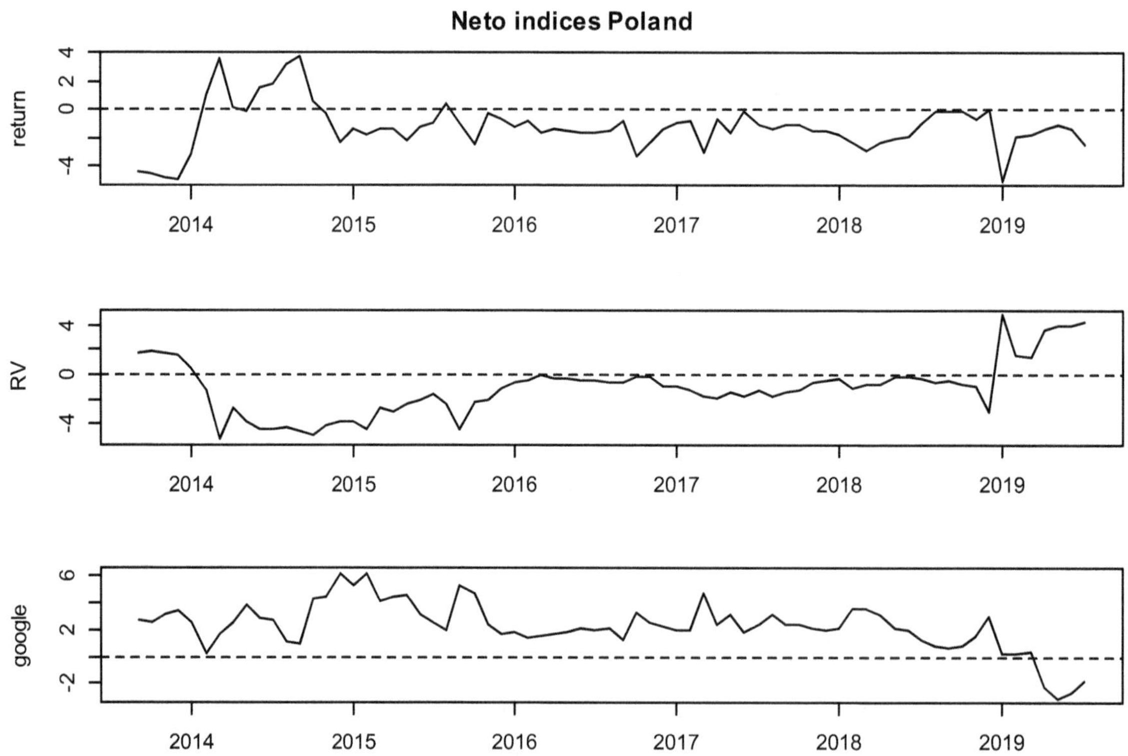


**Figure 11.** Net rolling indices, Poland.

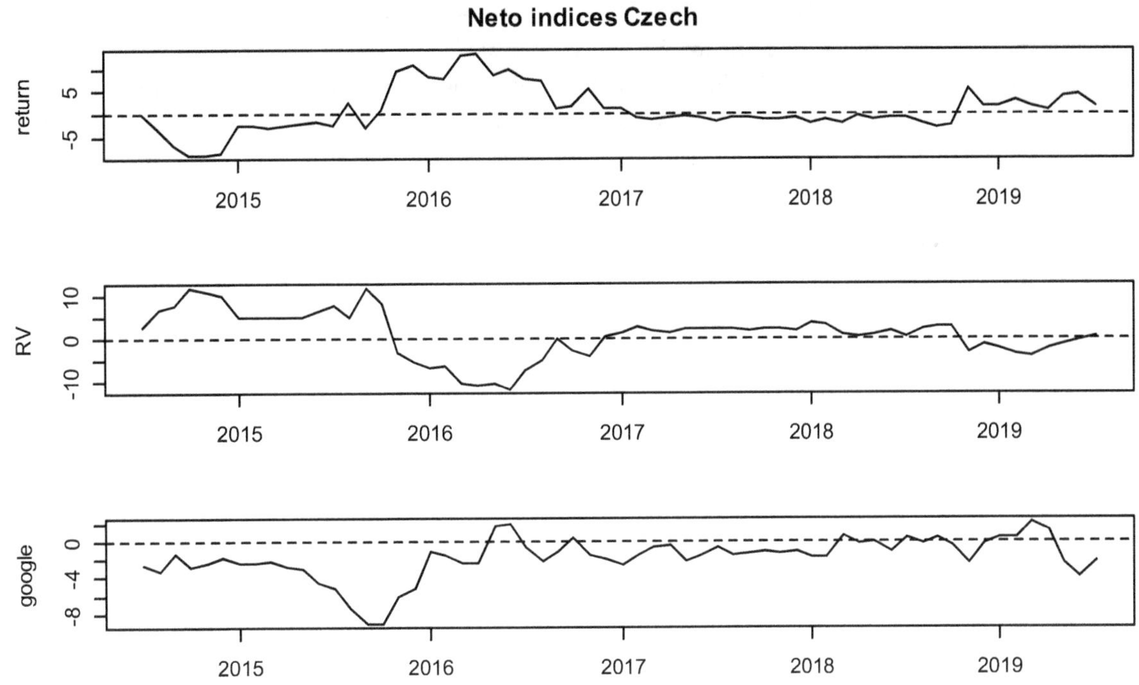


**Figure 12.** Net rolling indices, the Czech Republic.

## 5. Conclusions

Summarizing the previous results, several things could be said. The results somewhat indicated that some of the stock markets exhibited violation of the EMH to some extent. This included the Hungarian, Slovenian and Croatian markets, while some weaker evidence was found for the Bulgarian and Polish markets. This was based on the results of Granger causality tests and the spillover tables' results. The impulse response functions gave insights into (non) rejection of investor's attention hypothesis. Namely, the Hungarian, Polish, Slovenian and Croatian markets were found to have the majority of significant results here. An increase in the variable Google search volume led to a decrease of return series on the Croatian and Hungarian markets, which was in favor of Merton's (1987) theoretical findings. Moreover, sometimes the risk variable reacted even more to shocks in the search volume variable, which was in accordance with Andrei and Hasler (2014) and Vlastakis and Markellos (2012).

Violating the efficient market hypothesis in terms of investor's attention towards specific groups of stocks is getting more focus in research over the last couple of years. The empirical literature on testing the predictability of stock returns and volatilities by including the online search volume in existing models has been booming, especially in the last decade. This paper wanted to get initial insights into the relationship between the Google search volumes and risk and return series for selected CEE and SEE stock markets. Reasoning lies upon the facts that such markets are rarely observed in similar studies and getting more information on these markets can be useful for (potential) investors.

With the main results being mixed, depending on the observed market, recommendations for international investors have to be based on the findings for individual markets. For those markets in which we found predictability of selected variables to some extent, investors could utilize these results for future forecasting. This could enhance portfolio performance in terms of risk and return. Some shortfalls should be mentioned as well. Data unavailability on some indices did not enable a long-term analysis for some of the countries in the sample. Thus, the results could very well be influenced by it. With that in mind, future work should repeat this analysis in order to test the validity of results given here.

Contributions of the research are found in extending the VAR framework with spillover indices: Total and directional, both static and dynamic. The time varying shocks spillover enabled us to provide comments on the dynamics between the selected variables. Moreover, the dynamic net spillover indices were estimated, so the information on which variable is the net emitter or net receiver of shocks in the system was obtained as well. Future work should focus on individual countries in order to get detailed insights in the dynamics of risks, returns and search volumes specific to a given country. In that way, with detailed results we will be able to simulate and compare investment strategies tailored on individual specific results.

**Funding:** This research received no external funding. The APC was funded by institutions through the Knowledge Unlatched initiative and partially funded by MDPI.

**Acknowledgments:** The author would like to thank the two referees for useful comments that have contributed to the final quality of the paper.

**Conflicts of Interest:** The author declares no conflict of interest.

## Appendix A

**Table A1.** Unit root test results for variables, constant included.

| Country | Return | Excess Return | Realized Volatility | Google Search Volume |
|---|---|---|---|---|
| Hungary | −7.0149 *** | −5.789 *** | −4.2054 *** | −3.6045 *** |
| Croatia | −8.2586 *** | −9.922 *** | −6.4532 *** | −3.1011 ** |
| Ukraine | −9.077 *** | −9.500 *** | −7.123 *** | −4.1481 *** |
| Slovenia | −6.0497 *** | −9.233 *** | −6.1911 *** | −2.8907 ** |
| Poland | −7.3147 *** | −7.483 *** | −5.3317 *** | −4.5645 *** |
| Bosnia and Herzegovina | −5.4507 *** | −6.227 *** | −4.7188 *** | −5.3291 *** |
| Czech Republic | −8.8916 *** | −8.778 *** | −5.9225 *** | −3.633 *** |
| Slovakia | −7.1175 *** | −6.902 *** | −5.5583 *** | −4.295 *** |
| Bulgaria | −5.5037 *** | −6.945 *** | −6.279 *** | −2.6779 * |
| Serbia | −6.9199 *** | −6.622 *** | −5.4058 *** | −3.7528 *** |

Note: Results in Table A1 show empirical test values, where *, ** and *** denote statistical significance on 10%, 5% and 1% respectively. Constant is included in the ADF test as a deterministic regressor.

**Table A2.** Multivariate autocorrelation and heteroskedasticity tests.

| Country | Multivariate Test | |
|---|---|---|
| | ARCH Test | LM Test |
| Hungary | 413.320 (0.733) | 47.697 (0.092) * |
| Croatia | 400.230 (0.302) | 13.901 (0.126) |
| Ukraine | 14.959 (0.092) * | 38.405 (0.361) |
| Slovenia | 48.593 (0.078) * | 26.446 (0.090) * |
| Poland | 437.540 (0.417) | 99.827 (0.700) |
| Bosnia and Herzegovina | 396.000 (0.892) | 18.77 (0.406) |
| Czech Republic | 443.040 (0.346) | 10.973 (0.278) |
| Slovakia | 453.760 (0.226) | 119.68 (0.208) |
| Bulgaria | 438.880 (0.412) | 131.48 (0.062) * |
| Serbia | 396.000 (0.892) | 99.431 (0.710) |

Note: * denotes statistical significance on 1 0%. Test results are provided for the 12th order autocorrelation and heteroskedasticity. Table shows empirical test values for each test and each country with $p$-values given in brackets.

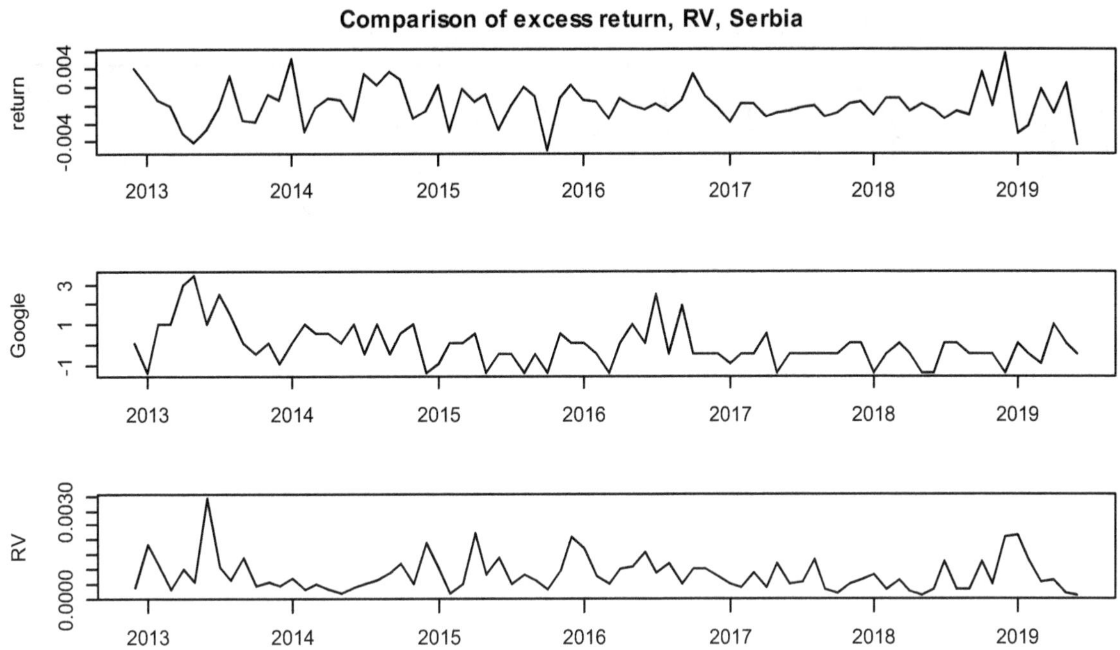


**Figure A1.** Comparison of monthly series: Excess return, RV and Google search volume, Serbia.

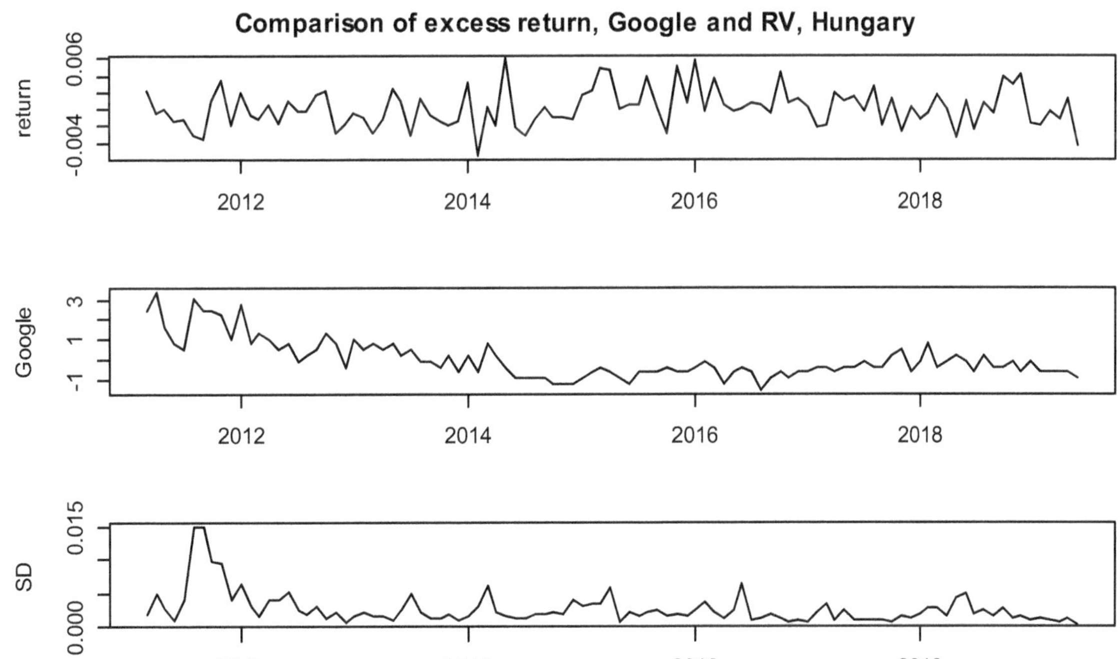


**Figure A2.** Comparison of monthly series: Excess return, RV and Google search volume, Hungary.

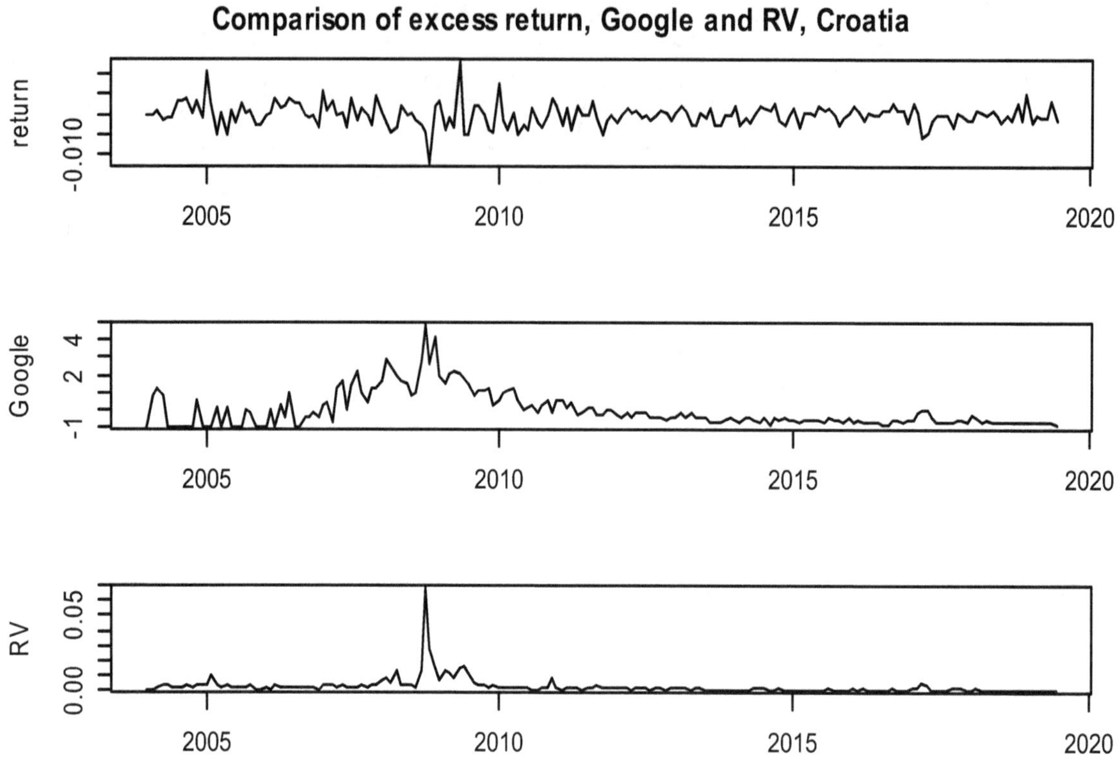


**Figure A3.** Comparison of monthly series: Excess return, RV and Google search volume, Croatia.

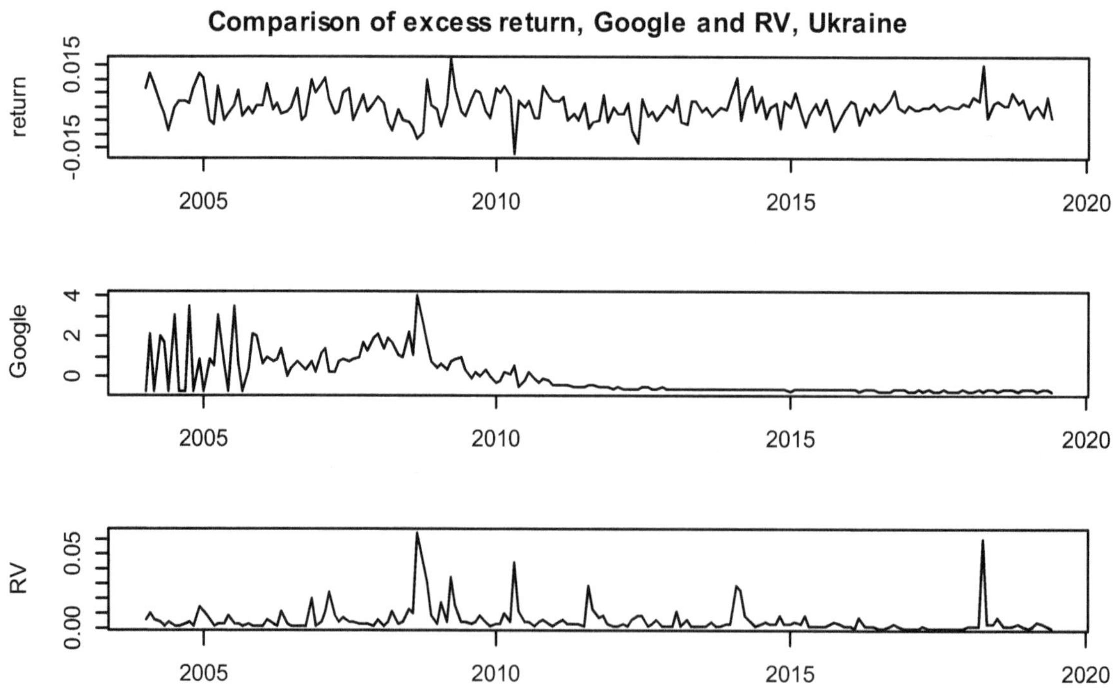


**Figure A4.** Comparison of monthly series: Excess return, RV and Google search volume, Ukraine.

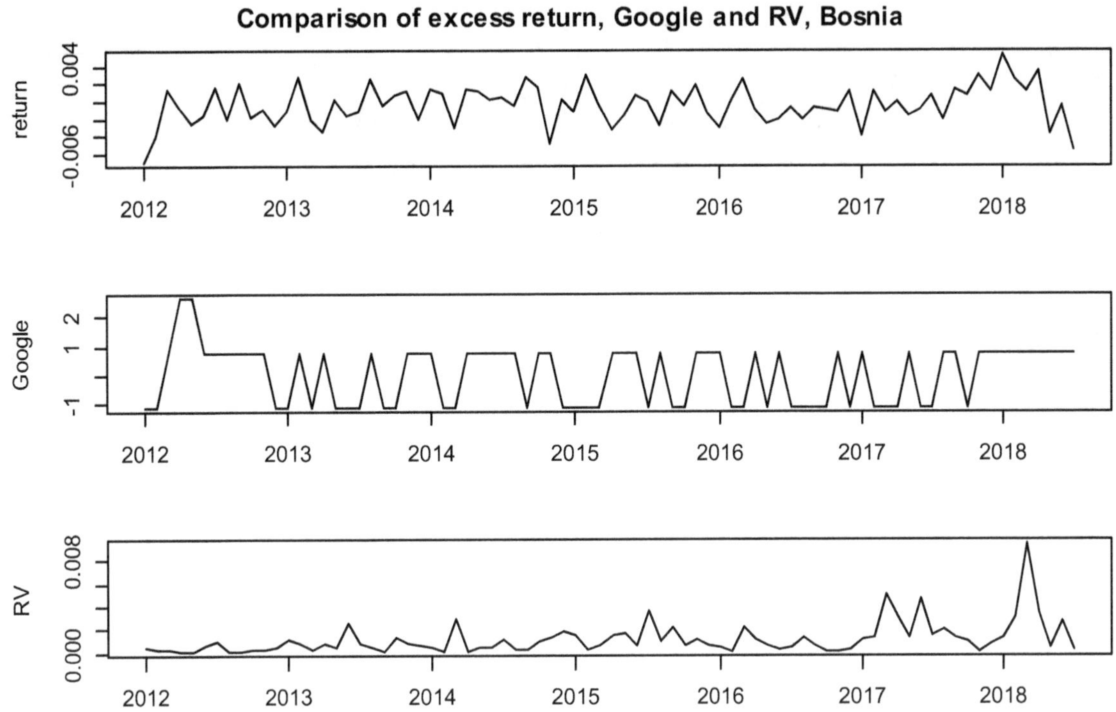


**Figure A5.** Comparison of monthly series: Excess return, RV and Google search volume, Bosnia and Herzegovina.

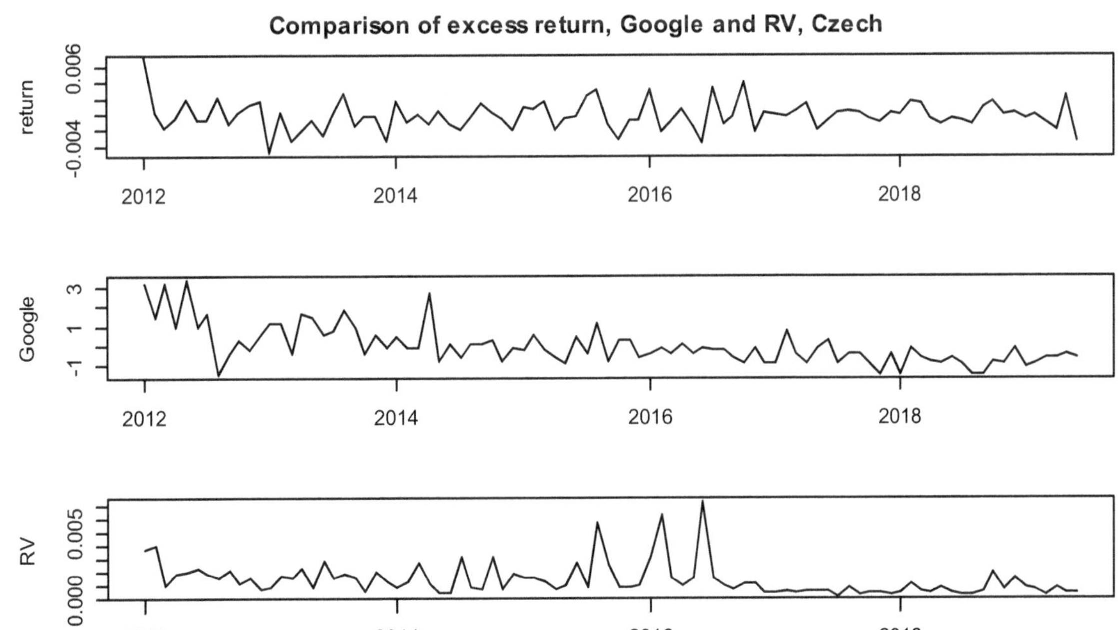


**Figure A6.** Comparison of monthly series: Excess return, RV and Google search volume, Czech Republic.

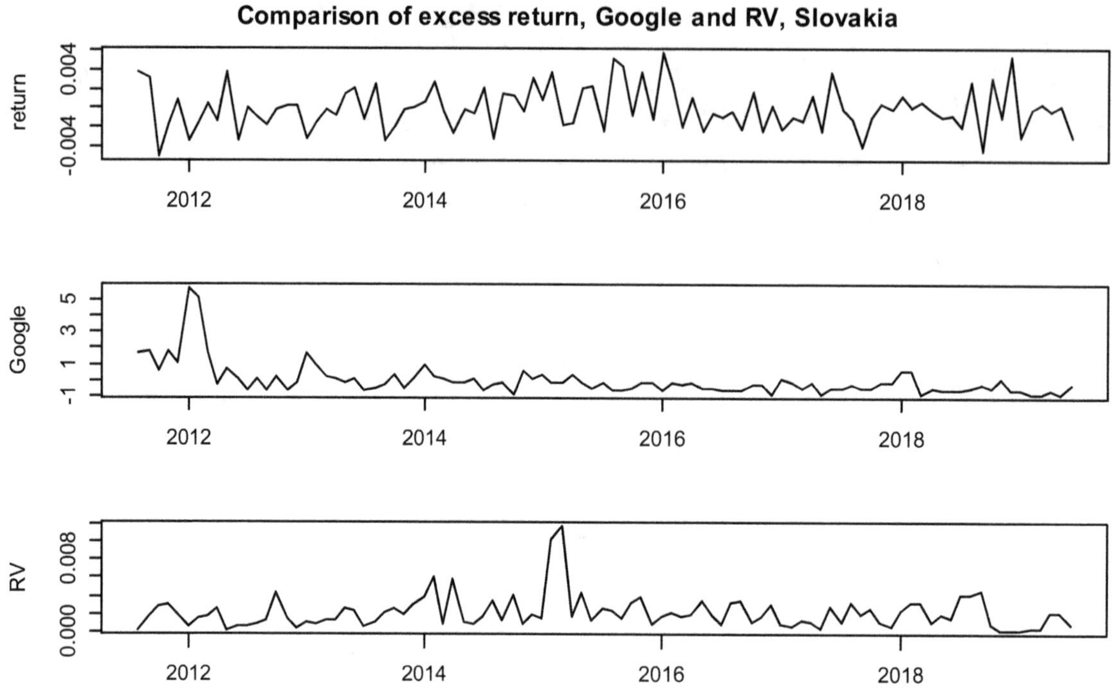


**Figure A7.** Comparison of monthly series: Excess return, RV and Google search volume, Slovakia.

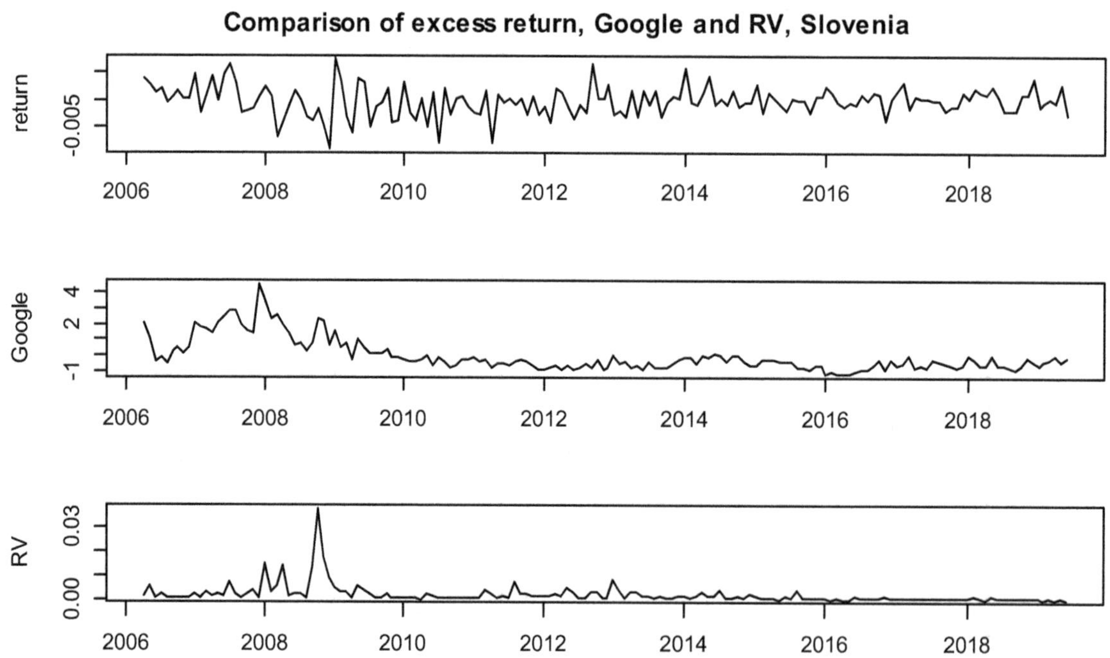


**Figure A8.** Comparison of monthly series: Excess return, RV and Google search volume, Slovenia.

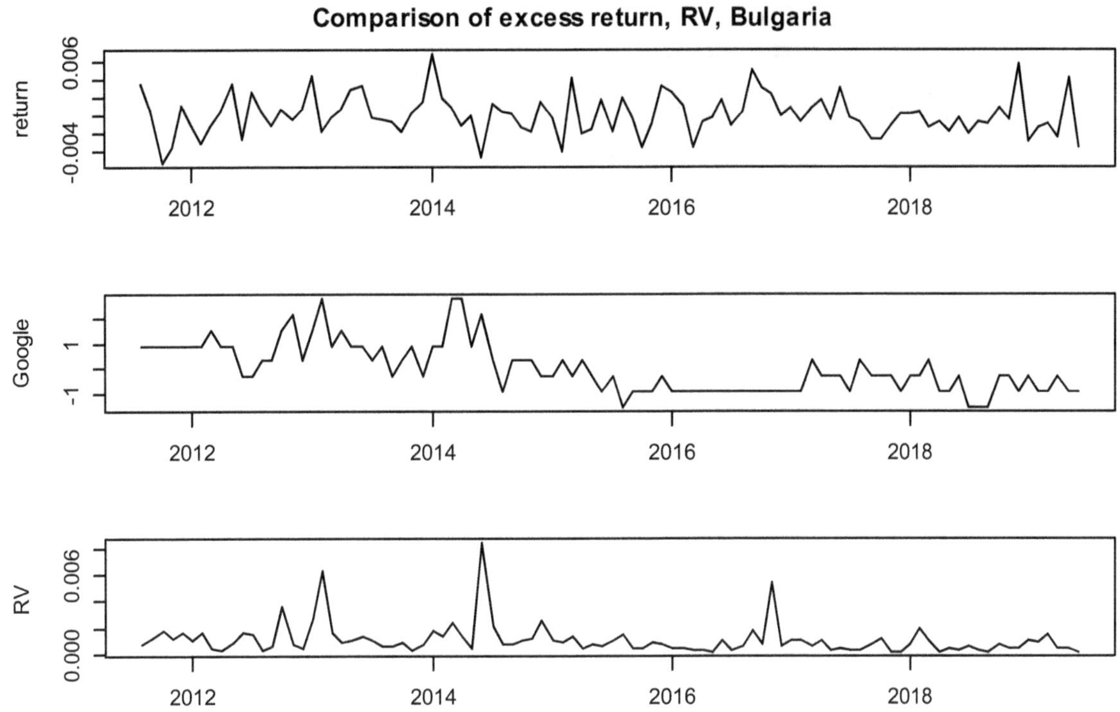


**Figure A9.** Comparison of monthly series: Excess return, RV and Google search volume, Bulgaria.

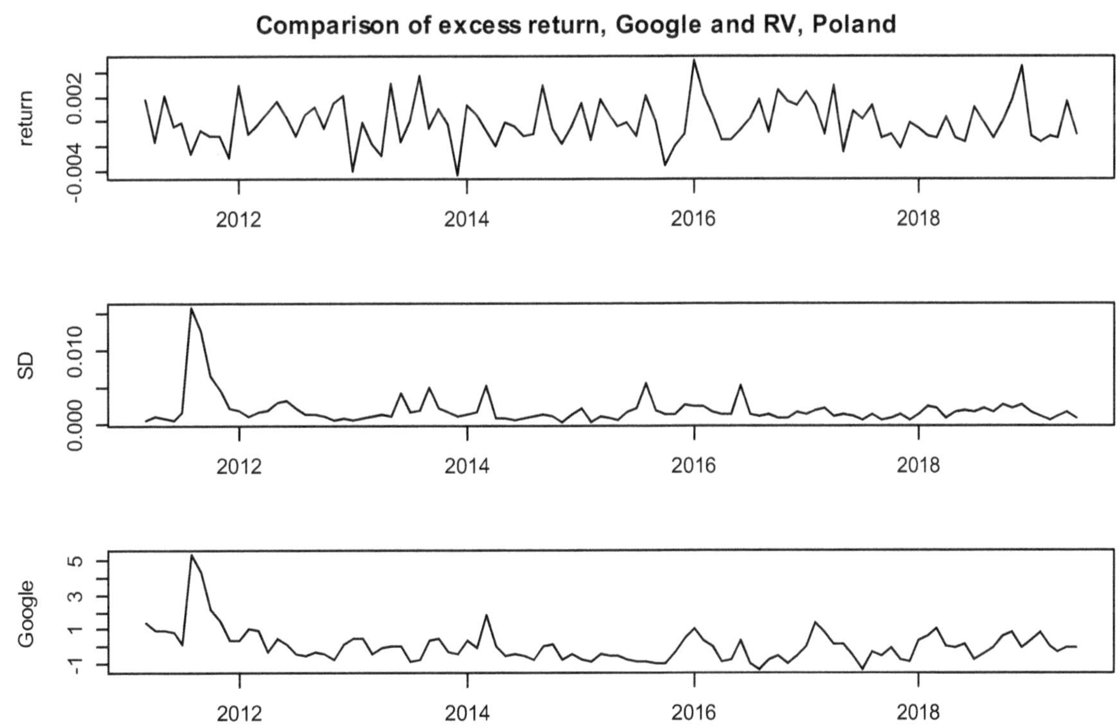


**Figure A10.** Comparison of monthly series: Excess return, RV and Google search volume, Poland.

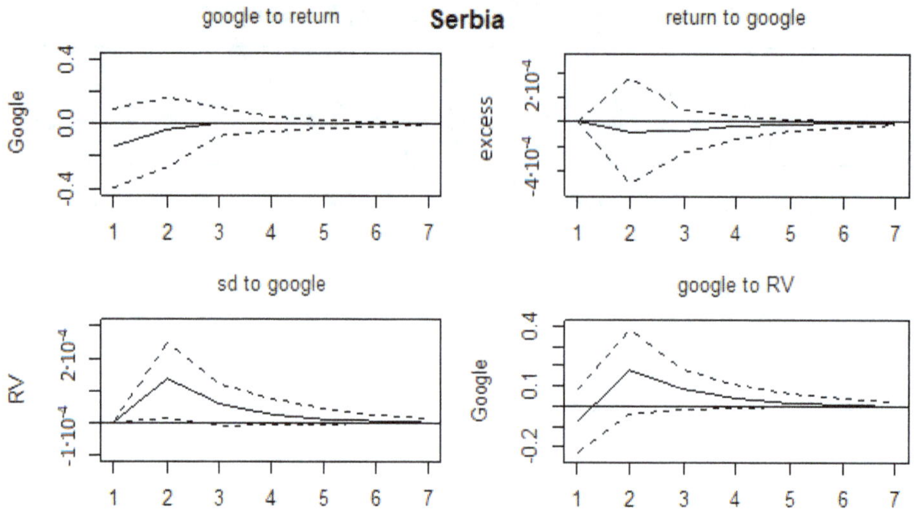


**Figure A11.** Impulse response functions, Serbia.

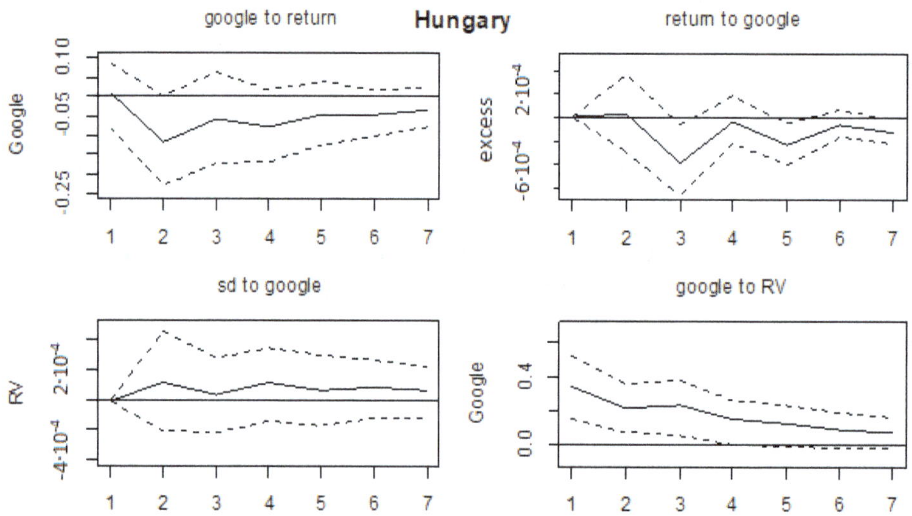


**Figure A12.** Impulse response functions, Hungary.

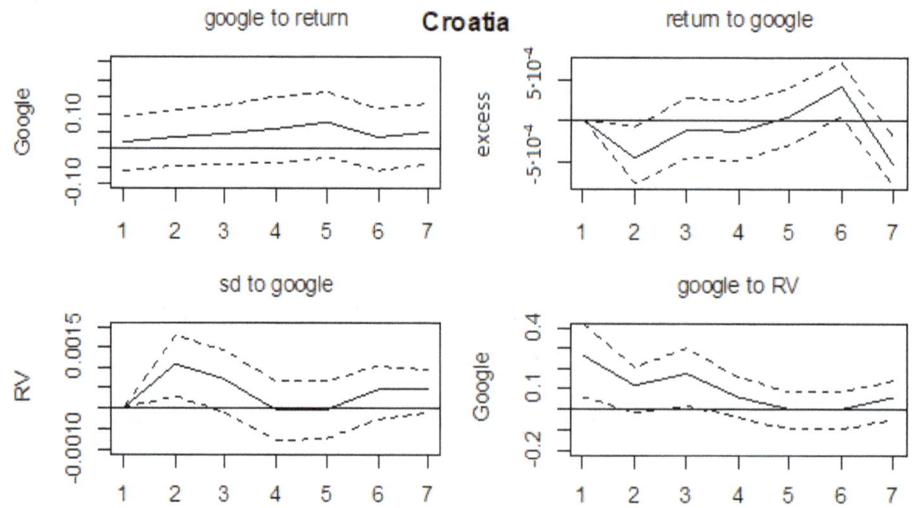


**Figure A13.** Impulse response functions, Croatia.

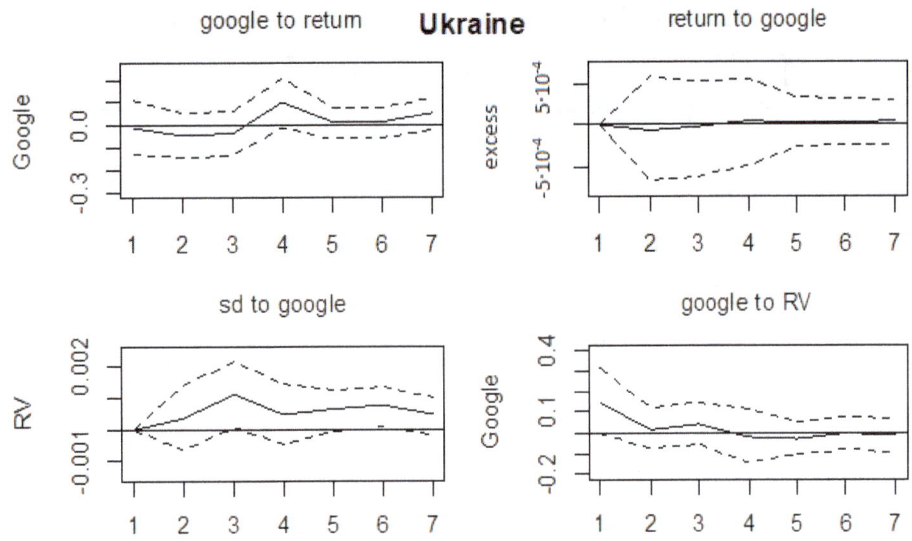


**Figure A14.** Impulse response functions, Ukraine.

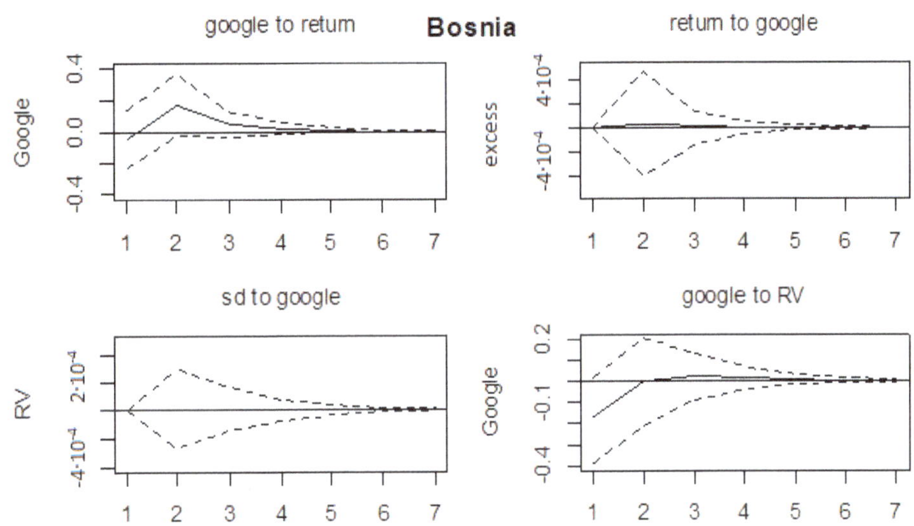


**Figure A15.** Impulse response functions, Bosnia and Herzegovina.

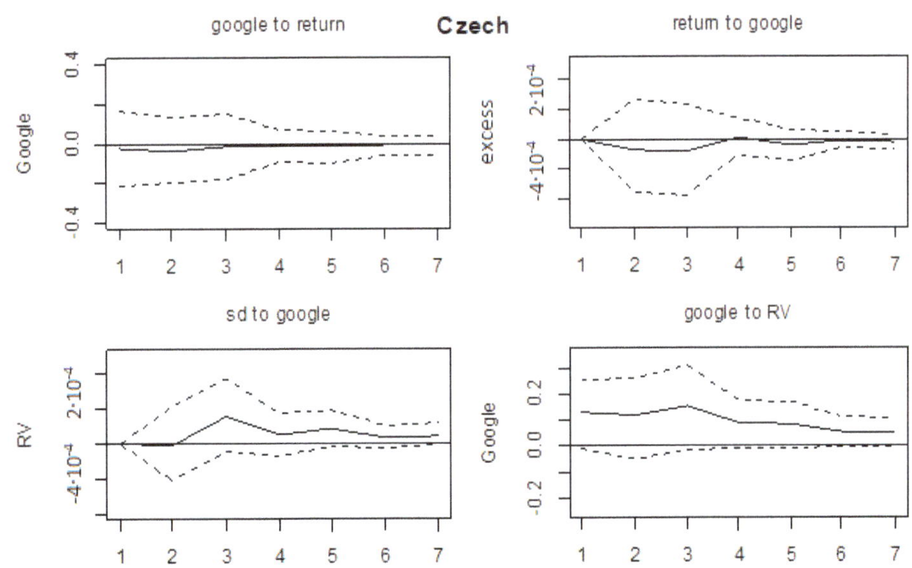


**Figure A16.** Impulse response functions, Czech Republic.

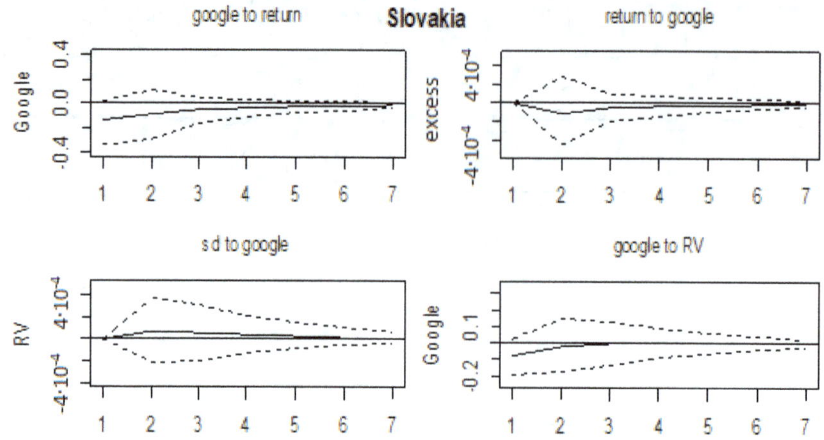


**Figure A17.** Impulse response functions, Slovakia.

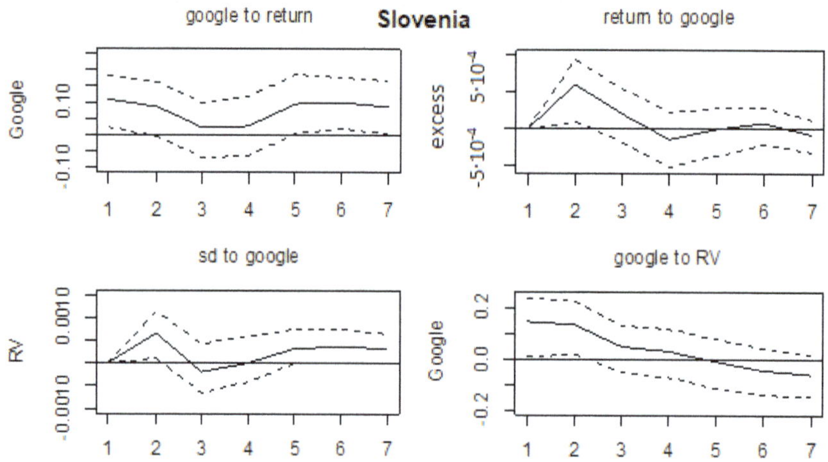


**Figure A18.** Impulse response functions, Slovenia.

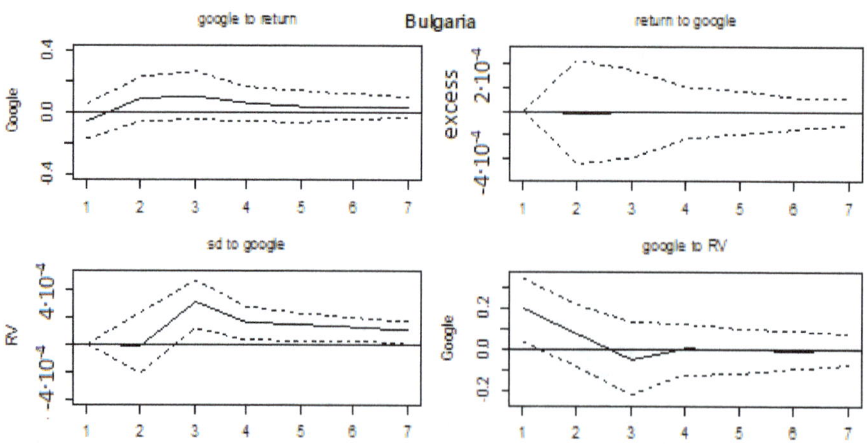


**Figure A19.** Impulse response functions, Bulgaria.

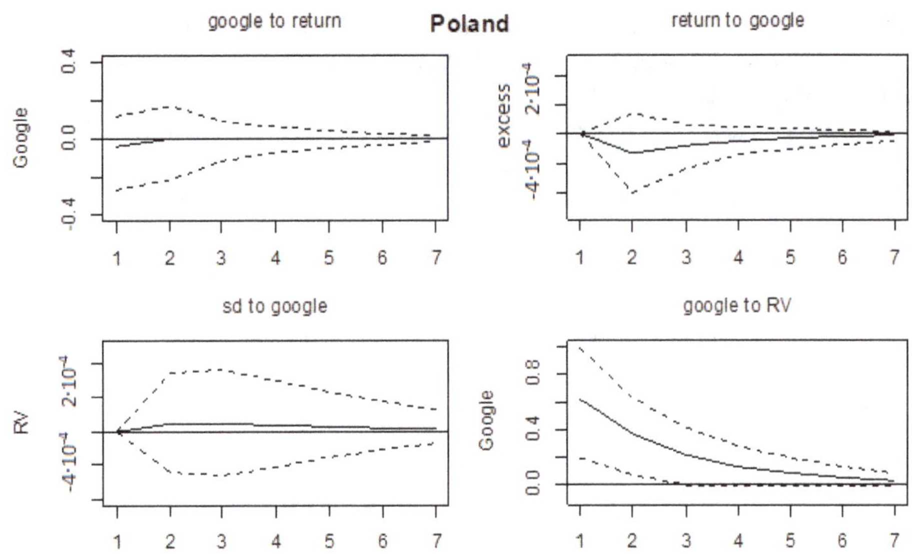


**Figure A20.** Impulse response functions, Poland.

## References


Aalborg, Halvor Aarhus, Peter Molnár, and Jon Erik de Vries. 2019. What can explain the price, volatility and trading volume of Bitcoin? *Finance Research Letters* 29: 255–65. [CrossRef]

Andersen, Torben, and Tim Bollerslev. 1998. Answering the sceptics: Yes standard volatility models do provide accurate forecasts. *International Economic Review* 39: 885–905. [CrossRef]

Andrei, Daniel, and Michael Hasler. 2014. Investor attention and stock market volatility. *The Review of Financial Studies* 28: 33–72. [CrossRef]

Andries, Alin Marius, Iulian Ihnatov, and Nicu Sprincean. 2018. Do seasonal anomalies still exist in central and eastern European countries? A conditional variance approach. *Romanian Journal of Economic Forecasting* 20: 60–83.

Antonakakais, Nikolas, Cristhophe Andre, and Rangan Gupta. 2016. Dynamic Spillovers in the United States: Stock Market, Housing, Uncertainty, and the Macroeconomy. *Southern Economic Journal* 83: 609–24. [CrossRef]

Baele, Lieven, Geert Bekaert, and Larissa Schäfer. 2015. *An Anatomy of Central and Eastern European Equity Markets.* Columbia Business School Working Paper, No. 15–71. Singapore: Columbia Business School.

Bank, Matthias, Martin Larch, and Georg Peter. 2011. Google search volume and its influence on liquidity and returns of German stocks. *Financial Markets and Portfolio Management* 25: 239–64. [CrossRef]

Barber, Brad, and Terrance Odean. 2007. All that glitters: The effect of attention and news on the buying behavior of individual and institutional investors. *Review of Financial Studies* 21: 785–818. [CrossRef]

Barndorff-Nielsen, Ole, and Neil Shephard. 2002. Econometric analysis of realised volatility and its use in estimating stochastic volatility models. *Journal of the Royal Statistical Society* 64: 253–80. [CrossRef]

Bijl, Laurens, Glenn Kringhaug, Peter Molnár, and Eirik Sandvik. 2016. Google searches and stock returns. *International Review of Financial Analysis* 45: 150–56. [CrossRef]

Black, Fischer. 1986. Noise. *The Journal of Finance* 41: 529–43. [CrossRef]

Bortoli, Clement, and Stephane Combes. 2015. Contribution from Google Trends for Forecasting the Short-Term Economic Outlook in France: Limited Avenues. Institut National de la Statistique et des Éstudes Économiques. Available online: https://www.insee.fr/en/statistiques/1408911?sommaire=1408916 (accessed on 25 May 2019).

Chen, Tao. 2017. Investor Attention and Global Stock Returns. *Journal of Behavioral Finance* 18: 358–72. [CrossRef]

Chen, Joseph, Harrison Hong, and Jeremy Stein. 2002. Breadth of Ownership and Stock Returns. *Journal of Financial Economics* 66: 171–205. [CrossRef]

Chen, Jian, Guohao Tang, Jiaquan Yao, and Guofu Zhou. 2019. Investor Attention and Stock Returns. Available online: https://ssrn.com/abstract=3194387 (accessed on 25 May 2019).

Da, Zhi, Joseph Engelberg, and Pngjie Gao. 2010. The Sum of All Fears: Investor Sentiment and Asset Prices, *SSRN eLibrary*. Available online: https://pdfs.semanticscholar.org/cc4f/6f4dba88381810412ea3d929715f38cb9ee0.pdf (accessed on 25 May 2019).

Da, Zhi, Joseph Engelberg, and Pengjie Gao. 2011. In search of attention. *The Journal of Finance* 66: 1461–99. [CrossRef]

De Long Bradford, James, Andrei Shleifer, Lawrence Summers, and Robert Waldmann. 1990. Noise trader risk in financial markets. *Journal of Political Economy* 98: 703–38. [CrossRef]

Demirer, Mert, Umut Gokcen, and Kamil Yilmaz. 2018. *Financial Sector Volatility Connectedness and Equity Returns*. Koc University-TUSIAD Economic Research Forum, Working Paper No. 1803. Istanbul: Koc University.

Dergiades, Theologos, Eleni Mavragani, and Bing Pan. 2018. Google trends and tourists' arrivals: Emerging biases and proposed corrections. *Tourism Management* 66: 108–20. [CrossRef]

Diebold, Francis, and Kamil Yilmaz. 2009. Measuring Financial Asset Return and Volatility Spillovers with Application to Global Equity Markets. *The Economic Journal* 119: 158–71. [CrossRef]

Diebold, Francis, and Kamil Yilmaz. 2011. Equity Market Spillovers in the Americas. In *Financial Stability, Monetary Policy, and Central Banking*. Bank of Chile Central Banking Series 5; Edited by Rodrigo Alfaro. Santiago: Bank of Chile Central Banking, pp. 199–214.

Diebold, Francis, and Kamil Yilmaz. 2012. Better to Give than to Receive: Predictive Directional Measurement of Volatility Spillovers. *International Journal of Forecasting* 28: 57–66. [CrossRef]

Dimpfl, Thomas, and Stephan Jank. 2016. Can Internet Search Queries Help to Predict Stock Market Volatility? *European Financial Management* 22: 171–92. [CrossRef]

Dzielinski, Michal. 2012. Measuring economic uncertainty and its impact on the stock market. *Finance Research Letters* 9: 167–75. [CrossRef]

Fama, Eugene. 1965. Random Walks in Stock Market Prices. *Financial Analysts Journal* 21: 55–59. [CrossRef]

Fama, Eugene. 1970. Efficient Capital Markets: A Review of Theory and Empirical Work. *The Journal of Finance* 25: 383–417. [CrossRef]

Fang, Lily, and Joel Peress. 2009. Media Coverage and the Cross-section of Stock Returns. *The Journal of Finance* 64: 2023–52. [CrossRef]

Ferreira, Paulo. 2018. Long-range dependencies of Eastern European stock markets: A dynamic detrended analysis. *Physica A* 505: 454–70. [CrossRef]

Frieder, Laura, and Avanidhar Subrahmanyam. 2005. Brand Perceptions and the Market for Common Stock. *Journal of Financial and Quantitative Analysis* 40: 57–85. [CrossRef]

Goddard, John, Arben Kita, and Qingwei Wang. 2015. Investor attention and FX market volatility. *Journal of International Financial Markets, Institutions & Money* 38: 79–96.

Goel, Sharad, Jake Hofman, Sebastien Lahaie, David Pennock, and Duncan Watts. 2010. Predicting consumer behavior with Web search. *Proceedings of the National Academy of Sciences of the United States of America* 107: 17486–90. [CrossRef]

Google Trends Data. 2019. Available online: https://trends.google.com/trends/ (accessed on 25 May 2019).

Grinblatt, Mark, and Matti Keloharju. 2000. The investment behavior and performance of various investor types: A study of Finland's unique data set. *Journal of Financial Economics* 55: 43–67. [CrossRef]

Grullon, Gustavo, George Kanatas, and James Weston. 2004. Advertising, breadth of ownership, and liquidity. *Review of Financial Studies* 17: 439–61. [CrossRef]

Habibah, Ume, Suresh Rajput, and Ranjeta Sadhwani. 2017. Stock market return predictability: Google pessimistic sentiments versus fear gauge. *Cogent Economics & Finance* 5: 1390897.

Hamid, Alain, and Moritz Heiden. 2015. Forecasting volatility with empirical similarity and Google Trends. *Journal of Economic Behavior & Organization* 117: 62–81.

Han, Liyan, Ziying Li, and Libo Yin. 2017. Investor Attention and Stock Returns: International Evidence. *Emerging Markets Finance and Trade* 54: 3168–88. [CrossRef]

Havranek, Tomas, and Ayaz Zeynalov. 2018. *Forecasting Tourist Arrivals: Google Trends Meets Mixed Frequency Data*. Munich Personal RePEc Archive, MPRA paper No. 90203. Munich: Munich University Library.

Investing Data Website. 2019. Available online: https://www.investing.com/ (accessed on 25 May 2019).

Joseph, Kissain, Babajide Wintoki, and Zelin Zhang. 2011. Forecasting abnormal stock returns and trading volume using investor sentiment: Evidence from online search. *International Journal of Forecasting* 27: 1116–27. [CrossRef]

Jun, Seung-Pyo, Hyoung Sun Yoo, and San Choi. 2018. Ten years of research change using Google Trends: From the perspective of big data utilizations and applications. *Technological Forecasting & Social Change* 130: 69–87.

Khan, Mehwish Aziz, and Eatzaz Ahmad. 2018. Measurement of Investor Sentiment and Its Bi-Directional Contemporaneous and Lead–Lag Relationship with Returns: Evidence from Pakistan. *Sustainability* 11: 94. [CrossRef]

Kim, Neri, Katarína Lučivjanská, Peter Molnár, and Roviel Villa. 2019. Google searches and stock market activity: Evidence from Norway. *Finance Research Letters* 28: 208–20. [CrossRef]

Koop, Gary, Mashem Pesaran, and Simon Potter. 1996. Impulse response analysis in nonlinear multivariate models. *Journal of Econometrics* 74: 119–47. [CrossRef]

Lehavy, Reuven, and Richard Sloan. 2008. Investor recognition and stock returns. *Review of Accounting Studies* 13: 327–61. [CrossRef]

Li, Jun, and Jiangfeng Yu. 2012. Investor Attention, Psychological Anchors, and Stock Return Predictability. *Journal of Financial Economics* 104: 401–19. [CrossRef]

Lütkepohl, Helmut. 1993. *Introduction to Multiple Time Series Analysis*. Berlin: Springer.

Lütkepohl, Helmut. 2006. *New Introduction to Multiple Time Series Analysis*. Berlin: Springer.

Lütkepohl, Helmut. 2010. *Vector Autoregressive Models*. Economics Working Paper ECO 2011/30. Fiesole: European University Institute.

Merton, Robert. 1987. A simple model of capital market equilibrium with incomplete information. *The Journal of Finance* 42: 483–510. [CrossRef]

Molnár, Peter, and Milan Bašta. 2017. Google searches and Gasoline prices. Paper presented at 2017 14th International Conference on the European Energy Market (EEM), Dresden, Germany, June 6–9; pp. 1–5.

Mondria, Jordi, Thomas Wu, and Yi Zhang. 2010. The determinants of international investment and attention allocation: Using internet search query data. *Journal of International Economics* 82: 85–95. [CrossRef]

Necula, Ciprian, and Alina-Nicoleta Radu. 2012. Long Memory in Eastern European Financial Markets Returns. *Economic Research* 25: 316–77. [CrossRef]

Netmarketshare. 2019. Available online: https://netmarketshare.com (accessed on 25 May 2019).

Odean, Terrance. 1998. Are investors reluctant to realize their losses? *The Journal of Finance* 53: 1775–98. [CrossRef]

Önder, Irem. 2017. Forecasting tourism demand with Google trends: Accuracy comparison of countries versus cities. *International Journal of Tourism Research* 19: 648–660. [CrossRef]

Padungsaksawasdi, Chaiyuth, Sirimon Treepongkaruna, and Robert Brooks. 2019. Investor Attention and Stock Market Activities: New Evidence from Panel Data. *International Journal of Financial Studies* 7: 30. [CrossRef]

Peng, Lin, and Wei Xiong. 2006. Investor attention, overconfidence and category learning. *Journal of Financial Economics* 80: 563–602. [CrossRef]

Pesaran, Hashem, and Yongcheol Shin. 1998. Generalized impulse response analysis in linear multivariate models. *Economics Letters* 58: 17–29. [CrossRef]

Preis, Tobias, Daniel Reith, and Eugene Stanley. 2010. Complex dynamics of our economic life on different scales: Insights from search engine query data. *Philosophical Transactions of the Royal Society A* 368: 5707–19. [CrossRef]

Preis, Tobias, Helen Susannah Moat, and Eugene Stanley. 2013. Quantifying Trading Behavior in Financial Markets Using Google Trends. *Scientific Reports* 3: 1684. [CrossRef]

Sibley, Steven, Yanchu Wang, Yuhang Xing, and Xiaoyan Zhang. 2016. The information content of the sentiment index. *Journal of Banking & Finance* 62: 164–79.

Škrinjarić, Tihana. 2018a. Mogu li Google trend podaci poboljšati prognoziranje prinosa na Zagrebačkoj burzi? (Can Google trend data enhance return forecasting on Zagreb Stock Exchange?). *Zbornik radova Ekonomskog fakulteta Sveučilišta u Mostaru (Journal of Economy and Business, University of Mostar)* 24: 58–76.

Škrinjarić, Tihana. 2018b. The value of food sector on Croatian capital market if the Agrokor crisis did not happen: Synthetic control method approach. *CEA Journal of Economics* 13: 53–65.

Škrinjarić, Tihana. 2018c. Testing for Seasonal Affective Disorder on Selected CEE and SEE Stock Markets. *Risks* 6: 140. [CrossRef]

Škrinjarić, Tihana, and Mirjana Čižmešija. 2019. Investor attention and risk predictability: A spillover index approach. Paper presented at the 15th International Symposium on Operations Research in Slovenia, Bled, Slovenia, September 25–27; pp. 423–28.

Škrinjarić, Tihana, and Zrinka Orlović. 2019. Effects of economic and political events on stock returns: Event study of Agrokor case in Croatia. *Croatian Economic Survey* 21: 47–86. [CrossRef]

Smith, Geoffrey Peter. 2012. Google Internet Search Activity and Volatility Prediction in the Market for Foreign Currency. *Finance Research Letters* 9: 103–10. [CrossRef]

Takeda, Fumika, and Takumi Wakao. 2014. Google search intensity and its relationship with returns and trading volume of Japanese stocks. *Pacific-Basin Finance Journal* 27: 1–18. [CrossRef]

Tan, Selin Düz, and Oktay Tas. 2019. Investor attention and stock returns: Evidence from Borsa Istanbul. *Borsa Istanbul Review* 19: 106–16.

Tantaopas, Parkpoom, Chaiyuth Padungsaksawasdi, and Sirimon Treepongkaruna. 2016. Attention effect via internet search intensity in Asia-Pacific stock markets. *Pacific-Basin Finance Journal* 38: 107–24. [CrossRef]

Tkacz, Greg. 2013. *Predicting Recessions in Real-Time: Mining Google Trends and Electronic Payments Data for Clues.* C.D. Howe Institute, Issue 387. Toronto: C. D. Howe Institute Commentary.

Urbina, Jilber. 2013. *Financial Spillovers across Countries: Measuring Shock Transmissions*. MPRA Working Paper. Munich: Munich Personal RePEc Archive.

Vlastakis, Nikolas, and Raphael Markellos. 2012. Information demand and stock market volatility. *Journal of Banking & Finance* 36: 1808–21.

Vosen, Simeon, and Torsten Schmidt. 2011. Forecasting Private Consumption: Survey Based Indicators vs. Google Trends. *Journal of Forecasting* 30: 565–78. [CrossRef]

Vozlyublennaia, Nadia. 2014. Investor attention, index performance, and return predictability. *Journal of Banking & Finance* 41: 17–35.

Woo, Jaemin, and Ann Owen. 2019. Forecasting private consumption with Google Trends data. *Journal of Forecasting* 38: 81–89. [CrossRef]

Yang, Tian, Jinsong Liu, Qianwei Ying, and Tahir Yousaf. 2019. Media Coverage and Sustainable Stock Returns: Evidence from China. *Sustainability* 11: 2335. [CrossRef]

Zhang Wei, Dehua Shen, Yongjie Zhang, and Xiong Xiong. 2013. Open source information, investor attention, and asset pricing. *Economic Modelling* 33: 613–619. [CrossRef]

Zhang, Junru, Hadrian Geri Djajadikerta, and Zhaoyong Zhang. 2018. Does Sustainability Engagement Affect Stock Return Volatility? Evidence from the Chinese Financial Market. *Sustainability* 10: 3361. [CrossRef]

# 10

# Hedge Fund Performance during and after the Crisis: A Comparative Analysis of Strategies 2007–2017

**Nicola Metzger** [1] **and Vijay Shenai** [2,*]

1 Independent Researcher, University of Westminster, London W1B 2HW, UK; nicola_metzger@t-online.de
2 Independent Researchert, University of Lincoln, Lincoln LN6 7TS, UK
* Correspondence: kvshenai11@gmail.com

**Abstract:** The performance of hedge funds is of interest to investors looking for ways of generating value over passive strategies, particularly in bad times. This study used the Hedge Index database with over 9500 hedge funds to analyse, in depth, the performance of ten major strategies, during and after the financial crisis (June 2007–January 2017). To the best of our knowledge, such a study covering the last ten years has not been published. Performance of the various strategies was analysed, using correlations, the Carhart's four factor model, persistence of performance, and reward-risk ratios. The findings are that some hedge fund strategies which have persistent performances are also able to outperform the benchmark in some periods. In the crisis period, value-wise, all strategies did better than the S&P500, thereby, conserving value for investors, better than passive investment in the S&P500. Over the entire period of the research (June 2007–January 2017), seven strategies performed better than the S&P500: Global Macro, Multi Strategy, Emerging Markets, Long/Short Equity, Event Driven, Convertible Arbitrage, and Fixed Income Arbitrage. As hedge funds typically have skewed return distributions, performance was analysed in different periods, within conventional and downside risk frameworks. This research contributes to the advancement of knowledge on the outcomes of hedge fund strategies in different market conditions and the reliability of alternative risk frameworks in their evaluation. Apart from the theoretical implications, this research provides practical knowledge to managers and investors on which strategies hold better value and in what circumstances.

**Keywords:** hedge funds; reward risk ratios; performance persistence

**JEL Classification:** G10; G19; G23

---

## 1. Introduction

According to Capital Market Theory, the Market Portfolio—made up of all the assets in the market—is the most mean-variance-efficient portfolio and investors make up their own portfolios, according to their appetite for risk, through investing more or less amounts in the Market Portfolio, with borrowing or lending. Such investment styles are known as passive. Real markets are not efficient, many imperfections exist, such as taxes, dealing charges; information is not simultaneously available to all participants, investors do not have homogeneous expectations and all assets are not equally scrutinised. Investment styles which exploit market imperfections and the opportunities therefrom, via mispriced assets, are classified as active, in contrast to the passive style.

Hedge funds have rapidly evolved as investment vehicles for active strategies, and are much sought after by investors, either for investment in themselves or as part of a portfolio. They were first created in 1949 and represent an alternative asset class that is closely related to mutual funds but exhibit some major differences. Hedge funds are not regulated as strictly as mutual funds which gives them the possibility to invest in traditional, as well as, alternative and more risky securities and derivatives. Furthermore, hedge funds are eligible for short-selling and leverage.

Another important characteristic of a hedge fund is that they generally invest in less liquid assets, compared to mutual funds. This can be done by generating "lockup periods" for investors. During these specified periods investors cannot redeem their investment. As a result of the specific characteristics and a high minimum investment (usually between US$500,000 and US$1million), access to hedge funds is limited to sophisticated investors, such as institutions or wealthy individual investors (Barclay Hedge 2018b). Nowadays, hedge fund assets can vary from traditional products, such as equities, bonds, real estate to alternative assets, such as paintings, artefacts, antiques, and other exoticities.

The hedge fund industry has been growing rapidly—from only US$118 billion in 1997 to over US$3 trillion in 2016 (Barclay Hedge 2018a). Many economies faced a crisis in 2007–2009, in the aftermath of the sub-prime mortgage market crash. Between 2007 and 2008, the beginning of the financial crisis, assets under management by hedge funds, worldwide, dropped by 25%, when many funds had to close (Barclay Hedge 2018a). As hedging has the meaning of adopting a strategy to reduce risk, it becomes meaningful to analyse the performances of hedge funds, during and after the crisis.

The aim of this research is, thus, to gain a deeper understanding of the risk-adjusted performance of major hedge fund strategies in different market conditions and then to ascertain which risk frameworks are most reliable for evaluating performance. To the best of our knowledge, such a study covering the last ten years has not been published.

To achieve the aim of this research, a literature review is first conducted in Section 2. The literature review covers a broad overview of hedge funds and their major strategies; this is followed by a summary of empirical research on hedge funds, a critical discussion of performance measurement models, persistence in performance, and alternative reward risk ratios. In Section 3, the methodology, data accessed and other relevant issues to this research are described. In Section 4, the, monthly performance data of ten major hedge fund strategies from 2007 to 2017 is analysed from various perspectives, with the S and P 500 as the market benchmark. Correlations of the different strategies with the entire market, and the results of Carhart's four factor model are studied. Persistence in performance is tested statistically and the reward-risk characteristics of the various hedge fund strategies are analysed in different periods, within traditional and downside risk frameworks. The findings are also discussed in this section. Finally, Section 5 concludes the paper and gives some ideas for further research on this topic.

## 2. Literature Review

### *2.1. Characteristics of Major Hedge Fund Strategies*

A short definition of hedge funds and the main characteristics have been given in the introduction. Travers (2012) defines hedge funds as "an investment pool that can invest in physical securities and derivatives markets". The most important and unique characteristic of hedge funds is the possibility to employ leverage and short selling, and their aim to generate absolute returns (Travers 2012). Different hedge fund strategies use a different approach to reach the aim. The major strategies, as indicated by Credit Suisse's Hedge Index database, will briefly be explained in the following.

#### 2.1.1. Convertible Arbitrage

Convertible arbitrage strategies aim to generate profit on price discrepancies of convertible securities, such as callable bonds. A common way to do so is to build a long position on the convertible security and short the stock or option of the underlying company. The goal, usually, is to hold the number of shares that makes the combined position market neutral. This way it will not fluctuate with the price of the underlying stock and profits are solely based on the price discrepancy (Credit Suisse 2018).

#### 2.1.2. Emerging Markets

Emerging Markets strategies typically invest in the securities of emerging or developing countries, such as China, India, Latin America, Southeast Asia, parts of Eastern Europe, and parts of Africa. These countries are not yet developed, and managers believe they are able to find arbitrage opportunities in these markets (Credit Suisse 2018).

#### 2.1.3. Equity Market Neutral

Equity market neutral strategies invest long and short in equities and try to keep their exposure risk neutral (matching long and short for 0 beta). Other methods include keeping the portfolio dollar neutral or factor neutral. This way managers can exploit opportunities in a specific group of stocks, without risk exposure to the broad stock market (Credit Suisse 2018).

#### 2.1.4. Event Driven

Event driven strategies focus on special events, like mergers and acquisitions, liquidation, bankruptcy or spin-outs. The strategy can be divided into three sub-strategies: Distressed, Multi Strategy, and Risk-Arbitrage.

Distressed managers trade credit securities of below-investment-grade companies. They profit from the high yields of these securities, as they usually trade at discounts. For this strategy it is crucial to investigate all available securities, across a company's capital structure, to identify the best risk/reward potential.

Multi Strategy event driven presents a mixture of event driven equity and credit strategies. Managers aim to take advantage of shifts in economic cycles by investing in different asset classes.

The event driven risk arbitrage strategies want to profit from the changing company value and spreads, related to mergers and acquisitions. The manager will typically buy shares of the company that is announced to be merged, and short sell shares of the corresponding acquirer in order to isolate the spread, while being market neutral (Credit Suisse 2018).

#### 2.1.5. Fixed Income Arbitrage

Fixed Income Arbitrage Managers aim to generate positive returns by identifying price anomalies in fixed income securities. They build up a long position in an undervalued security, while shorting a related overvalued one. A market neutral or interest rate neutral position could be created to reduce total volatility (Credit Suisse 2018).

#### 2.1.6. Global Macro

Global Macro strategies attempt to quickly react to changing market dynamics, to profit from the market movements. Managers employ top-down market analysis to exploit global market opportunities, by forecasting effects of political and macroeconomic trends. They go long if they expect bullish markets and short in bearish market conditions. Leverage is often applied to enhance the effect (Credit Suisse 2018).

#### 2.1.7. Long/Short Equity

In long/short equity strategies, managers try to exploit pricing inefficiencies, by investing long in undervalued equities and short in overvalued equities. The short portfolio can, therefore, be seen as a way to generate more returns or to hedge the long portfolio (Travers 2012).

#### 2.1.8. Managed Futures

Managed futures are often referred to as commodity trading advisors (CTAs). Investment decisions are made on global trends and historical price data. Managers can make use of many financial securities, such as equity, commodity futures or currency markets. A high degree of leverage can be applied (Credit Suisse 2018).

2.1.9. Multi Strategy

Multi Strategy funds have the ability to diversify their capital, over several strategies. This leads to reduced volatility and smoothed returns. Managers aim to generate positive return, independent of directional movements in the markets (Credit Suisse 2018).

### 2.2. Empirical Studies on Hedge Fund Performance

When public interest in hedge funds started to increase in the 1990s, more studies on hedge fund risk and return characteristics were published. Fung and Hsieh (1997), as well as Schneeweis and Spurgin (1997), focused on the correlation between hedge funds and standard asset classes. They observed a low correlation profile and concluded that alternative investments provide diversification and improve risk adjusted returns. Similar results are shown by Brown et al. (1999), Liang (1999), and Do et al. (2005), and more recently by Jordao and De Moura (2011), who analysed Brazilian hedge funds. Amenc et al. (2003) attribute the positive diversification effect to the various risk factors that hedge funds are exposed to. Brown et al. (1999) found that offshore hedge funds show a low correlation to U.S stock markets and show positive risk-adjusted returns. However, they attributed the positive returns to style effect rather than manager skills. Ackermann et al. (1999) compared risk adjusted performance of hedge funds and mutual funds and showed that hedge funds are able to consistently outperform mutual funds, but not the market indices. They also show that hedge funds are more risky than mutual funds and market indices. In contrast to that, Liang and Kat (2001), looking at data from 1990 to 1999, finds higher volatility in the market benchmark (S&P500) than in hedge funds. He attributes the lower volatility of hedge funds to the cross-style diversification. Consistent with other research, Liang and Kat (2001) concluded that hedge funds provide better risk-adjusted returns. However, this finding is challenged by later research conducted by Amin and Kat (2003). The authors' results show that hedge funds improve the portfolios risk return profile, when mixed with the S and P 500, but fail to do so as a standalone investment. Brown et al. (2001) observed that hedge funds tend to decrease volatility, following good performance in the first half of the year and increase volatility, following bad performance.

Liang and Kat (2001), Capocci and Hübner (2004), Strömqvist (2009), Schaub and Schmid (2013), had a closer look at hedge funds, during crises periods and financial distress. Liang and Kat (2001) showed that hedge funds were strongly affected by the economic crises in 1998 but concluded that this does not necessarily mean that hedge funds did not contribute as a trigger to the crisis. In case of the financial crisis in 2008, Strömqvist (2009) was unable to find any evidence of hedge funds having a greater impact on the crisis than other investors. Schaub and Schmid (2013) indicated that liquidity plays a crucial role in hedge fund performance, during crises periods. Their study showed that hedge funds with illiquid portfolios had lower returns and alphas, compared to hedge funds with more liquid portfolios, during crisis periods. Capocci and Hübner (2004) and Stoforos et al. (2016) analysed hedge fund performance during crises. Both concluded that hedge funds suffered from losses and could not reach their goal of higher absolute returns. Capocci (2002) identified Relative Value Arbitrage and Foreign Exchange as the only sub-strategies that benefited from the Asian crisis.

Do et al. (2005) studied data on the Australian hedge fund market (2001–2003) and advised that hedge funds included as a part of a portfolio, improved returns, irrespective of strategy. A study by Jordao and De Moura (2011) on the Brazilian hedge fund industry found that hedge funds were not able to generate significant alphas, under conditions of high volatility and financial stress. Data on the research by Boasson and Boasson (2011) on US hedge funds (1972–2005) showed that hedge funds have significant correlations with the market (high for all strategies, except Global Macro and Fixed Income), although they concluded that investments in hedge funds offer the benefits of diversification.

Stoforos et al. (2016) studied US hedge fund data on thirteen hedge fund strategies, for a period of 19 years (1995–2014), and found that the average dynamic correlations increased for hedge funds in crisis periods, a finding confirmed by Forbes and Rigobon (2002) and Guesmi et al. (2014). Their data also showed that dynamic correlation coefficients decreased significantly in the non-crisis period, only for Global Macro and Short Selling strategies. They concluded that most hedge fund strategies (with the exception of Global Macro and Short selling) were not able to outperform the S and P 500, during crisis periods and could, therefore, not protect their investors, like the S and P 500.

### 2.3. Performance Measurement Models

Measuring the performance of an investment is essential in evaluation. The Sharpe ratio (Sharpe 1966), which measures the excess return over the risk-free rate in relation to total risk, is the most widely known performance measure (Eling and Schuhmacher 2007). It is used by Ackermann et al. (1999), Liang and Kat (2001) and others, to measure hedge fund performance. However, since it assumes normally distributed returns and does not account for hedge funds' special characteristics, it is criticised as an inadequate measurement for hedge fund performance (Eling and Schuhmacher 2007; Capocci 2002). This is also stated by Brooks and Kat (2002), Amin and Kat (2003), Mahdavi (2004) and Murguia and Umemoto (2004), on the basis that Hedge fund returns typically have asymmetric distributions.

To solve this issue, Sortino and Price (1994) developed the Sortino ratio, which divides the excess return on a portfolio, with respect to a minimum acceptable return (MAR), by a term called the downside deviation (deviation of returns below the MAR). Later on, Sortino, Sortino et al. (1999) developed the Upside Potential ratio, which divides the positive excess returns of the portfolio by the downside deviation. Sortino et al. (2001) claimed that the downside risk framework was able to overcome the problems in ranking skewed return distributions, and found that the Upside Potential ratio was a more accurate evaluator than the Sharpe ratio, particularly when the strategies included the use of options. Studies by Rosenberg et al. (2004), and Scherer (2004), found the Sortino ratio to be a superior performance ratio compared to the Sharpe ratio. Chaudhary and Johnson (2008) in a simulation study of skewed distributions, also found that the Sortino ratio is a superior performance measure to the Sharpe ratio.

To analyse fund performance, in terms of various attributes, factor models were created over time. The models can broadly be divided into two categories—linear multi factor models and non-linear multi factor models.

Linear multi factor models were created by Sharpe (1992), Fama and French (1993) and Carhart (1997). They identified several factors to explain performance and returns (Capocci 2002). Sharpe (1992) implemented the asset class factor model that allows for style analysis. The model includes twelve asset classes and the degree of exposure to each asset class is used to explain the variation of returns in the specific period. Unfortunately, Sharpe's model can only be applied to funds pursuing a long-only strategy, while many hedge fund strategies use short selling and leverage. In 1993, Fama and French built their three-factor model. It expanded the Capital Asset Pricing Model (CAPM) by considering size (small and large cap) and value (book to market ratio) factors. Kothari and Warner (2001) consented to the improvement of the CAPM, by including the new factors, however, they criticised the Fama and French model by pointing out that it detects abnormal results that do not exist. Building up on this, Carhart (1997) came up with a four-factor model. He included momentum, which made his model superior to the CAPM, as well as the Fama and French. Linear multi factor models are used to measure hedge fund performance in several studies, like Schneeweis and Spurgin (1999), Capocci (2002) or Jordao and De Moura (2011). Despite the application to hedge fund performance, the linear models are more suitable to evaluate traditional funds because they fail to capture hedge fund characteristics like time variation (Stafylas et al. 2017). Furthermore, Slavutskaya (2013) concluded that linear factor models are not suitable for hedge funds as they lead to over-parameterisation, because many hedge funds have a life of three years.

Non-linear multi factor models include the asset factor model by Fung and Hsieh (1997, 2001) and models by Agarwal and Naik (2000) or Huber and Kaiser (2004). Fung and Hsieh (1997) extend the asset class factor model by Sharpe (1992) to make up for major hedge fund investment styles and consider hedge funds as option portfolios. In 2001, they used the trend-following strategy, to model hedge fund returns and demonstrated that the returns resemble lookback straddle returns. Huber and Kaiser (2004) arrived at the same conclusion. Agarwal and Naik (2000) introduced a general asset class factor model that is optimised for passive option-based strategies and buy-and-hold strategies. Agarwal and Naik (2004) later focussed on hedge funds that use these strategies and their risk exposure. Their findings suggest that hedge funds have a significant exposure to the Fama and French three-factor model and Carhart's four-factor model. More recently, Gregoriou et al. (2016) analysed hedge funds' returns and cross-sectional dispersion, using the Fama and French (1993) model, as well as Fung and Hsieh (1997, 2001) factors.

Although non-linear multifactor models can explain hedge fund returns in a more detailed way and account for special characteristics of hedge funds, they might not be best for investors' performance evaluation. This is mainly due to the fact that exposures are not static and, therefore, need to be adjusted and that the models and factors are complicated to replicate (Stafylas et al. 2017).

In another study, Fung and Hsieh (2004) attempted to model hedge fund returns in terms of seven asset-based style (ABS) factors—two equity ABS factors (market risk and the spread between small-cap stock returns and large-cap stock returns), two fixed income ABS factors (10-year treasury yields, change in the yield spread between 10-year T-bonds and Moody's Baa bonds), and three trend-following ABS factors (portfolios of lookback straddles on bonds, on currencies and on commodities), as an alternative to other models. Although they report success with high R-squares, it could be argued that introduction of too many factors introduces an arbitrariness in the analysis, which might not be robust when market conditions change. Moreover, there may be other factors which have a higher explanatory power over short horizons and such factors can change with time, making it burdensome to identify them.

### *2.4. Persistence in Performance*

Persistence in performance is a sought-after metric by Fund Managers and investors. Brown et al. (1999), using annual returns of offshore hedge funds, found virtually no persistence in their sample. Agarwal and Naik (2000) used a multi-period framework for evaluating persistence as a measure of evaluating manager skills, since fund managers might exhibit a different degree of persistence at different return horizons. They found maximum persistence at a quarterly horizon, indicating that persistence among hedge fund managers is short-term in nature. They also find that persistence, whenever present, is unrelated to the type of strategy (directional or non-directional) followed by the fund. Boyson (2003) finds that a portfolio of funds selected on past performance, alone, shows no persistence, but a portfolio that is long low-tenure/past good performers and short high-tenure/past poor performers, displays a quarterly persistence. Consistently poor performance among high-tenure/past poor performers drives this finding. Capocci (2002), on the other hand, concluded that there is no evidence of persistence in low performing and high performing hedge funds, but limited evidence of persistence for medium performing funds. Baquero et al. (2005) find positive persistence in hedge fund returns at the quarterly level, after correcting for investment style, however, with weak statistical significance. Manser and Schmid (2009) studying the performance persistence of equity long/short hedge funds find that funds with the highest raw returns in the previous year, continue to outperform over the subsequent year, although not significantly, and there is no persistence in returns, beyond one year. In contrast, they find performance to be persistent, based on risk-adjusted return measures, such as the Sharpe Ratio, and in particular, also with an alpha from a multifactor model. Funds with the highest risk-adjusted performance, continue to significantly outperform in the following year. The persistence does not last longer than a year, except for the worst performers. Sun et al. (2016) constructed two performance measures: Downside Returns and

Upside Returns. After controlling for the overall hedge fund market return and risk, and other fund characteristics, they find that hedge funds in the highest Downside Returns quintile, outperform funds in the lowest quintile, by 5%, in the subsequent year, whereas funds with better Upside Returns do not outperform subsequently.

### *2.5. Performance Rating Measures*

Fund performance has been earlier evaluated by the measures developed by Sharpe (1966), Treynor (1965) and Jensen (1968). The Sharpe ratio of a portfolio (Sp) measures the excess return of portfolio, relative to the risk-free rate divided by its standard deviation, and is defined as

$$\mathrm{Sp} = \frac{\mathrm{E(Rpi - rfi)}}{\sigma \mathrm{p}} \tag{1}$$

The Sharpe measure takes into account the total risk of returns, whilst the Treynor and Jensen measures rate a fund, just on its market risk. More recently, to account for asymmetricities in returns and not only the market risk, alternative reward-risk evaluation measures, such as the Sortino ratio (Sortino and Price (1994)), and Upside Potential ratio (Sortino et al. (1999)) were proposed.

The Sortino ratio of a portfolio is defined as

$$\mathrm{SORp} = \frac{\mathrm{E(Rpi - MAR)}}{\sqrt{\mathrm{E(Min(Rpi - MAR),0)^2)}}} \tag{2}$$

where Rpi is the return of the portfolio at time i, MAR is the minimum acceptable return, and $\sqrt{\mathrm{E(Min(Rpi - MAR),0)^2)}}$ is the Downside risk (DR).

The Upside Potential ratio of a portfolio is defined as

$$\mathrm{UPRp} = \frac{\mathrm{E(Max(Rpi - MAR),\ 0)}}{\sqrt{\mathrm{E(Min(Rpi - MAR),0)^2)}}} \tag{3}$$

The upside potential ratio divides the average of the excess positive returns, compared to the minimum acceptable return (MAR), by the downside risk (DR).

## 3. Methodology

### *3.1. General*

In this research, a deductive approach was used. Quantitative data on hedge fund performance was collected in the form of monthly returns of the major hedge fund strategies, between June 2007 to January 2017. The performance of each strategy, value-wise, was first visually inspected and then return data were analysed. The correlations of hedge fund strategies with the benchmark S and P 500 was also studied.

To ascertain explanatory factors for the performance of the various hedge fund strategies and the extent to which the strategies incorporate market risk, the strategies were tested via Carhart's four-factor model (1997). The four-factor model was chosen as it can provide additional explanations for performance over the traditional CAPM and Fama and French (1993) three-factor model, explained earlier. The four-factor model was an extension of the Fama and French (1993) model and included four risk factors to explain returns (excess market return, excess return of small cap over big cap stocks (SMB), excess return of value stocks over growth stocks (HML), and the excess return of the stocks that went up minus the stocks that went down (UMD) (Fama and French 1993; Carhart 1997).

Regressions were estimated as follows:

$$E(R) = R_f + \beta_1 \left(R_m - R_f\right) + \beta_2 * SMB + \beta_3 * HML + \beta_4 * UMD \tag{4}$$

To obtain further insights into the strategies which hold value for investors, tests for persistence and risk-reward rankings were also conducted. The traditional Sharpe ratio had been a useful metric to rank fund strategies, on the basis of reward and risk. Given asymmetricities in the returns of hedge funds, evaluation of performance was also made in a downside-risk framework, with reward-risk ratios, such as the Upper Potential Ratio and the Sortino Ratio.

Investors look at persistence in performance at two levels—consistent positive performance and consistent performance better than the market. While a lot of work has been done by various authors on the subject of persistence in performance of Hedge Funds, this research relied on the work of Agarwal and Naik (2000), who after extensive analysis of quarterly, half yearly and yearly returns, found maximum persistence at the quarterly horizon.

Taking these considerations into account, persistence tests were devised as follows:

(i) To test for persistence, t-tests were conducted, over a three-month rolling window.

(ii) The total number of statistically significant negative performance windows were subtracted from the total number of statistically significant positive performance windows, and the different strategies were ranked for persistent positive performance on this basis, then tested against the ranked total performance of the various strategies, to test for any relationship between persistence in positive returns and actual performance. A non-parametric test was used for this test.

(iii) The procedures in (i) and (ii) were repeated for excess performance, over the return of the S and P 500, for the whole period, during and after the crisis.

(iv) To test for any relationship between total performance and alternative reward-risk ratios, the Sharpe ratio, Upside Potential ratio (UPR), and Sortino ratios were computed for the different strategies, then ranked and tested in comparison with actual performance. The t-bill rate was taken as the minimum acceptable return (MAR) in these calculations. A non-parametric test was used for this test.

*3.2. Data*

To begin with, it is very important to mention that hedge fund performance data was provided on a voluntary basis and available to persons depending on the country only. Many hedge funds, however, do publish their monthly performance to inform existing clients and attract new investors. According to D'Alessio (2015), the top five online hedge fund databases are Barclay hedge, Eurekahedge, Hedge Fund Research and Hedge Index. Hedge Index is sponsored by Credit Suisse, and with over 9500 funds, it offers a reliable, large database of reporting funds.

For the purpose of this study, qualitative hedge fund performance data accessed from the Hedge index was used. Reasons for this were the large database, as mentioned above, as well as the easy accessibility. Hedge index defines ten major strategies, namely Convertible Arbitrage, Emerging Markets, Equity Market Neutral, Event Driven, Fixed Income Arbitrage, Global Macro, Long/Short Equity, Managed Futures, Multi Strategy and Short Biased. The indices are asset-weighted and created by Credit Suisse Hedge Index LLC. Hedge funds are chosen from the Credit Suisse Hedge Fund Database, which includes around 9500 funds. All funds feature a minimum twelve-month track record, a minimum of US$50 million, under management, and are able to provide an audited financial statement. The indices reflect net performance and are rebalanced and calculated on a monthly basis. Survivorship bias is limited, by including all funds in the index, until they are fully liquidated or unable to meet the financial reporting requirements. Fees including (but not limited to) management and incentive fees, as well as transaction costs, are considered in the return calculations (Credit Suisse 2018).

Data for the Carhart four-factor model was obtained from the website of French (2018). The four factors Mkt-Rf (market risk), SMB (Size), HML (Value) and UMD (Momentum) were created from six size/book-to-market benchmark portfolios. These portfolios neither include hold ranges nor transaction costs. The market return was represented by the value-weighted return on all NYSE, NASDAQ and AMEX stocks, obtained from CRSP. To calculate the excess return of small cap stocks over large cap stocks (SMB) the average return on three big portfolios was subtracted from the average return on three small portfolios (value, neutral and growth). The variable HML (high minus low) measured the excess return of the value stocks, over the growth stocks and was calculated by subtracting the average return on the two growth portfolios, from the average return on the two value portfolios (small and big). To calculate the momentum factor (UMD), French used "six value-weighted portfolios formed on size and prior (2–12) returns" (French 2018). UMD equalled the average return on the two high prior return portfolios, minus the average return on the two low prior return portfolios. Portfolios were updated monthly and rebalanced quarterly.

### *3.3. Market Performance and Risk-Free Return*

To evaluate the performance of the different hedge fund indices, a benchmark is needed. From an investor's perspective, in Capital Market Theory, the Market portfolio offered the best reward-risk performance in an efficient market. The S and P 500 has been used as a proxy for the Market Portfolio in many hedge fund studies. Examples are the studies performed by Liang and Kat (2001), Amin and Kat (2003) or Stoforos et al. (2016). Capocci (2002) used a value-weighted portfolio of all stocks on the NYSE, Amex and Nasdaq, instead of only using the largest 500. The risk-free rate (rf) is represented by the one-month Treasury-bill rate from Ibbotson Associates. The Standard and Poor's index is a value-weighted index and consist of stocks issued by 500 large cap companies listed on the NYSE or NASDAQ. Due to its large proportion of total market value, it widely reflects the entire U.S. equity market and the economic health of the United States (Nasdaq 2018). As a result of globalisation in the financial markets the S and P, furthermore, reflects international events, to a large extent (Stoforos et al. 2016).

## 4. Data Analysis, Findings and Discussions

In this section, data was analysed with various methods and the results of the tests are interpreted and discussed. The data consists of monthly returns of each of the 10 strategies mentioned, the risk-free rate and the market benchmark. It ranged from June 2007 to January 2017.

### *4.1. Descriptive Statistics, Visual Inspection, Other Diagnostics and Correlations*

(a) Tests for stationarity and distribution of the returns

As regressions were to be performed later, the data was first tested for stationarity. Results of the test for the presence of a unit root are summarised in Table 1 (details Appendix A). The null hypothesis of a unit root being present in the return series was rejected at the 1% level.

**Table 1.** Tests for the presence of a unit root (details presented in Appendix A).

| Strategy | | t-Statistic | Probability |
|---|---|---|---|
| Convertible Arbitrage | | −7.9293 | <0.01 |
| Short Bias | | −10.9196 | <0.01 |
| Emerging Markets | | −9.596 | <0.01 |
| Equity Market Neutral | | −17.7315 | <0.01 |
| Event Driven | | −7.6882 | <0.01 |
| Fixed Income Arbitrage | | −10.4436 | <0.01 |
| Global Macro | | −10.4389 | <0.01 |
| Long/Short Equity | | −9.5381 | <0.01 |
| Managed Futures | | −11.5436 | <0.01 |
| Multi Strategy | | −7.5482 | <0.01 |
| Test critical values | 1% level | −4.9491 | 1% |
| | 5% level | −4.4436 | 5% |
| | 10% level | −4.1936 | 10% |

Source: Authors' work.

Table 2 below summarises the descriptive statistics on the various hedge fund strategies (10) and the benchmark of S and P 500.

**Table 2.** Descriptive statistics for all 10 strategies and S&P 500 6/2007–1/2017.

| Strategy | Mean | Median | Maximum | Minimum | Std Dev | Skewness | Kurtosis | Jarque Bera | Prob |
|---|---|---|---|---|---|---|---|---|---|
| Convertible Arbitrage | 0.0031 | 0.0031 | 0.0581 | −0.1259 | 0.0024 | −2.4518 | 16.2970 | 970.817 | 0.0000 |
| Short bias | −0.0079 | −0.0139 | 0.1031 | −0.1128 | 0.0447 | 0.4462 | 2.9290 | 3.873 | 0.1442 |
| Emerging Markets | 0.0031 | 0.0042 | 0.0696 | −0.1363 | 0.0275 | −1.4139 | 8.6909 | 190.185 | 0.0000 |
| Equity Markets Neutral | −0.0017 | 0.0029 | 0.0366 | −0.4045 | 0.0402 | −8.1180 | 88.9230 | 37,184.510 | 0.0000 |
| Event Driven | 0.0026 | 0.0049 | 0.0422 | −0.0575 | 0.0190 | −0.8694 | 3.9609 | 19.075 | 0.0000 |
| Fixed Income Arbitrage | 0.0029 | 0.0049 | 0.0433 | −0.1404 | 0.0196 | −4.2558 | 29.0433 | 3628.401 | 0.0000 |
| Global Macro | 0.0044 | 0.0054 | 0.0444 | −0.0663 | 0.0161 | −0.8460 | 6.3701 | 68.731 | 0.0000 |
| Long Short Equity | 0.0030 | 0.0039 | 0.0523 | −0.0781 | 0.0225 | −0.7765 | 4.5441 | 23.183 | 0.0000 |
| Managed Futures | 0.0023 | 0.0023 | 0.0750 | −0.0581 | 0.0318 | 0.0789 | 2.0548 | 4.439 | 0.1087 |
| Multi Strategy | 0.0039 | 0.0060 | 0.0428 | −0.0735 | 0.0163 | −1.8300 | 9.9337 | 297.117 | 0.0000 |
| SP500 | 0.0034 | 0.0095 | 0.1023 | −0.1856 | 0.0453 | −0.8928 | 5.0006 | 34.755 | 0.0000 |

Source: Authors' work.

The mean return, standard deviation, median, minimum return and maximum return of each of the ten strategies, is stated in the table above, and can be contrasted with that of the benchmark SP 500 over the whole data period (June 2007–January 2017). The null hypothesis of normality of returns distribution was rejected at the 5% level, for all but two of the strategies (Short Bias and Managed Futures). There was evidence of negative skewness and leptokurtosis (kurtosis > 3), for nine of the eleven series tested.

(b) To visualise the performance of the different strategies in the period of the study (June 2007–January 2017), the value of all series on the various strategies, indexed at 100 at the beginning of the series, is plotted below in Figure 1:

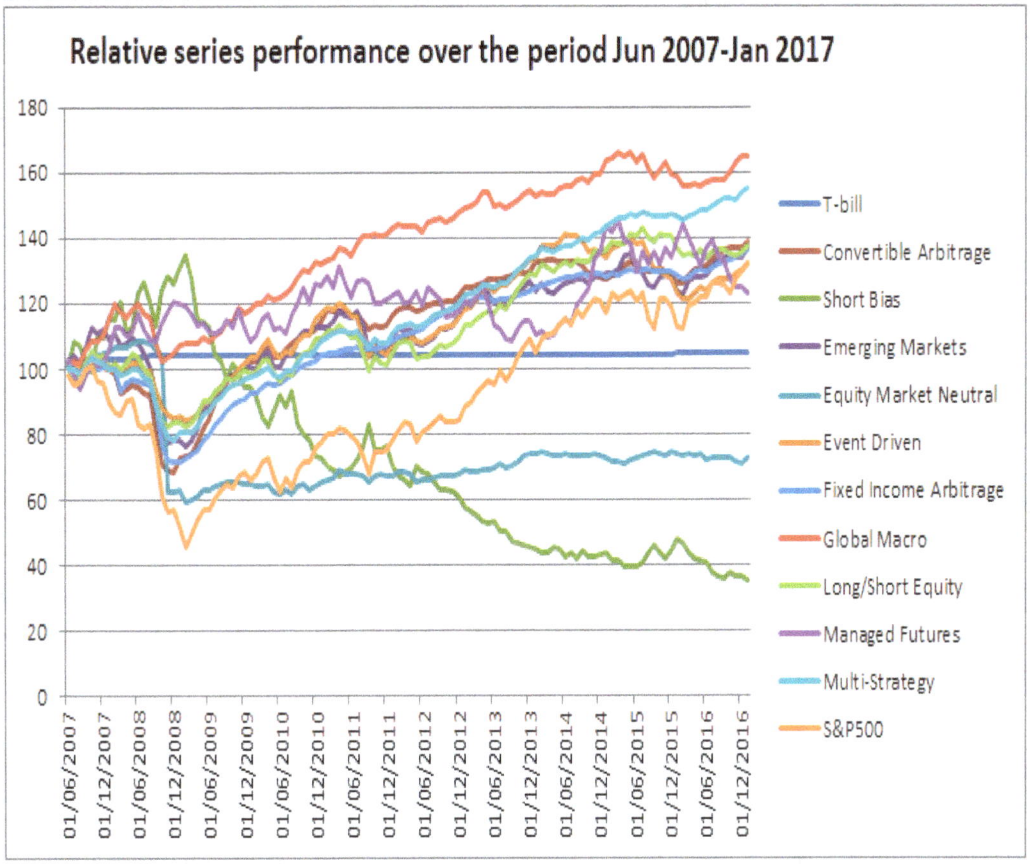


Source: Authors' work

**Figure 1.** Relative series performance over the whole period: June 2007–January 2017.

Visual inspection of the performance of the various strategies over the period of 2007–2017, shows that there was a downturn in 2008 and that there were clearly two different periods to analyse—a period of downturn from the middle of 2007, up till the end of the first quarter of 2009, and then on an upturn, up till the first month of 2017. Therefore, it was decided to study the entire period of June 2007 to January 2017, in two split periods (a) crisis period—June 2007–March 2009 (b) after crisis—April 2009–January 2017, and also the whole period.

The gross performance of the various strategies in each period, i.e., a value of $100 invested in a particular strategy, at the beginning of the period (whole period, during crisis and after crisis) are summarised in Table 3 below:

**Table 3.** Performance of strategies and (S&P 500) in the whole period, during crisis and after crisis.

| Period | Whole Period | | During Crisis | | After Crisis | |
|---|---|---|---|---|---|---|
| **Strategy/Rank *** | **Value** | **Rank** | **Value** | **Rank** | **Value** | **Rank** |
| Risk free rate | 104.70 | 3 | 104.16 | 9 | 100.52 | 2 |
| Convertible Arbitrage | 138.88 | 10 | 73.92 | 4 | 187.87 | 10 |
| Short Bias | 35.42 | 1 | 127.46 | 12 | 27.79 | 1 |
| Emerging Markets | 136.56 | 8 | 77.94 | 5 | 175.21 | 8 |
| Equity Market Neutral | 72.45 | 2 | 60.17 | 2 | 120.41 | 4 |
| Event Driven | 132.08 | 6 | 84.50 | 8 | 156.31 | 6 |
| Fixed Income Arbitrage | 136.44 | 7 | 73.71 | 3 | 185.11 | 9 |
| Global Macro | 164.47 | 12 | 107.66 | 10 | 152.77 | 5 |
| Long/Short Equity | 137.35 | 9 | 83.77 | 7 | 163.97 | 7 |
| Managed Futures | 123.10 | 4 | 116.89 | 11 | 105.31 | 3 |
| Multi-Strategy | 154.84 | 11 | 80.72 | 6 | 191.82 | 11 |
| SPX | 131.86 | 5 | 49.42 | 1 | 266.85 | 12 |

Source: Authors' work. * start value at beginning of period = 100; ranked in ascending order.

Table 3 shows that:

(i) Over the entire period, seven strategies performed better than the S and P 500: The Global Macro, Multi Strategy, Emerging Markets, Long/Short Equity, Event Driven, Convertible Arbitrage, and the Fixed Income Arbitrage; with Short Bias and Equity Market Neutral and Managed Futures doing much worse than the benchmark S and P 500.

(ii) In the crisis period (June 2007–March 2009), the S and P 500 was the worst performer, with an investment of $100 falling down to $49.42; while all the other strategies did better; the best performers being Managed Futures, Global Macro and Short Bias, with values above investment in the risk-free rate.

(iii) After the crisis: April 2009–January 2017; the worst performer was Short Bias while the S and P 500 was the best performer with the value of an investment of $100 at the beginning of the after-crisis period rising to $266.85; the next best being Multi Strategy, Convertible Arbitrage and Fixed Income Arbitrage.

To get a detailed overview of the strategies' performance, in the various periods, Table 4 contains the mean return and standard deviation in each period.

Table 4 shows that over the whole period, the highest mean return was achieved by Global Macro (0.44%) and Multi Strategy (0.39%), with the S and P 500's return being the third highest (0.34%). The lowest mean return was generated by the Short Bias strategy (−0.79%). The benchmark and Short Bias strategies exhibited a much higher standard deviation, compared to the other strategies in the sample. The table above gives further insights into the return risk profile of the strategies, during and after the crisis. Again, during the crisis, the benchmark S and P 500 had the lowest mean return and next highest standard deviation, with Short Bias having the highest mean return and third highest standard deviation. In the after-crisis period, Short Bias had the lowest return and highest standard deviation, while the benchmark S and P 500 had the highest return and next highest standard deviation.

Ackermann et al. (1999) found that hedge funds were riskier than the market indices. These results could not be confirmed by the findings of this study. Over the ten-year period of 2007–2017, the benchmark (and inversely, the Short Bias strategy) had the highest standard deviation and therefore, the highest risk. This was consistent with a study by Liang and Kat (2001) who found higher volatility in the market benchmark (S and P 500). He attributed the lower risk of hedge funds to the cross-style diversification. A major area of interest was the correlation of hedge fund strategies with the benchmark S and P 500.

**Table 4.** Mean and standard deviation of the strategies in the whole period, during the crisis and after.

| Period | Whole Period | | | | During Crisis | | | | After Crisis | | | |
|---|---|---|---|---|---|---|---|---|---|---|---|---|
| **Strategy** | **Mean** | **Rank+** | **Stdev** | **Rank+** | **Mean** | **Rank+** | **Stdev** | **Rank+** | **Mean** | **Rank+** | **Stdev** | **Rank+** |
| Convertible Arbitrage | 0.31% | 8 | 2.36% | 6 | −1.27% | 4 | 4.21% | 7 | 0.68% | 9 | 1.48% | 5 |
| Short Bias | −0.79% | 1 | 4.47% | 10 | 1.24% | 11 | 5.23% | 9 | −1.27% | 1 | 4.16% | 11 |
| Emerging Markets | 0.31% | 7 | 2.75% | 7 | −1.04% | 5 | 4.26% | 8 | 0.62% | 7 | 2.18% | 8 |
| Equity Market Neutral | −0.17% | 2 | 4.02% | 9 | −1.78% | 2 | 8.77% | 11 | 0.21% | 3 | 1.35% | 4 |
| Event Driven | 0.26% | 4 | 1.90% | 3 | −0.74% | 8 | 2.18% | 1 | 0.49% | 5 | 1.76% | 6 |
| Fixed Income Arbitrage | 0.29% | 5 | 1.96% | 4 | −1.30% | 3 | 3.78% | 6 | 0.66% | 8 | 0.87% | 1 |
| Global Macro | 0.44% | 11 | 1.61% | 1 | 0.37% | 9 | 2.79% | 3 | 0.46% | 4 | 1.20% | 3 |
| Long/Short Equity | 0.30% | 6 | 2.25% | 5 | −0.76% | 7 | 3.04% | 4 | 0.55% | 6 | 1.96% | 7 |
| Managed Futures | 0.23% | 3 | 3.18% | 8 | 0.77% | 10 | 3.41% | 5 | 0.10% | 2 | 3.13% | 9 |
| Multi-Strategy | 0.39% | 10 | 1.63% | 2 | −0.93% | 6 | 2.68% | 2 | 0.70% | 10 | 1.07% | 2 |
| SP500 | 0.34% | 9 | 4.53% | 11 | −2.96% | 1 | 6.16% | 10 | 1.12% | 11 | 3.68% | 10 |

Table 5 sets out the correlation of returns between the various strategies, in the whole period and during and after the crisis.

**Table 5.** Correlations of returns of various strategies with S&P 500 returns in the whole period and during and after crisis.

| Strategy/Period | Whole Period | During Crisis | After Crisis |
|---|---|---|---|
| Convertible Arbitrage | 0.56 | 0.55 | 0.54 |
| Short Bias | −0.77 | −0.64 | −0.85 |
| Emerging Markets | 0.71 | 0.71 | 0.73 |
| Equity Market Neutral | 0.34 | 0.30 | 0.58 |
| Event Driven | 0.71 | 0.65 | 0.76 |
| Fixed Income Arbitrage | 0.56 | 0.66 | 0.41 |
| Global Macro | 0.30 | 0.29 | 0.35 |
| Long/Short Equity | 0.80 | 0.73 | 0.87 |
| Managed Futures | −0.01 | −0.17 | 0.12 |
| Multi-Strategy | 0.66 | 0.60 | 0.71 |

Source: Authors' work

Three strategies showed a positive correlation above 0.7, over the whole period. During the crisis, two strategies showed a high correlation (>0.7) with the S and P 500 (Emerging Markets and Long/Short Equity). After the crisis, Emerging Markets, Event Driven and Long Short Equity, showed a high positive correlation with the benchmark, while Short Bias showed a high negative correlation. The lowest positive correlations, over the whole period and the benchmark, were Global Macro and Equity Market Neutral; while Short Bias and Managed Futures showed a negative correlation.

Although Fung and Hsieh (1997) or Schneeweis and Spurgin (1997) found that hedge funds exhibit a low correlation to the benchmark, the findings of this study were different. A test for difference of means in the correlation values, during and after the crisis showed that there was no significant difference (Appendix B). This meant that some strategies had increased their correlation with the S and P 500 after the crisis, whilst others had decreased, but overall, there was no significant difference. In sum, the results implied that some alternative investments provide diversification and can improve risk-adjusted returns, as stated in the literature.

### *4.2. Estimating Performance Using Carhart's Four-Factor Model*

The Carhart Four Factor Model was used to analyse performance over all three periods.

Over the entire period (Table 6), all models estimated were statistically valid with a $p$-value of the F statistic < 0.05. Looking at the performance over the whole data set (June 2007–January 2017) in Table 6, it is obvious that first almost all strategies had a significant positive degree of market risk, the highest being the Emerging Markets (0.47) and the Long/Short Equity (0.46); while Short Bias had a significant negative amount of market risk (−0.69) and Managed Futures were the exception. Only two strategies were able to generate a significant alpha over the whole period. These strategies were Global Macro and Multi Strategy. Both of them have a low significant positive correlation to the market and low significant negative correlation with the HML factor, which measures the return of value stocks, minus that of growth stocks. The negative sign of the HML coefficient shows that the portfolios were short in value stocks and long in growth stocks.

**Table 6.** Carhart's Four factor model estimations whole period: (6/2007–1/2017).

| Strategy | Alpha | Mkt Risk | SMB | HML | UMD | Adj $R^2$ | $p$ val F | Sigma |
|---|---|---|---|---|---|---|---|---|
| Convertible Arbitrage | 0.0022 | 0.2813 *** | −0.0168 | −0.2330 *** | −0.1251 *** | 0.3709 | 0.0000 | 2.31% |
| Emerging Markets | 0.0003 | 0.4740 *** | −0.0853 | −0.2587 *** | −0.0641 * | 0.568 | 0.0000 | 2.70% |
| Equity Market Neutral | −0.0028 | 0.2546 *** | 0.0476 | 0.1344 | −0.0193 | 0.0981 | 0.0030 | 3.92% |
| Event Driven | 0.0011 | 0.3234 *** | 0.0333 | −0.0809 | 0.0214 | 0.5318 | 0.0000 | 1.89% |
| Fixed Income Arbitrage | 0.0015 | 0.2380 *** | −0.0698 | −0.0845 | −0.0656 | 0.3163 | 0.0000 | 1.91% |
| Global Macro | 0.0038 *** | 0.1517 *** | −0.0907 | −0.1383 ** | 0.0094 | 0.1342 | 0.0003 | 1.58% |
| Long/Short Equity | 0.0004 | 0.4621 *** | −0.0141 | −0.2106 *** | 0.0331 | 0.7412 | 0.0000 | 2.22% |
| Managed Futures | 0.0021 | 0.1131 | −0.2486 * | −0.08 | 0.1672 ** | 0.0748 | 0.0110 | 3.22% |
| Multi-Strategy | 0.0025 ** | 0.2688 *** | −0.0265 | −0.1838 *** | −0.0197 | 0.497 | 0.0000 | 1.61% |
| Short Bias | −0.0027 | −0.6945 *** | −0.4783 *** | 0.0577 | 0.0478 | 0.7054 | 0.0000 | 4.37% |
| SP500 | | | | | | | | 4.40% |

Source: Authors' work. * significant at the 10% level, ** significant at the 5% level, *** significant at the 1% level.

In the crisis period (Table 7), seven models estimated were found to be statistically valid ($p$-value < 0.05), while three were not (Equity Market Neutral, Global Macro and Managed Futures). These strategies show a lack of relationship with the entire market, in this time. During the financial crisis (June 2007–March 2009) period, six strategies (Convertible Arbitrage, Emerging Markets, Event Driven, Fixed Income Arbitrage, Global Macro, Long/Short Equity and Multi Strategy) continued to bear a significant positive amount of market risk, whilst Short Bias had a significant negative amount of market risk (−0.55), and Equity Market Neutral and Managed Futures continued to have an insignificant amount of market risk. None of the ten strategies analysed were able to produce a significant alpha. Moreover, the relationship with the HML factor was significantly negative for many of the strategies (Convertible Arbitrage, Emerging Markets, Event Driven, Fixed Income Arbitrage, Global Macro and Long/Short Equity) showing the negative relationship to the return from Value stocks, compared to the Growth stocks.

In the after-crisis period (Table 8), all models estimated were statistically valid ($p$-value of F statistic < 0.05). The period after the financial crisis (April 2009–January 2017) was characterised by rising market prices. At this stage, almost all strategies had a significant positive amount of market risk (highest being the Long/Short (0.47), followed by the Emerging Markets (0.41)), with Short Bias continuing to have a significant negative amount of market risk (−0.81). Four out of ten strategies were able to generate a significant alpha, during this period (Convertible Arbitrage, Fixed Income Arbitrage, Global Macro and Multi Strategy) with Fixed Income Arbitrage being the highest (0.54%). Two of the strategies with significant positive alphas (Convertible Arbitrage and Fixed Income Arbitrage) had a significant negative UMD coefficient, showing that these strategies had a negative momentum factor—short in winners and long in losers.

Analysis with the Carhart model, yielded several insights. Only two strategies were able to generate significant alphas, over the whole period. These strategies were the Global Macro and Multi Strategy. During the crisis, none of the strategies yielded positive alphas. After the crisis, Global Macro and Multi Strategy continued to show positive alphas. The strategies which were the most successful had low but significant betas. Over the whole period, almost all strategies showed significant amounts of market risk to different degrees (except Short Bias which was significantly negative). The HML factor showed significant negative correlation to the strategies that were able to generate positive alphas, over the whole period, and also during the crisis, implying the underlying portfolio of these strategies were short in value stocks and long in growth stocks. The relationship with the HML factor was significantly negative for many of the other strategies, as well at different times. Although the SMB and UMD factors did not have an explanatory value for the better performing strategies, the SMB factor had a significant negative correlation with Short Bias, over the whole period and after the financial crisis, suggesting this portfolio was short on small stocks and long in large stocks; the UMD factor had a significant positive value for Managed Futures, over the whole period and after the financial crisis, suggesting that these portfolios invest in momentum stocks.

Consistent with the findings of Capocci (2002) and Stoforos et al. (2016), the study showed no fund manager was able to generate a significant alpha over the crisis period. However, market beta was significant for all strategies, except Equity Market Neutral and Managed Futures, in this period. It meant that the other strategies were not able to completely hedge against the market risk in the crisis period. In the after-crisis period, all strategies had a significant positive market risk, except Short Bias; although the ones with significant alphas also had the lowest market risk.

**Table 7.** Carhart's Four Factor Model estimations during the Financial Crisis (06/2007–03/2009).

| Strategy | Alpha | Mkt Risk | SMB | HML | UMD | Adj $R^2$ | *p* val F | Sigma |
|---|---|---|---|---|---|---|---|---|
| Convertible Arbitrage | −0.0079 | 0.4355 *** | 0.2507 | −0.7883 *** | −0.1632 | 0.6158 | 0.0003 | 3.88% |
| Emerging Markets | 0.0004 | 0.6480 *** | −0.1387 | −0.4291 ** | 0.1192 | 0.5965 | 0.0005 | 3.96% |
| Equity Market Neutral | −0.0101 | 0.1987 | 0.963 | 0.4371 | 0.1087 | −0.025 | 0.5031 | 7.95% |
| Event Driven | −0.0037 | 0.3025 *** | 0.1457 | −0.2767 *** | 0.0939 | 0.622 | 0.0003 | 2.25% |
| Fixed Income Arbitrage | −0.0041 | 0.4202 *** | 0.1943 | −0.3279 * | −0.1015 | 0.4089 | 0.0103 | 3.49% |
| Global Macro | 0.0051 | 0.2118 * | −0.0051 | −0.3356 * | 0.0318 | 0.129 | 0.1799 | 2.54% |
| Long/Short Equity | −0.0004 | 0.5009 *** | 0.0289 | −0.3848 *** | 0.1337 ** | 0.8099 | 0.0000 | 2.93% |
| Managed Futures | 0.0027 | −0.0782 | 0.0673 | 0.0693 | 0.2679 | 0.0464 | 0.3256 | 3.47% |
| Multi-Strategy | −0.0059 | 0.3153 *** | 0.1848 | −0.4469 *** | −0.0034 | 0.5884 | 0.0006 | 2.61% |
| Short Bias | −0.0044 | −0.5500 *** | 0.1196 | −0.1495 | 0.0247 | 0.3199 | 0.0302 | 4.81% |
| SP500 | | | | | | | | 5.64% |

Source: Authors' work. * significant at the 10% level, ** significant at the 5% level, *** significant at the 1% level.

**Table 8.** Carhart's Four Factor Model estimations after the Financial Crisis (04/2009–01/2017).

| Strategy | Alpha | Mkt Risk | SMB | HML | UMD | Adj $R^2$ | *p* val F | Sigma |
|---|---|---|---|---|---|---|---|---|
| Convertible Arbitrage | 0.0042 *** | 0.1671 *** | −0.024 | 0.0115 | −0.1027 *** | 0.3736 | 0.0000 | 1.48% |
| Emerging Markets | 0.0005 | 0.4113 *** | −0.0623 | −0.1393 ** | −0.1001 *** | 0.5677 | 0.0000 | 2.18% |
| Equity Market Neutral | −0.0008 | 0.2216 *** | −0.0654 | −0.0739 | −0.0137 | 0.3204 | 0.0000 | 1.35% |
| Event Driven | 0 | 0.3471 *** | −0.0023 | 0.0523 | 0.0151 | 0.5751 | 0.0000 | 1.76% |
| Fixed Income Arbitrage | 0.0054 *** | 0.0812 *** | −0.0461 | 0.0099 | −0.0486 *** | 0.2168 | 0.0000 | 0.87% |
| Global Macro | 0.0029 ** | 0.1418 *** | −0.1093 ** | −0.0082 | 0.0149 | 0.1238 | 0.0032 | 1.20% |
| Long/Short Equity | −0.0008 | 0.4715 *** | −0.0326 | −0.0818 * | 0.019 | 0.7673 | 0.0000 | 1.96% |
| Managed Futures | −0.0009 | 0.2299 ** | −0.3180 ** | −0.1339 | 0.1420 ** | 0.0877 | 0.0158 | 3.13% |
| Multi-Strategy | 0.0042 *** | 0.2070 *** | −0.0345 | −0.0452 | −0.0126 | 0.4875 | 0.0000 | 1.07% |
| Short Bias | −0.0006 | −0.8058 *** | −0.5272 *** | 0.1393 * | 0.0649 | 0.8378 | 0.0000 | 4.16% |
| SP500 | | | | | | | | 3.73% |

Source: Authors' work. * significant at the 10% level, ** significant at the 5% level, *** significant at the 1% level.

While the estimations using Carhart's model afford several insights, they do not provide an overall evaluation of the return versus the risk on the various strategies. Due to this, it is relevant to compare the strategies' performances using alternative measures, such as persistence in performance and reward-risk payoffs.

#### *4.3. Analysing Performance for Persistence and Its Relationship with Total Performance*

(i) Persistent Positive Returns

As stated in previous sections, persistence in performance is an attribute sought after by investors. Here, all eleven strategies were analysed for persistence in positive performance, and the results are presented in Table 9. The strategies are ranked in ascending order, in the column titled NETPP (Net persistent positive performance), following the procedure explained in the section on methodology.

Fixed Income Arbitrage had the highest rank for persistent performance rate with Multi Strategy being the next, over the whole period; in the crisis period, Global Macro and Equity Market Neutral Managed Futures had the highest rank; in the after-crisis period, Fixed Income Arbitrage had the highest rank, with Multi Strategy being the next. In the columns titled Performance, the strategies were ranked in ascending order, based on the end value of $100 invested at the beginning of the period. In the last row, the rank correlation coefficient was computed and showed a significant positive correlation between persistence in performance and total performance, only in the after-crisis period. Moreover, over the whole period, Global Macro, Multi Strategy, Fixed Income Arbitrage and Convertible Arbitrage had the highest net persistent positive performance (NETPP) and were well above the S and P 500, on this measure.

(ii) Persistent Returns above S&P500

In Table 10, the net persistent positive performance over the S&P500 is presented. Over a quarterly horizon, none of the strategies had a positive figure for net persistent performance (NETPOS), over the S&P500, either over the whole period or in the after-crisis period; though all strategies had a net persistent performance over the S&P500, during the crisis period.

The analysis showed that rankings on persistence in performance for performance over the benchmark S&P500, had a significant correlation with overall performance of that strategy in the after-crisis period (0.885), near significant correlation (0.721) over the whole period, but not in the crisis period (0.212).

#### *4.4. Analysis of the Risk-Adjusted Performances (Sharpe Ratio) and Actual Performances*

At first, the performance of all strategies on the Sharpe ratio, were ranked in ascending order, in the different periods (Table 11).

Over the whole period, seven strategies had done better than the benchmark S and P 500 (Convertible Arbitrage, Emerging Markets, Event Driven, Fixed Income Arbitrage, Global Macro, Long/Short Equity and Multi Strategy); in the crisis period, all ten strategies did better than the benchmark; finally, after the crisis period, four strategies had done better than the benchmark S and P 500 (Convertible Arbitrage, Fixed Income Arbitrage, Global Macro and Multi Strategy). Of these strategies, the Global Macro and the Multi Strategy were able to outperform the S and P 500, over the whole period.

Unlike Stoforos et al. (2016), the findings of the study showed that the mean risk-adjusted return of each strategy was above the mean risk-adjusted return of the benchmark, during the financial crisis. Every strategy was able to outperform the market. This meant that investing in hedge funds rather than the broad equity market (S and P 500) could have saved investors from higher losses.

**Table 9.** Net persistent positive performance.

| Period | Whole Period | | | During Crisis | | | After Crisis | | |
|---|---|---|---|---|---|---|---|---|---|
| **Strategy/Ranks** | **NETPP** | **Pers Rank** | **Perf Rank** | **NETPP** | **Pers Rank** | **Perf Rank** | **NETPP** | **Pers Rank** | **Perf Rank** |
| Convertible Arbitrage | 23 | 9 | 9 | 0 | 6 | 4 | 23 | 9 | 9 |
| Short Bias | −6 | 1 | 1 | 0 | 6 | 11 | −6 | 1 | 1 |
| Emerging Markets | 8 | 4 | 7 | 0 | 6 | 5 | 8 | 4 | 7 |
| Equity Market Neutral | 12 | 7 | 2 | 4 | 10 | 2 | 8 | 4 | 3 |
| Event Driven | 9 | 5 | 5 | −1 | 2 | 8 | 10 | 6 | 5 |
| Fixed Income Arbitrage | 47 | 11 | 6 | −1 | 2 | 3 | 48 | 11 | 8 |
| Global Macro | 14 | 8 | 11 | 4 | 10 | 9 | 10 | 6 | 4 |
| Long/Short Equity | 3 | 3 | 8 | −2 | 1 | 7 | 5 | 3 | 6 |
| Managed Futures | 2 | 2 | 3 | 2 | 9 | 10 | 0 | 2 | 2 |
| Multi-Strategy | 28 | 10 | 10 | −1 | 2 | 6 | 29 | 10 | 10 |
| S&P 500 | 9 | 5 | 4 | −1 | 2 | 1 | 10 | 6 | 11 |
| Rank Correlation | | | 0.5682 | | | 0.1545 | | | 0.7364 * |

Source: Authors' work. NPP: net persistent positive performance; Pers Rank is the Persistence Rank; Perf Rank is the Performance Rank; +Ranked in ascending order; * Significantly different from zero at 5% level, respectively.

**Table 10.** Net persistent positive performance over the S&P 500.

| Period | Whole Period | | | During Crisis | | | After Crisis | | |
|---|---|---|---|---|---|---|---|---|---|
| Strategy/Ranks | NETPOS | Pers Rank | Perf Rank | NETPOS | Pers Rank | Perf rank | NETPOS | Pers Rank | Perf Rank |
| Convertible Arbitrage | −2 | 6 | 8 | 0 | 1 | 3 | −2 | 8 | 9 |
| Short Bias | −6 | 2 | 1 | 0 | 1 | 10 | −6 | 3 | 1 |
| Emerging Markets | −1 | 8 | 6 | 3 | 9 | 4 | −4 | 7 | 7 |
| Equity Market Neutral | −7 | 1 | 2 | 1 | 3 | 1 | −8 | 1 | 3 |
| Event Driven | −3 | 4 | 4 | 2 | 6 | 7 | −5 | 4 | 5 |
| Fixed Income Arbitrage | −1 | 8 | 5 | 1 | 3 | 2 | −2 | 8 | 8 |
| Global Macro | −2 | 6 | 10 | 3 | 9 | 8 | −5 | 4 | 4 |
| Long/Short Equity | −3 | 4 | 7 | 2 | 6 | 6 | −5 | 4 | 6 |
| Managed Futures | −6 | 2 | 3 | 2 | 6 | 9 | −8 | 1 | 2 |
| Multi-Strategy | −1 | 8 | 9 | 1 | 3 | 5 | −2 | 8 | 10 |
| Rank Correlation | | | 0.721 | | | 0.212 | | | 0.8848 |

Source: Authors' work. NPPOSP: net persistent performance over SP500; +Ranked in ascending order; *, ** Significantly different from zero at 5% and 1% levels, respectively.

**Table 11.** Sharpe ratio for the various strategies and benchmark S&P 500 in the different periods.

| Period | Whole Period | | During Crisis | | After Crisis | |
|---|---|---|---|---|---|---|
| **Strategy/Rank+** | **SR** | **Rank** | **SR** | **Rank** | **SR** | **Rank** |
| Convertible Arbitrage | 0.131225 | 7 | −0.34792 | 5 | 0.459399 | 9 |
| Short Bias | −0.18672 | 1 | 0.201479 | 11 | −0.30595 | 1 |
| Emerging Markets | 0.113375 | 5 | −0.28964 | 7 | 0.283405 | 6 |
| Equity Market Neutral | −0.04096 | 2 | −0.22519 | 8 | 0.149315 | 3 |
| Event Driven | 0.158962 | 9 | −0.4317 | 2 | 0.276549 | 5 |
| Fixed Income Arbitrage | 0.128655 | 6 | −0.39652 | 4 | 0.751279 | 11 |
| Global Macro | 0.262124 | 11 | 0.067842 | 9 | 0.378203 | 8 |
| Long/Short Equity | 0.134646 | 8 | −0.31168 | 6 | 0.276392 | 4 |
| Managed Futures | 0.054348 | 3 | 0.169392 | 10 | 0.031262 | 2 |
| Multi-Strategy | 0.242318 | 10 | −0.42212 | 3 | 0.647783 | 10 |
| SP500 | 0.08658 | 4 | −0.51418 | 1 | 0.301515 | 7 |

Source: Authors' work. +ranked in ascending order.

Although many previous studies have used the Sharpe ratio to evaluate performance (Ackermann et al. (1999); Liang and Kat (2001)), Eling and Schuhmacher (2007), criticised the Sharpe ratio as being inadequate to explain hedge fund performance, as it does not account for hedge funds' special characteristics. This was also stated by Brooks and Kat (2002), Amin and Kat (2003), Mahdavi (2004) and Murguia and Umemoto (2004), on the basis that Hedge fund returns typically have asymmetric distributions.

### *4.5. Assessment of the Reliability of Alternative Reward-Risk Ratios in Risk-Adjusted Performance Evaluation*

Keeping in mind the asymmetry of returns in hedge funds, in the next part of this section, the Sharpe ratio, Upside Potential ratio and the Sortino ratio were compared for all strategies, for the whole period; the crisis period and the after-crisis period, ranked in each period and compared with the overall strategy performance in that period, as a test of reliability of these ratios.

Over the whole period, the Global Macro had the highest Sharpe ratio with Multi Strategy being ranked the next highest. The Sortino ratio ranking was similar and different from the Upside Potential ratio. The rank correlation coefficient showed a significant relationship at the 1% level, with both the Sharpe ratio rankings and the Sortino ratio rankings (Table 12).

**Table 12.** Overall performance rankings compared to reward risk ratio rankings in whole period.

| Strategy/Rank+ | Performance | Sharpe | Upside Potential | Sortino |
|---|---|---|---|---|
| Convertible Arbitrage | 5 | 7 | 3 | 7 |
| Short Bias | 1 | 1 | 4 | 1 |
| Emerging Markets | 9 | 5 | 5 | 6 |
| Equity Market Neutral | 2 | 2 | 1 | 2 |
| Event Driven | 6 | 9 | 9 | 9 |
| Fixed Income Arbitrage | 4 | 6 | 2 | 5 |
| Global Macro | 11 | 11 | 11 | 11 |
| Long/Short Equity | 8 | 8 | 8 | 8 |
| Managed Futures | 3 | 3 | 10 | 3 |
| Multi-Strategy | 10 | 10 | 7 | 10 |
| SPX | 7 | 4 | 6 | 4 |
| Rank correlation coefficient | | 0.8091 ** | 0.5364 | 0.8545 ** |

Source: Authors' work. +Ranked in ascending order; *, ** Significantly different from zero at 5% and 1% levels, respectively.

During the crisis period, Short Bias and Managed Futures had, the highest Sharpe and Sortino ratios and, overall, there was a high degree of correlation for all three measures, with the Sortino ratio having the most significant relationship with the overall strategy performances (Table 13).

**Table 13.** Overall performance rankings compared to reward risk ratio rankings during crisis.

| Strategy/Rank+ | Performance | Sharpe | Upside Potential | Sortino |
|---|---|---|---|---|
| Convertible Arbitrage | 4 | 5 | 3 | 5 |
| Short Bias | 9 | 11 | 8 | 10 |
| Emerging Markets | 6 | 7 | 7 | 8 |
| Equity Market Neutral | 2 | 8 | 10 | 6 |
| Event Driven | 8 | 2 | 5 | 3 |
| Fixed Income Arbitrage | 3 | 4 | 1 | 2 |
| Global Macro | 10 | 9 | 9 | 9 |
| Long/Short Equity | 7 | 6 | 6 | 7 |
| Managed Futures | 11 | 10 | 11 | 11 |
| Multi-Strategy | 5 | 3 | 4 | 4 |
| SPX | 1 | 1 | 2 | 1 |
| Rank correlation coefficient | | 0.6091 | 0.6182 * | 0.7727 ** |

Source: Authors' work. +Ranked in ascending order; *, ** Significantly different from zero at 5% and 1% levels, respectively.

In the after-crisis period, Fixed Income Arbitrage had the highest Sharpe ratio, while Convertible Arbitrage had the highest Upside Potential and Sortino ratios. Only the Sharpe and Sortino ratios had a significant correlation with the overall strategy performance, for all periods (Table 14).

**Table 14.** Overall performance rankings compared to reward risk ratio rankings in after crisis period.

| Strategy/Rank+ | Performance | Sharpe | Upside Potential | Sortino |
|---|---|---|---|---|
| Convertible Arbitrage | 9 | 9 | 11 | 11 |
| Short Bias | 1 | 1 | 1 | 1 |
| Emerging Markets | 7 | 6 | 5 | 6 |
| Equity Market Neutral | 3 | 3 | 2 | 2 |
| Event Driven | 5 | 5 | 6 | 4 |
| Fixed Income Arbitrage | 8 | 11 | 7 | 7 |
| Global Macro | 4 | 8 | 9 | 9 |
| Long/Short Equity | 6 | 4 | 8 | 8 |
| Managed Futures | 2 | 2 | 4 | 3 |
| Multi-Strategy | 10 | 10 | 10 | 10 |
| SPX | 11 | 7 | 3 | 5 |
| Rank correlation coefficient | | 0.7909 ** | 0.5091 | 0.6636 * |

+Ranked in ascending order; *, ** Significantly different from zero at 5% and 1% levels, respectively.

In summary, in all periods, only the Sortino ratio ranking had a significant relationship with the ranking in performances, making it the most reliable ratio. Such results were also confirmed by other researchers (Sortino et al. (2001); Rosenberg et al. (2004) and Scherer (2004); Chaudhary and Johnson (2008)). This emphasised the superiority of the downside risk framework in analysing hedge fund returns.

## 5. Conclusions

Using a large database of over 9500 hedge funds available from the Hedge Index, performances of ten major strategies, during and after the financial crisis, were investigated in this study. After visual inspection, the ten-year data-sample was divided into two sub-periods (June 2007–March 2009 and April 2009–January 2017) and was analysed for correlations, risk and return, persistence in performance, return attribution using Carhart's four-factor model (Carhart 1997) and reward-risk ratios.

Analysis with Carhart's model, showed that no strategy was able to produce a significant alpha during the financial crisis. It became obvious that the market was not the most efficient during the financial crisis, though it might well have been so, in the after-crisis period when the S and P 500 was the best performer. During the financial crisis, each hedge fund strategy offered risk-adjusted performance that was superior to the S and P 500's risk-adjusted performance. After the financial crisis, although four strategies (Convertible Arbitrage, Fixed Income Arbitrage, Multi Strategy and Global Macro) were able to outperform the S and P 500, in risk-adjusted terms, in absolute terms, the S and P 500 was the best value performer.

All strategies did better than the benchmark S and P 500, during the crisis, and over the whole period, seven strategies did better than the benchmark S and P 500 (Convertible Arbitrage, Emerging Markets, Event Driven, Fixed Income Arbitrage, Global Macro, Long/Short Equity, Multi Strategy). This meant that, for an investor, it is important to forecast downturns for a continued better performance than the benchmark S and P 500.

All this brings up an evaluation of whether hedge funds deliver better value for investors, which was one of the main aims of the current research. Correlations of various hedge fund strategies with the benchmark S and P 500, showed different behaviour in the during -crisis period versus the after-crisis period; the correlations of Emerging Markets, Equity Market Neutral, Global Macro, Long/Short/Equity and Multi Strategy and Managed Futures, increased in the after-crisis period; the strategies which showed a fall in correlation with benchmark S and P 500 in the after-crisis period, were the Convertible Arbitrage, Fixed Income Arbitrage and the Shortbias. The Carhart Model provided tremendous insights on which strategies generated positive alphas, the extent of market risk, strategies have, or had advantageous attributions to the SML, HML and UMD factors. Strategies which generated significant positive returns were related to a better overall performance, though none of the strategies were able to persistently perform better than the S and P 500, in a rising market. Of the reward-risk ratios, the Sortino ratio appeared to be the most reliable, as strategies ranked in this way, within a downside risk framework were significantly correlated with the ranking of performances of the strategies, either over the whole period, or during or after crisis. In falling markets, Short Selling and Managed Futures had a clear advantage for opportunities of better returns, just as in rising markets, Convertible Arbitrage and Fixed Income Arbitrage do. In rising markets, Managers of these strategies see 'arbitrage opportunities' through shorting shares for the related convertible, or locating underpriced bonds, as the yield curve changes are brought on by Central Bank interventions; though, of course, these are still speculative, under the strict definitions of 'arbitrage', as they bet on a rising market or increasing interest rates. By definition, Short Selling and Managed Futures result in a better predictable outcome than the benchmark, only in falling markets.

If hedging is about hedging against market risk (i.e., the risk of the S and P 500), all strategies did better than the S and P 500, in the crisis period; thereby, better conserving value for investors over passive investment in the S and P500. Global Macro with its top-down approach, and Multi Strategy, Long/Short Equity and Event Driven, with their active strategies, appeared to be the best performers. Emerging Markets was the fourth best performer over the whole period and also did better than the S and P 500 by offering diversification and risk reduction (higher Sharpe and Sortino ratios in the crisis and whole periods). However, over the whole period, only Global Macro and Multi Strategy had superior performances with positives alphas, and lowest positive correlations with the S and P 500, through active exploitation of opportunities, either in the same or alternative markets than the universe of the S and P 500.

Unlike previous studies, the conclusions of this research are that hedge fund strategies can generate superior returns over passive investments in the Market Portfolio (proxied by the S and P 500), particularly in crisis times, and depend on Investors' ability to forecast and select the appropriate strategy for that time. Furthermore, the downside risk framework is superior to the conventional one for evaluating reward-risk characteristics of Hedge Fund strategies.

## 6. Limitations and Further Research

The current research was done using the Hedge Index data base of over 9500 funds. These data agglomerated the performances of many individual hedge funds within the 9500 fund base and classified them by strategy. This raised the issue of caution in generalising results. Within each strategy, there are Managers who are better-performing or worse-performing than the average performer in that strategy. Again, with globalisation on the increase every year, it can be expected that correlations between markets will increase. So, it would be useful to micro-analyse individual hedge fund performances for more insights into what contributed to their particular performance. Analysis of hedge fund performance in different crisis scenarios, like the crisis in 1929 or the Asian crisis in 1997, also helps. By comparing the results in each crisis, it would be possible to find patterns and filter out strategies that can offer superior performance, in each crisis scenario. Furthermore, simulations for possible future crisis scenarios could be made to investigate how the strategies would perform. This is important, since past performance might not be a good indicator for future performance, especially in turbulent crisis scenarios.

**Author Contributions:** The contribution to this article is distributed as follows: N.M. 50%, V.S. 50%.

**Funding:** This research is not funded from any source.

**Acknowledgments:** The Authors are thankful to anonymous Peer Reviewer 2 for constructive comments which helped improve the paper.

**Conflicts of Interest:** The authors declare no conflict of interest.

## Appendix A

Test for unit root in returns of various strategies.

**Unit Root with Break Test on CONVERTIBLE_ARBITRAGE**

Null Hypothesis: CONVERTIBLE_ARBITRAGE has a unit root
Trend Specification: Intercept only
Break Specification: Intercept only
Break Type: Innovational outlier

Break Date: 2008M10
Break Selection: Minimize Dickey-Fuller t-statistic
Lag Length: 0 (Automatic - based on Schwarz information criterion, maxlag=12)

| | | t-Statistic | Prob.* |
|---|---|---|---|
| Augmented Dickey-Fuller test statistic | | -7.929327 | < 0.01 |
| Test critical values: | 1% level | -4.949133 | |
| | 5% level | -4.443649 | |
| | 10% level | -4.193627 | |

*Vogelsang (1993) asymptotic one-sided p-values.

**Figure A1.** Unit Root with Break Test Convertible Arbitrage.

**Unit Root with Break Test on EMERGING_MARKETS**

Null Hypothesis: EMERGING_MARKETS has a unit root
Trend Specification: Intercept only
Break Specification: Intercept only
Break Type: Innovational outlier

Break Date: 2008M10
Break Selection: Minimize Dickey-Fuller t-statistic
Lag Length: 0 (Automatic - based on Schwarz information criterion, maxlag=12)

| | | t-Statistic | Prob.* |
|---|---|---|---|
| Augmented Dickey-Fuller test statistic | | -9.596043 | < 0.01 |
| Test critical values: | 1% level | -4.949133 | |
| | 5% level | -4.443649 | |
| | 10% level | -4.193627 | |

*Vogelsang (1993) asymptotic one-sided p-values.

**Figure A2.** Unit Root with Break Test Emerging Markets.

**Unit Root with Break Test on EQUITY_MARKET_NEUTRAL**

Null Hypothesis: EQUITY_MARKET_NEUTRAL has a unit root
Trend Specification: Intercept only
Break Specification: Intercept only
Break Type: Innovational outlier

Break Date: 2008M11
Break Selection: Minimize Dickey-Fuller t-statistic
Lag Length: 2 (Automatic - based on Schwarz information criterion, maxlag=12)

| | | t-Statistic | Prob.* |
|---|---|---|---|
| Augmented Dickey-Fuller test statistic | | -17.73145 | < 0.01 |
| Test critical values: | 1% level | -4.949133 | |
| | 5% level | -4.443649 | |
| | 10% level | -4.193627 | |

*Vogelsang (1993) asymptotic one-sided p-values.

**Figure A3.** Unit Root with Break Test Equity Market Neutral.

**Unit Root with Break Test on EVENT_DRIVEN**

Null Hypothesis: EVENT_DRIVEN has a unit root
Trend Specification: Intercept only
Break Specification: Intercept only
Break Type: Innovational outlier

Break Date: 2008M09
Break Selection: Minimize Dickey-Fuller t-statistic
Lag Length: 0 (Automatic - based on Schwarz information criterion, maxlag=12)

| | | t-Statistic | Prob.* |
|---|---|---|---|
| Augmented Dickey-Fuller test statistic | | -7.688177 | < 0.01 |
| Test critical values: | 1% level | -4.949133 | |
| | 5% level | -4.443649 | |
| | 10% level | -4.193627 | |

*Vogelsang (1993) asymptotic one-sided p-values.

**Figure A4.** Unit Root with Break Test Event Driven.

**Unit Root with Break Test on FIXED_INCOME_ARBITRAGE**

Null Hypothesis: FIXED_INCOME_ARBITRAGE has a unit root
Trend Specification: Intercept only
Break Specification: Intercept only
Break Type: Innovational outlier

Break Date: 2008M10
Break Selection: Minimize Dickey-Fuller t-statistic
Lag Length: 0 (Automatic - based on Schwarz information criterion, maxlag=12)

| | | t-Statistic | Prob.* |
|---|---|---|---|
| Augmented Dickey-Fuller test statistic | | -10.44356 | < 0.01 |
| Test critical values: | 1% level | -4.949133 | |
| | 5% level | -4.443649 | |
| | 10% level | -4.193627 | |

*Vogelsang (1993) asymptotic one-sided p-values.

**Figure A5.** Unit Root with Break Test Fixed Income Arbitrage.

**Unit Root with Break Test on GLOBAL_MACRO**

Null Hypothesis: GLOBAL_MACRO has a unit root
Trend Specification: Intercept only
Break Specification: Intercept only
Break Type: Innovational outlier

Break Date: 2008M09
Break Selection: Minimize Dickey-Fuller t-statistic
Lag Length: 0 (Automatic - based on Schwarz information criterion, maxlag=12)

| | | t-Statistic | Prob.* |
|---|---|---|---|
| Augmented Dickey-Fuller test statistic | | -10.43890 | < 0.01 |
| Test critical values: | 1% level | -4.949133 | |
| | 5% level | -4.443649 | |
| | 10% level | -4.193627 | |

*Vogelsang (1993) asymptotic one-sided p-values.

**Figure A6.** Unit Root with Break Test Global Macro.

**Unit Root with Break Test on LONG_SHORT_EQUITY**

Null Hypothesis: LONG_SHORT_EQUITY has a unit root
Trend Specification: Intercept only
Break Specification: Intercept only
Break Type: Innovational outlier

Break Date: 2008M10
Break Selection: Minimize Dickey-Fuller t-statistic
Lag Length: 0 (Automatic - based on Schwarz information criterion, maxlag=12)

| | | t-Statistic | Prob.* |
|---|---|---|---|
| Augmented Dickey-Fuller test statistic | | -9.538091 | < 0.01 |
| Test critical values: | 1% level | -4.949133 | |
| | 5% level | -4.443649 | |
| | 10% level | -4.193627 | |

*Vogelsang (1993) asymptotic one-sided p-values.

**Figure A7.** Unit Root with Break Test Long/Short Equity.

**Unit Root with Break Test on MANAGED_FUTURES**

Null Hypothesis: MANAGED_FUTURES has a unit root
Trend Specification: Intercept only
Break Specification: Intercept only
Break Type: Innovational outlier

Break Date: 2015M01
Break Selection: Minimize Dickey-Fuller t-statistic
Lag Length: 0 (Automatic - based on Schwarz information criterion, maxlag=12)

| | | t-Statistic | Prob.* |
|---|---|---|---|
| Augmented Dickey-Fuller test statistic | | -11.54356 | < 0.01 |
| Test critical values: | 1% level | -4.949133 | |
| | 5% level | -4.443649 | |
| | 10% level | -4.193627 | |

*Vogelsang (1993) asymptotic one-sided p-values.

**Figure A8.** Unit Root with Break Test Managed Futures.

**Unit Root with Break Test on MULTI_STRATEGY**

Null Hypothesis: MULTI_STRATEGY has a unit root
Trend Specification: Intercept only
Break Specification: Intercept only
Break Type: Innovational outlier

Break Date: 2008M09
Break Selection: Minimize Dickey-Fuller t-statistic
Lag Length: 0 (Automatic - based on Schwarz information criterion, maxlag=12)

| | | t-Statistic | Prob.* |
|---|---|---|---|
| Augmented Dickey-Fuller test statistic | | -7.548245 | < 0.01 |
| Test critical values: | 1% level | -4.949133 | |
| | 5% level | -4.443649 | |
| | 10% level | -4.193627 | |

*Vogelsang (1993) asymptotic one-sided p-values.

**Figure A9.** Unit Root with Break Test Multi Strategy.

**Unit Root with Break Test on SHORT_BIAS**

Null Hypothesis: SHORT_BIAS has a unit root
Trend Specification: Intercept only
Break Specification: Intercept only
Break Type: Innovational outlier

Break Date: 2009M04
Break Selection: Minimize Dickey-Fuller t-statistic
Lag Length: 0 (Automatic - based on Schwarz information criterion, maxlag=12)

| | | t-Statistic | Prob.* |
|---|---|---|---|
| Augmented Dickey-Fuller test statistic | | -10.91956 | < 0.01 |
| Test critical values: | 1% level | -4.949133 | |
| | 5% level | -4.443649 | |
| | 10% level | -4.193627 | |

*Vogelsang (1993) asymptotic one-sided p-values.

**Figure A10.** Unit Root with Break Test Short Bias.

## Appendix B

**Table A1.** Correlations of returns of various strategies with S&P500 returns during and after crisis.

| Strategy/Period | During Crisis | After Crisis |
|---|---|---|
| Convertible Arbitrage | 0.55 | 0.54 |
| Short Bias | −0.64 | −0.85 |
| Emerging Markets | 0.71 | 0.73 |
| Equity Market Neutral | 0.30 | 0.58 |
| Event Driven | 0.65 | 0.76 |
| Fixed Income Arbitrage | 0.66 | 0.41 |
| Global Macro | 0.29 | 0.35 |
| Long/Short Equity | 0.73 | 0.87 |
| Managed Futures | −0.17 | 0.12 |
| Multi-Strategy | 0.60 | 0.71 |
| **t-Test: Paired Two Sample for Means** | | |
| **Strategy/Period** | **During Crisis** | **After Crisis** |
| Mean | 0.3688 | 0.42141 |
| Variance | 0.2017 | 0.24815 |
| Observations | 10 | 10 |
| Pearson Correlation | 0.9357 | |
| Hypothesized Mean Difference | 0.0000 | |
| df | 9.0000 | |
| t Stat | −0.9414 | |
| P(T<=t) one-tail | 0.1855 | |
| t Critical one-tail | 1.8331 | |
| P(T<=t) two-tail | 0.3711 | |
| t Critical two-tail | 2.2622 | |

## References


Ackermann, Carl, Richard McEnally, and David Ravenscraft. 1999. The performance of hedge funds: Risk, return, and incentives. *The Journal of Finance* 54: 833–74. [CrossRef]

Agarwal, Vikas, and Narayan Naik. 2000. Multi-period performance persistence analysis of hedge funds. *Journal of Financial and Quantitative Analysis* 35: 327–42. [CrossRef]

Agarwal, Vikas, and Narayan Naik. 2004. Risks and Portfolio Decisions Involving Hedge Funds. *Review of Financial Studies* 17: 63–98. [CrossRef]

Amenc, Noel, Lionel Martellini, and Mathhieu Vaissié. 2003. Benefits and risks of alternative investment strategies. *Journal of Asset Management* 4: 96–118. [CrossRef]

Amin, Gaurav S., and Harry M. Kat. 2003. Hedge fund performance 1990–2000: Do the "money machines" really add value? *Journal of Financial and Quantitative Analysis* 38: 251–74. [CrossRef]

Baquero, Guillermo, Jenke ter Horst, and Marno Verbeek. 2005. Survival, Look-Ahead Bias, and Persistence in Hedge Fund Performance. *Journal of Financial and Quantitative Analysis* 40: 493–517. [CrossRef]

Barclay Hedge. 2018a. Value of Assets Managed by Hedge Funds Worldwide from 1997 to 2016 (in Billion U.S. Dollars). Statista. Available online: https://www.statista.com/statistics/271771/assets-of-the-hedge-funds-worldwide/ (accessed on 5 February 2018).

Barclay Hedge. 2018b. What Is a Hedge Fund? Available online: https://www.barclayhedge.com/research/educational-articles/hedge-fund-strategy-definition/what-is-a-hedge-fund.html (accessed on 29 January 2018).

Boasson, Vigdis, and Emil Boasson. 2011. Risk and returns of hedge funds investment strategies. *Investment Management and Financial Innovations* 8: 110–21.

Boyson, Nicole. 2003. *Do Hedge Funds Exhibit Performance Persistence? A New Approach.* Working Paper. West Lafayette: Purdue University, Krannert Graduate School of Management.

Brown, Stephen J., William N. Goetzmann, and Roger G. Ibbotson. 1999. *Offshore Hedge Funds: Survival [and] & Performance 1989–1995.* Charlottesville: CFA Institute.

Brown, Stephen J., William N. Goetzmann, and James Park. 2001. Careers and survival: Competition and risk in the hedge fund and CTA industry. *The Journal of Finance* 56: 1869–86. [CrossRef]

Capocci, Daniel. 2002. *Analysis of Hedge Fund Performance*. Munich: University Library of Munich.

Capocci, Daniel, and Georges Hübner. 2004. Analysis of hedge fund performance. *Journal of Empirical Finance* 11: 55–89. [CrossRef]

Carhart, Mark M. 1997. On persistence in mutual fund performance. *The Journal of Finance* 52: 57–82. [CrossRef]

Chaudhary, Ashraf, and Helen L Johnson. 2008. The Efficacy of the Sortino Ratio and Other Benchmarked Performance Measures under Skewed Return Distributions. *Australian Journal of Management* 32: 485–502. [CrossRef]

Credit Suisse. 2018. Broad Hedge Fund Index. Credit Suisse Hedge Index LLC. Available online: https://lab.credit-suisse.com/#/en/index/HEDG/HEDG_GLMAC/overview (accessed on 24 February 2018).

D'Alessio, G. 2015. Review: Online Hedge Fund Database Providers in 2015. Available online: Sophisticatedinvestor.com (accessed on 12 February 2018).

Do, Viet, Robert Faff, and J. Wickramanayake. 2005. An empirical analysis of hedge fund performance: The case of Australian hedge funds industry. *Journal of Multinational Financial Management* 15: 377–93. [CrossRef]

Eling, Martin, and Frank Schuhmacher. 2007. Does the choice of performance measure influence the evaluation of hedge funds? *Journal of Banking & Finance* 31: 2632–47.

Fama, Eugene F., and Kenneth R. French. 1993. Common risk factors in the returns on stocks and bonds. *Journal of Financial Economics* 33: 3–56. [CrossRef]

French, Kenneth R. 2018. Dara Library. Available online: http://mba.tuck.dartmouth.edu/pages/faculty/ken.french/data_library.html (accessed on 15 July 2018).

Fung, William, and David Hsieh. 1997. Empirical characteristics of dynamic trading strategies: The case of hedge funds. *The Review of Financial Studies* 10: 275–302. [CrossRef]

Fung, William, and David Hsieh. 2001. The risk in hedge fund strategies: Theory and evidence from trend followers. *The Review of Financial Studies* 14: 313–41. [CrossRef]

Fung, William, and David Hsieh. 2004. Hedge Fund Benchmarks: A Risk-Based Approach. *Financial Analysts Journal* 60: 65–80. [CrossRef]

Gregoriou, Greg, Francois-Eric Racicot, and Raymond Théoret. 2016. The q-factor and the Fama and French asset pricing models: Hedge fund evidence. *Managerial Finance* 42: 1180–1207. [CrossRef]

Huber, Claus, and Helmut Kaiser. 2004. Hedge Fund Risk Factors with Option-like Structures: Examples and Explanations. *The Journal of Wealth Management* 7: 49–60. [CrossRef]

Jordao, Gustavo, and Marcelo L. De Moura. 2011. Performance analysis of Brazilian hedge funds. *Journal of Multinational Financial Management* 21: 165–76. [CrossRef]

Kothari, S.P., and Jerold B. Warner. 2001. Evaluating mutual fund performance. *The Journal of Finance* 56: 1985–2010. [CrossRef]

Liang, Bing. 1999. On the performance of hedge funds. *Financial Analysts Journal* 55: 72–85. [CrossRef]

Liang, Bing, and Harry M. Kat. 2001. Hedge fund performance: 1990–1999. *Financial Analysts Journal* 57: 11–18. [CrossRef]

Manser, Samuel, and Markus M. Schmid. 2009. The Performance Persistence of Equity Long/Short Hedge Funds. *Journal of Derivatives & Hedge Funds* 15: 51–69. [CrossRef]

Nasdaq. 2018. Other Index Descriptions. Available online: http://www.nasdaq.com/reference/index-descriptions.aspx (accessed on 19 February 2018).

Rosenberg, Mark, James F. Tomeo, and Sam Y Chuang. 2004. Hedge Fund of Fund Allocations Using a Convergent and Divergent Strategy Approach. *The Journal of Alternative Investments Summer* 7: 44–53.

Schaub, Nic, and Markus Schmid. 2013. Hedge fund liquidity and performance: Evidence from the financial crisis. *Journal of Banking & Finance* 37: 671–92.

Scherer, Bernd. 2004. An alternative route to performance hypothesis testing. *Journal of Asset Management* 5: 5–12. [CrossRef]

Schneeweis, Thomas, and Richard Spurgin. 1997. Managed Futures, and Hedge Fund and Mutual Fund Return Estimation: A MultiFactor Approach. Available online: https://www.researchgate.net/publication/251901666_Managed_Futures_Hedge_Fund_and_Mutual_Fund_Return_Estimation_A_MultiFactor_Approach (accessed on 15 July 2018).

Schneeweis, Thomas, and Richard Spurgin. 1999. Quantitative Analysis of Hedge Fund and Managed Futures Return and Risk Characteristics. Available online: https://pdfs.semanticscholar.org/ee20/b8a6323c7d1c7625e37570d61ab18e0f23db.pdf (accessed on 15 July 2018).

Sharpe, William F. 1966. Mutual fund performance. *The Journal of Business* 39: 119–38. [CrossRef]

Sharpe, William F. 1992. Asset allocation: Management style and performance measurement. *Journal of Portfolio Management* 18: 7–19. [CrossRef]

Slavutskaya, A. 2013. Short-Term Hedge Fund Performance. *Journal of Banking and Finance* 37: 4404–31. [CrossRef]

Sortino, Frank A., and Lee N. Price. 1994. Performance measurement in a downside risk framework. *Journal of Investing* 3: 59–64. [CrossRef]

Sortino, Frank, Robert van der Meer, and Auke Plantinga. 1999. The Dutch Triangle: A Framework to Measure Upside Potential relative to Downside Risk. *Journal of Portfolio Management* 26: 50–58. [CrossRef]

Stafylas, Dimitrios, Keith Philip Anderson, and Moshafique Uddin. 2017. Recent Advances in Explaining Hedge Fund Returns: Implicit Factors and Exposures. *International Review of Financial Analysis* 43: 48–61. [CrossRef]

Stoforos, Chrysostomos E., Stavros Degiannakis, and Theodosios Palaskas. 2016. *Hedge Fund Returns under Crisis Scenarios: A Holistic Approach.* MPRA Paper 80161. Munich: University Library of Munich.

Strömqvist, Maria. 2009. Hedge Funds and Financial Crises. *Sveriges Riksbank Economic Review.* Available online: https://papers.ssrn.com/sol3/papers.cfm?abstract_id=1631893 (accessed on 19 February 2018).

Sun, Zheng, Ashley W. Wang, and Lu Zheng. 2016. Only Winners in Tough Times Repeat: Hedge Fund Performance Persistence over Different Market Conditions. *Journal of Financial and Quantitative Analysis* 53: 2199–225. [CrossRef]

Travers, Frank J. 2012. *Hedge Fund Analysis an In-Depth Guide to Evaluating Return Potential and Assessing Risks.* New York: Wiley.

# 11

# Risk Taking and Fiscal Smoothing with Sovereign Wealth Funds in Advanced Economies

**Snorre Lindset and Knut Anton Mork ***

Department of Economics, Norwegian University of Science and Technology, 7491 Trondheim, Norway; snorre.lindset@ntnu.no

* Correspondence: knut.anton.mork@ntnu.no

**Abstract:** In an economy with a sovereign wealth fund (SWF), the government may draw on the fund to supplement other government revenues. If the fund is invested in risky assets, this introduces a new stochastic element into the government's budget. We analyze the interaction between the draw from and risk taking in the SWF. Using non-expected utility preferences, we distinguish between intended changes and stochastic changes in the SWF draws over time. We show that the desire for smoothness in taxes and public services translates into smoothing of SWF draws and lower risk taking. It can even lead to procyclical rebalancing of the SWF portfolio. Future interest rates are associated with interest-rate risk. We show that this risk may lead to a higher optimal equity share in the SWF portfolio. Policy makers can use the draws from the SWF to smooth over time variation in risk-free rates.

**Keywords:** fiscal policy; sovereign wealth funds; portfolio choice

**JEL Classification:** G11; G23

---

## 1. Introduction

For a country with a large enough sovereign wealth fund (SWF), its financial returns can fund substantial parts of government spending. Blissful as this situation may seem, it raises a fundamental dilemma in that the financial returns are procyclical whereas the fiscal needs are fairly stable over time or even countercyclical. This dilemma carries important implications for the fund's desired risk profile.

Whereas some of today's SWFs date back to the 1970s (Kunzel et al. 2011; Baldwin 2012; Paltrinieri and Pichler 2013), the number of such funds grew significantly in the 1990s and especially after the Asian financial crisis towards the end of that decade. Whereas some such funds remain relatively small, others have grown to become very large, such as those owned by the United Arab Emirates, Saudi Arabia, China, and Norway. Decisions regarding fund management and draws on the fund naturally grow in importance as the fund grows in magnitude. The authors' interest in SWFs has been inspired by the policy debate surrounding the Norwegian Government Pension Fund Global (GPFG), whose market value at the time of writing is reported to be $940 billion.[1] However, as other SWFs grow as well, we believe the issues we study could be of equal interest to many other countries.

SWFs have been funded from a variety of sources. In some cases, especially after the Asian financial crisis, large trade surpluses have been added to the foreign-exchange reserves of some countries, notably China, so as to substantially exceed the normal needs for foreign-exchange

---

[1] One of us participated in two government-appointed commissions related to the investment strategy and the fiscal rule associated with this SWF; Norwegian Ministry of Finance (2015, 2016).

stabilization. In other cases, such as Singapore, government pension systems have accumulated substantial reserve funds. The currently most typical, however, are SWFs funded by revenues from harvesting non-renewable natural resources, such as oil and gas.

The asset composition of the SWFs' investment portfolios affects portfolio risk and may also restrict draws from the funds. The funds have been established for a variety of purposes, as documented by Bernstein et al. (2013), Dreassi et al. (2017), as well as the references listed above and the literature surveyed by Alhashel (2015). Some, such as the Canada Pension Plan Investment Board, have been established as pure pension funds tied to future pension obligations.[2] They are typically managed more or less like private pension funds, sometimes with sizeable positions in non-listed assets. Others, such as the China Investment Corporation, have been established more or less as instruments of the government's foreign policy and thus take risk profiles that serve these purposes (Johan et al. 2013). The emergence of such funds has been the source of some apprehension about reversed colonialism, as discussed by Baldwin (2012). A third group consists of stabilization funds, exemplified by Chile's Economic and Social Stabilization Fund. This fund is maintained as a buffer against copper price fluctuations, allowing the government to draw on the fund to cover budget deficits when copper prices are low, subsequently to be refilled when copper prices recover. The fourth group, which interests us the most, consists of the funds accumulated by petroleum exporting countries. The first big wave of such funds came in the 1970s as leading oil exporting countries, mainly in the Middle East, accumulated revenues faster than they were able to spend meaningfully or invest domestically. Later there followed similar funds in Azerbaijan, Kazakhstan, Norway, and Russia.

These oil funds, in short, were established as a way to convert the financially concentrated wealth of below-ground natural resources into a balanced portfolio of liquid financial assets in support of future fiscal obligations. The channeling of extraordinary revenues into SWFs, furthermore, serves as protection against the so-called Dutch disease, analyzed by Van Wijnbergen (1984), Corden (1984), Krugman (1987), and many others. That is, they are supposed to shield the economy from a temporary expansion of domestic spending that risks depleting the stock of human capital in traditional export industries and thus leave the economy worse off when the non-renewable resources are depleted than before they were discovered. At the same time—and more or less by the same token—these funds are also intended as saving funds to allow the financial benefits of the finite resource stock to be shared by future generations.

The challenge raised by this strategy is that the string of future generations starts with the current one. Thus, it is arguably desirable to allow part of the resource revenue to fund current government spending while saving the lion's share for future use. This challenge is easily managed as long as the fund is small. However, the Norwegian GPFG has, as one example, grown from 80% of the country's annual GDP in 2006 to two and a half times that currently. During the same period, the share of public spending funded by draws on the GPFG increased from 8% to no less than 19% in 2018.

The challenges facing a government with a SWF of this magnitude are similar to those of many university endowment funds: on the one hand, one will want the fund to take considerable risk so as to generate large average yields to fund government services. But on the other hand, one will want the same services to be as smooth as possible over time, as argued, for example, Barro (1979). In addition—and in contrast to university endowments—variations in public spending or taxation may have considerable adverse macroeconomic consequences. In fact, it is easy to make a macroeconomic argument that the government deficit—apart from the SWF—should be countercyclical. This is hard to reconcile with high SWF risk taking, which tends to make the SWF budget contribution procyclical. The nature and possible handling of this dilemma is the focus of the present paper.

This dilemma appears to have been ignored by the SWF literature so far. Chambers et al. (2012) argue that "The Norway Model" makes the GPFG especially able to harvest risk premia because its

---

2 The Norwegian GPFG has, despite its name, no special role in funding future pensions obligations.

investment horizon is effectively infinite. However, a fiscal rule, adopted in 2001, allows an annual draw on the fund as a regular source of fiscal revenue corresponding to the expected real financial return, initially estimated as 4%, from 2018 on lowered to 3%. Although Chambers et al. note this rule, they do not pursue its consequences for the SWF to take on risky positions.

The Norwegian fiscal rule has been motivated by the permanent-income theory in macroeconomics (e.g., Hall 1978). Its great weakness is that it ignores risk. Simple extensions to the risky case can be found in the classical analyses by Phelps (1962), Samuelson (1969), and Merton (1969) of an individual's optimal spending and portfolio allocation. However, these studies ignore the fiscal need for smooth tax rates and government services, which we refer to as backward smoothing. Thus, we believe that SWF investing should be analyzed in the broader framework of asset liability management, as in Choudhry (2007). As yet another complication, the substantial movements in risk-free interest rates in recent decades raise the question of how such movements should influence the rules for drawing from an SWF, such as the lowering of the Norwegian rule from 4% to 3%. Our paper addresses all of these concerns.

These considerations contrast starkly with the challenge of sovereign debt management for countries with net debt positions. Although a net asset position may seem obviously preferable, we show in this paper that the simultaneous tasks of investing the fund and using it as a source of fiscal revenue is far from trivial. The normative literature on SWF management has mainly focused on emerging economies, where the majority of SWFs are located. Thus, Van der Ploeg and Venables (2011) focus on the cases where limited access to global financial markets may present an argument for investing a disproportionate part of the fund domestically. Carroll and Jeanne (2009) and Sá and Viani (2013) follow the same vein by focusing on the effects on global balances and exchange rates of SWF development in emerging economies. Guerra-Salas (2014) compares the effects of fiscal responses, including SWF investing as well as domestic public investment to oil price changes in Mexico and Norway. In a slightly different context, Collier and Gunning (2005) argue for using an oil windfall primarily to reduce domestic debt.

In a somewhat different vein, Van den Bremer et al. (2016) focus on the interaction between the financial portfolio and the value of the natural resources that fund that portfolio. Although we find this issue important, we bypass it in our study, which then can best be interpreted as an analysis of SWF management and spending once the natural resource has been depleted.

Once an SWF of the type we study has been established, policy makers have to decide on at least three important issues: first, how much risk to assume in the asset portfolio, and second, how much to draw from the fund to support current spending. A third decision will be equally important, namely, how to distribute the draws from the fund over time. The goal of this paper is to address all three of these issues and how they fit into the overall fiscal policy framework. The issues are related and we address them simultaneously. Although risk premia may motivate high risk taking, our observations suggest that policy makers have low tolerance for non-stochastic, or planned, variation over time in tax rates and public services as well as a strong desire to preserve value for future generations. This combination of attitudes cannot be reconciled within the standard expected utility framework. To encompass the stylized facts, we use non-expected utility preferences as proposed by Epstein and Zin (1991). These preferences allow us to distinguish between risk aversion and willingness to undertake intertemporal substitution. Furthermore, we borrow the tools of habit formation (see e.g., Constantinides 1990; Campbell and Cochrane 1999) to include preferences for smooth changes in public services. We derive closed-form solutions for the portfolio selection problem. Interestingly, the preferences for planned variation over time do not affect the portfolio choice, i.e., the distribution between risky and non-risky assets. Although this insight has already been established in the literature going back to Svensson (1989) for the basic case of a constant riskless rate and no habit formation, we show that it holds also when these assumptions are relaxed.

Ideally, we would have carried out a complete modeling of policy makers' desire for smooth tax rates as well as government services. Unfortunately, such a complete analysis does not generally lend itself to informative, closed-form solutions. As an introduction of the issue in the paper, we choose instead to approximate policy makers' preference as a case of habit formation regarding SWF draws. Under this assumption, we derive closed form solutions for how the preferences for maintaining the spending habit affect the spending rate. Because, in contrast, risk taking feeds volatility, we find habit-influenced preferences to have a profound effect on the portfolio selection problem. They reduce short-term risk taking because a larger part of the investment portfolio must be used to safeguard the habit level of consumption.

A side effect of this smoothing of public spending and taxes is that the portfolio risk for the long run increases. We find that this increased portfolio risk spills over into public spending and can increase the long-run spending risk considerably. For short-horizon portfolio-selection problems, treasury STRIPS or other zero-coupon bonds can be good substitutes for risk-free investments. For portfolio-selection problems with long horizons, like the infinite horizons for many SWFs, "risk-free investments" are risky because interest rates fluctuate randomly. We address the effect of interest rate uncertainty on the optimal draw from the fund and on the portfolio-selection problem.

Our analysis is partial in the sense that it treats policy makers as a representative investor and consumer, but does not present a model for the underlying macro economy. Carroll and Jeanne (2009) and Sá and Viani (2013) analyze related topics to what we analyze. While they include a model for the macro economy, their asset-price dynamics and preference specification are simpler than ours. Parts of our analysis follows from results in the existing literature, but the generalization to the case of non-expected utility is, to the best of our knowledge, novel for the cases of habit formation and time-varying risk-free rates. This generalization is particularly important for decisions regarding portfolio allocation for SWFs and the use of such funds as budget revenues. Yang (2015) includes habit formation and long-run risks in a non-expected utility framework. While his analysis is methodologically related to our analysis, his focus is not on portfolio choice and spending, but rather to analyze asset market phenomena from the macro-finance literature.

There have been several studies of Norway's GPFG, but they all have a different focus than ours. Two of the studies that have received the most attention (Ang et al. 2009; and Dahlquist and Ødegaard 2018), analyze empirically the performance of the fund's investment portfolio. Only a small fraction of the fund is actively managed, and the choice of benchmark index has, therefore, been most important for the fund's (absolute) performance.

Our paper is organized as follows: Section 2 uses Svensson (1989) generalization to Epstein-Zin preferences of the Merton model with a constant risk-free rate and no backward smoothing to gain some preliminary insights into the respective roles of risk aversion and intertemporal substitution for decisions about portfolio allocation and use of the proceeds of a SWF. Section 3 studies the implications of backward smoothing of tax rates and public services based on a generalization of the model of Constantinides (1990). Such smoothing turns out to have implications for the normal rebalancing of the fund as well as its long-term performance, which we consider in Section 4. Section 5 extends the analysis to the case of time variation in the risk-free rate. Section 6 presents our conclusions and some plans for further research.

## 2. Risk Aversion vs. Intertemporal Substitution

We start by considering the different roles of risk aversion and intertemporal substitution for the owner of an SWF. For this purpose, we use the Epstein–Zin formulation of non-expected utility, which in discrete time can be expressed by the following value function:

$$V_t(W_t) = \max_{c_t,\alpha_t}\{c_t^{1-\delta} + e^{-\rho}E_t[V_{t+1}(W_{t+1})^{1-\gamma}]^{(1-\delta)/(1-\gamma)}\}^{1/(1-\delta)}. \quad (1)$$

Here, $\rho$ is the subjective discount rate, $\gamma$ is the standard measure of relative risk aversion, and $\delta \equiv 1\varepsilon$, where $\varepsilon$ is the elasticity of intertemporal substitution. Thus, $\delta$ can be interpreted as a measure of aversion against non-stochastic or planned time variations of consumption $c$, which we interpret as the annual draw on the fund. $W$ denotes wealth, i.e., the total value of the SWF portfolio. A fraction $\alpha$ of the fund's assets is invested in a risky asset (equity) and a fraction $1 - \alpha$ in a safe asset. As is well known, this formulation simplifies to standard power expected utility if $\gamma = \delta$. However, we will not make this assumption because these two parameters serve rather substantially different functions in our present context, and we believe policy makers' attitudes towards risk and non-stochastic time variation can be quite different.

Although decision making with non-expected utility is more easily analyzed in discrete time, continuous-time analysis yields more informative solutions. For this reason, we carry out our analysis in continuous time, but leave most of the mathematical derivations to Appendix A.

As shown in Appendix A.1, after transformation, taking the limit as the discrete time intervals approach zero, the value function (1) is equivalent to the Bellman equation:

$$0 = \max_{c(t),\alpha(t)} \left\{ c(t)^{1-\delta} - \rho U(W(t))^{(1-\delta)/(1-\gamma)} + \frac{1}{dt}[E_t dU(W(t))]^{(1-\delta)/(1-\gamma)} \right\}, \tag{2}$$

where $U(W(t)) \equiv V(W(t))^{1-\gamma}$.

Equation (2) needs to be supplemented by a dynamic budget constraint. In this section, we assume that the risk-free return $r$ is constant over time. In continuous-time notation, the flow budget constraint is given by:

$$dW(t) = [(r + \alpha(t)\mu)W(t) - c(t)]dt + \alpha(t)\sigma W(t) dB(t), \tag{3}$$

where $B(t)$ is a Wiener process. The risky asset has return $z(t) \sim NIID(r + \mu, \sigma^2)$, where $\mu$ is the time-invariant equity premium. Then, $r + \alpha(t)\mu$ is the expected portfolio return and $\alpha(t)^2\sigma^2$ its variance. This formulation ignores the possibility of stock-price mean reversion (e.g., Fama and French 1988), as well as uncertainty about long-term trends (Bansal and Yaron 2004; and Yang 2015). We offer some informal comments on these issues below.

**Proposition 1.** *Under the assumptions given in (2) and (3), the optimal equity share $\alpha$ is constant and the optimal consumption is a constant share $\eta$ of wealth, where,*

$$\alpha = \frac{\mu}{\gamma\sigma^2} \equiv m \tag{4a}$$

and,

$$\eta = \varepsilon\rho + (1-\varepsilon)\left(r + m\mu - \frac{1}{2}\gamma m^2\sigma^2\right) = \varepsilon\rho + (1-\varepsilon)\left(r + \frac{1}{2}m\mu\right). \tag{4b}$$

This proposition was originally proved by Svensson (1989). Our proof, which is somewhat different than his in order to facilitate our subsequent analysis, is provided in Appendices A.1 and A.2.

The solution for the equity share is identical to that derived by Merton (1969) for the expected-utility case. Although known from previous research such as Svensson's, it may be worth noting that this part of Merton's results is not influenced by the double duty served by the risk-aversion parameter $\gamma$ as the reciprocal of the elasticity of substitution in the expected-utility case.[3]

Our main interest concerns the optimal draw on the fund. The draw rate in our case differs from the draw rate derived by Merton. Thus, while we have the same equity share as in the Merton model, going forward, the different draw rate makes the value of the investment portfolio, and thereby the amount invested in equity, different from the corresponding investments by the Merton investor. The draw rate is expressed as a linear combination—if $0 \leq \varepsilon \leq 1$ as a weighted average—of what

3 It is also worth noting that the optimal equity share is not bounded above by unity. This is a feature of the model's partial nature, however.

Giovannini and Weil (1989) and Campbell and Viceira (2002) refer to as a myopic and an annuity component, respectively. The myopic component may be large if the investor is impatient, so that $\rho$ is large. For policy makers, we believe this would be roughly equivalent to a desire to favor current generations over future ones. However, policy makers would then also need to be willing to plan for draws on the fund to vary non-stochastically over time, so that $\varepsilon > 0$.

In his seminal empirical study, Hall (1988) concludes that the intertemporal elasticity of substitution is likely to be small. This observation indicates that the income effect is more important than the substitution effect. Later studies, like Bansal and Yaron (2004) and Thimme (2016) have found larger values of $\varepsilon$, indicating that the substitution effect of reactions to changes in rates of return is important. However, our casual observations of policy-maker behavior in advanced-economy countries with sovereign wealth funds suggest that their overriding concern is about preserving the fund for future generations. We believe that, if anything, this attitude reveals lower elasticities of intertemporal substitution than those estimated for households. Acknowledging that $\varepsilon$ is likely to be close to zero, we thus read SWF decision-makers as focusing mainly on the annuity component. This attitude would also be consistent with a desire for smoothness in the time-series behavior of public services and tax rates, as argued by Barro (1979) and many others. In Section 3 we return to further implications of this literature.

A near-zero elasticity of intertemporal substitution does not imply high risk aversion, however. Rational decision makers can be highly averse to planned variations in consumption over time and yet be highly tolerant of variations that result from stochastic movements in stock prices. On the other hand, we note that the annuity component in (4b) contains a risk adjustment. The permanent-income theory in its simplest form ignores uncertainty and recommends consumption of the entire expected return. When risk is considered, this would naturally be optimal only with risk neutrality, i.e., $\gamma = 0$. In general, the greater the risk aversion, the smaller the draw rate should be. More specifically, the safety buffer should correspond to half the expected return of the optimally chosen risky portion of the portfolio. For example, if the equity premium is 4% and the equity share has been optimally chosen as 60%, we can conclude that the annuity component of the optimal draw is 1.2 percentage points higher than the risk-free rate or, equivalently, 1.2 percentage points lower than the expected return on the entire portfolio. This difference is far from trivial.

Mean reversion in stock returns would make this correction smaller. Mean reversion has been noted by Fama and French (1988) and Poterba and Summers (1988) and discussed further in Campbell and Viceira (2002). However, Bansal and Yaron (2004) argue, convincingly, in our view, that a proper explanation of observed risk premia requires recognition of uncertainty, not only about current returns, but also about their long-term trend. Swanson (2016) implements Bansal and Yaron's specification in a complete macro model with apparent success and concludes similarly. Trend uncertainty would naturally add to the optimal risk correction of the annual draw. Thus, we do not believe that our derivation overstates it.

As we shall see in the following sections, the results in Formula (4a) and (4b) will have to be modified if taxes and public spending are smoothed or if the risk-free rate varies over time. However, the desirability of a safety buffer is a general finding, which we summarize as:

**Observation 1.** *As a provision against risk, the annuity part of the optimal draw rate should be lower than the expected return on the portfolio.*

### 3. Backward Smoothing

As the owner of a SWF, the government will want to use it to enhance government services and/or keep a lid on taxes. Barro (1979) and others have presented convincing arguments that both the tax system and the stream of government services ought to be smooth. This smoothness should work backward as well as forward. That is, policy makers should not only plan for smoothness in future services and tax rates, they should also avoid sudden changes from past patterns in response to unexpected shocks. In practice, policy makers often have only limited leeway when it comes to changing government services from one period to the next.

In our framework, forward smoothing is ensured by a low value of the elasticity of intertemporal substitution $\varepsilon$. Backward smoothing is provided to some extent by risk aversion because low risk taking limits the effects of negative random shocks. However, in the model as specified so far, the degree of (relative) risk aversion is independent of the level of consumption and wealth. A more natural assumption would be that this aversion becomes stronger the more strained the government's finances are compared to recent experience. This assumption can be approximated by introducing habit formation in the model. We naturally do not mean that policy decisions are governed by habits in a literal sense, but that models of habit formation offer a suitable technique for modelling variations in risk aversion and hence backward smoothing.

The consumption literature distinguishes between external and internal habits. External habits refer to people's valuation of their own consumption relative to that of others: "catching up with the Jones'," cf. Abel (1990) or Campbell and Cochrane (1999). Internal habits refer instead to how people tend to get used to their standard of living and derive utility only from consumption over and above that standard. We believe the latter formulation of habit formation is the most relevant for our purpose because our decision maker is the government deciding for the entire nation.

Constantinides (1990) has introduced habit formation in a model of portfolio investment in continuous time with expected-utility preferences. We extend his analysis to Epstein–Zin preferences by letting the consumption variable in the Bellman Equation (2) be replaced by consumption $y$ over and above a habit level $x$, so that $y = c - x$. The habit level is assumed to start from an exogenously given initial level $x_0$ and to develop over time according to:

$$dx(t) = [bc(t) - ax(t)]dt \equiv by(t)dt + (b-a)x(t)dt,\ a \geq 0,\ b \geq 0,\ b < r + a. \tag{5}$$

Appendix A.3 extends Constantinides' results for this specification to the case of Epstein–Zin non-expected utility. We show there that, in this case, the SWF can be thought of as consisting of two portfolios, one part with value $\mathcal{X}(t)$, providing safe financing for the minimum consumption level defined by the habit $x(t)$ and a remaining part with value $\mathcal{Y}(t)$ financing the rest. The portfolio with value $\mathcal{X}(t)$ needs to be risk free because otherwise a bad random draw could make consumption fall below $x(t)$, which would make utility drop to negative infinity. Safe funding of this minimum level of consumption turns out to require $\mathcal{X}(t) = x(t)/(r + a - b)$.

Relative risk aversion in this setup is defined by the transformed value function $U(W)$ defined after Formula (2) above. Without habit formation, it is simply:

$$RRA_{NH} = -\frac{U_{ww}W}{U_w} = \gamma.$$

For the analysis of behavior under habit formation, this transformed value function is replaced by $U(\mathcal{Y})$. Thus, relative risk aversion is then defined as:

$$RRA_H = -\frac{U_{ww}W}{U_w} = -\left(\frac{U_{\mathcal{Y}\mathcal{Y}}\mathcal{Y}}{U_{\mathcal{Y}}}\right)\frac{W}{\mathcal{Y}} = \gamma W/\mathcal{Y} = \gamma W/(W - \mathcal{X}). \tag{6}$$

For $\mathcal{X} > 0$, this measure is unambiguously larger than for the case without habit formation. It is larger the smaller the difference between total wealth and the wealth needed to maintain safe funding for the minimum habit level of consumption. The more "squeezed" public finances are, the more risk averse policy makers will be. This is the property that we wanted our preference specification to have.

Under these conditions, the optimal equity share is no longer constant, and the optimal draw on the fund is no longer proportional to wealth. Instead, they follow the same rules that Constantinides shows for expected utility and which Appendix A.3 shows hold also with the more general Epstein–Zin preferences. We summarize them as:

**Proposition 2.** *With Epstein–Zin preferences and Constantinides habit formation as defined in (5), the optimal equity share and the optimal SWF draw are given by the following formulae:*

$$\alpha(t) = m[W(t) - \mathcal{X}(t)]/W(t) \tag{7a}$$

*and,*

$$c(t) = x(t) + \left(1 - \frac{b}{r+a}\right)\eta[W(t) - \mathcal{X}(t)], \tag{7b}$$

*where $\eta$ is defined as in (4b).*

Risk taking now clearly is limited by the need to be able to maintain the habit level $x(t)$ of consumption without risk. The equity share is proportional to the ratio of "free" wealth $W(t) - \mathcal{X}(t)$ to total wealth $W(t)$. An adverse development in the equity market should be followed by a reduction of the equity share. Put differently, the amount of wealth invested in the risky asset is a fixed proportion of the free wealth:

$$\alpha(t)W(t) = m[W(t) - \mathcal{X}(t)].$$

Draws from the fund must be large enough to permit consumption to at least equal the habit level of consumption. However, it also needs to be limited by the need to retain sufficient wealth to fund the habit level of consumption without risk. First, the "free" level of consumption (over and above the habit level) is a fixed proportion of only the "free" wealth. Second, this proportion is a little lower than the one in Section 2 because of the need continuously to set aside some money to ensure the continued safe funding of the habit level of consumption. This is the price to be paid for the opportunity to maintain at least the habit level of consumption no matter what happens to the return on risky assets.

For optimization with habit formation to be feasible, the initial habit level obviously cannot be too large. As a minimum, it cannot exceed the riskless return on the entire fund. It also makes sense to assume $b \leq a$ because otherwise the habit level would tend to rise autonomously over time, which would have required an even larger riskless portfolio to finance habit consumption over time.

We summarize these insights as:

**Observation 2.** *A wish to keep taxes and public services smooth over time should make risk aversion for SWF investment greater in general, and risk aversion should move in the opposite direction of the equity market. However, the extent of smoothing will have to be somewhat limited in order to be feasible.*

Cochrane (2017) argues that models with habit formation and models with non-expected utility (as well as other models used in macro-finance) in many ways provide similar modifications, technically speaking, of the classical power expected-utility model in terms of providing better explanations of observed data for equity premia and riskless rates. However, in the context of optimal portfolio choice and optimal spending decisions in a SWF context, our results in Proposition 2 demonstrate that these two modifications complement rather than substitute each other. Whereas the portfolio allocation is determined by the habit level, spending is determined by habits as well as the intertemporal elasticity of substitution provided by the non-expected utility model.

## 4. Rebalancing and Long-Term Volatility

We furthermore note the following implication of (7a):

**Observation 3.** *If the government wants to maintain a smooth flow of taxes and government services, the rules for SWF portfolio rebalancing after asset price changes should be formulated so as to safeguard the funds needed to secure this smoothness.*

As a response to price changes in the risky part of the asset portfolio, the portfolio has to be rebalanced to obtain the optimal portfolio weights. Recall that, without habit formation, the risky share of the portfolio should always be the constant $m$. In this case, maintaining the optimal portfolio weights leads to counter-cyclical rebalancing: the fund buys more of the risky asset when its price falls and sells it when the price increases. With backward smoothing modelled as habit formation, counter-cyclical rebalancing may not always be optimal. Consider the following stylised example: An SWF has 100 to invest (e.g., $100 billion). It can be invested in a risky asset with price 100 or in a risk-free asset also with price 100. The price of the risky asset then falls to 98, making it necessary for the portfolio manager to rebalance the asset portfolio of the SWF. The portfolio holdings before and after rebalancing are illustrated in Table 1. In the first two cases, the price decrease makes the portfolio manager invest more in the risky asset (Δrisky investment > 0). While in the first case the fraction of the wealth invested in the risky asset is constant, in the second case the optimal fraction is slightly reduced after the price decrease. In the third case, with a lower risk aversion to begin with than in the second case, the price decrease lowers the total portfolio value so much that it starts to threaten the habit level of consumption. The government investor responds to this threat by reducing the investment in the risky asset (Δrisky investment < 0). As in the second case, the optimal fraction of the wealth invested in the risky asset is reduced after the price fall. This example illustrates that, under habit formation, counter-cyclical rebalancing need not always be the optimal response to a price change in the risky asset. We note that Chambers et al. (2012) also state that portfolio management based on excessively procyclical investing is a common error that should be avoided.

**Table 1.** Example of portfolio rebalancing after a decline in the risky-asset price from 100 to 98. Parameter values: $r = 0.05$, $\mu = 0.05$, $\sigma = 0.2$, $a = 0.3$, $b = 0.25$.

| | Price Risky | Price Risk-Free | Investment before Rebalancing | | Investment after Rebalancing | |
|---|---|---|---|---|---|---|
| **Non-Habit ($\gamma = 2$)** | | | | | | |
| | | | **Risky** | **Risk-Free** | **Risky** | **Risk-Free** |
| Before price change | 100 | 100 | 62.5 | 37.5 | | |
| After price change | 98 | 100 | 61.25 | 37.5 | 61.72 | 37.03 |
| Δrisky investment | | | | | 0.47 | |
| **Habit ($\gamma = 2$, $x = 4$)** | | | | | | |
| | **Price Risky** | **Price Risk-Free** | **Investment before Rebalancing** | | **Investment after Rebalancing** | |
| | | | **Risky** | **Risk-Free** | **Risky** | **Risk-Free** |
| Before price change | 100 | 100 | 37.5 | 62.5 | | |
| After price change | 98 | 100 | 36.75 | 62.5 | 37.03 | 62.22 |
| Δrisky investment | | | | | 0.28 | |
| **Habit ($\gamma = 1.2$, $x = 4$)** | | | | | | |
| | **Price Risky** | **Price Risk-Free** | **Investment before Rebalancing** | | **Investment after Rebalancing** | |
| | | | **Risky** | **Risk-Free** | **Risky** | **Risk-Free** |
| Before price change | 100 | 100 | 62.5 | 37.5 | | |
| After price change | 98 | 100 | 61.25 | 37.5 | 61.2 | 37.55 |
| Δrisky investment | | | | | −0.05 | |

As shown by Sundaresan (1989) and Constantinides (1990), smoothing, such as modelled in Section 3, reduces the volatility of consumption on the short horizon. Indeed, habit formation has been invoked as a mechanism to help explain the empirical smoothness of consumption. The time series of consumption has lower volatility because the consumption level responds less to changes in wealth, compared to the standard model without habit formation. When the wealth increases, the consumption level increases relatively less and similarly for decreases in wealth. The direct effect of this smoothing is a higher variance for the fund value. Although this effect is partially countered by the more conservative investment portfolio, our numerical investigations indicate that the fund's value eventually becomes more volatile. This steeper rise in the long-horizon volatility of the fund value may then even be translated into a higher long-horizon volatility of consumption itself. Thus, although the short-horizon variance is lower with habit formation, the long-horizon variance can be higher for consumption as well as for the fund itself. These insights can be gleaned from inspection of the formulae involved. However, numerical simulations presented in Figure 1 show that the variance of future log-wealth for the case of habit-formation type of smoothing rises much more quickly with the length of the horizon than in the case without such smoothing (in the figure labelled "Non-Habit").[4] The figure shows four different sets of parameter configurations. For all four configurations, the parameters are set so that the investor with habit preferences has the same initial portfolio composition as the investor without habit formation and a coefficient of relative risk aversion of $\gamma = 2$.

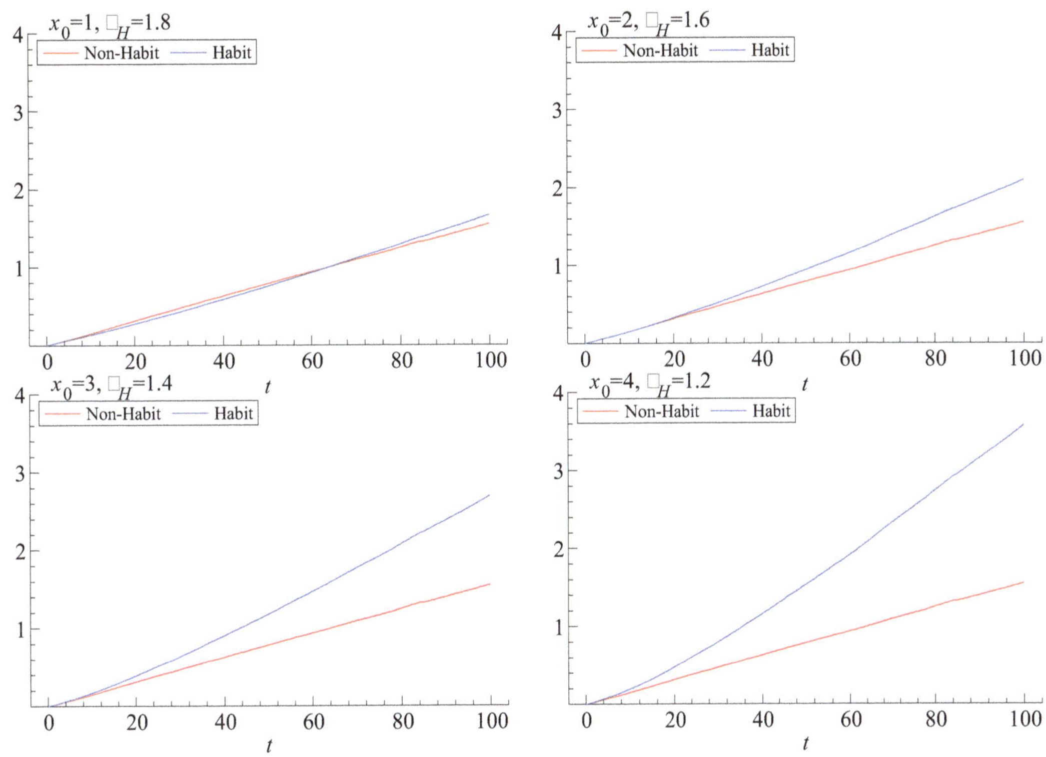


**Figure 1.** Variance of log-wealth at different time horizons t for the investor with non-expected utility, non-habit preferences (Non-habit) and for the investor with non-expected utility, habit preferences (Habit). Parameter values are $\mu = 0.05, \sigma = 0.20, r = 0.05, a = 0.30, b = 0.25, \rho = 0.03, \gamma = 2$, $\varepsilon = 0.1$, and $W_0 = 100$. The variances are estimated from 10,000 simulated observations at each point in time. We use 10 time points per year. The parameter $x_0$ shows the initial habit level, and $\gamma_H$ shows the $\gamma$ coefficient for the investor with habit preferences.

The long-horizon uncertainty of consumption is illustrated in Figure 2. Here, we plot the variances of log-consumption for different time horizons and for different parameter configurations. In three of the cases, we see lower consumption volatility for "short" horizons (say, less than 20 to 50 years) for the smoothing case than for the base case. However, for longer horizons the smoothing investor can face far more variation in consumption. This increase comes as a consequence of the riskier wealth illustrated in Figure 1.

This exercise teaches us an important lesson: smoothness comes at a price. We can smooth current consumption by using the fund as a buffer. But then we tamper with the fund's principal. In so doing, we affect future consumption indirectly and hence future habit levels, which in turn influence consumption even further out. Short-term convenience carries long-term costs.

---

4 Calculations are performed using Ox, see Doornik (2007).

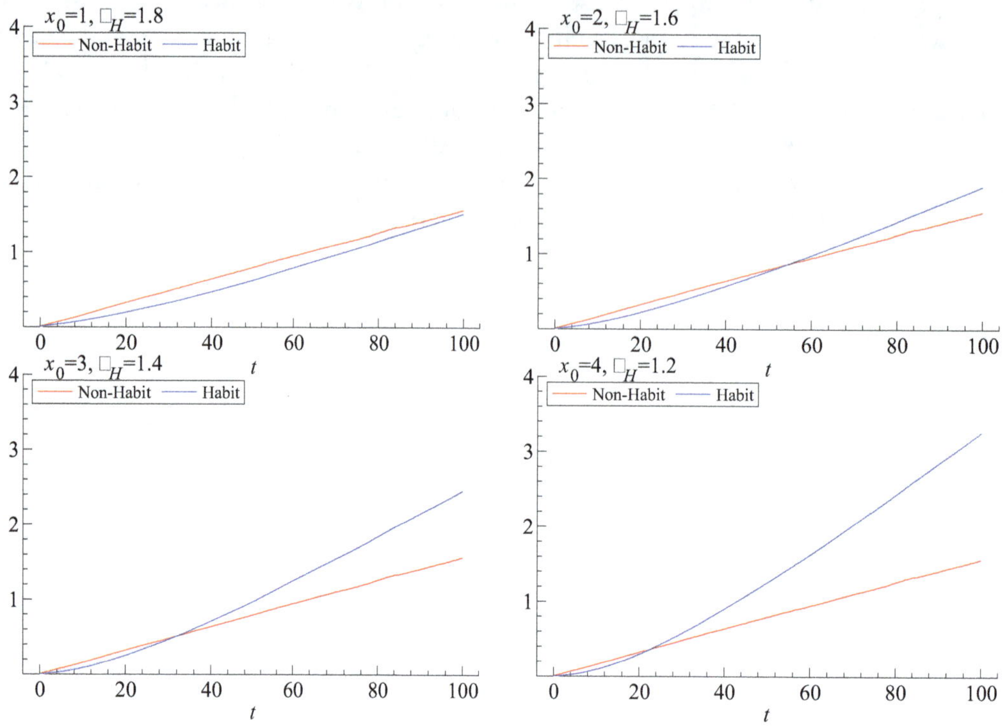


**Figure 2.** Variance of log-consumption at different time horizons t for the investor with non-expected utility, non-habit preferences (Non-habit) and for the investor with non-expected utility, habit preferences (Habit). Parameter values are $\mu = 0.05$, $\sigma = 0.20$, $r = 0.05$, $a = 0.30$, $b = 0.25$, $\rho = 0.03$, $\gamma = 2$, $\varepsilon = 0.1$, and $W_0 = 100$. The variances are estimated from 10,000 simulated observations at each point in time. We use 10 time points per year. The parameter $x_0$ shows the initial habit level and $\gamma_H$ shows the $\gamma$ coefficient for the investor with habit preferences.

Provided the smoothing modelled as habits really is part of preferences, the trade-off between short-term smoothness and long-term uncertainty is done optimally. Figure 3 shows what would happen to the variance of log-consumption at various time horizons if the investment and spending decisions were separated so that the risky share of the portfolio were kept constant even though spending is based on the above implications of the habit model. The separation of spending and investment decisions leads to higher variability of consumption. At least as interesting is the fact that the separated rules eventually become inconsistent in all four examples, illustrated by the fact that the graph for the variance of log-consumption ends prematurely for the case of constant equity share (labelled "Habit mixed" in the figure). This phenomenon arises because keeping the risky share fixed fails to safeguard the funding of the minimal, habit-determined rates of future spending for some states of the world. Thus, the investor/consumer ends up in what Lax (2002) refers to as the insolvency range.[5]

We summarize these observations as:

**Observation 4.** *The smoothing of consumption tends to carry a price in the form of a wider uncertainty of the long-run prospects for consumption. This uncertainty is mitigated by the optimal modification of portfolio rebalancing, but it is not removed.*

5 Out of the 10,000 simulated consumption paths used to construct each of the four graphs for the variance of log-consumption (labeled "Habit mixed"), insolvency happens in 178, 227, 288, and 387 consumption paths, respectively, with the number increasing in the initial habit level $x_0$.

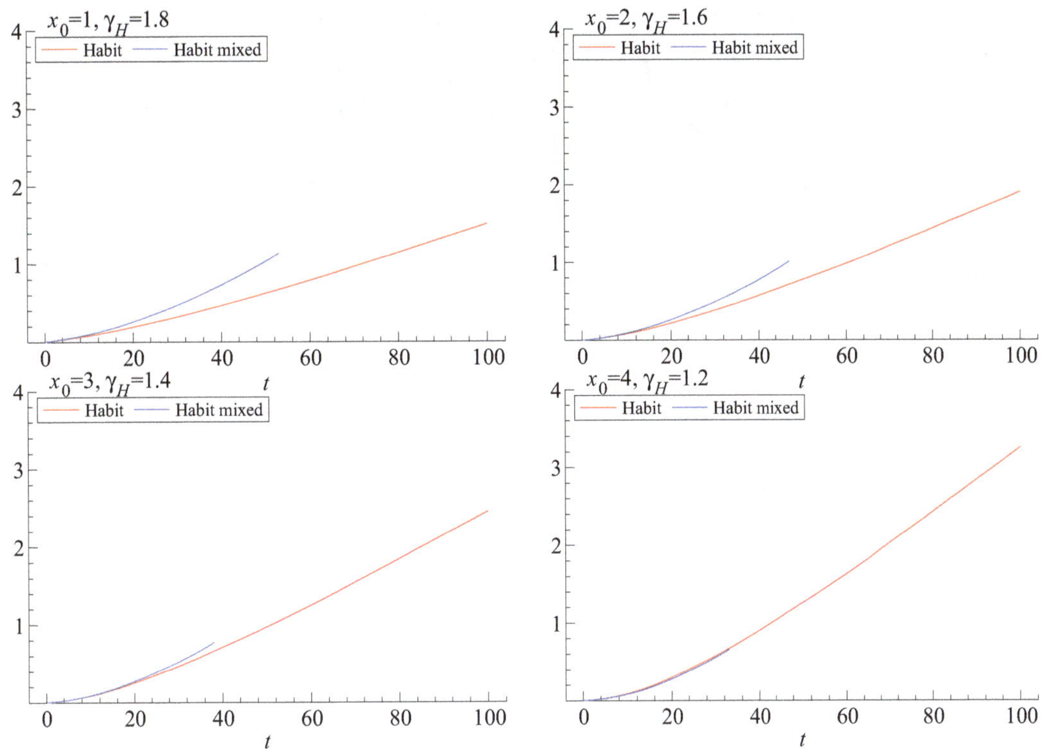


**Figure 3.** Variance of log-consumption at different time horizons t for two investors. The first is for the investor with non-expected utility, habit preferences (Habit). The second is for an investor with non-expected utility, habit preferences. This investor consumes as the habit-investor, but uses the portfolio weights for the investor with non-habit preferences (Mixed habit). Parameter values are $\mu = 0.05$, $\sigma = 0.20$, $r = 0.05$, $a = 0.30$, $b = 0.25$, $\rho = 0.03$, $\gamma = 2$, $\varepsilon = 0.1$, and $W_0 = 100$. The variances are estimated from 10,000 simulated observations at each point in time. We use 10 time points per year. The parameter $x_0$ shows the initial habit level and $\gamma_H$ shows the $\gamma$ coefficient for the investor with habit preferences.

## 5. Time-Varying Risk-Free Rates

In this section we extend the analysis to account for interest-rate uncertainty. In practice, risk-free rates are not constant over time. In fact, recent decades have seen a long global trend of falling real interest rates since the mid-1980s, as documented, e.g., by King and Low (2014) and Rachel and Smith (2015). With a less than unit elasticity of intertemporal substitution, a permanent drop in the risk-free rate should obviously imply a corresponding reduction of the optimal draw on an SWF, as indicated by (4b). However, some authors, such as the Organization for Economic Co-operation and Development (OECD 2014), argue that the recent long decline is likely to be reversed, at least partially. We now turn to the question of what the optimal draw should be under these conditions.

For this purpose, we need a specification of the dynamically stochastic variation in the instantaneous risk-free rate. For tractability, we use the mean-reverting diffusion process introduced by Vasicek (1977):

$$r(t) = \theta(r^* - r(t))dt + \zeta d\xi(t),\ \theta \geq 0, \tag{8}$$

where $\xi(t)$ is a Wiener process, possibly correlated with $B(t)$, $r^*$ is the steady-state riskless return rate, $\theta$ the speed of return towards this rate after deviations (also known as the force of gravity), and $\zeta$ is the instantaneous standard deviation of $r(t)$. This specification is consistent with the OECD's expectation.

When the risk-free rate varies over time, the question also arises whether the equity premium stays constant or whether the expected equity return stays constant instead, so that the equity premium varies inversely with the risk-free rate. We choose to remain agnostic about this issue and use a specification of the equity premium that encompasses both cases:

$$\mu(t) = \mu(r(t)) = \lambda\overline{\mu} + (1-\lambda)(\varphi - r(t)), \;\; 0 \leq \lambda \leq 1, \tag{9}$$

where $\overline{\mu}$ denotes the risk premium if constant ($\lambda = 1$) and $\varphi$ the expected equity return if that is constant instead ($\lambda = 0$). With this modification, the diffusion process for wealth now becomes,

$$dW(t) = \{[r(t) + \alpha(t)\mu(t)]W(t) - c(t)\}dt + \alpha(t)\sigma W(t)dB(t). \tag{10}$$

In Appendices A.1 and A.4, we carry out the analysis of this case in the absence of habit formation. In Appendix A.5 we show that an extension to habit formation yields results that are closely approximated by those without habit formation provided that the elasticity of intertemporal substitution is small.

In the absence of habit formation, we note that the Bellman Equation (2) also needs to be modified to allow for the time variation in the riskless rate:

$$0 = \max_{c(t),\alpha(t)} \left\{ c(t)^{1-\delta} - \rho U(W(t), r(t))^{(1-\delta)/(1-\gamma)} + \frac{1}{dt}[E_t dU(W(t), r(t))]^{(1-\delta)/(1-\gamma)} \right\}. \tag{11}$$

As shown in Appendix A.1, the time variability of the risk-free rate does not change the result that the optimal draw is proportional to the wealth level. However, the proportionality factor is now a function of the risk-free rate. This function is the solution to a non-linear, second-order differential equation. Although a closed-form solution to this equation may exist, our interest focuses on its semi-elasticity with respect to the risk-free rate. As shown in Appendix A.4, this elasticity can be approximated around the steady-state risk-free rate of return $r^*$ by means of the method used by Campbell and Viceira (2002) in their Chapter 5. Appendices A.1, A.4 and A.5 thus prove the following:

**Proposition 3.** *If the risk-free return varies over time according to (14), the optimal SWF draw, as a ratio of wealth, should respond to time variations in the risk-free rate according to:*

$$d\ln\eta(r)/dr \cong (1-\varepsilon)[1-(1-\lambda)\alpha^*]/(\eta^* + \theta) < (1-\varepsilon)/\eta^* = d\ln\eta^*/dr^*, \tag{12}$$

*provided $\varepsilon < 1$, where $\eta^*$ denotes the value of $\eta$ if the risk-free rate is constant at its steady-state value, as defined in (4b), and $\alpha^*$ is the optimal equity share for $r = r^*$. This result holds as a close approximation even with habit formation provided $\varepsilon$ is small.*

This intuitive formula shows that the reaction to dynamically stochastic variation in the risk-free rate should have the same sign as the comparative-static response, but be smaller in absolute value because of the expectation of an eventual mean reversion.[6] The difference between the two responses depends positively on $\lambda$ and negatively on $\theta$. $\lambda = 0$ means that an increase in the risk-free rate lowers the equity premium and thus reduces the incentive for risk taking, so that the portfolio return is raised by somewhat less than the rise in the riskless rate, which in turn dampens the effect on the optimal draw rate. In contrast, $\lambda = 1$ means that the equity premium is unaffected by the variation in the risk-free rate, so that this dampening disappears.

---

6 We also note that, in both cases, the response has the sign as $1 - \varepsilon$. This is because the effect on consumption is dominated by the wealth effect when $\varepsilon < 1$. When $\varepsilon > 1$, the substitution effect dominates, so that the investor will want to postpone consumption when the risk-free rate rises, so that current consumption falls. We believe, however, that SWF decision makers tend to think mainly in terms of the wealth effect in this regard, which is consistent with our presumption that epsilon can be assumed to be quite small in the context of SWF management.

As expected, the effect on the optimal draw rate is furthermore dampened by $\theta$, the speed of the mean-reversion adjustment. Thus, the expectation that the risk-free rate eventually returns to normal allows for a smoothing of SWF draws relative to movements in this rate. This is true even if the return path is rocky in the sense of a large $\zeta$. The larger the speed of this mean-reversion adjustment, the stronger the smoothing. If the deviation from the steady state is truly ephemeral ($\theta \to \infty$), the smoothing is complete. If, however, the mean reversion is expected to take very long, the smoothing should be very modest.

We summarize this insight as:

**Observation 5.** *The rule for SWF draws should smooth over changes in the risk-free return provided they are temporary. The strength of the optimal smoothing depends on the expected speed of return to normal, even if the return path is rocky. The smoothing should be even stronger if the movements in the risk-free return leaves the expected return on equity unchanged.*

**Proposition 4.** *If the risk-free return varies over time according to (14), the optimal equity share becomes:*

$$\alpha(r(t)) = \mu(r(t))/\left(\gamma\sigma^2\right) - (1 - 1\gamma)\beta\left[1 - (1 - \lambda)\alpha^*\right](\eta^* + \theta), \tag{13}$$

*where $\beta$ denotes the theoretical regression coefficient of $\zeta d\xi$ on $\sigma dB$.*

Again, the proof is contained in Appendices A.1 and A.4. The first term indicates an inverse relationship between the risk-free rate and the equity share if a drop in the risk-free rate implies a higher equity premium. That would be the case if, as argued by Hall (2016) and Caballero et al. (2008) regarding the recent long decline in real interest rates, such a decline is due to an increase in the risk aversion of the marginal investor in global markets.

Compared to (4a), this formula furthermore has an additional term which reflects the dynamic risk of future changes in the risk-free rate. We assume $\beta \leq 0$ because a drop in the risk-free rate tends to coincide with higher stock valuations, other things being equal. The entire second term, including the minus sign in front of it, is positive provided $\gamma > 1$, which we view as the normal case. Thus, the risk of a future drop in the risk-free rate calls for a somewhat higher equity share as a dynamic hedge against such a drop. Not surprisingly, this effect is weaker if risk aversion is lower and is actually reversed if risk aversion is very low ($\gamma < 1$).[7]

We summarize these insights as

**Observation 6.** *A temporary decline in the risk-free rate calls for an increase in the equity share if this change leaves the expected equity return unchanged. For a reasonably risk-averse investor, the uncertainty of future risk-free rates, furthermore, calls for a somewhat higher equity share as a dynamic hedge provided a drop in the risk-free rate is associated with a higher equity return.*

## 6. Conclusions and Future Work

Using the proceeds of a SWF as a regular supplement to other government revenues makes sense in an advanced economy with a sizeable SWF. However, this practice offers greater complications than it may seem at first.

A rule permitting annual draws corresponding to the expected real return is optimal only under highly restrictive conditions. Our analysis uses Epstein–Zin preferences, which allows us to distinguish between risk aversion and aversion to planned changes over time. Within this framework, we find that

---

7 Indeed, if the inverse link between innovations in equity prices and the risk-free rate is strong enough, a risk neutral investor could decide to hold a short net equity position so as to take advantage of the ensuing fall in equity prices as well as the rise in the riskless rate should the latter occur. We do not pursue this extreme case, however.

a fiscal rule derived from the expected real return is optimal if policy makers' elasticity of intertemporal substitution is small. However, unless risk is negligible or risk aversion extremely low, the annual draws should be considerably lower than the expected real return as an allowance for risk.

Furthermore, in the presence of risk, such a rule makes fiscal policy bumpy as either tax rates or government services (or both) must move in response to the vagaries of financial markets. This problem can be mitigated by introducing the responses to market returns gradually over time, which we refer to as backward smoothing and the model as habit formation. However, backward smoothing requires lower risk taking, which in turn implies lower return on average. Thus, smoothing can be bought at the expense of lower average SWF draws. Moreover, risk taking must not only be lower, but should move countercyclically relative to the financial markets. Rebalancing should be modified as well so that, in some instances, the SWF should sell rather than buy equity after a stock market decline. Ignoring this implication may lead to premature depletion of the fund. As a final implication, backward smoothing, although dampening short-term uncertainty about SWF draws, will typically increase long-term uncertainty about future draws.

These insights make us critical of the Norwegian fiscal rule. By allowing draws corresponding to the expected real return it ignores risk. By permitting temporary deviations from the real-return rule, it does allow backward smoothing; but it ignores its implications for risk taking and rebalancing.

Our conclusions are somewhat more upbeat in regard to the implications of stochastic movements in the riskless rate over time. When this rate declines, as has been observed in recent years, the SWF draws should decline as well; however, in this case, smoothing does indeed make sense. Moreover, dynamic risks to the instantaneously riskless rate actually call for a somewhat higher equity share as a hedge against the dynamic risk.

We believe these insights to be important food for thought for policy makers in developed countries with sizeable SWFs. However, we also realize that the analysis in this paper only scratches the surface. Just as most households receive labor income in addition to capital income, a government collects taxes. Furthermore, tax revenues as well as spending needs tend to vary with the business cycle, which in turn tends to correlate with stock returns as well as real interest rates. Active, countercyclical fiscal policy adds further volatility to these fluctuations. In the context of an SWF, this means that the policy makers not only want to smooth the draws on the fund relative to returns; they may even want the draws to fluctuate in the opposite direction. Such opposite fluctuations would translate into attacks on the fund's principal in bad economic times, which could add to the long-term fluctuations and jeopardize the fund's solvency if caution is not taken.

We intend to take up these and other issues in our future research. As is well known from the context of household behavior, the presence of non-capital income sources presents no new complication if markets are complete. However, this assumption is especially problematic in the context of government finances, as moral hazard, dynamic inconsistency, and poor contract enforceability mean that a government's future tax revenues cannot be capitalized. As is well known, exact analytical solutions are then no longer available except in uninteresting cases like quadratic utility.

Viceira (2001) has worked out approximate solutions for optimal consumption and investment for an individual with stochastic labor income under the assumption that permanent changes in labor income are the main determinants of spending behavior. Benzoni et al. (2007) similarly study co-integration between stock and labor markets. However, these approaches are unsuitable for studying the implications of cyclical variations in government spending and revenues. Thus, we expect that we will need to rely on simulation exercises to obtain numerical solutions.

**Author Contributions:** Conceptualization, K.A.M. and S.L.; methodology, K.A.M.; software, S.L.; validation, K.A.M. and S.L.; formal analysis, K.A.M.; investigation, K.A.M. and S.L.; writing—original draft preparation, K.A.M.; writing—review and editing, S.L. and K.A.M.; visualization, S.L.

**Funding:** This research received no external funding.

**Acknowledgments:** Valuable comments by John Campbell, Espen Henriksen, Hans Jørgen Tranvåg, NTNU colleagues, and seminar participants at BI Norwegian Business School and the Norges Bank Investment Management. Egil Matsen provided valuable encouragement at the beginning of the project.

**Conflicts of Interest:** The authors declare no conflict of interest.

## Appendix A. Optimal Investment and Consumption with Epstein–Zin Preferences in Continuous Time, with Time-Changing Risk-Free Rate and/or Habit Formation

### Appendix A.1. General Setup

We start with the value function for Epstein–Zin preferences in discrete time:

$$e^{\rho t}V_t(W_t,r_t)^{1-\delta} = \max_{c_t,\alpha_t}\left\{e^{\rho t}c_t^{1-\delta}\Delta t + e^{\rho(t+\Delta t)}E_t[V_{t+\Delta t}(W_{t+\Delta t},r_{t+\Delta t})^{1-\gamma}]^{(1-\delta)/(1-\gamma)}\right\}. \tag{A1}$$

Define $U_t(W_t,r_t) = V_t(W_t,r_t)^{1-\gamma}$. Then, the value function may be rearranged and written as,

$$0 = \max_{c_t,\alpha_t}\left\{e^{\rho t}c_t^{1-\delta}\Delta t + e^{\rho(t+\Delta t)}E_t[U_{t+\Delta t}(W_{t+\Delta t},r_{t+\Delta t})]^{(1-\delta)/(1-\gamma)} - e^{\rho t}U_t(W_t,r_t)^{(1-\delta)/(1-\gamma)}\right\}.$$

Division by $e^{\rho t}\Delta t$ and taking the limit as $\Delta t \searrow 0$ now gives us the Bellman equation in continuous time:

$$0 = \max_{c,\alpha}\left\{c^{1-\delta} - \rho U(W,r)^{(1-\delta)/(1-\gamma)} + \frac{1}{dt}[E_t dU(W,r)]^{(1-\delta)/(1-\gamma)}\right\}. \tag{A2}$$

where dates $t$ have been omitted except for the expectations operator.

The dynamic budget constraints are as follows:

$$dW = [(r+\alpha\mu)W - (1+\tau)c]dt + \alpha W\sigma dB(t), \;\; \mu = \lambda\overline{\mu} + (1-\lambda)(\varphi - r), \tag{A3}$$

$$dr = \theta(r^* - r)dt + \zeta d\xi(t), \; \theta \geq 0. \tag{A4}$$

Here, $B$ and $\xi$ are Wiener processes for equity returns and the risk-free rate, respectively. $\mu$ is the equity premium, which is time invariant and equal to $\overline{\mu}$ if $\lambda = 1$. If $\lambda = 0$, the expected equity return, is time invariant instead and equal to $\varphi$, so that the equity return moves one for one in opposite directions of the risk-free rate. $\tau$ is a consumption tax whose significance will be apparent in Appendix A.3.

We follow Campbell and Viceira (2002) by working with a second-order expansion of the value function under the conjecture that,

$$V(W,r) = \Phi(r)W. \tag{A5}$$

Then, ignoring higher-order terms, we have:

$$\begin{aligned} dV &= V_W dW + V_r dr + \tfrac{1}{2}V_{WW}dW^2 + \tfrac{1}{2}V_{rr}dr^2 + V_{Wr}dWdr \\ &= \Phi(r)dW + \Phi'(r)Wdr + \tfrac{1}{2}\Phi''(r)Wdr^2 + \Phi'(r)dWdr. \end{aligned}$$

Substituting from the budget constraints, this can be further written as:

$$\begin{aligned} dV = \Phi(r)W\Big\{\Big[&(1-\alpha(1-\lambda))r + \alpha(\lambda\overline{\mu} + (1-\lambda)\varphi) - (1+\tau)c/W + \frac{\Phi'}{\Phi}\theta(r^* - r) + \frac{1}{2}\frac{\Phi''}{\Phi}\zeta^2 \\ &+ \frac{\Phi'}{\Phi}\alpha\sigma\zeta\rho_{B\xi}\Big]dt + \alpha\sigma dB + \frac{\Phi'}{\Phi}\zeta d\xi\Big\}, \end{aligned}$$

where $\rho_{B\xi}$ is the correlation coefficient between $dB$ and $d\xi$.

By Itô's lemma, this gives us:

$$E_t dU = (1-\gamma)U\Big\{(1-\alpha(1-\lambda))r + \alpha(\lambda\overline{\mu} + (1-\lambda)\varphi) - (1+\tau)c/W + \frac{\Phi'}{\Phi}\theta(r^* - r) + \frac{1}{2}\frac{\Phi''}{\Phi}\zeta^2 + \frac{\Phi'}{\Phi}\alpha\sigma\zeta\rho_{B\xi} - \frac{1}{2}\gamma\left[\alpha^2\sigma^2 + \left(\frac{\Phi'}{\Phi}\right)^2\zeta^2 + 2\frac{\Phi'}{\Phi}\alpha\sigma\zeta\rho_{B\xi}\right]\Big\}dt.$$

Using polynomial expansion, ignoring higher-order terms of $dt$, this furthermore gives us:

$$E_t dU^{(1-\delta)/(1-\gamma)} = (1-\delta)U\Big\{(1-\alpha(1-\lambda))r + \alpha(\lambda\overline{\mu} + (1-\lambda)\varphi) - (1+\tau)c/W + \frac{\Phi'}{\Phi}\theta(r^* - r) + \frac{1}{2}\frac{\Phi''}{\Phi}\sigma^2 + \frac{\Phi'}{\Phi}\alpha\sigma\zeta\rho_{B\xi} - \frac{1}{2}\gamma\left[\alpha^2\sigma^2 + \left(\frac{\Phi'}{\Phi}\right)^2\zeta^2 + 2\frac{\Phi'}{\Phi}\alpha\sigma\zeta\rho_{B\xi}\right]\Big\}dt.$$

After dividing through by $U^{(1-\delta)/(1-\gamma)}$, this allows us to write the Bellman equation as:

$$\begin{aligned} 0 = \max_{c,\alpha}\Big\{& c^{1-\delta}\Phi^{-(1-\delta)}W^{-(1-\delta)} - \rho \\ &+ (1-\delta)\left[(1-\alpha(1-\lambda))r + \alpha(\lambda\overline{\mu} + (1-\lambda)\varphi) - \tfrac{1}{2}\gamma\alpha^2\sigma^2 - (1+\tau)c/W\right] \\ &+ (1-\delta)\frac{\Phi'}{\Phi}[\theta(r^* - r) + \alpha(1-\gamma)\beta\sigma^2] + \tfrac{1}{2}(1-\delta)\left[\frac{\Phi''}{\Phi} - \gamma\left(\frac{\Phi'}{\Phi}\right)^2\right]\zeta^2\Big\}, \end{aligned} \tag{A6}$$

where $\beta \equiv \rho_{B\xi}\zeta/\sigma$ is the theoretical regression coefficient of $\zeta d\xi$ on $\sigma dB$.

The first- order condition for $c$ is now easily obtained as:

$$c = (1+\tau)^{-1/\delta}\Phi(r)^{1-1/\delta}W. \tag{A7}$$

Define $\eta(r) = (1+\tau)^{1-1/\delta}\Phi(r)^{1-1/\delta}$, so that,

$$c = \left(\frac{1}{1+\tau}\right)\eta(r)W. \tag{A8}$$

Then, obviously,

$$\Phi(r) = (1+\tau)\eta(r)^{-\delta/(1-\delta)},$$

which implies,

$$\frac{\Phi'}{\Phi} = -\frac{\delta}{1-\delta}\eta'/\eta \tag{A9a}$$

$$\frac{\Phi''}{\Phi} = -\frac{\delta}{1-\delta}\left[\left(\frac{1}{1-\delta}\right)(\eta'/\eta)^2 - \eta''/\eta\right]. \tag{A9b}$$

Then,

$$\frac{1}{2}(1-\delta)[\frac{\Phi''}{\Phi} - \gamma\left(\frac{\Phi'}{\Phi}\right)^2]\zeta^2 = \frac{1}{2}\delta\left[\left(\frac{1-\gamma\delta}{1-\delta}\right)(\eta'/\eta)^2 - \eta''/\eta\right]\zeta^2.$$

Substituting, we can now write the Bellman equation as:

$$\begin{aligned} 0 = \max_{\alpha}\Big\{&\delta\eta - \rho + (1-\delta)\left[(1-\alpha(1-\lambda))r + \alpha(\lambda\overline{\mu} + (1-\lambda)\varphi) - \tfrac{1}{2}\gamma\alpha^2\sigma^2\right] \\ &- \delta[\theta(r^* - r) + \alpha(1-\gamma)\beta\sigma^2]\eta'/\eta + \tfrac{1}{2}\delta\left[\left(\tfrac{1-\gamma\delta}{1-\delta}\right)(\eta'/\eta)^2 - \eta''/\eta\right]\zeta^2\Big\}. \end{aligned}$$

Maximization with respect to $\alpha$ gives:

$$\alpha = \frac{\mu(r)}{\gamma\sigma^2} - \left(\frac{\delta}{1-\delta}\right)\left(\frac{1-\gamma}{\gamma}\right)\beta\eta'/\eta, \quad \mu(r) = \lambda\overline{\mu} + (1-\lambda)(\varphi - r). \tag{A10}$$

Define now $\mu^* = \mu(r^*)$, so that $\mu(r) = \mu^* + (1-\lambda)(r^* - r)$).

After substitution of these formulae, the Bellman equation boils down to:

$$\begin{aligned} 0 &= \eta - \varepsilon\rho - (1-\varepsilon)r - \theta(r^* - r)\eta'/\eta \\ &-(1-\varepsilon)\left[\tfrac{\mu^*}{\gamma\sigma^2} + \tfrac{1-\lambda}{\gamma\sigma^2}(r^* - r) - \tfrac{1-1/\gamma}{1-\varepsilon}\beta\eta'/\eta\right][\mu^* + (1-\lambda)(r^* - r)] \\ &+(1-\varepsilon)\tfrac{1}{2}\left[\tfrac{\mu^*}{\gamma\sigma^2} + \tfrac{1-\lambda}{\gamma\sigma^2}(r^* - r) - \tfrac{1-1/\gamma}{1-\varepsilon}\beta\eta'/\eta\right]^2 \gamma\sigma^2 \\ &-\left\{1-\gamma\right)\left[\tfrac{\mu^*}{\gamma\sigma^2} + \tfrac{1-\lambda}{\gamma\sigma^2}(r^* - r) - \tfrac{1-1/\gamma}{1-\varepsilon}\beta\eta'/\eta\right]\beta\sigma^2\eta'/\eta \\ &+\tfrac{1}{2}\left[\left(\tfrac{\gamma-\varepsilon}{1-\varepsilon}\right)(\eta'/\eta)^2 - \eta''/\eta\right]\zeta^2, \end{aligned} \tag{A11}$$

where $\varepsilon \equiv 1/\delta$ is the elasticity of intertemporal substitution.

*Appendix A.2. Constant Risk-Free Rate*

In this case, $r = r^*$ and $\zeta^2 = 0$ Thus, $\Phi$ and $\eta$ are constants. From (A10) and (A11), we then find:

$$\alpha = \frac{\mu}{\gamma\sigma^2} \equiv m \tag{A12}$$

$$\eta = \varepsilon\rho + (1-\varepsilon)\left(r + m\mu - \frac{1}{2}\gamma m^2\sigma^2\right) = \varepsilon\rho + (1-\varepsilon)\left(r + \frac{1}{2}m\mu\right). \tag{A13}$$

From (A8), we see that the optimal consumption level as a share of wealth is $\eta$ divided by one plus the consumption tax rate, if any. These results generalize those of Merton (1969). To our knowledge, they were first derived by Svensson (1989), with the exception of the consumption tax. However, we find our slightly different derivation method to be more amenable to applications with a time-varying riskless rate and habit formation.

*Appendix A.3. Habit Formation*

In this section, we assume a constant risk-free rate. We model habit formation by letting $y \equiv c - x$ replace $c$ in the preference ordering, where $x$ is the habit level. Following Constantinides (1990), we assume that the habit level moves over time according to the constraint:

$$x = e^{-at}x_0 + b\int_0^t e^{a(s-t)}c(s)ds,\ a \geq 0,\ b \geq 0,\ b < r + a, \tag{A14}$$

where $x_0$ is exogenous, which implies,

$$dx = (bc - ax)dt \equiv bydt + (b-a)xdt. \tag{A15}$$

Constantinides has derived formulas for optimal consumption and equity with this specification of habit formation with expected utility. We now proceed to show that these results also hold under the specification of non-expected utility in Appendix A.1.

Our proof starts with the observation that, with our specification of habit formation, utility becomes infinitely negative if $y = c - x < 0$. With normally distributed equity returns, there is a non-zero probability that the return on equity at some point will be less than any arbitrarily negative number. It then follows that the habit level of consumption must be funded by investment in the safe asset only.

Thus, we may think of the investor-consumer as managing two separate portfolios. One portfolio, whose value we denote $\mathcal{X}$, is held for the exclusive purpose of funding the habit level $x$. The other portfolio, denoted $\mathcal{Y}$, is invested in order to fund the "surplus" level of consumption, $y$. We continue to let $W$ denote total wealth, so that:

$$W = \mathcal{X} + \mathcal{Y}. \tag{A16}$$

Because the habit level in general will move over time, the value of its funding portfolio, $\mathcal{X}$, will generally need to move as well. Thus, it is not sufficient to maintain $\mathcal{X} = x/r$ because then the entire return on this portfolio will be absorbed by the current habit level. This means that the investor-consumer must make a regular transfer from the "surplus" portfolio $\mathcal{Y}$ to the "habit" portfolio $\mathcal{X}$. If $a > b$ these transfers may be negative, but that does not change the argument.

Let $v$ denote the transfer. We may then specify the budget constraints for the two portfolios as:

$$d\mathcal{Y} = [(r + \alpha'\mu)\mathcal{Y} - y]dt - vdt + \alpha'\mathcal{Y}\sigma dB \tag{A17}$$

and

$$d\mathcal{X} = r\mathcal{X}dt - xdt + vdt. \tag{A18}$$

where $\alpha'$ now denotes the equity share of the surplus portfolio $\mathcal{Y}$, not necessarily constant. Here, we have implicitly assumed that the consumption tax on $c$ is zero.

Based on Constantinides' results for the case of expected utility, we conjecture that optimization requires:

$$\mathcal{X} = x/(r + a - b). \tag{A19}$$

Under this conjecture, (A18) implies:

$$dx = (b - a)xdt + (r + a - b)vdt.$$

This condition is equivalent to the flow condition for habit formation (A15) if and only if,

$$v = \left(\frac{b}{r + a - b}\right)y. \tag{A20}$$

Consider now an arbitrary path for $y$. Given (A20) and (A17), this path for $v$ is just sufficient to fund the path of the habit level as given by (A15). If, at any time, a lower value of $v$ is chosen, the implied size of the habit portfolio $\mathcal{X}$ will be insufficient to fund the habit level implied by (A15), so it is not feasible. If, on the other hand, a higher value is chosen, it will be wasted because the habit portfolio will become excessively large. Thus, (A20) indicates the optimal path for the transfer amount v for an arbitrary path of $y$.

Next, consider the optimal surplus consumption path $y$. Note, then, that the optimal transfer level $v$, given by (A20), is linear in $y$. Thus, it has the same form as a consumption tax with:

$$\tau = b/(r + a - b).$$

From (A8), we then see that the optimal level of surplus consumption must be:

$$y = \left(\frac{r + a - b}{r + a}\right)\eta\mathcal{Y}.$$

Thus, using (A16), the definition of $y$, and the conjecture in (A19), we find,

$$c = x + \left(\frac{r + a - b}{r + a}\right)\eta[W - x/(r + a - b)]. \tag{A21}$$

For the conjecture in (A19) to hold, it suffices that the investor-consumer at time 0 sets aside:

$$X_0 = x_0/(r + a - b) \tag{A22}$$

as the initial habit portfolio.

Thus, habit formation according to (A14) requires two kinds of set-aside into the habit portfolio. First, at time 0, the investor-consumer must set aside the initial amount in (A22). Then, for $t > 0$, a transfer into this portfolio must continuously be made as indicated by (A20)

It is worth noting that the continuous transfers for $t > 0$ disappear if $b = 0$. The reason is that the habit level $x$ then will shrink over time, as can be seen from (A15), so that the habit portfolio can be allowed to shrink as well. If both $a = 0$ and $b = 0$, the habit level of consumption is given once and for all, and the habit portfolio will remain constant at $x_0/r$.

Lastly, consider the optimal equity share in this context. From (A12), we find $\alpha'(t) = m$, so that:

$$\alpha = m\mathcal{Y}/W = m\left[\frac{W - x/(r+a-b)}{W}\right]. \tag{A23}$$

This completes our proof that Constantinides' results generalize to the case of an Epstein–Zin non-expected preference ordering in continuous time.

*Appendix A.4. Time-Varying Risk-Free Rate*

For this section, the consumption tax plays no role, so that we assume $\tau = 0$. We start with Equation (A11), which is a second-order non-linear differential equation in $\eta(r)$. Rather than trying to derive an exact solution, we follow Campbell and Viceira in approximating this function around $r^*$ as follows:

$$\eta \approx \eta^* + \eta^* \ln \eta(r - r^*),$$
$$\ln \eta(r - r^*) \approx C_0 + C_1(r - r^*).$$

We then readily find,

$$\eta'/\eta \approx C_1$$
$$\eta''/\eta \approx C_1^2$$

Substituting this into (A11) and ignoring quadratic terms in $(r^* - r)$, we obtain the following equation:

$$0 = \eta^*[1 + C_0 + C_1(r - r^*)] - (1-\varepsilon)r - \theta(r^* - r)C_1 - (1-\varepsilon)(1-\lambda)\alpha^*(r^* - r)$$
$$+ \text{ terms independent of } r.$$

This equation must hold as an identity in $r$, which means that we can use the method of undetermined coefficients to identify the parameters $C_0$ and $C_1$. In particular, the coefficients multiplying $r$ must sum to zero. Thus,

$$C_1 = \eta'/\eta = (1-\varepsilon)[1 - (1-\lambda)\alpha^*]/(\eta^* + \theta) \leq (1-\varepsilon)/\eta^*, \tag{A24}$$

where $\alpha^* = \frac{\mu^*}{\gamma\sigma^2} - \left(\frac{1-1/\gamma}{1-\varepsilon}\right)\beta\eta'/\eta$.

*Appendix A.5. Time-Varying Risk-Free Rate with Habit Formation*

This analysis is carried out for the simplified case of $a = b$, so that:

$$dx = aydt.$$

However, the analysis carries over to the more general case. For the sub-portfolio $\mathcal{X}$ to support the habit, we must have:

$$x = r(t)\mathcal{X},$$

so that,

$$dx = r(t)d\mathcal{X} + \mathcal{X}dr.$$

Also, as before,

$$d\mathcal{X} = r(t)\mathcal{X} - xdt + vdt.$$

Thus,

$$dx = \mathcal{X}dr + r(t)d\mathcal{X} = \mathcal{X}dr + r(t)^2\mathcal{X} - r(t)xdt + r(t)vdt$$
$$= \mathcal{X}dr + r(t)xdt - r(t)xdt + r(t)vdt = r(t)vdt + \mathcal{X}dr.$$

Equating the two equations for dx, we find:

$$vdt = \left(\frac{a}{r(t)}\right)ydt - \left(\frac{x(t)}{r(t)}\right)dr.$$

This means that $v(t)$ will not be proportional to $y(t)$ with a fixed proportionality factor. Thus, the implicit consumption tax rate,

$$\tau = \frac{v(t)}{y(t)}$$

will not be constant, but a function of $r(t)$. This function is decreasing because, with a higher interest rate, the safe sub-portfolio $\mathcal{X}$ can fund a larger habit level of consumption, so that less needs to be set aside for this purpose.

The question is the extent to which the general properties of the model are affected by this change. In Section A.1, the derivations are unaffected by this change until the first-order condition (A17), which we now write as:

$$c = (1+\tau(r))^{-1/\delta}\Phi(r)^{1-1/\delta}W.$$

If we again define $\eta(r) = (1+\tau(r))^{1-1/\delta}\Phi(r)^{1-1/\delta}$, the subsequent derivations will be riddled with various terms containing the derivative $\tau(r)$. However, we can avoid this complication by redefining:

$$\eta(r) = \Phi(r)^{1-1/\delta}.$$

Then, although the optimal consumption follows the somewhat more complicated formula,

$$c = (1+\tau(r))^{-1/\delta}\eta(r)W,$$

Equations (A9a) and (A2) will continue to hold. Furthermore, the exponent $-1/\delta = -\varepsilon$, is the negative of the intertemporal substitution, which we have assumed to be small.

The terms involving $c$ in the Bellman Equation (A6) become:

$$c^{1-\delta}\Phi^{-(1-\delta)}W^{-(1-\delta)} - (1-\delta)(1+\tau)c/W$$
$$= (1+\tau)^{-(1-\delta)/\delta}\eta^{1-\delta}W^{1-\delta}W^{-(1-\delta)} - (1-\delta)(1+\tau)^{1-1/\delta}\eta$$
$$= \delta(1+\tau)^{1-1/\delta}\eta.$$

As a result, in (A11), the first term $\eta$ is replaced by $(1+\tau)^{1-1/\delta}\eta = (1+\tau)^{1-\varepsilon}\eta$.

In Appendix A.4, we can use the same approximation for $\eta$ as before. However, we need to consider the dependence of $\tau$ on $r$. For this we can use the first-order approximation:

$$(1+\tau(r))^{1-\varepsilon} \approx (1+\tau(r^*))^{1-\varepsilon} + (1-\varepsilon)(1+\tau(r^*))^{-\varepsilon}\tau'(r^*)(r-r^*).$$

This gives us the following first-order approximation for the product $(1+\tau)^{1-\varepsilon}\eta$:

$$(1+\tau)^{1-\varepsilon}\eta \approx \left[(1+\tau(r^*))^{1-\varepsilon} + (1-\varepsilon)(1+\tau(r^*))^{-\varepsilon}\tau'(r^*)(r-r^*)\right] \times \eta^*[1+C_0+C_1(r^*-r)]$$
$$\approx (1+\tau(r^*))^{1-\varepsilon}\eta^*[1+C_0+C_1(r^*-r)] + \eta^*(1+C_0)(1-\varepsilon)(1+\tau(r^*))^{-\varepsilon}\tau'(r^*)(r-r^*).$$

The equation preceding (A24) becomes:

$$0 = (1+\tau(r^*))^{1-\varepsilon}\eta^* C_1(r-r^*) + \eta^*(1+C_0)(1-\varepsilon)(1+\tau(r^*))^{-\varepsilon}\tau'(r^*)(r-r^*)$$
$$-(1-\varepsilon)r - \theta(r^*-r)C_1 - (1-\varepsilon)(1-\lambda)\alpha^*(r^*-r) + \text{ terms independent of } r.$$

For this equation to hold identically for all values of $r$, the following two conditions must be satisfied:

$$C_0 = -1,$$
$$C_1 = \eta'/\eta = (1-\varepsilon)\frac{1-(1-\lambda)\alpha^*}{(1+\tau(r^*))^{1-\varepsilon}\eta^*+\theta} \leq (1-\varepsilon)/\eta^*,$$

where the inequality holds provided $\varepsilon \leq 1$.

With the above re definition of $\eta$, $\eta'/\eta$ is no longer exactly the semielasticity of the consumption-wealth ratio with respect to the interest rate. Rather, we have:

$$\frac{d\ln(c/W)}{dr} = \eta'/\eta - \varepsilon\frac{\tau'(r^*)}{1+\tau(r^*)}.$$

Recall that the "tax" for the set-aside is a decreasing function of the interest rate, so that $\tau'(r^*) <$. Thus, the semielasticity of the consumption-wealth ratio is slightly higher than $\eta'/\eta$. Again, if $\varepsilon$ is low, this correction will be small.

## References


Abel, Andrew B. 1990. Asset prices under habit formation and catching up with the Joneses. *American Economic Review* 80: 38–42.

Alhashel, Bader. 2015. Sovereign Wealth Funds: A literature review. *Journal of Economics and Business* 78: 1–13. [CrossRef]

Ang, Andrew, William N. Goetzmann, and Stephen Schaefer. 2009. Evaluation of Active Management of the Norwegian Government Pension Fund—Global. Available online: https://www0.gsb.columbia.edu/faculty/aang/papers/report%20Norway.pdf (accessed on 26 December 2018).

Baldwin, Christopher. 2012. *Sovereign Wealth Funds: The New Intersection of Money and Politics*. Oxford: Oxford University Press.

Bansal, Ravi, and Amir Yaron. 2004. Risks for the Long Run: A Potential Resolution of Asset Pricing Puzzles. *Journal of Finance* 59: 1481–509. [CrossRef]

Barro, Robert J. 1979. On the determination of the public debt. *Journal of Political Economy* 87: 940–71. [CrossRef]

Benzoni, Luca, Pierre Collin-Dufresne, and Robert S. Goldstein. 2007. Portfolio choice over the life-cycle when the stock and labor markets are cointegrated. *Journal of Finance* 62: 2123–67. [CrossRef]

Bernstein, Shai, Josh Lerner, and Antoinette Schoar. 2013. The Investment Strategies of Sovereign Wealth Funds. *Journal of Economic Perspectives* 27: 219–37. [CrossRef]

Caballero, Ricardo J., Emmanuel Farhi, and Pierre-Olivier Gourinchas. 2008. An Equilibrium Model of 'Global Imbalances' and Low Interest Rates. *American Economic Review* 98: 358–93. [CrossRef]

Campbell, John, and John Cochrane. 1999. By force of habit: A consumption-based explanation of aggregate stock market behavior. *Journal of Political Economy* 107: 205–51. [CrossRef]

Campbell, John Y., and Luis Viceira. 2002. *Strategic Asset Allocation: Portfolio Choice for Long-Term Investors*, 1st ed. Oxford: Oxford University Press.

Carroll, Christopher, and Olivier Jeanne. 2009. A Tractable Model of Precautionary Reserves, Net Foreign Assets, or Sovereign Wealth Funds. NBER Working Paper No. 2824. Cambridge, CA, USA: NBER.

Chambers, David, Elroy Dimson, and Antti Ilmanen. 2012. The Norway Model. *The Journal of Portfolio Management* 38: 67–81. [CrossRef]

Choudhry, Moorad. 2007. *Bank Asset and Liability Management: Strategy, Trading, Analysis*, 1st ed. Singapore: Wiley Finance.

Cochrane, John H. 2017. Macro-Finance. *Review of Finance* 21: 945–85. [CrossRef]

Collier, Paul, and Jan Willem Gunning. 2005. Asset Policies During an Oil Windfall: Some Simple Analytics. *The World Economy* 28: 1401–15. [CrossRef]

Constantinides, George. 1990. Habit formation: A resolution of the equity premium puzzle. *Journal of Political Economy* 98: 519–43. [CrossRef]

Corden, Warner Max. 1984. Boom Sector and Dutch Disease Economics: Survey and Consolidation. *Oxford Economic Papers* 36: 362. [CrossRef]

Dahlquist, Magnus, and Bernt Arne Ødegaard. 2018. A Review of Norges Bank's Active Management of the Government Pension Fund Global. Available online: https://papers.ssrn.com/sol3/papers.cfm?abstract_id=3114175 (accessed on 26 December 2018).

Doornik, Jurgen. 2007. *Object-Oriented Matrix Programming Using Ox*, 3rd ed. London: Timberlake Consultants Press and Oxford, Available online: www.doornik.com (accessed on 26 December 2018).

Dreassi, Alberto, Stefano Miani, and Andrea Paltrinieri. 2017. Sovereign Pension and Social Security Reserve Funds: A Portfolio Analysis. *Global Financial Journal* 34: 43–53. [CrossRef]

Epstein, Larry G., and Stanley E. Zin. 1991. Substitution, Risk Aversion, and the Temporal Behavior of Consumption and Asset Returns: An Empirical Analysis. *Journal of Political Economy* 99: 263–86. [CrossRef]

Fama, Eugene F., and Kenneth R. French. 1988. Permanent and temporary components of stock prices. *Journal of Political Economy* 96: 246–73. [CrossRef]

Giovannini, Alberto, and Philippe Weil. 1989. Risk Aversion and Intertemporal Substitution in the Capital Asset Pricing Model. NBER Working Paper No. 2824. Cambridge, MA, USA: NBER.

Guerra-Salas, Juan F. 2014. *Government Investment and the Business Cycle in Oil-Exporting Countries*. Bronx: Fordham University.

Hall, Robert E. 1978. Stochastic implications of the life cycle-permanent income hypothesis: Theory and evidence. *Journal of Political Economy* 86: 971–87. [CrossRef]

Hall, Robert E. 1988. Intertemporal Substitution in Consumption. *Journal of Political Economy* 96: 339–57. [CrossRef]

Hall, Robert E. 2016. *The Role of the Growth of Risk-Averse Wealth in the Decline of the Safe Real Interest Rate*. Stanford: Stanford University.

Johan, Sofia A., April Knill, and Nathan Mauck. 2013. Determinants of Sovereign Wealth Fund Investment in Private Equity vs. Public Equity. *Journal of International Business Studies* 44: 155–72. [CrossRef]

King, Mervyn, and David Low. 2014. Measuring the 'World' Real Interest Rate. NBER Working Paper 19887. Cambridge, MA, USA: NBER.

Krugman, Paul. 1987. The Narrow Moving Band, the Dutch Disease, and the Competitive Consequences of Mrs. Thatcher. *Journal of Development Economics* 27: 41–55. [CrossRef]

Kunzel, Peter, Yinqiu Lu, Iva Petrova, and Jukka Pihl. 2011. Investment Objectives of Sovereign Wealth Funds—A Shifting Paradigm. IMF Working Paper WP/11/19. Available online: https://www.imf.org/en/Publications/WP/Issues/2016/12/31/Investment-Objectives-of-Sovereign-Wealth-Funds-A-Shifting-Paradigm-24598 (accessed on 26 December 2018).

Lax, Yoel. 2002. *Habit Formation and Lifetime Portfolio Selection*. Available online: https://ssrn.com/abstract=325043 (accessed on 26 December 2018).

Merton, Robert C. 1969. Lifetime portfolio selection under uncertainty: The continuous time case. *Review of Economics and Statistics* 51: 247–57. [CrossRef]

Norwegian Ministry of Finance. 2015. *Finanspolitikk i en oljeøkonomi (Fiscal Policy in an Oil Economy)*. Official Norwegian Report NOU 2015:9. Available online: https://www.regjeringen.no/no/dokumenter/nou-2015-9/id2423507/?q=2015:9 (accessed on 8 January 2019).

Norwegian Ministry of Finance. 2016. *Aksjeandelen i Statens pensjonsfond utland (The Equity Share of the Government Pension Fund Global)*. Official Norwegian Report NOU 2016:20. Available online: https://www.regjeringen.no/no/dokumenter/nou-2016-20/id2516269/?q=2016:20 (accessed on 8 January 2018).

OECD. 2014. *The Long-Term Global Outlook for Interest Rates*. Report Commissioned by the Norwegian Ministry of Finance. Available online: https://www.regjeringen.no/no/dokumenter/nou-2015-9/id2423507/sec9 (accessed on 8 January 2019).

Paltrinieri, Andrea, and Flavio Pichler. 2013. Asset Management Issues in Sovereign Wealth Funds: An Empirical Analysis. In *Bank Performance, Risk and Securitization*. Edited by Joseph Falzon. London: Palgrave Macmillan.

Phelps, Edmund S. 1962. The accumulation of risky capital: A sequential utility analysis. *Econometrica* 30: 729–43. [CrossRef]

Poterba, James M., and Lawrence H. Summers. 1988. Mean reversion in stock returns: Evidence and implications. *Journal of Financial Economics* 22: 27–60. [CrossRef]

Rachel, Lukasz, and Thomas Smith. 2015. Secular Drivers of the Global Real Interest Rate. Bank of England, Staff Working Paper No. 571. Available online: https://www.bankofengland.co.uk/-/media/boe/files/working-paper/2015/secular-drivers-of-the-global-real-interest-rate.pdf?la=en&hash=AC63431DCC1F424EE322014DF858C860C148817D (accessed on 26 December 2018).

Sá, Filipa, and Francesca Viani. 2013. Shifts in Portfolio Preferences of International Investors: An Application to Sovereign Wealth Funds. *Review of International Economics* 21: 868–85. [CrossRef]

Samuelson, Paul A. 1969. Lifetime portfolio selection by dynamic stochastic programming. *Review of Economics and Statistics* 51: 239–46. [CrossRef]

Sundaresan, Suresh. 1989. Intertemporally dependent preferences and the volatility of consumption and wealth. *Review of Financial Studies* 2: 79–89. [CrossRef]

Svensson, Lars E. O. 1989. Portfolio Choice with Non-Expected Utility in Continuous Time. *Economic Letters* 30: 313–17. [CrossRef]

Swanson, Eric. 2016. *A Macroeconomic Model of Equities and Real, Nominal, and Defaultable Debt*. Irvine: University of California.

Thimme, Julian. 2016. Intertemporal Substitution in Consumption: A Literature Review. *Journal of Economic Surveys* 31: 226–57. [CrossRef]

Van den Bremer, Ton, Frederick van der Ploeg, and Samuel Wills. 2016. The Elephant in the Ground: Managing Oil and Sovereign Wealth. *European Economic Review* 82: 113–31. [CrossRef]

Van der Ploeg, Frederick, and Anthony J. Venables. 2011. Harnessing Windfall Revenues: Optimal Policies for Resource-Rich Developing Economies. *The Economic Journal* 121: 1–30. [CrossRef]

Van Wijnbergen, Sweder. 1984. The 'Dutch Disease': A Disease After All? *The Economic Journal* 94: 41–55. [CrossRef]

Vasicek, Oldrich. 1977. An equilibrium characterization of the term structure. *Journal of Financial Economics* 5: 177–88. [CrossRef]

Viceira, Luis M. 2001. Optimal portfolio choice for long-horizon investors with nontradable labor income. *Journal of Finance* 56: 433–70. [CrossRef]

Yang, Wei. 2015. Intertemporal Substitution and Equity Premium. *Review of Finance* 20: 403–45. [CrossRef]

# Permissions

All chapters in this book were first published in IJFS, by MDPI; hereby published with permission under the Creative Commons Attribution License or equivalent. Every chapter published in this book has been scrutinized by our experts. Their significance has been extensively debated. The topics covered herein carry significant findings which will fuel the growth of the discipline. They may even be implemented as practical applications or may be referred to as a beginning point for another development.

The contributors of this book come from diverse backgrounds, making this book a truly international effort. This book will bring forth new frontiers with its revolutionizing research information and detailed analysis of the nascent developments around the world.

We would like to thank all the contributing authors for lending their expertise to make the book truly unique. They have played a crucial role in the development of this book. Without their invaluable contributions this book wouldn't have been possible. They have made vital efforts to compile up to date information on the varied aspects of this subject to make this book a valuable addition to the collection of many professionals and students.

This book was conceptualized with the vision of imparting up-to-date information and advanced data in this field. To ensure the same, a matchless editorial board was set up. Every individual on the board went through rigorous rounds of assessment to prove their worth. After which they invested a large part of their time researching and compiling the most relevant data for our readers.

The editorial board has been involved in producing this book since its inception. They have spent rigorous hours researching and exploring the diverse topics which have resulted in the successful publishing of this book. They have passed on their knowledge of decades through this book. To expedite this challenging task, the publisher supported the team at every step. A small team of assistant editors was also appointed to further simplify the editing procedure and attain best results for the readers.

Apart from the editorial board, the designing team has also invested a significant amount of their time in understanding the subject and creating the most relevant covers. They scrutinized every image to scout for the most suitable representation of the subject and create an appropriate cover for the book.

The publishing team has been an ardent support to the editorial, designing and production team. Their endless efforts to recruit the best for this project, has resulted in the accomplishment of this book. They are a veteran in the field of academics and their pool of knowledge is as vast as their experience in printing. Their expertise and guidance has proved useful at every step. Their uncompromising quality standards have made this book an exceptional effort. Their encouragement from time to time has been an inspiration for everyone.

The publisher and the editorial board hope that this book will prove to be a valuable piece of knowledge for researchers, students, practitioners and scholars across the globe.

# List of Contributors

**Woon Leong Lin**
Faculty of Economics and Management, Universiti Putra Malaysia; Selangor 43400, Malaysia

**Iman Harymawan and Mohammad Nasih**
Department of Accountancy, Universitas Airlangga, Surabaya 60286, Indonesia

**Brian Lam**
Division of Business and Management, BNU-HKBU United International College, Zhuhai 519087, China

**Rumayya Rumayya**
Department of Economics, Universitas Airlangga, Surabaya 60286, Indonesia

**David Yechiam Aharon**
Department of Business Administration, Ono Academic College, Haifa 55000, Israel

**Yossi Yagil**
Department of Business Administration, University of Haifa, Haifa 3498838, Israel
Department of Business Administration, Western Galilee College, Akko 2412101, Israel

**Ragnar Nymoen**
Department of Economics, University of Oslo, 0315 Oslo, Norway

**Kari Pedersen and Jon Ivar Sjåberg**
The Financial Supervisory Authority of Norway, 0107 Oslo, Norway

**Manuela Ender**
Campus Urstein, Salzburg University of Applied Sciences, Urstein Süd 1, 5412 Puch/Salzburg, Austria

**Finn Brinckmann**
Biogena Management Holding GmbH, Strubergasse 24, 5020 Salzburg, Austria

**Keith Pilbeam**
Department of Economics, City, University of London, Northampton Square, London EC1V 0HB, UK

**Hamish Preston**
S&P Dow Jones Indices, 55 Water Street, New York, NY 1004, USA

**Peter Arendas and Jana Kotlebova**
Department of Banking and International Finance, Faculty of National Economy, University of Economics in Bratislava, 852 35 Bratislava, Slovakia

**Chaiyuth Padungsaksawasdi**
Thammasat Business School, Department of Finance, Thammasat University, Bangkok 10200, Thailand

**Sirimon Treepongkaruna**
University of Western Australia Business School, Accounting and Finance, The University of Western Australia, 6009 Perth, Australia

**Robert Brooks**
Monash Business School, Department of Econometrics and Business Statistics, Monash University, Clayton VIC 3800, Australia

**Tihana Škrinjarić**
Faculty of Economics and Business, University of Zagreb, 10000 Zagreb, Croatia

**Nicola Metzger**
Independent Researcher, University of Westminster, London W1B 2HW, UK

**Vijay Shenai**
Independent Researchert, University of Lincoln, Lincoln LN6 7TS, UK

**Snorre Lindset and Knut Anton Mork**
Department of Economics, Norwegian University of Science and Technology, 7491 Trondheim, Norway

# Index

www.ingramcontent.com/pod-product-compliance
Lightning Source LLC
LaVergne TN
LVHW060940220926
848485LV00015B/1144
*9781639895151*